英·韓
글로벌 비즈니스 사전

ENGLISH-KORAN DICTIONARY
OF GLOBAL BUSINESS

김영래 · 조강필 · 임달호 편저

법영사

머 리 말

세계는 지금까지 소위 3Bs(국경: border, 경계: boundary, 장벽: barrier)로 인하여 경영자원의 국제간 이동이 자유롭지 못하여 기업경영 활동에 많은 제한을 받아왔다.

그러나 최근 수년간 글로벌 환경은 3Bs가 철폐 내지 완화되는 시대가 되어가고 있다. 즉, Less 3Bs 시대를 맞이하고 있다. 이런 변화는 좁은 국내시장을 지향하는 국내기업으로서는 치열한 경쟁에서 생존하기 위한 전략을 마련해야 하는 반면, 넓은 글로벌 시장을 지향하는 글로벌 기업에게는 새로운 시장에 도전할 수 있는 기회를 제공하고 있다. 즉, 글로벌 기업환경의 변화는 위협인 동시에 기회이기도 하다. 여기서 강조되고 있는 것은 기업이 글로벌하게 배치한 사업단위를 어떻게 네트워크하고, 그를 위한 하드 인프라 스트럭쳐를 어떻게 정비할 것인가, 그리고 이러한 네트워크를 유효하게 만들어 경쟁력우위를 구축할 것인가, 또한 경쟁력 우위를 갖춘 네트워크를 어떻게 효율적으로 경영할 것인가 등이 오늘날 글로벌 경영환경의 과제이다. 본서는 그런 의미에서 글로벌 환경을 헤쳐 나가는 프론티어들이 개념을 정립하는데 도움이 되는 사전일 것이다.

우리나라 기업의 경우에도 국내거래 단계를 지나 1960년대부터 본격적으로 해외무역 단계를 왕성히 전개하여, 1980년대까지는 그로 인하여 1인당 국민소득 1만달러를 달성하였고, 1990년대 들어서는 무역뿐만 아니라 해외에서 직접생산, 현지 및 제3국에 수출하는 국제경영 단계로 옮겨갔다.

그러나 2000년대에 들어서 한국 기업은 한국 본사든 해외 자회사든 세계를 하나의 시장으로 보고 각기 핵심 역량을 가진 부분을 특화하고, 그렇지 못한 부분은 아웃소싱에 의해서 효율성을 높일 뿐만 아니라, 네트워킹을 통해 시너지 효과를 올리는 글로벌 비즈니스를 전개하고 있다.

우리나라 기업의 발전 단계에서 볼 때도, 이 사전은 매우 시의 적절한 비즈니스 사전일 것이다. 뿐만 아니라 요즈음 새로운 약어나 용어가산더미 같이 쏟아져 나오고 있는 현실에서는 일반 사전이나 컴퓨터의 검색 만으로는 전문적인 분야를 커버할 수가 없다.

본사전의 내용을 편저함에 있어 *THE DICTIONARY OF NEWEST INTERNATIONAL BUSINESS TERMS* (English-Japaness), Tokyo, Kinokuniya, 2002년도판을 많이 참고로 하였고, 영국의 Hoogvelt, Ankie, M.M., 교수가 저술한 *MULTI NATIONAL ENTERPRISE : AN ENCYCLOPDIC DICTIONARY OF CONCEPTS AND TERMS*, London Macmilliam, 1987년도판 중 중요용어를 취사 선택하여 보완하였다. 그 외에 최근 시사 용어는 IMIDAS 編, 時事用語辭典, 集英社, 2004, 2005, 2006년도 판을 참조 삽입하였다.

그러나 아직 우리말로 옮길 수 없거나 한국에서 쓰지 않고 있는 용어, 영어 그대로를 쓰고 있는 용어는 통상 쓰는 발음대로 표기하였다.

이 사전은 발간 기획으로부터 이미 5년의 세월이 흘렀다. 편저자들의 나태함을 묵묵히 인내 해주신 법영사의 고준영사장님께 무어라 죄송한 말씀을 올려야 될지 모르겠다. 늘 시작했다가 멈추곤 한 것은 사전의 특성상 한번 막히면 좀체로 진전이 어렵다. 그 까닭은 너무나도 광범위하고 다양한 분야로 전문화 되어 있고 빠른 속도로 변하고 있기 때문이다. 이 같은 사정에서도 편저자들이 나름대로 최선을 기울였지만, 너무나도 미흡한 점이 많다. 따라서 만약 본 책자의 잘못이 있다면 그것은 모두 편저자들 책임에 속할 것이다.

또한 본 사전은 국제무역, 국제금융, 국제경영, 국제전략경영 그리고 일반경영까지 총 망라 커버하고자 하였다. 부디 글로벌 비즈니스 학계에 종사하는 연구자 및 학생들 그리고 글로벌 비즈니스에 종사하는 비즈니스맨들에게 꼭 도움이 되는 사전이길 기원한다.

끝으로 다시 한번 법영사의 고준영 사장님과 편집부 정정희 팀장께 이 같이 말끔히 책자를 꾸며 주심에 감사드린다.

2006. 8. 8 입추

김영래, 조강필, 임달호 씀

차 례

英・韓
글로벌 비즈니스 사전

ENGLISH-KORAN DICTIONARY
OF GLOBAL BUSINESS

《 A 》

a derivative suit	주주대표 소송
a private legislature	사적 입법자
ab initio	처음부터
abandonment of action	소송포기
abandonment of right	권리포기
abatement	감액
abbreviation	약어
ABC inventory management	ABC 재고관리
abide by	지키다, 따르다
abiding conviction	결정적 확신
ability	능력
ability to pay	지급능력
ability to pay basis	지급능력기준
ability to pay dividend	배당능력
ability to pay principle	지급능력원칙
abishering	벌금면제
abnormal growth model	이상성장모형
abnormal item	이상(異常)항목
abnormal returns	이상수익
abolition	폐지
above par	액면 이상의
above the line	어보브 더 라인
above the market strategy	고가격 시장 전략
abridged life table	간이생명표
abridgment	적요
abrogation	폐지

absence	부재
absence of demand	수요부재
absentee ownership	부재소유권
absolute	무조건의
absolute advantage	절대우위
absolute beneficiary	변경불능보험금수취인
absolute conveyance	절대적 양도
absolute cost	절대원가
absolute delivery	무조건인도
absolute fixed capital	절대적 고정자본
absolute frequency	절대빈도
absolute income hypothesis	절대소득가설
absolute liability	결과책임
absolute profit	순익
absolute sales	무조건 판매
absolute total loss	절대 전손(全損)
absolute value	절대치
absolutism	절대주의
absorbed bond	완매채권
absorbed burden	배부제 제조간접비
absorbed corporation	흡수되는 회사
absorbed cost	회수제 원가
absorption	흡수합병, 완매(完賣)
absorption account	흡수계정
absorption approach	어섭션 어프로치
absorption cost	전부원가
absorption costing	전부원가계산
abstention	회피
abstract	개요
abstract of account	발췌계산서
abstract of financial statements	재무제표의 요약
abstract of register	초본

abstract of title	권리서
absurdity	불합리
abuse	남용
abuse of confidence	배신
abut	접근하다
accelerated benefits	사망보험금의 선지급
accelerated depreciation	특별상각
accelerated method	가속법
acceleration	기한이익상실
acceleration claims	촉진크레임
acceleration clause	변제기일 앞당김조항
acceleration coefficient	가속도계수
acceleration of registration	등록앞당김
acceleration principle	가속도원리
acceptable price	지급가능가격
acceptance	승낙, 인수
acceptance commission	인수수수료
acceptance credit	인수조건부의 신용공여
acceptance criteria	합격기준
acceptance line	인수한도
acceptance notice	인수통지
acceptance on security	담보부 인수
acceptance payable	지불수표
acceptance price of net assets	순자산인수액
acceptance process	수용과정
acceptance rate	수입수표결제율
acceptance receivable	수취수표
acceptance slip	인수슬립
acceptance system	엑셉턴스 방식
acceptance theory	권한수용설
acceptance bank	수표인수은행
acceptance house	수표인수상사

acceptance rate of exchange	환인수율
acceptor	인수인
access	교접, 접근
access card	엑세스 카드
access charge	엑세스 차지
access point	엑세스 포인트
access to books	장부열람
access to counsel	변호사의뢰권
access to courts	재판을 받을 권리
access to market	마켓 엑세스, 시장접근
accessibility of store	접근용이성
accession	부합
accessorial service	부대서비스
accessories	부속품
accessory building	부속건물
accessory contract	부수적 계약
accessory obligation	부종채권
accessory product	부산물
accessory to tax evasion	탈세종범
accessory use	부속용도
accident	사고
accident and health insurance	상해 · 건강보험
accident and indemnity insurance	상해 · 보상보험
accident and sickness insurance	상해 · 질병보험
accident at work	근무중 사고
accident compensation	재해보험
accident insurance	상해보험
Accident Offices' Association	재해보험회사 해외협회
accident prevention	방재
accidental cost	우발경비
accidental death benefit	사고사 급부금
accidental grounding	우발적

accomenda	적하매각위탁계약
accommodation	융동
accommodation area	특설서비스 장소
accommodation bill	융통수표
accommodation lands	증가토지
accommodation line	영업정책 맞춘 인수계약
accommodation maker	융통수표의 진출인
accommodation works	편익공작물
accompanying document	첨부서류
accord	동의
accord and satisfaction	대물변제
accordance	일치
accordant	일치하여
account	계산서, 고객
account analysis	계정분석
account book	출납부
account chart	계정과목일람표
account closing procedure	결산수속
account current	당좌계정
account day	결산일
account due from sales on approval	시용판매미수금
account due on consignment-out	위탁판매미수입금
account executive	어카운트 이그제큐티브
account form	계정식
account form income statement	계정식 손익계산서
account form profit and loss statement	계정식 손익계산서
account headings	계정과목
account in arrears	잔업수당계정
account in transit	미달계정
account method	장부방식

account number	계정과목번호
account number plan	계정과목번호표시법
account of business	영업보고서
account of credit sales	외상매출계정
account of sale	매출계산서
account opener	신규거래처 획득경품
account owed to employees	종업원에 대한 채무
account paid	지급계정
account payable	외상채무
account planner	어카운트 플래너
account receivable	수취계정
account receivable discounted	할인수취계정
account receivable due from affiliated company	관계회사 외상대금
account receivable insurance	외상대금 보험
account receivable ledger	거래처원장
account reconcilement	계정대조표
account record	보고서
account rendered	확정계정
account report service	어카운트 리포트 서비스
account sales	매출계산서
account stated	확정계정
account statement	계산서
account system	계정시스템
account title	계정과목
account transfer	계좌이체
accountability	책임
accountability unit	책임단위
accountable condition	회계 사상
accountable officer	회계담당관
accountable person	책임자
accountable receipt	수령증

accountable warrant	회계 워런트
accountancy	회계학, 회계업무
accountancy service	회계감사업무
accountant	회계사
accountant in bankruptcy	파산청산인
accountant in charge	주임회계사
accountant liability policy	회계사배상책임보험
accountant report	감사보고서
accountant's inspection	회계감사
accountant's office	회계사 사무소
accountant's responsibility	회계사 책임
accountbook	장부
accountee	신용장 발행의뢰인
accounting beta value	회계 베타치
accounting book	회계장부
accounting by month	월별계산
accounting control	회계관리
accounting convention	회계원리
accounting data process	회계사무처리
accounting department	경리과
accounting division	회계과
accounting earnings	회계적 이익
accounting entity	회계실체, 회계주체
accounting evidence	회계증거
accounting firm	회계사무소, 회계법인
accounting for branch office	지점회계
accounting for business combinations	기업결합회계
accounting for changing prices	화폐가치변동회계
accounting for compensated absences	유급휴가회계
accounting for income tax allocation	세금배포회계
accounting for income taxes	세효과회계

accounting for internal reporting	내부보고회계
accounting for inventories	재고자산회계
accounting for leases	리스 회계
accounting for pension plan	연금회계
accounting for price-level change	가격수준변동회계
accounting for tax allocation	세금배분회계
accounting function	회계직능, 회계기능
accounting identity	회계등식
accounting information system	회계정보시스템
accounting manual	회계매뉴얼
accounting organization	회계조직
accounting period	사업년도
accounting period in case of merger	합병사업년도
accounting policy	회계방침
accounting postulate	회계공준
accounting practice	회계실무
accounting principle	회계원칙
accounting principles	회계기준
Accounting Principles Board	회계원칙심의회
accounting principles for business enterprise	기업회계원칙
accounting procedures	회계수속
accounting profession	회계사업(業)
accounting ratio of profits to net worth	회계적 자기자본이익률
accounting records	회계기록
accounting regulation	회계규정
accounting report	회계보고
Accounting Research Bulletin	회계연구공보
accounting rules	회계통칙
accounting section	회계과
Accounting Series Release	회계연속통첩(會計連續通牒)

accounting sheet of collected amount	징수액계산서
accounting standards	회계기준
Accounting Standards Committee (ASC)	회계기준위원회
accounting system	회계제도
accounting terminology	회계용어
accounting transactions	회계상 거래
accounting treatment	회계처리
accounting unit	회계단위
accounting valuation	회계적 평가
accounting year	회계년도
accounts due	미수금
accounts receivable insurance	외상보험
accounts to receive	수취계정
accredit	신임장 부여
accredited investor	적격투자가
accredited party	신임장발행 의뢰인
accreting swap	원금증가스왑
accretion	재산의 증가
accrual	발생, 미지급금, 예정액, 미실현
accrual account	발생항목, 예정계정
accrual accounting	발생주의회계
accrual basis	발생주의, 발생기준
accrual item	예상항목
accrual of cause of action	소송원인의 발생
accrual of discount	할인액기간대응할부
accrued account	예정계정
accrued assets	예정자산
accrued basis	발생주의
accrued bonuses	미지급상여금, 상여충당금
accrued charge	미지급비용, 예정손비
accrued commission	미지급수수료

accrued depreciation	감가상각발생액
accrued dividend	미지급배당
accrued donation	미지급 기부금
accrued employees retirement benefit	미지급 퇴직급여, 퇴직급여 충당금
accrued expenses payable	미지급비용
accrued income	미수수익
accrued income taxes	미지급 법인세
accrued interest	경과이자
accrued interest on loan	대부미수이자
accrued liabilities	미지급부채, 예정부채
accrued payroll	미지급급료
accrued premium	계상보험료
accrued rent	미수임대료
accrued revenue	미수수익
accrued salaries	미지급급료
accrued severance indemnities	퇴직급여 충당금
accrued taxes on income	납세충당금
accrued wages	미지급임금
accruing costs	추가비용
acculturation	문화적응
accumulated amount	누적액
accumulated assets	적립자산
accumulated benefit obligation	누적급부채무
accumulated depreciation	감가상가 누적액
accumulated dividend	누적배당
accumulated dividend deposit	배당예탁
accumulated earning tax	유보이익세
accumulated earnings	유보이익, 적립이익
accumulated fund	적립금
accumulated income	누적이익
accumulated investment	누적투자

accumulated preferred stock	누적배당우선주식
accumulated surplus	잉여금 누계액
accumulation	누적
accumulation clause	전보액누증약관
accumulation of capital	자본축적
accumulation process	집적과정
accumulation system	어큐물레이션방식
accumulation trust	이익의 원금투입형 투자신탁
accumulations	이자적립
accumulative	누적적
accumulative investment period	누적투자기간
accumulative investment plan	누적투자계획
accumulative investment unit	누적투자단위
accumulative judgment	누적판결
accumulative risk	누적위험
accumulative stock	누적배당형 주식
accusation	고발
accusatory body	기소결정기관
accusatory instrument	기소서류
accusatory part	기소부분
accused	피고인
accuser	기소자
achievement	업적
achievement level	달성수준
achieving need	달성동기
acid ratio	당좌비율
acid test ratio	당좌비율
acknowledgement of declaration	보험인수증
acknowledgment	승인
acknowledgment of order	응낙
acquest	취득재산
acquiescence	묵인

acquired needs	후천성 니즈
acquired right	기득권
acquired surplus	취득잉여금
acquirement of properties	자산의 취득
acquisition	취득
acquisition agent	취득대리점
acquisition commission	취득수수료
acquisition cost	취득원가, 조달원가
acquisition cost adjustment	취득원가조정
acquisition cost method	취득원가법
acquisition cost of depreciable assets	감가상각자산의 취득가액
acquisition cost of inventory	재고자산의 취득가액
acquisition cost of leasehold	차지권의 취득가액
acquisition cost of securities	유가증권취득가액
acquisition cost price	조달가격
acquisition for value	유상취득
acquisition multiple method	매수사례비교법
acquisition of concessions	이권획득
acquisition of debenture	사채취득
acquisition of right	권리취득
acquisition of stock	주식취득
acquisition of the application right	출원권의 취득
acquisition opportunity	매수기회
acquisition value	취득가격
acquisitive prescription	취득시효
acquittal	채무면제
acquittance	채무의 완제
acreage	지적
across the board	일괄의
act	행위, 제정법
act of bankruptcy	파산행위
act of God	불가항력

act of grace	사면령
act of honor	참가인수
act of incorporation	설립법
act of indemnity	면책법
act of insolvency	지급불능행위
act of law	법적 행위
act of parliament	국회제정법
act of sale	매매기록
act of state	국가행위
act of stealing	절취행위
act of war	전쟁행위
act tax	행위세
action	상장활동
action for accounting	계산소송
action for damages	손해배상청구소송
action in personam	대인소송
action in rem	대물소송
action of detinue	동산인도청구소송
action program	액션 프로그램, 행동 강령
action quasi in rem	준대물소송
actionable fraud	사기
actionable negligence	소송을 야기하는 과실
actionable words	명예훼손이 되는 표시
active account	활동계정
active bond	이자부채권
active bond management	적극적 운용
active buying	구매활동
active conduct of business	사업활동
active dealer	적극적 딜러
active debt	채권
active employee	현재종업원
active investment management theory	적극적 투자이론

active life fund	현직자기금
active management	적극적 운용
active market	호황시장
active method	액티브 방식
active portfolio	액티브 포트폴리오
active return	액티브 리턴
active risk	액티브 리스크
active risk aversion	액티브 리스크 회피도
active stock	인기주
active trust	적극신탁
activity accounting	활동회계
activity analysis	업무분석
activity rates	활동률
actual acquisition cost basis	실제취득원가주의
actual annual percentage rate	실질연리
actual assets	실제자산
actual basis	발생주의
actual basis accounting	실제주의회계
actual burden rate	실제배부율
actual cash value	실제현금가치
actual cost	실제원가
actual cost accounting system	실제원가계산제도
actual costing	실제원가계산
actual deaths	실제사망수
actual delivery	현물수수
actual delivery of stock sold	현물매도
actual demand rule	실수요원칙
actual expenses	실비
actual instruction	실효명령
actual inventory	실지재고
actual life	실제내용년수
actual loss	실제손해
actual market	현재시장

actual price	실제가격
actual product	실제제품
actual production	생산실적
actual purchase price	실제구입가격
actual quantity of mining	실제채굴량
actual rate of growth	실제성장률
actual results of recent stock transactions	주식취득실적
actual return on plan assets	연금자산 실제운용수익
actual total loss	현실전손
actual trading behavior	실제거래
actual transfer price	실제양도가격
actual useful life	실제내용년수
actual value	실제가치
actual value method	실가법, 개별법
actually expected standard cost	실제 예측표준원가
actuals	원자산
actuarial contribution	수리적 보험료
actuarial cost method	연금수리비용계산방식
actuarial expectation	보험수리상의 기대치
actuarial gains or losses	수리적 손익
actuarial hours	평균실질노동시간
actuarial mathematics	액츄어리얼 수학
actuarial method	연금이회법
actuarial relationship	액츄어리얼 관계
Actuarial Society of America	미국 액츄어리얼 협회
actuarial soundness	보험수리적 건전성
actuary	보험계리인, 액츄어리
ad damnum	손해배상청구문헌
ad hoc	임시의
ad hoc arbitration	개별중재
ad interim	임시의
ad litem	소송을 위하여

ad opus	(~의)위하여
ad valorem	종가세
ad valorem storage	종가보관료
ad valorem tariff	종가세율
ad valorem tax	종가세
adaptation level	적응수준
adaptive behavior	적응행동
adaptive product	시장적응제품
adaptive strategy	적응전략
add-back method	가감법
add-on charge	추가요금
add-on markup	추가 마크업
add-on rate	추가 금리
add-on system	애드 온 방식
added discount	추가할인
added value	부가가치
addenda	추가문서
adding to holdings	매입증가
addition	부가
addition to reserve	충당금 산입
addition to retained earnings	이익잉여금으로 대체
additional amount to a refund of national tax	국세환급 가산액
additional arrearage charge	연체가산금
additional benefit	부가급부(付加給付)
additional budget	보정예산(補正豫算)
additional call	추가부담금
additional capital	증가자본, 증자
additional charge	추가비용
additional charge for deficient return	과소신고가산금
additional charges	운송비할증

additional collateral	추가담보
additional conditions	추가조항
additional depreciation deduction	할증상각
additional establishment	추가설정
additional expenses	추가비용
additional expenses clause	추가비용약관
additional extended coverage endorsement	확장담보배서
additional freight	할증운임
additional interest	추가이해관계자
additional investment	추가출자
additional issue	추가설정
additional living expense insurance	임시생계비보험
additional margin	추가증거금
additional markup	추가가격인상
additional paid-in capital	자본준비금
additional premium	추가보험료
additional security	추가보증
additional tax	가산세
additional tax due to failure to file a return	무신고가산세
additional tax for deficient returns	과소신고가산세
additional tax on nonpayment	미납가산세
additions and omissions	추가 및 생략
additions to plant and equipment	설비신규구입액
additions to reserves	적립금이월
additions to tax	부대세
additive substruction	가법적 감산(加法的減算)
addressee	수신인
adduce	인증하다
adequate	상당한
adequate liquidity	적정유동성

adequate protection	충분한 보호
adjacent	근접의, 인접한
adjacent experience	근접경험, 인접경험
adjective law	수속법
adjoining	접근의, 인접하는
adjourned sale	발매연기
adjournment	연기
adjudge	사법적 판단을 하다
adjudication	재판
adjudication of bankruptcy	파산선고
adjudication order	파산명령
adjunct account	부가계정
adjuration	서약
adjust	조정하다
adjustable basket technique	비대칭 바스켓 방식
adjustable fire policy	조정가능 화재보험증권
adjustable life policy	조정가능 생명보험증권
adjustable peg system	조정가능 고정환율
adjustable policy	조정보험
adjustable rate	변동이자
adjustable rate mortgage	변동금리모기지
adjustable rate mortgage loan	조정금리저당론
adjustable rate preferred stock	변동이율우선주
adjusted	조정필
adjusted basis	수정기초액
adjusted beta value	수정베타값
adjusted capital gain	수정후 양도소득
adjusted central bank money stock	수정후 중앙은행 스톡
adjusted death rate	정정사망률
adjusted debit balance	신용거래융자잔고
adjusted dividend increase	수정후 배당증가율
adjusted gross income	수정된 총소득

adjusted historical cost	수정된 취득원가
adjusted income	수정된 소득금액
adjusted net profit	수정된 순이익
adjusted premium	조정보험료
adjusted regression analysis	수정회귀분석
adjusted to seasonal variations	계절변동조정필
adjusted trial balance	조정후 시산표
adjuster	손해사정인
adjusting entry	수정분개
adjusting journal entry	수정분개기법
adjustment	손해사정
adjustment account	대조계정
adjustment at term-end	기말정산
adjustment bond	정리사채
adjustment bureau	손해사정국
adjustment costs	손해사정비
adjustment entry	정리기입
adjustment for price fluctuations	가격변동조정
adjustment for taxable income	세무조정
adjustment in filing a final tax return	신고조정
adjustment in settling accounts	결산조정
adjustment inflation	조정인플레이션
adjustment item	조정항목
adjustment of accounts	계정조정
adjustment of business income	기업이익조정
adjustment of capital	자본수정
adjustment of cost variance	원가차액조정
adjustment of debts	채무조정
adjustment of supply to demand	수급조정
adjustment of surplus	잉여금조정
adjustment of the carrying amount	부가수정

adjustment premium	조정보험료
adjustment process of balance of payments	국제수지조정과정
adjustment securities	조정증권
admeasurement	배분
administered price	관리가격
administered-price inflation	관리가격 인플레이션
administration	사무관리
administration estate	유산관리
administration in bankruptcy	파산관재(破產管財)
administration of insurance contract	보험계약의 보전(保全)
administration suit	유산관리소송
administrative accounting	관리회계
administrative act	행정행위
administrative and maintenance expenses	유지관리비용
administrative appellate law	행정불복심사법
administrative audit	관리적 감사
administrative discretion	행정재량
administrative disposition	행정처분
administrative dispute	행정쟁송(行政爭訟)
administrative expenses	일반관리비
administrative expenses budget	일반관리비 예산
administrative expenses variance	일반관리비 차이
administrative fiat	경영관리명령
administrative fit	관리적합
administrative guidance	행정지도
administrative interpretation	행정해석
administrative law	행정법
administrative legislation	행정입법
administrative litigation	행정소송
administrative officer	행정직원

administrative order	행정명령
administrative power	행정권
administrative protest	불복신청
administrative reform	행정개혁
administrative remedy	행정구제
administrative review	불복심사
administrative uncertainty	관리상 불확실성
administrator	관재인
administrator cum testamento annexo	유언에 따른 유산관리인
administrator de bonis non	후임유산관리인
administrator in bankruptcy	파산관재인
administrator of bequest	유산관리인
administrator of tax payment	납세관리인
admiralty bond	해사사건보증증권
admiralty court	해사재판소
admissible	허용해야 할
admission	보석허가명령
admission tax law	입장세법
admissions	입장자 수
admitted assets	인용자산
admonition	충고, 경고, 훈계
adopted concept	차용개념
adoption curve	채용곡선
adoption model	채용모델
adoption order	양자결정
adoption process	채용단계
adoptive act	임의법
adoption for purchase	매입전도금
adoptive provisions	임의규정
adult	성년자
adulteration	조악화(粗惡化)

advance	선급금
advance account	선급금계정
advance by customers	거래처선수금
advance call	선지급분담금
advance collection	조기징수
advance demand	조기청구
advance dividend	사전계약자배당
advance freight	선지급운임
advance from controlled companies	종속회사 선수금
advance funding method	사전적립방식
advance made for purchase of material	원료매입 선급금
advance made on contract	계약선급금
advance made to salesmen	판매원 가지급금
advance money	선급금
advance of salary	급료선불
advance on a promissory note	어음대부
advance on account of sellers	납입선지급대금
advance on consignment-in	수탁매매입체금
advance on construction	건설공사 전도금
advance on indent	주문선수금
advance on subscription	예약선급금
advance payment	선급금
advance payment bond	선급금 반환 보증증권
advance premium	선납보험료
advance pricing agreement	사전가격확인제도
advance received	선수금
advance received on contract	계약선수금
advance received on indents	주문 선수금
advance received profit	선수수익
advance refunding	사전조정
advance salary	선급급여

advance sale	예약판매
advance seizure	조기차압
advance to subcontractor	하청선급금
advance to vendor	판매대리점 선급금
advance wages	선급임금
advance-decline line	등락선
advanced accounting	고급회계학
advanced collection on sale contracts	매매계약선수금
advanced countries	선진국
advanced depreciation	압축기장
advanced depreciation deduction	압축손해
advanced depreciation limit	압축한도액
advanced money	선수금
advanced processed goods	고도가공품
advanced redemption	조기상환
advanced television	선진 텔레비전
advancement barrier	진입장벽
advances received on consignments out	적송품선수금(積送品先受金)
adventure	절정, 고비
adversary party	상대방당사자
adversary proceeding	대심수속(對審手續)
adversary system	당사자과실책임제도
adverse claim	이의신청
adverse effects	악영향
adverse element	마이너스 요인
adverse financial selection	금융상 역선택
adverse interest	상반이익
adverse opinion	부정적 의견
adverse physical conditions claims	지하조건 크레임
adverse possession	취득시효
adverse selection	역선택

advertised price 광고표시가격
advertisement 광고
advertisement agency 광고대행사
advertisement exposure 광고노출
advertisement for bid 입찰공고
advertisement media 광고매체
advertisement mix 광고활동통합
advertisement source 광고 소스
advertisement tax 광고세
advertisement theme 광고 테마
advertising allowance 광고원조금
advertising and general publicity expenses 광고선전비
advertising appeals 광고소송
advertising appropriation 광고예산
advertising budgeting 광고예산편성
advertising campaign 광고캠페인
advertising copy 광고원고
advertising criticism 광고비판
advertising decision 광고결정
advertising differentiation 광고차별화
advertising effect 광고효과
advertising evaluation 광고의 평가
advertising expenses 광고비
advertising fantasy 광고의 환상
advertising group 광고집단
advertising media 광고매체
advertising message 광고메세지
advertising network 광고대리점망
advertising objectives 광고목표
advertising opportunity 광고기회
advertising psychology 광고심리학

advertising regulation	광고규제
advertising research	광고조사
advertising sales ratio	광고비비율
advertising society	광고회사
advertising specialty	광고노벨리티
advertising strategy	광고전략
advertising technology	광고기술
advertising testing	광고효과테스트
advertising theme	광고테마
advertising unexpired	미경과광고료
advice of credit	입금
advice of shipment	선적통지
advice of subrogation	대위통지서
advice slip	통지전표
advising bank	통지은행
advisory	조언의
advisory committee	자문위원회
advisory opinion	조언적인 의견
advisory organization	요율자문기관
advisory rates	권고요율
advisory service	투자자문업
advisory tax board	세무자문위원회
advocacy advertisement	어드보카시 광고
advocate	변호사, 옹호자
Advocate General	법무관
aerial transport	항공수송
affairs	업무
affect	영향을 미치다
affection	담보설정
affectional drives	감정적 동기
affectivity	감성
affidatio	충성서약

affidavit 선서서, 선서진술서
affiliate 관계자
affiliated company 관계회사, 계열사
affiliated family corporations 동족관계회사
affiliated financial institute 계열금융기관
affiliated loan 제휴론
affiliated middleman 가맹중간업자
affiliated store 가맹점
affiliation 계열화
affine transformation 아핀 변환
affirmance 시인, 확언
affirmant 확약증언자
affirmation 확약
affirmation of fact 사실의 확인
affirmative 긍정적인
affirmative charge 긍정표시
affirmative covenants 긍정적인 서약
affirmative defense 적극적 항변
affirmative statute 명령적 법률
affix 서명하다
affluent economy 풍요로운 경제
affordable growth 여유있는 성장
affranchise 개방하다
affreightment 해상운송계약
affreightment contract 해상화물운송계약
African Development Bank 아프리카개발은행
Afro-Asian Common Market 아시아 · 아프리카 공동시장
after cost 사후경비
after effective tax 실효세과세후
after image lag 잔상
after market 신규발행후시장
after maturity endorsement 만기후 이서

after tax	세후
after tax profit rate	세후이익률
after-acquired clause	사후취득조항
after-acquired property	사후취득재산
after-loan	애프터 론
after-tax income	세후 이익
after-tax yield	세후 이윤
afternoon session	후장
aftershock	여진
against all risks	전위험담보
against the will	의지에 반해서
age at entry	가입연령
age at expiry	만기시 연령
age distribution	연령분포
age limit	연령제한
age of discretion	분별연수
age of retirement	퇴직연령
age of vessel	연령
age setback	연령후퇴조정
aged account	연체보험료
aged dependent	노인부양친족
aged person	노년자
agency	대리점
agency account receivable	대리점
agency accounts	대리점계정
agency activity	대리점활동
agency agreement	대리점계약서
agency backed securities	정부기관증권담보증권
agency bookkeeping	대리인부기
agency commission	대리점수수료
agency contract	대리점 계약
agency cost	대리점 경비

agency department	외무부
agency fee	대리점수수료
agency filing	회원회사의 대리요금신청
agency find	대리인자금
agency ledger	대리점원장
agency loan	대리대부
agency market	에이전시 시장
agency network	광고대리점망
agency note	정부기관비
agency problem	대리인 문제
agency system	대리점제도
agency theory	대리인 이론
agency to receive tax	수납기관
agency transaction	위탁거래
agency work	보험모집활동
agenda	협의사항
agent	대리인
agent account	대리점계정
agent bank	간사은행
agent commission	대리수수료
agent development era	외무원개발의 시대
aggravation	가중사유
aggregate	총계
aggregate active risk	총 액티브 리스크
aggregate average	총평균
aggregate concentration	일반집중
aggregate corporation	사단법인
aggregate face amount	액면총액
aggregate gross margin	조이익총계
aggregate limit	총전보한도액
aggregate managed portfolio	총운송포트폴리오
aggregate market value	시가총액

aggregate net sales	순매출액총계
aggregate normal	총 정상 포트폴리오
aggregate of depreciation deduction	감가상각비누계
aggregate response curve	총반응곡선
aggregate supply	총공급량
aggregate supply function	총공급함수
aggregate table	총합표
aggregate theory	집합이론
aggregated shipment	일괄운송
aggregation mentium	의견일치
aggregation	합산
aggregation of income amount	소득금액의 합산
aggregation of profit and loss	손익통산
aggregation problem	집계문제
aggressive investment	공격적 투자
aggressive portfolio	적극적 운용
aggressive securities	공격적 증권
aggressively held up	약간 높은 유도
aggrieved party	불복당사자
aging	연령조사
agio	환전수수료
agreed case	합의사항
agreed insured value	협정보험가액
agreed interest rate	약정금리
agreed statement of facts	합의사실진술서
agreed value	보험평가액
agreed yield to maturity	약정만기이자
agreement	계약, 약정
agreement among underwriters	인수업자간 계약
agreement corporation	협정회사
agreement for overdraft	당좌대월약정서
agreement jurisdictional court	합의관할재판소

Agreement of the International Bank for Reconstruction and Development 국제개발부흥은행협정
Agreement of the International Monetary Fund 국제통화기금협정
agribusiness 농업관련사업, 기업농업
agricultural bank 농업은행
agricultural bookkeeping 농업부기
agricultural credit 농업금융
agricultural goods markets 농산물시장
agricultural income 농업소득
agricultural insurance 농업보험
agricultural lien 농업선취특권
agricultural machinery and equipment floater 농기구포괄보험
agricultural machinery insurance 농업기계보험
agricultural production corporation 농업생산법인
agricultural society 농업조합
aid 상납금
aid and abet 현장방조(現場幇助)
aid and comfort 조력(助力)
aid bond 보조공채
aid prayer 원조청원
aid societies 공제조합
aids 원조금
ailing 업체부진의
air carrier 항공화물운송업자
air fare 항공요금
air right 상공권
air transport insurance 항공운송보험
air transportation 공수
air waybill 항공화물운송장
air-borne cargo insurance 항공운송보험

aircraft hull insurance	항공기체보험
aircraft liability insurance	항공기책임보험
aircraft passenger insurance	항공상해보험
aircraft third party liability insurance	항공책임보험
airport owner's or operator's liability insurance	공항관리자배상책임보험
airway	항공로
airway freight	항공운임
alba firma	자지대(自地代)
alcohol bond	주정보증증권
alcoholic beverage	주류
ale-silver	주류판매세
aleatory contract	사행계약
alias	별명
alien	외국인
alien corporation	외국법인
alien insurer	외국보험회사
alien juris	타주권자
alien property	외국인재산
alien tax	입국세
alien taxpayer	외국인납세자
alienable	이전가능한
alienation	이전
alienation clause	양도무효조항
alienator	양도인
alienee	양수인
alieni juris	사람의 감독하에 있는
alignment	제휴
alimony and separate maintenance payment	부조료 및 별거수당
all amounts invested in capital	총출자금액
all and singular	예외없이 전부

all buyers	구입일색
all gone	매진
all issued stocks	발행완료 주식총액
all lines insurance	생손보상호보험
all lines insurer	전보험종목 인수회사
all lines organization	전보험종목 인수기구
all purpose card	범용카드
all risks clause	올 리스크 담보약관
all risks coverage	올 리스크 담보
all risks dwelling house insurance	주택종합보험
all risks insurance	올 리스크 담보보험
all sold	매진
all states endorsement	전미담보특약
all totaled	총계에서
all-inclusive basis	포괄주의
all-inclusive income concept	포괄주의적 이익개념
all-inclusive income statement	포괄손익계산서
all-or-none order	일괄매매주문
all-purpose	만능의
all-purpose financial statement	다목적 재무제표
all-time high	신고치(新高值)
allegation	주장
allege	주장하다
allegiance	충성주의
alleging diminution	기록흠관(記錄欠款)의 주장
allergist	알러지전문의
alliance	제휴
allied company	제휴사
allied line cover	계열위험담보계약
allied line risks	계열위험
allied members	증권거래소 준회원
allocated benefit	표정급부

allocated funding instrument 할당적립방식
allocating function 배분기능
allocation and execution of budget 예산의 배분과 집행
allocation by market potential 시장잠재능력별 할당
allocation of cost 원가배분
allocation of new shares to a third party 제3자 할당
allocation on bases 배분기준
allocation procedure 배부수순
allocatur 비용사정증
allodial 자유보유토지의
allodium 사유지
allograph 비자서(非自署)
allot 분할하다
allotment 증권할당
allotment certificate 할당증
allotment ledger 할당예산원장
allotment letter 할당서
allotment note 선원급료수취 선지도서
allotment of shares 주식할당
allotment system 토지배분제도
allotment to shareholders 주주할당
allotment warden 배분지 관리인
allotted amount in constructing public facility 공공시설건설부담액
allow 허용하다
allowable limit for depreciation amount 상각한도액
allowable maximum amount 허용한도액
allowance 협정손해율, 준비금
allowance for bad debt 대손충당금
allowance for bad loan 대손충당금

allowance for dependent	부양공제
allowance for depreciation	감가상각충당금
allowance for dismissal without notice in advance	해고수당
allowance for doubtful accounts	대손충당금
allowance for old person	노인공제
allowance for promotion of employment	취직촉진수당
allowance for repairs	수선충당금
allowance for spouse	배우자공제
allowance for uncollectable accounts	대손충당금
allowance for undistributed profits	유보공제액
allowance for widow	과부공제
allowance for working student	근로학생공제
allowance in kind	현물지급
allowed amortizable limit	상각한도액
allowed cost	허용원가
allowed depreciation	상각범위
allowed limit of accumulation	적립한도액
allowed retirement income deduction	퇴직소득공제
alms	의손금
alongside delivery	자체취득
alpha value	알파값
alphabet fund	알파벳 펀드
already-issued bond	기발채
alter ego doctrine	분신의 이론
alteration	변경, 개조
alteration bordereau	변경각서
alteration of species	성질의 상실
alternate preference beneficiaries	순차우선수취인
alternate product	대체제품
alternation	교체

alternative accounting principles	대체회계원칙
alternative contract	선택계약
alternative costs	대체원가
alternative duties	선택세
alternative health care delivery system	대체의료서비스공급시스템
alternative mixes	대체믹스
alternative obligation	선택채무
alternative order	택일주문
alternative plan	대체안
alternative price change	대체적 가격변경
alternative pricing	선택형 가격결정
alternative remedy	선택적 구제
alternative sources	대체사입선
alternative technology	대체기술
alternative withholding tax on dividends	배당원천선택과세
alternatives	대체안
altogether	총계로
altruistic	이타주의
always open basis	상시유효
amalgamation	합병
amalgamation on an equal basis	대등합병
amalgamation procedures	합병수속
amalgamation surplus	합병잉여금
ambience	분위기
ambient light	엔비언트라이트
ambiguity	애매, 모호
ambit	권한범위
ambulatory	일시적인
amelioration	개선
amend	수정하다

amended budget 수정예산
amended return 수정신고
amendment 수정
amendment of articles of corporation 정관변경
amendment to a contract 계약내용수정
amercement 벌금
American Academy of Actuaries 미국계리인학회
American Accounting Association 미국회계학회
American Annuitants Mortality Table 미국연금가입자사망표
American Arbitration Association 미국중재협회
American Association of Medical Social Workers 미국의료사회사업자협회
American Association of Social Workers 미국사회사업가협회
American Association of University Teachers of Insurance 미국보험교수협회
American Bar Association 미국법조협회
American Bar Endowment 미국법조기금
American clause 중복보험의 순위주의약관
American Council of Life Insurance 미국생명보험협회
American Federation of Labor 미국노동총연맹
American Institute Cargo Clauses 미국협회화물약관
American Institute of Accountants 미국회계사협회
American Institute of Certified Public Accountants 미국공인회계사협회
American Institute of Marine Underwriters 미국해상보험업자협회
American Intellectual Property Law Association 미국공인회계사협회
American Judicature Society 미국사법협회
American Law Institute 미국법률협회

American Life Insurance Association	미국생명보험협회
American Management Association	미국경영자협회
American Mutual Insurance Alliance	미국상호보험회사협회
American National Standards Institute	미국규격협회
American option	미국옵션
American Risk and Insurance Association	미국보험학회
American selling price	미국국내판매가격
American Standard Code for Information Interchange	미국정보교환표준코드
American Stock Exchange	미국증권거래소
American type	미국식
Amex Commodity Exchange	아맥스 상품거래소
AMEX Index	미국증권거래소 주가지수
amicable action	우의적 소송
amicus curiae	법정조언자
Amnesty International	국제암네스티
amortization	채무상환, 정액상각
amortization cost	상각비용
amortization fund	부채상각준비금, 감채기금, 연부기금
amortization loan	분할반제형 대부
amortization of bond premium	사채할인발행차금상각
amortization of deferred assets	이연자산상각
amortization of goodwill	영업권상각
amortization of initial expenses	창업비상각
amortization of intangibles	무형자산감가상각
amortization of prior service cost	과거근무채무의 상각액
amortization of taxes	세금의 환원
amortization schedule	채무상환 스케줄
amortize	상각하다
amortized balance	미상각잔액

amortized cost	상각원가
amortizing diffusion model	절대확산모델
amortizing swap	원금 감소스왑
amortion	박탈
amount added to capital	증자
amount advanced	대부금액
amount assessed	평가액
amount billed	청구액
amount carried forward	차기이월액
amount claimed	청구액
amount covered	보험금액
amount deducted	공제액
amount due	만기지급액
amount financed	대출액
amount imposed	부과액
amount in arrears	미불금
amount in hand	보유액
amount insured	보험금액
amount invested	출자액
amount issued	발행액
amount of annuity certain	확정연금종가
amount of claim	구상액
amount of clearing	어음교환고
amount for the first payment	初回金
amount on hand	보유액
amount on hand goods in stock	재고상품보유액
amount outstanding	미지급액, 잔고
amount overbought	매(買)입액
amount oversold	매(賣)출액
amount paid	지급액
amount paid out to the outside by distribution of net profit	이익처분에 의한 사외유출액

amount paid per new stock	신주한주당 불입가액
amount receivable	수취금
amount received	수입금액
amount subscribed	응모금액
amount withheld	원천맡김
amoveas manus	재산반환영장
amplitude	음량
amusement	오락설비
amusement and restaurant tax	유흥음식세
amusement expenses	접대비
anagraph	기록
analog method	아날로그
analog to digital conversion	아날로그의 디지털 전환
analogy	유사, 비슷함
analysis	분석
analysis of budget variance	예산차이분석
analysis of cost variances	원가차이분석
analysis of credit	신용분석
analysis of lender's preference	대수분석
analysis of problem	문제해석
analysis of routes	루트분석
analysis of securities	증권분석
analysis of the affairs of a business	경영분석
analyst	분석자
analytic system	위험비율분석방식
analytical data	분석 자료
analytical forecast	분석적 예측
analytical jurisprudence	분석법학
analytical model	분석모형
analytical tools	분석수단
anamnesis	병력(病歷)
anchorage	정박세

ancient lights	채광권
ancient rent	임대료
ancient watercourse	고수로
ancient writing	고문서
ancients	고참변호사
ancillary	보조의
ancillary attachment	가차압
ancillary bill or suit	부수적 소송
ancillary product	보조제품
Andean Common Market	안데스 공동시장
Andean Group	안데스 그룹
Andean Pact Countries	안데스 조약국
angle of view	화각
anglers' insurance	낚시보험
animal insurance	동물보험
animus et factum	의사와 행위
animus furandi	절도의사
animus manendi	수주의사
animus revocandi	철회의사
annates	초년도 수익
annex	부속서류
annexation	병합
annexed letter	부속서류
annexed structure	부속설비
annire	소환
anniversary date	계약응당일
annotation	주석
announcement	공시
announcement effect	고지효과
annoyance	성가신 일
annual accounting	연차결산
annual audit	연도감사

annual audited financial statement	감사필 연차재무보고
annual basis	연환산
annual bonus agreement	임시급여협정
annual closing	마감, 연도말 마감
annual club due	연회비
annual compounding	유럽식 복리이자상환
annual coupon	연불 쿠폰
annual dues	연회비
annual earnings	연간소득
annual economic review	경제연보
annual expenditure	세출
annual financial statements	연차재무제표
annual income	연수
annual installment	연부
annual interest rate	연리
annual meeting	연차총회
annual member	연회원
annual payment	연일회 후불
annual payment budget facilities	연부불방식
annual percentage rate	연율 퍼센트
annual premium adjustment	보험료조정정산
annual profit disposition amount	연간이익처분액
annual rate of returns	연수이익
annual report	연차보고서
annual revenue	세입
annuitant	연수수취인
annuity bond	무상환채권
annuity certain	확정연금
annuity certain due	기한부 연금
annuity consideration	연금괘금
annuity insurance	연금보험
annuity purchase fund	연금구입기금

annuity purchase rates	연금구입요율
annuity refund	상환식연금
annuity repayment method	원리균등상환방식
annuity unit	연금유니트
annul	취소하다
annulment	무효
annulment of a contract	계약해제
annulment right	취소권
anomaly	아노말리
anonymous association	익명조합
another debt	기존채무
anstalt	엔스털트
answer	답변
answering time	응답시간
ante-nuptial	혼인전의
antedated	소급발행
antedated check	소급발행한 수표
antenna shop	안테나샾
anthropological jurisprudence	문화인류학적 법학
anti-dilution clause	희박화 방지조항
anti-monopoly law	독점금지법
anti-positivism	반실증주의
anti-rebate law	리베이트 금지법
anti-trust acts	반트러스트법
Anti-Trust Division	반트러스트국
anti-trust law	독점 금지법
anti-trust legislation	반트러스트 법규제
anticipated acceptance	만기전 인수 반트러스트 법안
anticipated cost	예정원가
anticipated profit	기대이익
anticipation	기한전 처분
anticipation discount	기한전 할인

anticipation of falling market	염가대기
anticipatory breach of contract	기한전의 계약위반
anticipatory demand	가수요
antiqua statuta	고법률
antique customa	구관세
antique customs	구관습법
antiselection	역선택
antithetic variable	대칭변수
apartment dwellers' comprehensive insurance	단지보험
aperture grille	어퍼투어 그릴
aperture grille pitch	어퍼투어 그릴피치
apology	사과, 사죄
apparatus	기구
apparel industry	어패럴 산업
apparent	표현적, 명백한
apparent agency	표현대리
apparent danger	명백한 위험
apparent easement	명시지역권
apparent heir	법정추정상속인
appeal	공소
appeal bond	상소보증금증서
appeal of felony	중죄소추
appeal power	소구력
appeals judge	국제심판관
appear	재판소에 출두
appearance	응소
appellant	상소인
appellate court	소송재판소
appellate jurisdiction	소송관할
appellee	피상소인
appendix	첨부서류

appetite	흥미
appliance	설비
applicable	적용할 수 있는
applicable law	준거법
applicable statutory useful life	적용법정내용연수
applicable useful life	적용가능한 내용연수
applicant	신청인
application	채무변제의 충당, 보험계약자의 사실고지, 신입요항
application for approval	승인신청
application for listing	상장신청서
application form for income tax convention	조세조약에 관한 제출서
application form for stock	주식청약신청서
application money	청약증거금
application money for stock	주식청약증거금
application of funds statement	자금운용표
application program	응용프로그램
application rate of overhead cost	간접비 배부율
application right	출원권
application to list	상장신청서
applied cost	적용원가
applied manufacturing expenses account	제조간접비배부계정
applied research	응용조사
appointed day	기일
appointed goods	지정상품
appointee	피임명자
appointing authority	중재인 선정기관
appointment	지정
appointment of depreciation	상각비배부
appointment sales	어포인트상법

appointor	지정권자
apportion	분할
apportionable part	보험가액 할당가능부분
apportioned tax	배부세
apportionment	분할(계약의)
apportionment of cost variance	원가차액조정
apportionment of loss	손해의 분담
apportionment of valuation	보험가액할당
appraisal	감정
appraisal loss	평가손
appraisal method	평가법
appraisal of assets	자산평가
appraisal of securities	유가증권평가
appraisal profit	평가익
appraisal profit or loss	평가손익
appraisal report	감정서
appraisal rights of shareholder	주식매수청구권
appraisal standard	평가기준
appraisal surplus	재평가적립금
appraisal system	업적평가제도
appraisal value	평가액
appraised price	산정가격
appraisement	재산평가
appraisement method of securities	유가증권평가방법
appraiser	평가인
appreciated market price	시가의 상승
appreciation	등귀
appreciation duty	증가세
appreciation surplus	재평가잉여금
apprehension	체포, 우려
approach	수법
appropriability theory	전유이론

appropriate	계상하다
appropriate cash supply for economic growth	성장통화
appropriate technology	적정기술
appropriated earned surplus	처분된 이익잉여금
appropriation	공용징수
appropriation account	이익처분계정
appropriation of profit	이익처분
appropriation of refund	환부금충당
appropriation section	이익처분부(部)
appropriation surplus	목적적립금
approval	승인
approval of special liquidation	특별청산승인
approval sales	시용판매
approval bidder	지정입찰자
approval list of investment	투자승인목록
approval pension contract	적격퇴직연금계약
approval pension funds	적격퇴직연금적립금
approval person	승인역원
approval retirement annuity	적격퇴직연금
approved society	인가조합
approved superannuation fund	적격퇴직연금
approved tender	지정입찰
approvement	개량지 수익
approximate cost	개산원가
approximate market price	시가개산액
approximate price	개산가격
approximate value	개산가격
appurtenance	재산에 부속하는 권리
appurtenant	부속물
apt time	적절한 시기
aptitude test	적성검사

aquatic rights	용수권
Arab League	아랍연맹
Arab Maghreb Union	아랍마그레브연합
arbi-loan	아비 론
arbiter	중재인
arbitrage	재정거래, 차익거래
arbitrage house	외국환중개인, 차액을 취득하는 중개인
arbitrage margin	재정보증금
arbitrage operation	재정조작, 중개매매
arbitrage opportunity	재정기회
arbitrage position	재정 포지션
arbitrage pricing theory	재정가격결정이론
arbitrage pricing theory (APT)	재정가격 경쟁 설정이론
arbitrage trader	재정거래자
arbitrage transaction	재정거래
arbitrageur	재정거래인
arbitral tribunal	중재법정
arbitrament	중재판단
arbitrament and award	중재판단의 항변
arbitrary	자의적인, 독단적인
arbitrated rate of exchange	재정환상장
arbitration	중재
arbitration clause	중재조항
Arbitration Commission	중재조정위원회
arbitration of exchange	환재정
arbitration proceedings	중재수속
arbitrator	중재인
architect's liability policy	건축가배상책임보험
archives	공문서
area of normal curve	정규곡선의 범위
area of welcome enterprise	기업유치지역
area polluted with soot and smoke	대기오염지구

area selection	지역선정
arena	입회장
arguendo	논쟁을 목적으로
argument	변론
arithmetic average	산술평균
arithmetic stock price average	단순평균주가
arm's length price	독립기업간 가격
arm's length principle	독립기업의 원칙
armchair theory	궤상의 공론
arm's length	암스랭스
arpentator	토지측량자
arranged total loss	협정전손
arrangement	채무정리
arranger	알선인(斡旋人)
arrearage	연체금
arrears	체납
arrears coupon	조연이찰
arrears of local tax	지방세의 연체금
arrears swap	지체되는 상환거래
arrest of judgment	판결의 저지
arrestment	체포, 억류
arrival	착선
arrival draft	도착후 일람불어음
arrival of shipment	착하
arrived damaged value	총손품가액
article	조항
article in custody	보관품
article of confederation	연합규약
article of the peace	안전보증신입
article on the free list	관세면제품
article subject to taxation	과세품
articled clerk	실무수습생

articles	정관
articles of agreement	계약각서
articles of association	통상정관
articles of confederation	연합규약
articles of impeachment	탄핵조항
articles of incorporation	회사정관
articles partnership	조합정관
articles of union	연합개조
artificer	명장
artificial	법
artificial environment	인공환경
artificial intelligence	인공지능
artificial life	인공생명
artificial person	법인(法人)
artificial presumptions	법률적 추정
artificial statement	다항식계산서
artificially	전문적인
as at	인취적으로, 부자연스럽게
ascendants	직계존속
ascending	상승
ascending curve	상승곡선
Asiadollar	아시아 달러
Asia Pacific Economic Cooperation	아·태경제협력회의
Asia Monitor Resource Center (AMRC)	아시아 감시정보센터
Asian Clearing Union	아시아결제동맹
Asian Currency Market	아시아 통화시장
Asian Currency Unit	아시아통화단위
Asian Development Bank	아시아개발은행
Asian Development Fund	아시아개발기금
Asian dollar bond	아시아달러채
Asian Insurance Commissioners Association	아시아보험감독관협회

Asian Monetary Unit	아시아통화단위
Asian Payment Union	아시아지불동맹
Asian Reinsurance Pool	아시아재보험공동기금
Asian Reserve Bank	아시아준비은행
Asian-dollar market	아시아달러시장
asked rate	매수인 지정가격
aspect ratio translation	종횡비환산
aspiration	원망
aspiration level	요구수준
aspirin theory	아스피린이론
assart	임지개척
assay office	순분검정소
assecurator	보험자
assembly cost system	조립원가계산
assembly department	조립부분
assembly lindustry	조립산업
assembly order	조립지시서
assembly order sheet	조립순위표
assembly process	조립공정
assembly production order	조립생산지시서
assembly service	집하서비스
assent	수락
assertory covenant	확인적 약속
assess	부과하다, 평가하다, 사정하다
assessable income	과세소득
assessed amount	검정액
assessed income	검정소득액
assessed tax	과세금
assessed valuation	평가가치
assessed value	사정가액
assessing organ	사정기관
assessment	부과액, 사정액, 추징금

assessment and collection 부과징수
assessment and decision 부과결정
assessment insurance 부과식 보험
assessment mutual association 부과식 상호보험조합
assessment of income tax 신고소득세
assessment plan 부과식 보험
assessment roll 과세원부
assessment system accumulation 부과식적립제
assessor 감정인, 평가인
asset accounting 자산회계
asset acquisition 자산취득
asset allocation technique 자산분배법
asset and liability management 자산・부채종합관리
asset approach 에셋 어프로치
asset backed securities 자산담보부증권
asset class target 자산종류별 목표액
asset coverage 자산담보율
asset income 자산소득
asset out of books 부외자산
asset position 자산상태
asset preference 자산충당금
asset reshuffling 자산이체
asset revaluation 자산재평가
asset revaluation tax 자산재평가세
asset sales 자산매각
asset settlement 자산결제
asset swap transaction 자산교환거래
asset turnover ratio 자산회전률
asset utilization 자산활용
asset valuation reserve 자산평가준비금
asset value 자산가치
asset-utilization ratios 자산활용률

assets	자산
assets and equities	자산과 지분
assets differentials	자산격차
assets effect	자산효과
assets money	자산화폐
assets not admitted	비인용자산
assets producting interest	운용자산
assets revaluation law	자산재평가법
assets share method	자산할당방법
assets subject to lien	담보차입자산
assets turnover	자산회전률
asseveration	엄숙한 선언
assign	양도하다
assigned accounts	양도채권
assigned counsel	국선변호사
assigned risk plans	불량물건할당계획
assigned surplus	특별적립잉여금
assignee	수탁자
assignment	양도
assignment and transfer	양도이전
assignment clause	양도조항
assignment fee	양도수수료
assignment in blank	백지양도
assignment of business	영업권양도
assignment of claim	채권양도
assignment of responsibility	신뢰계약
assignment of sales contract	매매계약의 양도
assignment of stock	주식양도
assignor	양도자
assigns	양수인
assimilation theory	동화이론
assistance	원조

assistant certified public accountant	회계사보
assisted acquisition	구제합병방식
assize of mort d'ancestor	상속부동산점유회복소송
associate	제휴하다
Associated Aviation Underwriters	항공보험협회
associated company	계열회사
associated gas	천연가스, 부수가스
associated person	특수관계인
Association Cambiste Internationale	상업회의소
association captive	자가보험취급기관
association group insurance	협회단체보험
Association of Average Adjusters	해손정산인보험
Association of South-East Asian Nations	동남아시아국가연합
association test	연상테스트
assoile	사면하다
assorting	분배
assortment	상품구성
assortment structure	구색구조
assumed bond	인수사채
assumed liability	인수부채
assumed rate of interest	예정이율
assumed settling day	가결산일
assumption	채무인수
assumption of risk	위험가정
assumption reinsurance	계약이전재보험
assumptions	가정, 공준
assurance	보험
assured	피보험자
at cost	원가로
at issue	계쟁 중의, 논쟁 중의
at low ebb	쇠퇴기에 있는

at par 액면가격으로
at risk 위험한 상태에
at sight bill 일람불어음
at sight buyiing rate 일람불어음매상장
at sight buying rate with credit 신용장일람불어음사장
at the market 시가로
at-home nursing service 재택간병서비스
attached document 첨부서류
attached goods 차압물건
attachment 첨부
attachment of privilege 소환수속
attainder 사권(私權)박탈
attained age 현재연령
attendance 입회
attendant term 연기임차권
attest 증명하다
attestation 증명, 입증
attestation clause 증명문언
attested copy 인증등본
attested witness 증명증인
attitude change 태도변용
attitude change research 태도변용조사
attitude measurement 태도측정
attitude study 태도연구
attitude survey 태도조사
attorney 변호사
attorney at law 변호사
Attorney General 법무장관
attornment 토지양도승인
attraction of factory 공장유치
attractive nuisance 유인적 방해물
attributable income principle 귀속주의

attribute	속성
attribute listing	속성열거법
attribution	직권
attribution analysis	요인분석
attrition rate	감소율
auction	경쟁매매
auction market	경매시장
auction sale	경매
auction system	경매조직망
auctioneer	경매인
audience analysis	시청자분석
audio-visual display	시청각기기
audio-visual education	시청각교육
audit	감사
audit adjustment	감사결정
audit after the contract award	계약체결후 감사
audit and criminal investigation	세무감사
audit certificate	감사증명
audit corporation	감사법인
audit fee	감사보수
audit frequency	감사의 빈도
audit objective	감사목적
audit on bank account	은행조사
audit on property	재산의 조사
audit opinion	감사의견
audit policy	감사정책
audit premium	감사결제보험료차액
audit procedure	감사절차
audit program	감사계획
audit report	감사보고서
audit year	감사연도
auditee	피감사자

auditing	회계감사
auditing organization	감사기관
auditing standards	감사기준
auditor	감사역
auditor's opinion	감사인의 의견
augmentation	수입증가
augmentation of earnings	수익증가
augmented product	확장제품
austere budget	긴축예산
austere fiscal policy	긴축재정
Australia-Asia Worker Links (AAWL)	호주 아시아 노동연합
Australian National Bond	오스트레일리아 국채
autarky	자급자족경제
authentic	인증된
authentic act	인증행위
authentication	인증
authorities	당국
authority	권한
authority bond	공사공단채
authority of correction or determination	경정 · 결정의 처분청
authority to inquire and inspect	질문검사권
authority to purchase	어음매입수권서
authorization	승인
authorization by law	법률의 위임
authorization number	승인번호
authorization procedures	인가수속
authorization test	허가시험
authorize	허가하다
authorized capital	수권자본
authorized dealer	정부공인딜러
authorized deferred payment	연납

authorized foreign exchange bank	외국환공인은행
authorized insurer	면허보험자
authorized shares	수권주식
auto sales	자동차판매대수
auto tax	자동차세
automated clearinghouse	자동결제기구
automated customer account transfer	고객계좌자동이전
automated reservation service	자동예약서비스
automated teller machine	현금자동입출금기
automatic approval system	자동인가방식
automatic call distributor	자동호출분산기
automatic collection service	자동집금서비스
automatic fund transfer	구좌자동이체
automatic increase in tax revenue	자연증수
automatic increased value clause	자동증액보험약관
automatic increasing annuity	자동증액연금
automatic markdown	자동가격할인
automatic premium loan	보험료자동이체대부
automatic reinstatement clause	보험금액자동복원조항
automatic renewal system	자동갱신제도
automatic renewal time deposit	자동갱신정기예금
automatic settlement	자동결제
automatic stay	자동정지
automatic transfer account	자동이체계좌
automatic transfer service	자동이체서비스
automaticity	자동성
automobile acquisition tax	자동차취득세
Automobile Association	자동차연맹
automobile bodiliy injury liability insurance	대인배상보험
automobile comprehensive liability policy	자동차종합손해배상책임보험

automobile driver's liability insurance	자동차운전자손해배상책임보험
automobile insurance	자동차보험
Automobile Insurance Rating Association of Japan	일본 자동차보험요율산정회
automobile liability insurance	자동차손해배상책임보험
automobile liability insurance certificate	자동차손해배상책임보험증명서
automobile passengers' personal accident insurance	탑승자상해보험
automobile physical damage insurance	차량보험
automobile property damage liability insurance	대물배상보험
automobile repair costs index	자동차수리비지수
automobile sales finance	자동차판매금융
automobile tax	자동차세
automobile tonnage tax	자동차중량세
autonomic decision	자주결정
autonomous investment	독립투자
autonomous item	자발적 항목
autonomous tariff	자주관세
autonomously strong	자율반등
autonomy	자율성
autoregressive model	자기회귀모형
autre action pendant	소송계속의 항변
auxiliary	보조(副)
auxiliary book	보조부
auxiliary journal	보조장부
auxiliary ledger	보조원장
availability	이용도
availability clause	가용성 약관

availability of bank	금리의 가용성
availability risk	가용성 위험
available	이용가능한, 유효한
available assets	이용가능자산
available bond	이용가능채권
available profit	가처분이익
avails	수익
average	비례전보
average absolute deviation	평균절대편익
average adjuster	해손정산인
average balance outstanding	평균발행잔고
average bond	공동해손맹약서
average claim	분손손해
average collection	평균회수기간
average collection period	매출채권회수기간
average condition	비례전보조항
average contracted rates on loans and discounts	대출약정평균금리
average cost	평균원가
average cost method	평균원가법
average cost of claims	평균손해가액
average current cost method	평균시가법
average earnings	평균수익
average future lifetime	평균여명
average growth rate	평균신장률
average income	평균소득
average index monthly earnings	평균표준보수월액
average interest rate cap	평균금리 캡
average inventory	평균재고
average life	평균잔존년수
average loss settlement	분손계산
average markup percentage	평균치입률

average maturity of debts 부채평균기간
average period of production 평균생산기간
average policy 비례전보계약
average premium 평균보험료
average premium system 평균보험료방식
average rate 평균요율
average rate of dividend 평균배당률
average return on investment 평균투자수익
average risk 표준체
average tax rate 평균세율
average taxation 평균과세
average term to maturity 평균상환년수
average unless general 비공동해손손해
average volatility 평균변동률
average warranty 분손약관
average yield 평균잔존기간
averaged type forward contract 평균형 선도거래
averaging 에버리징
averaging clause 비례전보조항
aviation cargo insurance 항공운송보험
aviation fuel tax 항공기연료세
aviation hull insurance 항공기체보험
Aviation Insurance Offices' Association 항공보험회사협회
avoidable cost 회부가능원가
avoidable risk 회부가능위험
avoidance of recurrence 재발방지
avoidance of sections 과제폐지
avoir fiscale (프랑스법 상의) 세액공제
avowry 정당점유의 주장
avulsion 토지의 전위
award 재정

≪ B ≫

BA rate	BA율
Babbage's Table	바베이지 생명표
baby bond	소액채권
baby fund	베이비 펀드
back away	백 어웨이
back bond	손실보상증서
back dating	실제보다 전일 날짜로 한 것
back dividend	역지급배당금
back door listing	뒷문상장, 우회상장
back money	연체금
back office	백 오피스
back pay	역급여
back rent	체납가임
back spread	백 스프레드
back tax	체납세
back to back credit	백 투 백 크레디트 신용장
back-door selling	후문판매
back-end load	백 앤 로드
back-end rights	백 앤 라이트
back-haul allowance	상품거래할인
back-to-back loan	백 투 백 론
back-up facility	백업 퍼실러티
back-up inventory	예비재고
back-up merchandise	예비상품
backbond	처분제한증서
background information	배경적 사항
backing	배서

backlighting	역광
backlog of orders	수지주문
backup line	백업 라인
backward channel	후방유통경로
backward countries	후진국
backward difference	후방차분 근사치
backward integration	후방통합
backward linkages	후방관련
backward needs	후방 니즈
backward vertical integration	후방수직통합
backwardation	수도연기금, 역전
bad	부적법의
bad account	대손처리하는 계정
bad debt	불량채권
bad debt loss	미회수금손실
bad debt provision	대손충당금
bad debt ratio	불량채권율
bad debt reserve	대손충당금
bad debt written-off	미회수금상각
bad delivery	불완전
bad faith	악의
bad loan	미회수채권
bad member	불량회원
bad news	악재
bad risk	불량물건
bad standing	불완전자격
badger	강매
bail	보석금
bail bond	보석보증증권
bail-piece	보석계약금
bailee	수여자
bailee clause	수여자약관

bailees' customers floater	수여자고객포괄포험
bailees' liability policy	수여자배상책임보험
bailment	기탁
bailor	기탁자
bailout	구제조치
bait advertising	미끼광고
bait and switch	미끼권유
bait pricing	미끼가격설정
balance account	잔고계정
balance at the bank	은행예금잔액
balance book	잔고장
balance due	부족액
balance form	잔고식
balance in hand	수주잔액
balance of accounts	계정잔액
balance of clearing	정산잔액
balance of current account	경상계정수지
balance of international indebtedness	국제대차
balance of international payments	국제수지
balance of loans	융자잔액
balance of monetary movements	금융계정
balance of payment	국제수지
balance of payments statistics	국제수지통계
balance of stock loans	차주잔액
balance of the amount charged to special account	특별계정잔액
balance of trade	무역수지
balance on current account	경상수지
balance on invisible trade	무역외수지
balance on ledger	원장잔액
balance on nonmonetary transactions	비금융적 거래수지
balance order	수금지불명령

balance renewal	론의 개서
balance sheet	대차대조표
balance sheet analysis	대차대조표 분석
balance sheet hedge	대차대조표 헷지
balance sheet program	BS 조정문제
balance sheet reserve system annuity	적립방식연금
balanced budget	균형예산
balanced budget theorem	균형예산정리
balanced finance	균형재정
balanced form	계정식
balanced fund	밸런스 펀드
balanced fund portfolio	밸런스 펀드 포트폴리오
balanced growth	균형성장
balanced manager	밸런스형 매니저
balanced power	균형세력
balanced stock	균형재고
balances	잔채
ballast	바닥짐, 저하(底荷)
balloon payment	벌룬 페이먼트
ban	공고
ban call	밴 콜
band and crawl	밴드 앤드 크롤
band wagon effect	밴드 웨건 효과
bandwidth compression	대역압축
banishment	추방
bank account	은행계좌
bank act	은행법
bank balance	은행예금잔고
bank bill	은행어음
bank bookkeeping	은행부기
bank check	은행수표
bank clearing	어음교환결제

bank credit card	은행계 신용카드
bank crisis	은행공황
bank dealer	은행딜러
bank debenture	은행채
bank deposit	은행예금
bank discount method	은행할인방법
bank discount rate	은행할인율
bank examination	은행검사
Bank for International Settlements	국제결제은행
bank full dealing	은행 풀 딜링
bank guarantee	은행보증
bank holding company	은행지주회사
bank holiday	은행휴무일
bank interest	은행이자
bank line	뱅크라인
bank liquidity	은행유동성
bank loan-deposit ratio	예대율
bank loans	단기차입금
bank loans payable	은행차입금
bank loans secured by mortgage	담보에 의한 은행차입
bank note	은행권
bank of issue	발행은행
Bank of Japan Act	일본은행법
Bank of Japan credit	일본은행신용
Bank of Japan note issue tax	일본은행권 발행세
bank point-of-sales	은행 POS
bank rate	은행이율
bank reference	은행조회
bank reserve	은행준비
bank's automatic accounts transfer system	은행자동
banker's acceptance	은행인수어음

banker's acceptances	은행인수어음
banker's blanket bond	은행포괄보증
banker's credit	은행신용장
bankers forgery bond	은행위조보증증권
banking accounts of all banks	전국은행계정
banking business	은행업무
banking day	은행거래일
banking facilities	금융기관
banking principle	은행주의
banking syndicate	은행단
banking transaction contract	은행거래약정서
bankrupt	파산자
bankrupt law	파산법
bankrupt's estate	파산재단
bankruptcy	파산
bankruptcy administrator	파산관재인
bankruptcy and composition	화의(和議)
bankruptcy court	파산재판소
bankruptcy debtor	파산채무자
bankruptcy law	파산법
bankruptcy notice	파산고지
bankruptcy proceedings	파산수속
bankruptcy rules	파산규칙
bankwire	뱅크와이어
bar	소송
bar association	법조협회
bar chart	바 차트
Barcelona Traction Case	바로셀로나 거래사건
bare body	나본문
bare trustee	수동적 수탁자
bargain	매매
bargain counter	본래가격보다

bargain purchase option	할인구입권
bargain stock	할인주
bargainee	매(買)수인
bargaining agreement	노동협약
bargaining cost	계약비용
bargaining power	교섭력
bargainor	매(賣)도인
barometer stock	표준주
barratry	소송교사
barrier free	배리어 프리
barriers to entry	진입장벽
barter	물물교환
base case	규범사례
base company	베이스 컴퍼니
base cost estimate	기초적 비용견적
base courts	하급재판소
base currency	기준통화
base date for assessment	부과기일
base earnings	기초수익
base free	제한부동산권
base money	베이스 머니
base of taxation	과세표준
base pay	기본급
base period	기준기간
base premium	기준보험료
base price	기준가격
base rate	기본율
base series	기준계열
base standard cost	기준표준원가
base year	기준년도
base-stock method	기준재고정리법
basement merchandise	특매상품

basic allowance	기초공제
basic assortment	기본적 진열
basic automobile policy	일반자동차보험
basic balance	기초수지
basic deduction	기초공제
basic deduction for bequest	유산에 대한 기초공제
basic discount rate	기준할인율
basic exemption	기초공제
basic needs	기본적 니즈
basic period	기본기간
basic rate	기본율, 기본요율
basic retirement funds	기초퇴직연금기금
basic salary	기본급
basic service	기본서비스
basic stockholder	판정의 기초가 되는 주주
basic taxable year	기준년도
basing-point pricing	원점가격제
basis	베이시스
basis for conclusions	결론의 논거
basis for recording sales	외상계산기준
basis gap	베이시스 갭
basis of calculation	계산기초
basis on the amount of salary	급여기준
basis point	베이시스 포인트
basis risk	베이시스 리스크
basis swap	베이시스 스왑
basis to prorate local tax	분할기준
basis trading	베이시스 거래
basket	바스켓
basket purchase	일괄구입
basket system	바스켓 방식
Basel Agreement	바젤협정

batch file	배치파일
batch processing	베치처리
batch production	연속생산
batch trading system	배치거래시스템
battle of the brands	브랜드 경쟁
bear	낳다
bear bond	베어 본드
bear call spread	베어 콜 스프레이트
bear hug	베어 허그
bear index bond	베어 인덱스채
bear market	하락시세
bear raiding	베어 레이딩
bear spread trading	베어 스프레드 거래
bear the market	하락장
bear-squeeze	주가의 상승세
bearer	지참인
bearer bond	무기명채권
Bearer Depositary Receipts	무기명예탁증권
bearer form	무기명식
bearer instrument	무기명증권
bearer share	무기명주식
bearish	약세의
bearish channel	약한 채널
bearish consolidation patterns	약한 컨설리테이션 패턴
bearish market	약세시장
bearish resistance line	약세저항선
bearish reversal patterns	약세리버설 패턴
bearish sentiment	약세시세
bearish support line	약세지지선
bearish tone	약세시황
become due	기한이 오다
before due endorsement	만기전 배서

before tax	세포함, 세전
beggar-my-neighbor policy	근린궁핍화 정책
beginning balance	기초잔액
beginning day of the taxable year	사업년도개시일
beginning inventories	기초재고
beginning of period	기초
behavior approach	행동적 어프로치
behavior criteria	행동기준
behavior science	행동과학
behavior-primacy theory	행동우선이론
behavioral modification	행동수정
behavioral theory	행동이론
belated claims	청구지체손해
bell and whistle	증권의 특전
bell-shaped curve	벨형 곡선, 종형 곡선
bellwehter issue	지표유가증권
belly up	무가치증권
belongings	재산
below cost	원가 이하에서
below par	액면이하, 평가이하
below the market	빌로우 더 마켓
below-cost sale	원가이하판매
benchmark	표준
benchmark portfolio	벤치 마크 포트폴리오
benchmark rate	표준가격권
benchmark securities	지표증권
benchmark survey	벤치마크 조사(기준조사)
bending	곡손
beneficial association	상호부조단체
beneficial duty	편익관세
beneficial interest	수익권
beneficial owner	실질소유자

beneficiary	신탁수익자, 보험금수취인
beneficiary certificate	수익증권
beneficiary company	수익기업
beneficiary of the retirement annuity	퇴직연금의 수취인
beneficiary right	수익권
beneficiary securities	수익증권
benefit	급부
benefit association	공제단체
benefit formula	연금급부액 산정방식
benefit of insurance clause	보험이익형수약관
benefit principle	수익부담의 원칙
benefit segmentation	베네비트 세그먼테이션
benefit society	공제조합
benefit taxation	부조료과세
benefits for survivor	유족급부금
benevolent association	상호부조조합
benign failure	고장의 영향완화
bequest	동산유증
Berne Union	베른 유니온
besoin	예비지불인
best evidence	최고증거
best-efforts basis	최선노력원칙
best-efforts selling	위탁판매
beta	베타
beta coefficient	베타지수
beta value	베타치
betterment	개선
betterment expense	개장비
bid	가격을 제시하다
bid and offer	매수호가와 매도호가
bid ask spread	매매치 폭
bid bond	입찰보증증서

bid by advertising	경쟁입찰
bid price	입찰가격
bid rate	매입효율
bid-offer spread	매입-매도 가격차
bidder	입찰자
bidding	입찰
bidding for public offering	공모입찰
bidding up	경매에 의한 가격상승
Big Bang	빅뱅
Big Board	뉴욕증권거래소
big jump	폭등
big shareholder	대주주
big ticket merchandise	고가상품
bilateral clearing arrangement	쌍무청산협정
bilateral contract	쌍무계약
bilateral investment agreement	쌍무투자협정
bilateral monopoly	쌍방독점
bilateral trade	쌍무무역
bilateral trade agreement	상호무역협정
bilged	해저침수
bill	청구서, 법안
bill accepted	인수된 환어음
bill bearer	어음소지인
bill bought	매입환
bill broker	어음 브로커
bill buying and selling rate	어음매매율
bill buying system	어음매입제도
bill clearing	어음교환
bill collection	추심어음(bill for collection)
bill discounted account	할인어음계정
bill drawn for sale	매출어음
bill for foreclosure	환수권상실소장

bill foreign currency	외화어음
bill in domestic currency	방화어음
bill obligatory	강제채무증서
bill of advocation	재심리상신서
bill of certiorari	이송영장청구소송
bill of complain	소장
bill of credit	신용증권
bill of debt	채무증서
bill of exceptions	항의취지서
bill of exchange	환어음(수출어음)
bill of lading	선하증권
bill of mortality	사망기록
bill of others	타행인수
bill of particulars	청구명세서
bill of quantities	수량표
bill of rights	권리장전
bill of sale	양도담보증서
bill pass	빌 패스
bill payable	지불어음
bill payable at a fixed date	확정일 지급어음
bill payable to bearer	지참인 지급어음
bill payable to order	지시인 지급어음
bill receivable	역환
bill sent	발송지 송금환
bill sold	매도환
bill-book	어음계정 장부
bills bought	매도환
bimetallism	복본위제
binary file	바이너리 파일
binational enterprise	2국간베이스기업
binder	각서
binding	구속력 있는

binding clause	구속조항
binomial coefficient	이항계수
binomial expansion	이항전개
binomial model	이항분포 모형
bio computer	바이오 컴퓨터
biorhythm	생체리듬, 바이오리듬
birth rate	출산율
bit guarantee insurance	입찰보증보험
bit-ask spread	매매의 폭
black box	블랙박스
black box auction	블랙박스 옥션
black check	납치 방치
black knight	블랙 나이트
black market	암시장
black market dealing	암 딜링
Black Monday	블랙 먼데이
"black out" period	공백기간
Black-Scholes model	블랙숄스 모형
blacklist	블랙 리스트
blank	백지배서
blank acceptance	백지인수
blank book	미기입장부
blank endorsement	백지배서
blank stock	백지주식
blanket bond	포괄저당권부 채권
blanket brand	통일상표
blanket clause	포괄조항
blanket mortgage	포괄적 저당권
blanket order	일괄주문
blanket policy	포괄보험계약
blanket pricing agreement	포괄가격계약
blanket system	포괄담보설정방식

blazing a trail	신기축을 열다
blind	익명의
blind advertisement	익명광고
blind bidding	익명입찰
blind check	발췌검사
blind pool	일임펀드
blind test	눈 가린 테스트
bloc economy	블록 경제
block exemption	집단적용면제
block flow	블록 플로우
block offer	일괄매출, 블록오퍼
block policy	일괄담보보험계약
block positioner	블록 포지셔너
block registration system	일괄등록제도
block sales	대량매매거래
block trading	블록 거래
block transaction	대량거래
blockade	봉쇄
blocked currency	동결통화
blocked funds	동결자산
blood relationship	혈연
blotter	일일계획표
blotting book	거래 일일계획표
blue chips	우량주
blue form return	청색신고
blue return system	청색신고제도
blue sky law	청공법
blue-collar	블루 칼라
Board of Audit	회계검사원
board of directors	이사회
Board of Governors of the Federal Reserve System	연방준비제도이사회

board of pardons	사면위원회
Board of Review	과세평가심사위원회
broad of supervisors	감리위원회
board of trade	상공회의소
board room	입회장
board trading	보드거래
bodily injury	신체손상
bodily injury liability cover	인적배상책임담보
body copy	본문
body of an instrument	문서의 본문
bogus dividend	배당의제, 제꼬리배당
bogus stock	유령주
boilerplate	상투적인 문구
bona fide contracts	선의의 계약
bona fide cost	진짜원가
bona fide creditor	선의의 채권자
bona fide holder	선의의 소지자
bona fide purchaser	선의취득자
bona fides	성질
bona vacantia	무생물
bonanza	대성공
bond	채권
bond account	채권계정
bond and debenture	채권
bond anticipation notes	장기채 차환예정증권
bond authorized	사채최고발행한도
bond broker	채권브로커
bond call provision	채권의 임의상환조항
bond certificate	사채권
bond collateral loans	공사채 담보금융
bond credit rating	채권등급
bond creditor	채권권리자

bond dealer 채권딜러
bond demand 채권수요
bond discount 채권할인
bond dividend 사채배당
bond flotation 기채
bond flotation market 기채시장
bond for distrain of rent 지대차압보증증권
bond form 보증증권양식
bond fund 채권펀드
bond futures 채권선물
bond futures option 채권선물옵션
bond held 보유채권
bond holder 사채권자
bond holding 채권보유
bond in a pipeline 발행예정채권
bond in portfolio 보유채권
bond interest 사채이자
bond inventory 재고채권
bond investment business 증권투자사업
bond investment trust 공사채투자신탁
bond issue 채권발행
bond issue costs 사채발행비용
bond issued 발행된 채권
bond issued by government related agency 정부관련 기관채권
bond issuing bank 채권발행은행
bond market 채권시장
bond market equilibrium 채권시장균형
bond of affiliated company 관계회사사채
bond of international agency 국제기관채권
bond of international creditors 파산신고채권자 보증증권
bond on tap 탭 채

bond option	채권옵션
bond option at over-the-counter	채권점두옵션
bond outstanding	미상환채권
bond premium	채권상승액
bond price	채권가격
bond purchase	채권구입
bond rating	채권평가
bond refunding	채권차환
bond register	사채원부
bond return	채권이율
bond selection option	채권선택옵션
bond subscription	채권응모
bond swap	채권스왑
bond switching	채권교환거래
bond trader	본드 트레이더
bond trust indenture	채권신탁증서
bond underwriting	채권인수
bond unissued	사채미발행고
bond unit trust	단위형 채권투자신탁
bond valuation	사채평가
bond washing	윤리에 반하는 거래
bond with debt warrant	데트 워런트 채
bond with stock purchase warrant	주식매수권부 사채
bond with subscription warrant	신주인수권부 사채
bond with voting right	의결권부 사채
bond with warrant	워런트 채
bond yield	채권이율
bond-equivalent yield	채권환산이율
bond-stock mixes	채권 · 주식조합
bonded area	보세지역
bonded debt	채권발행차입금
bonded goods	보세창고내 화물

bonded warehouse	보세창고
bonding company	계약이행보증회사
bonus	특별배당
bonus paid per employee	1인당 상여
bonus paid to director	임원상여
bonus payment entered into expenses	손금산입상여
bonus payment reserve	상여충당금
bonus reserve	이익배당준비금
bonus scheme	이익배당계획
bonus stock	특별배당주
book	장부
book account	당좌계정
book balance	장부잔액
book binding	제본
book credit	대변계정
book entry	장부기입
book entry security	은해계좌기장증권
book inventory	장부상 재고
book keeper	부기계
book money	장부화폐
book of final entry	최종기입부
book of original entry	원시기입부
book runner	사무간사회사
book value	장부가격
book-entry securities	등록정부증권
book-entry system for bond	채권대체결제제도
book-keeper	장부담당
book-keeping machine	기장기
booking	장부기입
booking center	기장장소
bookkeeping	부기
bookkeeping by double entry	복식기장법

bookkeeping by single entry 단식부기
boom 호황
boom and bust 큰시세
boom town 신흥도시
boomerang effect 부메랑효과
boost 증대
boosting 자극하다
booth 부스
bootstrap acquisition 부스트랩 매수
borax goods 값싼 상품
border tax adjustment 국경세조정
bordereau 재보험계약 명세서
borderless economy 국경 없는 경제
borderline risk 경계체
borough courts 市재판소
borrowed capital 차입자본
borrowed money 차입금
borrowed reserves 대출
borrowed securities 차입유가증권
borrowed share 차입 주식
borrowing 차입금
borrowing account 차입금계정
borrowing cost 차입비용
borrowing demand 차입수요
borrowing in advance 전차
borrowing rate 조달금리
borrowing requirements 차입필요액
borrowing short 단기차입
Bottin International 보틴 인터내셔널
bottle-neck inflation 바틀넥 인플레이션
bottom 바닥
bottom line 당기이익

bottom price	최저가격
bottom straddle	하향제한 스트래들
bottom vertical combination	보통 버티컬 콤비네이션
bottom-up approach	바텀 업 어프로치
bottom-up forecasting	바텀 업형 예측
bottom-up process	바텀 업형
bottoming out	최저시세까지 떨어짐
bottomry bond	모험임차증권
bought and sold note	매매보고서
bought deal	매입인수
bought for cash	현금매입
bounce	되살아나다
boundary	경계선
boundary representation	바운더리 리프리젠테이션
boundary strategy	경계전략
bounds	경계
bounty	교부금
bourse	환거래소
bourse tax	거래소 거래세
bourse transaction tax	거래소세
boutique	전문증권회사
Box-Jenkins	박스잰킨스법
bracket	서열
bracket creep	요율단계의 변경
brag and boast commercial	과장광고
brain drain	두뇌 유출
branch	지점
branch office	지점
branch plant	분공장
branch accounting	지점회계
branch banking system	지점은행제도
branch handling foreign exchange business	외국환거래지점

branch ledger	지점원장
branch line	지선
branch office	지점
branch system	지사제도
brand acceptance	브랜드 수용
brand advertising	브랜드 광고
brand awareness	브랜드 인지
brand comparison	브랜드 비교
brand equity	브랜드 애퀴티
brand image	브랜드 이미지
brand label	브랜드 레벨
brand loyalty	브랜드 충성도
brand management	상표관리
brand merchandising	브랜드상품의 머천다이징
brand naming	브랜드 네이밍
brand policy	상표정책
brand preference	상표선호
brand recognition	브랜드 인지
brand strategy	상표전략
brand switch	브랜드 변경
brand switching	브랜드 추이
brand-extension strategy	브랜드 확충전략
brand-named item	명품
Brand Commision	브랜트 위원회
branding	브랜드 설정
brass plate company	브래스 플레이트 컴퍼니
brass-plate office	표찰만의 오피스
breach	위반
breach of confidence	신뢰위반
breach of contract	계약위반
breach of covenant	날인증서 계약위반
breach of duty	의무위반

breach of law	법률위반
breach of privilege	특권남용
breach of warranty	담보위반
breadth	넓이
breadth of assortment	진열정도
break-down	내역
break-even analysis	손익분기분석
break-even chart	손익분기도표
break-even line	채산수준
break-even point	손익분기점
break-even yield	투자수익률이 동일
break-up value	청산가치
breakage	파손
breakdown	붕괴
breaking bulk	양화개시
breakthrough	돌파, 약진
breakup value	분산가치
Bretton Woods	브렛튼 우즈
Bretton Woods monetary system	브렛튼 우즈 통화체제
brewery-tax	주조세
bribery	뇌물행위
bridal market	혼례식장
bridge finance	연결융자
bridge loan	브릿지 론
bridging exchange	계환
brief	준비서면
brief rally	일시적 반등
bring forward	이월하다
bring over	인도하다
brisk market	활황시장
brisk recovery	순조로운 회복
British Banker's Association	영국은행협회

British Export Trade Research Organization	영국무역진흥회
British Insurance Association	영국보험협회
British Stock Exchange	영국증권거래소
broad based stock index	종합주가지수
broad form	종합보험증권
broad market	큰 장사
broad market index	광범위 시장 인덱스
broad tape	전광 정보판
broadcast advertising	방송광고
broadcast commercials	커머셜
broadcast media	방송매체
broadcaster	방송업자
broadcasting satellite	방송위성
broadened marketing concept	확장마케팅 개념
broken term	특정기간
broker	중개업자
broker agent	주식거래인
broker's business	브로커업자
broker's loan	브로커즈 론
broker's market	업자에 의한 투기상장
brokerage	브로커업자
brokerage commission	위탁수수료
brokered market	브로커시장
brokers blanket bond	브로커 포괄보증보험
broking business	중개업자
brought-in capital	지입자본
brown goods	브라운 상품
Brussels Tariff Nomenclature (BTN)	브럿셀 관세품목분류표
bucket shop	장외거래점
budget	예산
budget allotment	예산배분

Budget Committee	예산위원회
budget deficit	재정적자
budget principle	예산원칙
budget system	예산제도
budget variance	예산차이
budgetary account	예산계정
budgetary control	예산통제
budgetary process	예산편성
budgeted balance sheet	견적대차대조표
budgeted cost	예산원가
buffer stock	완충재고
buffer stock financing facility	완충재고융자
bug	버그
builders' risks insurance	건설보험
building account	건축계정
building and loan association	건축대부조합
building and loan blanket bond	건물 및 대부금포괄 보증증권
building block	구성부문
building expenses	건축비
building lease	건축임차권
building lot	건물용 부지
building lots for sale	분양지
building societies	건축조합
building tax	건축세
building under construction	건설중인 건물
built-in flexibility	빌트인 프렉시빌리티
built-in stabilizer	자동안정장치
bulk buying	생산전량구입
bulk discount	대량광고할인
bulk marking	대량
bulk order	일괄주문
bulk purchase	대량구입

bull	강세쪽
bull and bear index	강약지수
bull bear bond	강약채
bull clique	강세매수
bull market	강세시장
bull speculation	투기매수
bull spread transaction	불 스프레드 거래
bull the market	부채질하다
bulldog bond	불독채
bullet	일시불행
bullet bond	만기일괄상환채
bullet maturity	만기일괄상환
bullet swap	브래트 스왑
bulletin board system	뷸리틴 보드 시스템
bulletin report	보고서
bullish	강세의
bullish channel	강한 채널
bullish factor	강세재료
bullish resistance line	강한 저항선
bullish support line	강한 지지선
bullish tone	마음이 강함
bunched cost	일괄원가
buoyant market	급상승장
burden	부담
burden charge	부담금
burden of paying tax	납세부담
burden of proof	입증책임
burden on cost	간접비(원재료와 노무비 이외의 것)
bureau adjuster	손해사정인
bureau company	요율산정회 가맹회사
bureau filing	요율신청
bureau rates	산정회요율

burglary insurance	도난보험
Burke-Hartke Bill	버크 하트케 법안
burning ratio	재보험지불액
bus	버스
business	사업
business accountability	독립채산제
business accounting	기업회계
Business Accounting Deliberation Council	기업회계심의회
business accounting principle	기업회계원칙
business adjustment	경기조정
business analysis	경영분석
Business and Industry Advisory Committee (BIAC)	경제산업자문위원회
business annuity	기업연금
business attitude	기업태도
business audit	업무감사
business automation	비즈니스 오토메이션
business barometer	경기지수
business buying	기업의 구매활동
business canvasser	보험권유원
business circle	업계
business climate	경기
business combinations	기업통합
business commencement expenses	개업비
business concern	기업
business conditions	경기
business consumer	기업소비자
business continuation insurance	사업계속보험
business corporation	사업회사
business cycle	경기순환
business cyclical company	경기순환형 기업

business cyclical stock	경기순환주
business day	영업일
business environment risk index	사업환경 리스크지수
Business Environment Risk Index (BERI)	경기환경 리스크지수
business establishment	사업소
business expansion	사업확장
business expenses	영업비
business finance	기업금융
business finance company	사업금융회사
business finder	사업발견자
business forecast	경기예측
business fund	사업자금
business game	비즈니스게임
business growth	기업성장
business hours	영업시간
business income	사업소득
business indicator	경기지수
business information	경제정보
business information service	경제정보서비스
business insurance	사업보험
business interception	사업방해
business interruption insurance	영업중계보험
business inventory	기업재고
business investment	기업투자
business judgment principle	경영판단원칙
business law	사업법
business liability insurance	영업책임보험
business life insurance	사업생명보험
business line	영업과목
business loan	사업융자
business meeting	영업회의

business name	상호
business of renting property	부동산 대부업
business of underwriting	인수업무
business office tax	사업소득
business operations audit	업무감사
business opportunity	사업기회
business place	사업소
business plan	경영계획
business portfolio	사업포트폴리오
business practice	상관습
business profit	영업이익
business profit tax	영업수익설
business proprietor	사업주
business reciprocity	호혜거래
business report	영업보고
business responsibility	기업책임
business results	영업성적
business risk	비즈니스 리스크
business round table	비즈니스 라운드 테이블
business statistics	경영통계
business stimulating measure	경기진작책
business structure	기업구조
business survey	경기동향조사
business tax	사업세
business terms	거래조건
business transaction	기업거래
business trust	사업신탁
business unit	사업단위
business year	사업년도
businessman's orientation	경영자 지향
bust-up proposal	회사청산요구
but-for income	가정이익

butterfly spread trading	버터플라이 스프레드 거래
butting	버팅
buy and hold strategy	장기보유전략
buy back	되사다
buy-back deal	바이 백 딜
buy high	고가매입
buy on close	염가매입
buy on opening	오전 동시호가 매수
buy on reaction	반락시매입
buy on scale	분할매수
buy out	매수하다
buy signal	매수신호
buy-back	되사다
buy-down loan	보조부 융자
buy-out arrangement	지수매수협정
buyer	매수자
buyer behavior	구매자 행동
buyer segmentation	구매자 세분화
buyer's credit	바이어 크레디트
buyer's guide	구입자 가이드
buyer's market	구매자 시장
buyer's risk	구매자 부담
buyer's surplus	구매자 잉여
buying	매입
buying ability	매입능력
buying agent	매입대리점
buying and selling	매매
buying at top price	상투잡기
buying by institutional investors	기관매수
buying calendar	매입 칼렌다
buying commission	매수수수료
buying cost	매입원가

buying criteria	매입기준
buying energy	매입에너지
buying error	매입실패
buying exchange	매입환
buying for resale	재판매입
buying habit	구매습관
buying hedge	매입 헷지
buying information	정보
buying offer	신청
buying on an yield basis	이율
buying on commission	위탁
buying on credit	외상
buying operation	오퍼레이션
buying opportunity	장
buying order	주문
buying over	매수
buying period	매입기간
buying power	매입에너지
buying power index	구매력 지수
buying price	매입가격
buying procedure	매입수속
buying process	매입과정
buying psychology	구매심리학
buying rate without credit	무신용장 어음매입률
buying side	매입측
buying support	매입지지
buying terms	매입조건
buying title	권원매입
buying trip	매입부 여행
buying up	매점
buzz session	버즈 세션
buzz word	점잖 빼는 말투

by deed	증언에 의한
by judgment	판결에 의한
by-laws	정관세칙
by-product	부차적 결과
bystander	방관자
byte	바이트

≪ C ≫

cabinet offer	캐비닛 오퍼
cabinet order	시행령
cabinet security	소액매매 상표
cable	펀드 대미 달러 상장
cable address	성명약호
cable credit	케이블 크레디트
cable television	케이블 TV
cable transfer	전신송금
Caborn Report	카본 보고
cadaster	토지대장의
calculate	계산하다
calculated tax amount	산출세액
calculation	산정
calculator	계산
calendar day	달력상의 하루
calendar month	달력상의 한달
calendar spread	칼렌다 스프레드
calendar spread transaction	칼렌다 스프레드 거래
calendar year	달력상의 한해, 경상연도
calender month delivery rate	달력월제 선물상장
calender month delivery rates with option	달력 월도 상장
calibration	캘리브레이션
calibration data	공정데이터
California Public Employees' Retirement Systme (CalPERS)	직원연금 기금
call	조상상환, 콜

call and bill market	콜 어음시장
call loan	콜 론, 단자(단기투자), 당좌차입금
call loan broker	단자업자
call loan dealer	단자회사
call loan market	단자시장
call market	콜시장
call money	콜머니
call money and discount market	단자시장
call money discount markets	콜 어음 매매시장자금
call money rate	콜 레이트
call option	콜 옵션
call option valuation and dividend	콜 옵션 평가와 배당
call premium	콜 옵션의 옵션료
call price	상환가격
call provision	임의상환 조항
call rate	콜 레이트
call ratio back spread transaction	콜 레티오 백 스프레드 거래
call sprad	콜 스프레드
call swaption	콜 스왑션
callable boun	임의상환채권
callable debt	조상상환 가능한 채권
callable loan	콜러블 론
callable preferred stock	상환가능주식
callable shares	상환주식
callable swap	콜러블 스왑
callable swaption	콜러블 스왑션
calling the jury	배심원 호출
calling the plaintiff	원고호명
call-sales merchant	방문판매업자
Calvo Clause	칼보 조항
cambist	어음취급업자
campaign advertising	캠페인 광고

campaign concept	캠페인 컨셉트
Canadian-dollar long-term bond	캐나다 달러 장기국채
cancel money	위약금
cancel order	취소주문
cancelable swap	취소가능형 스왑
canceled order	출합주문
canceling date	해약기일
cancellation	해약
cancellation before maturity	중도해약
cancellation card	캔슬레이션 카드
cancellation clause	계약해제약관
cancellation money	해약금
cancellation of a contract	중도해약
cancellation of approval of filing a blue return	청색신고의 승인취소
cancellation of contract	계약해약
cancellation of debts of directors	직원의 채무면제
cancellation of shares	주식 소거
cancellation request	해약청구
cancellation return	해약반환금
cancer insurance	암보험
cannibalization	자기잠식효과
canons of descent	부동산 상속순위법칙
canvasser	보험권유원, 보험설계사
cap	캡, 상한
cap and floor	캡 & 플로어
cap interest rate	상한금리
capacity	계약인수능력, 행위능력
capacity to contract	계약능력
capacity utilization rate	설비가동률
cape	토지회복영장
capias ad audiendum judicium	판결년도를 위한 출정명령

capital	자본
capital account	자본계정
capital account balance	자본수지
capital adequacy requirements	자기자본비율규제
capital adjustment	자본의 수정
capital and liabilities ratio	자본부채비율
capital appreciation	가격상승이익
capital arrangement	고정성배열법
capital asset pricing model (CAPM)	자본자산가격모형
capital assets	자본자산
capital balance	자본계정
capital budget	자본예산
capital budgeting	설비투자계획
capital coefficient	자본계수
capital composition	자본구성
capital consumption	자본소비
capital consumption adjustment	자본소비의 조정
capital consumption allowance	자본감모저당
capital contribution	자본의 출처
capital cost	자본비용
capital decrease	감자
capital disposition	자본지출
capital duty	자본세
capital equipment	자본적 설비
capital equipment ratio	자본장비율
capital expenditure	자본지출
capital export	자본수출
capital export neutrality	자본수출의 중립성
capital flight	자본도피
capital flow	자본이동
capital formation	자본형성
capital formation account	자본형성계정

capital formula	자본등식
capital gain	캐피탈 게인, 매매익
capital gain free of taxation	비과세의 양도소득
capital gain fund	캐피탈 게인 펀드
capital gain taxation	캐피탈 게인 과세
capital gearing	캐피탈 기어링
capital goods	자본재
capital import	자본수입
capital improvement	자본적 지출로 볼 수 있는 개량
capital in excess of par or stated value	자본준비금
capital in excess of par value	액면초과금
capital income	자본소득
capital increase	증자
capital increase by new shares at market price	시가발행증자
capital inflow	자본유입
capital interest	자본이자
capital interest tax	자본이자세
capital investment	설비투자
capital investment intention	설비투자의욕
capital lease	캐피탈 리스
capital levy	자본과세
capital liabilities	자본부채
capital liberalization	자본자유화
capital loan	캐피탈 론
capital loss	캐피탈 로스
capital market	자본시장
capital market line	자본시장선
capital meeting for merger	합병을 위한 주주총회
capital outflow	자본유출
capital outlay	자본지출
capital paid-up	불입자본

capital participation 자본참가
capital productivity 자본생산성
capital profit 자본이윤
capital ratio 자기자본비율
capital receipt 자본적 수입
capital redemption 자금상환업무
capital redemption business 원금상각보험사업
capital reduction 감자
capital requirement 자기자본규제
capital reserve 자본준비금
capital risk 캐피탈 리스크
capital saving technical progress 자본절약적 기술진보
capital spending 자본투자
capital stock 발행제 주식총수
capital stock account 자본계정
capital stock adjustment 자본스톡조정
capital stock adjustment principle 자본스톡 조정원리
capital stock issued 발행제 자본금
capital stock preferred 우선주 자본금
capital stock registered 공칭 자본금
capital stock subscribed 인수제 자본금
capital stock tax 자본세
capital stock unpaid 미불입액
capital structure 자본구성
capital subscription 출자
capital sum 최고급부금, 자본액
capital supplier nation 자본공급국
capital surplus 자본잉여금
capital surplus reserve 자본잉여금 적립, 자본적립금
capital tax 자본세
capital transaction 자본거래
capital transfer 자본이전

capital turnover	자본회전율
capital utilization	설비가동률
capital working rate	자본가동률
capital-intensive merchandise	자본집약적 상품
capital-output ratio	자본·산출액 비율
capital-reconciliation statement	자본조정표
capitalism	자본주의
capitalist	자본가
capitalist bracket	자본가 계급
capitalization	자본전입
capitalization issue	선주발행
capitalization of accumulated earnings	이익적립금의 자본전입
capitalization of interest cost	차입이자의 자산계상
capitalization of market price	시가총액
capitalization rate	자본환원율
captialization unit	자산화 단위
capitalization weighted	시장가치가중
capitalization weighted indices	시가총액가중 지수
capitalized surplus	자본화된 잉여금
capitalized value of stock	배당환원가액
capitation tax	인두세
capped floating rate note	캡트 부채
capped loan	캡트 론
capped swap	캡트 스왑
capping	캡핑
capsized	전복
capsule shop	캡슐 점포
caption	캡션
captive audience	갇힌 시청자
captive finance company	금융자회사
captive insurance company	전속보험회사
captive market	전속시장

card counterfeiting	카드위조
card criminal fraud	카드범죄
card discrimination code	카드식별코드
card issuer	카드회사
card loan	카드 론
card member	카드사원
card of accounts	감정료 목표
card renewal	카드갱신
card replacement	카드 재발행
card standardization	카드 표준화
card system	카드 시스템
card system of bookkeeping	카드식 기장법
card-holic	다중채무
care and custody	관리책임, 재물관리
care of works	공사관리
career agency system	전속외무원제도
career average	전기간 평균
career development program	캐리어 발전 프로그램
career plateau	캐리어 플래튜
cargo capacity	화물적재능력
cargo damage survey	화물손해검사
cargo insurance	화물해상보험
Cargo Loss Prevention Committee	화물손해방지위원회
cargoworthiness	재화적성
Caribbean Community and Common Market	캐리비안 공동체 공동시장
Carlisle Mortality Table	칼라일 생명표
Carpenter cover	카펜터 식재보험
carriage	운송비
carriage and insurance paid to	운송비 · 보험료 포함
carriage paid to	운송비 포함
carried forward	이월

carried interest	이월지분
carrier's risk	상업과실
carriers liability insurance	운송인 책임보험
carry forward	이월
carry income	캐리 인컴
carry on	경영하다
carryback of deficit	결손금의 반복
carryback of loss	손실의 반복
carryback of net loss	순손실의 반복
carrying broker	고객감정을 갖는 브로커
carrying charge	이월일보, 재산보유비용
carrying cost	이월비용
carrying firm	증거금 취급업자
carrying value	이월가액
carrying-in expenses	반입비
carrying-over contract	연기 계약
carryover of casualty loss	잡손실의 이월공제
carryover of deficit	결손금의 이월
carryover of expense	이월사용
carryover of foreign tax credit	외국세액의 이월공제
carryover of loss	손실의 이월
cartage	운임
Cartagena Agreement	카르타헤나 협정
carte blanche	백지위임
cartel	카르텔
cartel tariffs	카르텔 관세
carucate	지조기준면적
cascade process	폭포 이론
cascade tax	누적세
cascade-type turnover tax	누적형 거래 고세
case	준비서면, 소송
case administration	파산의 관리

case law	판례법
case method	사례연구법
case of first impression	선례 없는 소송사건
case on appeal	상소사실 기재서
case reserved	합의를 위한 사실기재서
case stated	사실기재서
cash account	금융계정
cash advance	캐쉬 어드밴스
cash and carry	현금지불
cash and carry system	캐쉬와 캐리 시스템
cash and carry trade	캐쉬와 캐리 거래
cash and carry wholesaler	현금도매상
cash and deposits banks accounts	현금예금계정
cash and deposits with banks	현금예금
cash asset value	현금자산가치
cash assets	현금자산
cash at bank	당좌예금
cash audit	현금감사
cash balance	현금잔고
cash basis	현금주의
cash basis accounting	현금주의 회계
cash before delivery	선급
cash book	현금출납장
cash break-even point	수지분기점
cash buying rate	현찰매입율
cash credit	당좌임대
cash currency	현금통화
cash delivery	당일 수수
cash deposit	현금예금
cash deposited for bond interest	사채이자불입금
cash disbursed	지출
cash disbursement	현금지불

cash disbursement book	지불장
cash discount	현금할인
cash dispenser	현금지급기
cash dividend	현금배당
cash dividend declared	현금배당 결의액
csh earnings	현금수입
cash equivalent	현예금
cash flow	현금흐름
cash flow analysis	수지분석
cash flow coverage ratio	현금흐름 부담배율
cash flow interest	현금흐름 이자
cash flow projection	현금흐름 예측
cash flow ratio	현금흐름률
cash flow ratio to capital expenditures	對설비투자 현금흐름률
cash flow ratio to long-term liabilities	對장기부채 현금흐름률
cash flow return	현금흐름 반환
cash flow statement	자금운용표
cash flow to current liabilities	현금흐름 대 유동부채
cash flow-back	현금회수
cash forecasts	수지예측
cash forward contract	현금 포워드 콘트랙트
cash forward transaction	현물선도거래
cash immediate market	전가-증권청산시장
cash in advance	선급금
cash in bank	은행예금
cash in banks and hand	예금현금
cash in hand	수중현금보유액
cash in transit	미달현금
cash income	현금수입
cash items	현금항목

cash journal	현금출납분개장
cash letters	현금송장
cash liabilities	현금부채
cash loan	현금대부
cash loss	즉시지불 재보험금
cash management	캐쉬 매니지먼트
cash management bill	단기재무성 어음
cash management service	현금 매니지먼트 서비스
cash market	현금시장
cash on delivery	대금상환도
cash on hand	보유현금
cash on shipment	선적지불
cash option	현물옵션
cash outlays	현금지출
cash over and short account	현금과부족계정
cash payment	현금지불
cash payment journal	현금지불분개장
cash position	현금포지션
cash price	현금가격
cash purchase	현금매입
cash ratio	현금비율
cash receipt	현금수취
cash receipt book	현금수납장
cash receipt journal	현금수납분개장, 현금수납장
cash received	수입현금
cash records	현금기록
cash redemption	현금상환
cash remittance	현금송금
cash reserve ratio	예금지급준비금
cash reserves	현금준비금
cash sale	현금매매
cash selling rate	현금판매율

cash settlement	현금결제
cash slips	출납전표
cash statement	현금계산서
cash surrender value	계약반환금
cash take	현금거래
cash to current liabilities ratio	현금유동부채비율
cash transactions	당일결제거래
cash value	운용부분
cash with order	현금주문
cash-book	출납부
cash-disbursement journal	지불사역장
cash-matching	현금 매칭
cash-matching techniques	현금 매칭 기술
cash-sale	현금매매
cashability goods	환금성 상품
cashier	현금출납계
cashier's check	은행수표
cashier's department	현금출납과
cashing	현금화
casset execution	집행정지명령
cassetur breve	소송종료 판결
casting vote	결정표
casual expenses	임시지출
casual loss	우발손실
casual profit	우발이익
casualty	재해
casualty and surety insurance	신종보험, 손해・보증보험
casualty insurance	재해보험
casualty loss	잡손
casualty loss deduction	잡손공제
casualty losses carried over	이월재해손실
casus fortuitus	우연의 재해

casus major 재해
casus omissus 실수사항
catastrophe reinsurance 이상손해재보험
catastrophe reserve 이상손해준비금
catch-up adjustments 소급수정
catching bargain 부당계약
category killer 카테고리 킬러
category of business 업종
category width 카테고리의 폭
cats and dogs stock 불량주식
causa causans 직접원인
causa inducement 동기
causa remota 간접원인
causa sine qua non 필요조건
causal analysis 인과분석
causal credit 원인채권
causal path analysis 인과 패스 분석
causal relationship 인과관계
causality 인과관계
cause 원인
cause list 사건목록
cause of action 소송원인
cause of bankruptcy 파산원인
cause proximate 근인주의
cause-books 사건부
caution 등기변경예고
caution money 보증금
cautionary 보증채권의
cautious stance 경계의 자세
caveat 수속차지 신청자
caveat emptor 사는 사람의 주의의무
caveat venditor 파는 사람의 주의의무

CD market	CD시장
cease orders	정지명령
cedant	출재보험자
cede back	려재보험(원상태로 되돌아가는 재보험)
ceded reinsurance	매 재보험
cedel	세델
ceding commission	출재수수료
ceding company	출재회사
ceding reinsurer	재보험자
ceiling	상환
ceiling price	천정상장
ceiling system	셀링 시스템
celebration of the beginning of operation	조업개시의 기념 축연
Celler-Kefauver Amendment	셀러-키퍼버 개정법
cellular approach	셀룰러 어프로치
cellular communication system	셀룰러 방식
census of commerce	상업통계
census register	호적
center of demand	수요중심점
Central American Common Market	중미공동시장
central bank	중앙은행
central bank intervention	평형개입
central bank rate	중앙은행 할인비율
central buying	본부집중구입
central death rate	중앙사망률
Central European Free Trade Association	중구자유무역연합
central market	중앙시장
central rate	센트럴 레이트
central tendency	중심경향
centralization	집권화

centralized management	집권관리
centralized organization	집권조직
centrifugal market	원심적 시장
centripetal market	구심적 시장
cepi corpus	체포보고서
cepit	탈취
certain assets	확실성 자산
certainty	명백성
certificate	증명서
certificate of analysis	분석증명서
certificate of automobile receivables	자동차론 저당증서
certificate of bank balances	은행예금잔고증명서
certificate of beneficial interest	부분수익증권
certificate of compliance	납세제증서
certificate of deposit	양도가능 정기예금증서
certificate of financial security	손해배상자력증명서
certificate of incorporation	회사설립면허
certificate of indebtedness	채무증서
certificate of insurance	보험인수증
certificate of origin	원산지 증명
certificate of registry	선박증명서
certificate of seal impression	인감증명서
certificate of share	주권
certificate of tax payment	납세증명서
certificate of time deposit	정기예금증서
certificate of weight and measurement	중량용적증명서
certificated financial statement	감사제 재무제표
certificated share	주권있는 주식
certification body	인증기관
certification market	인증마크
certification of audit	감사증명

certification of payment	지급보증
certified check	지불인수수표
certified copy	인증등본
certified copy of commercial registration	상업등기부 등본
certified copy of real estate register	부동산 등기부 등본
certified equipment	인정장지
certified public accountant	공인회계사
certified public accountant Law	공인회계사법
certified tax accountant	세무사
certified tax accountant association	세무사회
certified tax accountant law	세무사법
certifying bank	지급보증은행
certiorari	이송명령
cessation of payment of premium	보험료지불정지
cesser	태만
cesset execution	집행정지명령
cession	재산인도
cession of an obligation	채권양도
cession of portfolio	포트폴리오 양도
cestui que trust	신탁수익자
chafing	마찰손
chain banking	체인 뱅킹
chain break	체인 브레이크
chain of command	명령계통
challenge	(배심원에 대한) 기피
chamber of commerce	상공회의소
chambers	사실(私室)
champerty	소송원조
chancellor of a university	대학총장
Chancellor of the Exchequer	대장대신
change	환산

change claims	변경요구
change in employment	전적
change in growth rate	성장률의 변화
change in par value	액면변경
change in valuation method	평가방법의 변경
change in work	변경공사
change of business	사업전환
change of category of land	지목변환
change of depreciation method	상각방법 변경
change of risk	위험의 변동
change of tax computation basis	세액계산기준 변경
change of taxable year	사업년도의 변경
change of the place of tax payment	납세지의 변경
change of valuation method	평가방법의 변경
change of venue	관할의 이전
change over	체인지 오버
changes in accounting principles	회계원칙의 변경
changes in estimates	견적금액변경
changes in gross margin	조이익의 증감
changes of owners of the principal	원본소유자 변동
channel control	경로통제
channel cost analysis	경로비용분석
channel development	경로개발
channel efficiency	경로효율
channel environment	경로환경
channel line	채널라인
channel of distribution	유통경로
channel system	경로시스템
channeling back	환류
channeling of liability	배상책임의 집중
chaos	카오스
characteristic line	특성선

characteristic of goods theory	상품특성론
characteristics	특징
charge	수수료
charge account	외상거래계정
charge against revenues	손금
charge back	입금의 취소
charge coupled device	차쥐 커플드 디바이스
charge extra	부대비용
charge for collection	징수수수료
charge for collection of bill	어음징수수수료
charge for demand for tax in arrears	체납독촉수수료
charge for development	개발부담금
charge for installment payment	할부수수료
charge on the declining balances	잔채방식
charge-off	대손상각
charges for custody	보관료
charges for remittance	환 수수료
charges forward	입체지불
charitable trust	공익신탁
charities and donations	자선기부금
chart	차트
chart pattern	차트 패턴
chart reading	케이선 분석
charta	날인증서
charter	기본정관
charter party B/L	차트 파티 B/L
charter provision	회사 설립허가서
charter-land	특허보유지
charterage	차트료
chartered	공인의
chartered accountant	칙허회계사

chartered financial analyst	공인증권분석사
Chartered Life Underwriters in Japan	인정생명보험사회
chartered property casualty underwriter	공인재산재해보험사
chartered public accountant	공인회계사
chartering broker	갑중
charterparty	용선계약
chartist	차티스트
chat	챗트
chattel	동산
chattel loan	동산대부
chattel mortgage	동산저당
cheapest-to-deliver	최할안상표
cheat	사기
check	수표, 전표
check act	수표법
check book	수표장
check drawee	수표지불인
check drawer	수표발행인
check guarantee card	체크 개런티 카드
check holder	수표지시인(지정인)
check mark	조합제기호
check register	수표기입장
check to bearer	지참인불 수표
check to order	지시수표(지정수표)
check-off	지급하기 전에 일정액을 공제함
check-out counter	감정구
cherry picking	체리 픽킹
checkable deposit	결제성 예금
checkbook stub	수표장 사본
checking	조합

checking account	당좌계정
checking deposits	당좌예금
checking inventory	조합재고조사
checking system	수표제도
Chicago Board of Trade	시카고 상품거래소
Chicago Board Options Exchange	시카고 옵션거래소
Chicago International Money Market	시카고 국제통화시장
Chicago Mercantile Exchange	시카고 상업거래소
chicken market	치킨 마켓
chief	주석
chief accountant	회계주임
chief actuary	보험계리인
chief examiner	통괄국세 조사관
chief executive officer	경영최고책임자(CEO)
chief financial officer	재무담당사원
chief investigator	통괄국세사찰관
chief justice	수석재판관
chief of the taxation office	세무서장
chief operating officer	최고업무책임자
chief revenue officer	통괄국세징수관
child's deferred insurance	유아거치보험
children's insurance	유아보험
chilling effect	냉각효과
china eggs	사지는 않고 가격만 묻고 다니는 손님
Chinese wall	차이니즈 월
chirograph	자필증서
chit	전표
chit system	전표(지)불제도
chitbook	송달부
choice of law clause	법선택조항
chose	물산
chose in action	무체동산

chose in possession	유체동산
chroma	채도
chroma key	크로마 키
chrominance signal	채도신호
chronic	만성적
chronic absenteeism	만성 적태업
chronic deflation	만성적 디플레이션
chronic inflation	만성적 인플레이션
chumming	가장매매
churning	과도한 매매권유
CIF price	원가·보험료 또는 운임포함가격
circuit breaker	동시거래 정지
circuit court	순회재판소
circuitswitching	순회 교환
circular flow of economic system	경제환경
circular note	신용장
circulating assets	유동자산
circulating capital	유동자본
circulating fund	운전자금
circulation	발행부수, 유통
circulation of cost	원가배부
circulation of national income	국민소득순환
circulation tax	유통세
circumstantial evidence	정황증거
circus swap	써커스 스왑
citation	소환
citizen	시민
citizen bond	대중용의 채권
City	도시
city bank	도시은행
city planning tax	도시계획세
civil	민사의

civil action	민사소송
civil code	민법
civil death	법률상의 사망
civil engineering	토목
civil engineering works	토목공사
civil law	민법
civil rights	공민권
civil servant	공무원
civil service	공무, 공무원
civilian demand	민간수요
civilian enterprise	민간사업
claim	채권, 청구
claim adjustment	손해의 청산
claim and delivery	동산회복소송
claim expenses	손해사정비용
claim for a refund	환부청구
claim for compensation	구상(배상)
claim for correction	경정의 요구
claim for damage	손해배상청구
claim for examination	심사청구
claim for guarantee	미수보증금
claim for reimbursement	상환청구
claim for tax refunds	조세환부청구권
claim frequency analysis	손해빈도분석
claim in bankruptcy	파산채권
claim in foreign currency	외화표시채권
claim note	보험금청구자
claim notice clause	손해통지조항
claim of prepayment of income tax	예정납입세액의 독촉
claim of recourse	상환청구
claim of redemption	상환청구권
claim paid	지불제보험금

claim paid or payable 전보액, 보험금
claim payable abroad clause 보험금해외지불약관
claim payable to a specific person 지명채권
claim period 구상기간
claim probability 손해발생확률
claim ratio 손해율
claim reserve 지불준비
claim right insurance 청구권보험
claim settlement 보험금지불
claim settlement analysis 손해결제분석
claim settlement fund 보험금지불자금
claim settling fee 보험금지불수수료
claimant 보험금청구자
claiming bank 구상은행
claims 배상금
clamor 신청
clandestine theft 은밀한 절도
clarification 설명
class action 집단소송
class cost 조별원가
class cost system 조별원가계산
class media 특정한 층을 대상으로 한 매체
class mutual 직업별 상호보험
class of insurance 보험의 종류
class of risk 위험의 종류
class-product production 급별생산물 생산
classes of stocks 주식의 종류
classical corporation tax system 고전적 법인세제도
classical school of economics 고전파 경제학
classification of a taxpayer 납세의무자의 구분
classification of account 계정과목일람표
classification of goods 상품분류

classification of item of accounts	계정과목분류표
classification of land	지목
classification of media	매체분류
classification of motives	동기분류
classification of securities	유가증권의 구분
classification of shares	주식의 종류
classification of tax	조세의 분류
classified advertising	안내 광고
classified income	각종소득
classified income tax	분류소득세
classified stock	종류로 분류된 주식
classified trial balance	구분식 시산표
clause	조항
clausula rebus sic stantibus	사정변형원칙
clausum fregit	부동산의 점유침해
Clayton Act	클레톤 법
clean bill of lading	클린 B/L: 무고장 선하증권
clean credit	무담보신용장
clean cut system	클린 컷 시스템
clean draft	신용어음
clean float	클린 플롯트
clean letter of credit	클린 신용장
clean loan	클린 론
clean opinion	클린 옵션
clear band	클리어 밴드
clear days	정미일수
clear space clause	공지조항
clearance	어음교환
clearance fee	출항수수료
clearance goods	재고품
clearing	청산
clearing account	어음교환감정

clearing agency	청산기관
clearing agreement	청산협정
clearing balance	어음교환고
clearing bank	어음교환소가맹은행
clearing contract	청산거래
clearing corporation	청산회사
clearing for nonmember	대리교환
clearing function	청산기능
clearing fund	클리어링 펀드
clearing house	클리어링 하우스
clearing member	청산회원
clearing organization	청산기관
clearing price	청산가격
clearing procedure	청산절차
clearing system	어음교환제도
clearing time	결제시
clearing transaction	청산거래
clearing-house balance	교환잔고표
clearinghouse	어음교환소
clearinghouse of commodity futures	상품선물거래청산소
clearinghouse proof	어음교환결산표
clerical mistake	오기
click-on contract	클릭온 계약
client and server	클라이언트와 서버
clientele effect	고객효과
clients	의뢰인
climbing angle	상승각
climbing power	상승력
clique	파벌
clock frequency	시계주파수
clone fund	클론 펀드
close	장부를 마감하다

close down	종가가 전일종가와 비교해서 저가이다
close of the session	끝
close one's position	전매·환매를 끝마쳐 거래관계를 완료하다
close up	종가가 전일종가와 비교해서 고가이다
close-out	창고떨이
closed account	마감제 계정
closed corporation	동족회사
closed door membership store	회원제 점포
closed economy	폐쇄경제
closed market	폐쇄시장
closed out method	전매·환매를 끝마쳐 거래관계를 완료
closed period	클로즈드 기간
closed-circuit system	클로즈드 써킷 시스템
closed-end dual fund	클로즈드 엔드형 펀드
closed-end fund	클로즈드 엔드형 펀드
closed-end mortgage	폐쇄식 담보
closed-end mortgage bond	폐쇄식 담보부사채
closed-end trust	클로즈드 엔드 신탁
closed-end type	클로즈드 엔드형
closely-held company	비공개회사
closing	계약내용의 실행, 끝, 종결
closing account	결산
closing adjustment	결산정리
closing all accounts in the ledger	원장의 각 계정을 마감하는 것
closing balance	기말잔액
closing business	사업의 폐쇄
closing date	결산일
closing entries	결산자동분류
closing high	상종가로 거래가 마감됨
closing inventories	기말재고조사액
closing lower	그날 중 가장 싼값으로 거래가 마감됨
closing meeting	최종회의

closing of the ledger	원장마감
closing price	그날의 파장 때 시세
closing quotation	그날의 파장 때 시세
closing sale	클로우징 판매
closing the ledger	원장마감
closing transaction	반대매매
closing trial balance	마감식 계산
closing-out	결제
clothing and shelter expenses	의식주의 비용
club deal	클럽 딜
club dues	회비
Club of Roma	로마 그룹
cluster analysis	클러스터 분석, 군집분석
cluster marketing	클러스터 마케팅
clutter position	클러터 포지션
co-branded card	제휴카드
co-existing cover clause	중복보험약관
co-finance	공동융자
co-heir	공동법정상속인
co-lead-manager	공동주간사
co-maker	공동진출인
co-manager	부간사
co-movement of earnings	이익의 공변동
co-ownership	공유
coal stock	저탄
Coase theorem	코스 정리
coast-to-coast	전미
coastwise cargo insurance	내항적하보험
coaxial cable	동축케이블
Cobb-Douglas production function	콥 더글러스 생산함수
cobweb cycle	거미집순환
cocket	관세서

cocktail swap	칵테일 스왑, 복합 스왑
code	법전
code division multiple access	부호분할 다원접속
code of civil procedure	민사소송법전
code of ethics	윤리규정
code of legal procedure	소송법
code of liberalization	자유화규약
Code of Procedure for Handling Trade Practice Complain	전미증권업협회분쟁처리규칙
Code of Liberalization of Capital Movements	자본이동자유화규약
codicil	추가조항
coefficient	계수
coefficient of correlation	상관계수
coefficient of determination	결정계수
coefficient of elasticity	탄력성 계수
coefficient of income sensitivity	소득감응계수
coefficient of multiple correlation	다중상관계수
coefficient of variation	변동계수
coercive power	강제력
cogeneration	코제너레이션
cognitive judgment	인지적 판결
cognitive science	인지과학
cognizance	승인
cognovit actionem	채무인지 승낙
cognovit note	원고청구의 인지승낙서
cohort analysis	코호트 분석
coincident indicator	일치지수
coincident series	일치계열
coinsurance	공동보험
coinsurance account payable	공동보험지불계정
coinsurance account receivable	공동보험수취계정

coinsurance limit	공동보험인수한도
coinsurance share	공동보험인수비율
coinsurer	공동보험자
cold call	전화에 의한 거래권유
cold canvassing	갑작스런 방문판매, 갑작스런 모집
cold chain	저온유통조직
collaboration	제휴
collapse	폭락
collapse in oil prices	원유가격의 하락
collar	콜러
collared swap	콜러드 스왑
collateral	담보
collateral bond	부대증서
collateral commodity	상품담보
collateral condition	부대조건
collateral consanguinity	방계혈족
collateral deposit	담보예금
collateral estoppel	부수적 금반언
collateral import	담보수입
collateral issue	방계쟁점
collateral loan	담보부 대부
collateral note	담보부 약속어음
collateral on loans on bills	어음대부담보
collateral on property	물적담보
collateral promise	부수적인 약속(담보)
collateral security	대용증권
collateral source rule	배상금중복회수의 원칙
collateral trust bond	담보부 신탁채권
collateral value	담보가치
collateral value of substitute security	대용증권의 담보가치
collateralized mortgage obligations	저당부 모기지 증서
collation	조합

collation of seals	날인의 인장조사
collect	징수하다
collected amount	징수액
collectible	회수 가능한
collecting agent	징수의무자
collecting commission	징수수수료
collecting tax	징수
collection	회수
collection agency	회수업자
collection bank	징수은행
collection basis	회수기준
collection bill	징수어음
collection charge	징수경비
collection cycle	회수순환
collection expenses	징수비용
collection fee	징수료
collection floater	수집물 포괄보험
collection letter	독촉장
collection management technique	회수기술
collection of bad debts deducted	상각제 대손금의 회수
collection of bill	외상대금 회수
collection of claim	채권회수
collection of loans	대부금회수
collection of premiums	보험료의 모집
collection of securities by purchase	유가증권 매집
collection of taxes	조세징수
collection period	회수기간
collection practices	회수업무
collective accident insurance	단체상해보험
collective self-reliance	집단적 자력갱생
collective accumulation	집단적립제
collective agreement	노동협약

collective bargaining	단체교섭
collective bargaining agreement	단체협약
collective insurance	단체보험
collective investment fund	합동운용형 펀드
collective leadership	집단지도
collective mark	단체마크
collective name schedule policy	단체기명식 보험
collective personal accident insurance	단체상해보험
College Retirement Equities Fund	미국대학교직원 퇴직 변액 연금기금
collision	충돌
collusion	담합, 순합소송, 공모
color	시황, 표시
color chart	컬러차트
color dynamics	컬러 다이나믹스
color lookup table	컬러 룩업 테이블
color naming system	색명법
color of office	표현상의 직권
color proof	색교정
color separation	색분해
color system	표색계
color temperature	색온도
color video signal	컬러 비디오 신호
colorable alteration	외견상의 변경
column measure	컬럼 폭
column number	컬럼 수
combination of causes	연계원인
combination plan reinsurance	조합방식 재보험
combination policy	조합보험
combination sale	두 가지를 묶어서 하는 판매
combine	합동
combine committee	통합위원회
combined	총계의

combined balance sheet	결합대차대조표
combined depreciation	결합상각법
combined financial statement	결합재무제표
combined house	주거겸용주택
combined income statement	합병손익계산서
combined marine surcharges	종합할증보험료
combined policy	복합보험증권
combined profit and loss statement	결합손익계산서
combined single limit	한 사고당 전보한도액
combined transport documents	복합운송서류
come to terms	만남
comecon	코메콘
comfort letter	각서
comfort letter	컴퍼트 레터
comity principle	국제예양원칙
commanding	지휘명령
commemorative dividend	기념배당
commerce and industry finance company·	상공업 금융회사
commerce clause	통상조합
commercial accounting	상업회계
commercial agent	대리점
commercial arbitration	상사중재
commercial automobile policy	상업용 자동차 보험
commercial bank	시중은행, 상업은행
commercial bank credit	시중대출
commercial banker	상업은행가
commercial bill	상업어음
commercial blanket primary bond	상업포괄신원보증증권
commercial block policy	판매업자 일괄보험
commercial bookkeeping	상업부기
commercial business	영리사업

commercial code 상법
commercial company 영리회사
commercial court 상업재판소
commercial credit 상업신용
commercial credit insurance 상업신용보험
commercial discount 상업할인
commercial enterprise 영리사업
commercial expenses 영업비
commercial finance 상업금융
commercial forgery policy 상업용 위조보험
commercial guarantee 상업보증
commercial insurance 영리보험
commercial invoice 상업인보이스
commercial letter of credit 상업신용장
commercial law 상법
commercial loan 상업대출
commercial mortgage 상업용 모기지
commercial paper 상업어음
commercial registration 상업등기
commercial risk 신용위험
commercial statistics 상업통계
commercial trader 상업 트레이더
commercial transaction 상행위
commingled fund 합동운용펀드
commingled investment account 혼합투자계정
Commissaires aux Comptes (프랑스 법상의) 감사역
commission 위임, 수수료
commission account 수수료 계정
commission agent 위탁매매인
commission broker 커미션 브로커
commission del credere 보증부위임
commission earned 수취수수료

commission for purchase	매입수수료
commission income	수수료수입
commission of authority	위탁계약서
commission on consignment	위탁수수료
Committee on International Investment and Multinational Enterprises (CIME)	국제투자 다국적기업위원회
Commission on Transnational Corporations	다국적기업위원회
commission payable	미지급수수료
commission receivable	미수수수료
commission sale	수수료매매
commission system	비율제
commission to consignee	위탁판매수수료
commission to examine witnesses	증인질문촉탁서
commissioners for oaths	선거관리관
commissioning	시운용
commitment	계약채무, 계약의무
commitment fee	약정수수료
committee	위원회
committee bond	후견인 보증증권
committee of inspection	검사위원회
Committee of Lloy's	로이즈 위원회
Committee on Accounting Procedure	회계절차위원회
committee on auditing procedure	감사수속위원회
commodities investment trust	상품투자신탁
commodity	상품
commodity account	상품계정
commodity approach	상품적 접근
commodity backed bond	상품담보채권
commodity customers agreement	상품고객계약
commodity demand	상품수요
commodity exchange	상품거래소

commodity exchange act	상품거래법
commodity exchange responsibility reserve	상품거래책임준비금
commodity excise	상품세
commodity flow method	상품흐름법
commodity futures	상품선물
commodity futures index	상품선물지수
commodity futures price	상품선물거래가격
commodity futures trading adviser	상품선물어드바이저
Commodity Futures Trading Commission	미국상품선물거래위원회
commodity market	상품시장
commodity money	상품화폐
commodity option	상품옵션
commodity pool	상품 풀
commodity pool operator	상품 풀 운영자
commodity price	물가
commodity rate	상품운임
commodity statistics	상품통계
commodity swap	상품 스왑
commodity tax	상품세
commodity tax law	상품세법
commodity trading adviser	상품거래고문
commodity transaction	상품거래
commodity transaction responsibility reserve	상품거래책임준비금
common account	공동계정
common assurance	양도증서
common background	공통의 기반
common carrier	일반운송업, 공중전기통신사업자
common carriers liability insurance	운송사업자책임보험
common collateral	공통담보

common cost	공통원가
common counts	일반항목
common dividend	보통배당
common dollar statements	안정가치에 수정한 재무제표
common employment	공동작업
common external tariff	대외공통관세
common factor risk	공통요인리스크
common fund	공통기금
common gap	공통갭
common informer	정보제공자
common injunction	보통차지명령
common law	관습법
common liquidation	통상해산
common market	공동시장
common nuisance	공적 불법방해
common property	공유자산
common recovery	담합부동산 회복소송
common signaling channel	공통선 신호방식
common stock	보통주식
common stock book value	보통주의 장부가격
common stock equivalents	주식적 증권
common stock for treasury	자기주식
common stock outstanding	사회발행보통주식
common stock preemptive right	신주인수권
common vouchee	권리담보자
common-law action	인사소송
common-law trust	관습법 신탁
common-law corporation	관습법 주식회사
common-size balance sheet	백분율대차대조표
common-size financial statements	백분율재무제표
commons	입회지
commorancy	가주소

commorientes	동일사고사망자
communication analysis	커뮤니케이션 분석
communication barrier	커뮤니케이션 장해
communication channel	커뮤니케이션 채널
communication charges	통신비
communication control procedure	통신제어수준
communication control unit	통신제어장치
communication gap	커뮤니케이션 갭
communication satellite	통신위성
communication strategy	커뮤니케이션 전략
communicator	커뮤니케이터
community	커뮤니티
community involvement	지역활동참가
community paper	커뮤니티 페이퍼
community reinvestment	지원에의 재투자
community trust	커뮤니티 트러스트(지역공익신탁)
commutation	환산
commutation function	계산기수
compact disk	컴팩트 디스크
compact disk read only memory (CD-ROM)	CD-ROM
company demand	자사수요
company law	회사법
company limited	주식회사
company limited by guarantee	유한책임보증회사
company limited by shares	주식회사
company organization	회사조직
company rehabilitation law	회사갱생법
company representative	회사대리인
company union	고용조합
company with reduced capital	감자회사
company's own stock	자사주

company-administered annuity	순수자가연금
company-specific	개별기업 특유의
comparability	비교가능성
comparable transaction	비교 대상 거래
comparative advantage	비교우위
comparative advantage theory	비교우위이론
comparative advertising	비교광고
comparative analysis	비교분석
comparative balance sheet	비교대차대조표
comparative cost	비교원가
comparative cost studies	비교원가조사
comparative financial statement	비교재무제표
comparative income statement	비교손익계산서
comparative influence	비교작용
comparative marketing	비교마케팅
comparative profit and loss statement	비교손익계산서
comparative statement	비교계산서
comparative statement of cash flows	비교수지계산서
comparative statistics	비교통계학
comparison	조합
comparison of beta values of funds	펀드베타의 가치비교
comparison slip	조합표
comparison table	비교표
compatibility	양립성
compensated absence	유급휴가
compensating balance	구속성 잔액
compensating error	상계오차
compensating interest	상계이자
compensating trade or transactions	구상무역
compensation	보수
compensation criminum	죄의 상계
compensation culpae	과실상계

compensation for damage 손해배상
compensation for eviction 퇴거료
compensation for expense and loss 경비보상금
compensation for expropriation 수용에 의한 보상금
compensation for injuries and deaths 부상사망보상금
compensation for residual land 잔지보상금
compensation for revenue 수익보상금
compensation paid to directors 직원보수
compensation plan 보수방식
compensation plans based on assets 운용자산액비례보수방식
compensation principle of taxation 조세의 수익자 부담원칙
compensation system 보상제도
compensation trade 구상무역
compensatory budget policy 보정적 예산정책
compensatory deposit 양건예금
compensatory effect 보정효과
compensatory financing facility 보상융자
compensatory fiscal policy 보정적 재정정책
compensatory item 보정적 항목
compensatory model 보정 모델
compensatory surplus 보정적 잉여
compete 경합
competence 직권
competence center 능력센터
competency 능력 있는 것
competent 소할(관할)
competent authority 권한 있는 당국
competent parties 능력 있는 당사자
competent taxation office 관할세무서
competent witness 증인능력 있는 증인
competition strategy 경쟁전략
competitive access provider 시내경쟁사업자

competitive advertising	경쟁광고
competitive depreciation	경쟁적 평가절차
competitive intelligence	경합타사정보
competitive market maker system	경합 마켓 메이커 시스템
competitive pattern	경합패턴
competitive pressure	경쟁압력
competitive price	경쟁가격
competitive sale	경쟁판매
competitive tender	경쟁입찰
competitor analysis	경쟁자 분석
compilation	편집
complainant	원고
complaint	고정(불평), 고소
complementary color	보색
complementary demand	보완적 수요
complementary goods	보완재
complete annuity	완전연금
complete audit	완전감사
complete competition	완전경쟁
complete life table	완전생명표
complete specialization	완전특화
complete stripping between interest and principal	완전금리의 완전분리
completed audit	기말감사
completed contract method	완성기준
completed operations hazard	완성작업위험
completely adaptive strategy	완전적합전략
completely knocked down (CKD)	완전 넉다운
completeness fund	보완펀드
completion basis	공사완성기준
completion bonus	완공 보너스
completion guarantee	완성보증

complex instruction set computer	시스크(CISC)
complex salvage operation	복잡구조작업
complex transportation	복합수송
compliance	준수, 위법
compliance accounting	준거회계
compliance program	수출관리규정
component analysis	구성비율분석
component percentages	구성비율
component ratio	구성비
component signal	컴포넌트 신호
components of cost	원가의 구성요소
composing	조판
composite depreciation	종합감가상각
composite depreciation assets	종합상각자산
composite index	경기종합지수
composite insurer	복수보험자
composite office	종합보험회사
composite price	컴포지트 프라이스
composite quotation system	종합거래정보시스템
composite signal	컴포지트 신호
composite stock price index	종합주가지수
composite stock price tables	종합주가표
composite useful life	종합내용연수
composition	화의
composition law	화의법
composition of inventory	재고자산의 범위
composition of working capital	운전자본구성
compound annual rate	복리연율
compound annual return	연복리이익률
compound discount	복리할인
compound duty	복합세
compound entry	복합기입

compound interest	복리
compound interest bonds	할인지방채
compound interest method	복리방식
compound interest yield	복리이자
compound transaction	복합거래
comprador	컴프래더, 매판
comprehensive	컴프리헨시브
comprehensive bonded area	종합보세지역
comprehensive dwelling policy	주택종합보험
comprehensive general liability policy	종합배상책임보험
comprehensive income taxation	종합과세
comprehensive insurance	종합보험
comprehensive major medical insurance	종합고액의료비보험
comprehensive marketing system	포괄적 마케팅시스템
comprehensive personal liability insurance	종합개인배상책임보험
comprehensive system model	컴프리헨션 모델
comprehensive trade bill	포괄통상법안
compromise	타협
compromise method	절충방식
compromised total loss	협정전손
comptroller	감사역
comptroller in bankruptcy	파산감사관
compulsory	강제적
compulsory accident insurance	강제상해보험
compulsory audit	강제감사
Compulsory Automobile Liability Insurance Council	자동차손해배상책임보험위원회
compulsory bond	강제재판보증증권
compulsory cancellation	강제해약

compulsory composition	강제화의
compulsory conversion into money	강제환가
compulsory deposit as a condition for loans	대부조건부 강제예금
compulsory execution	강제집행
compulsory insurance	강제보험
compulsory liability insurance	강제배상보험
compulsory liquidation	강제청산
compulsory or involuntary transfer of property	자산의 강제양도
compulsory sale by auction	강제경매
compulsory surplus	강제잉여금
compulsory third party liability insurance	제3자 강제배상책임보험
compulsory winding-up	강제청산
compurgation	면책선서
CompuServe	컴퓨서브
computation	산정
computation of business income	사업소득의 계산
computation of tax amount	세액의 계산
computation of useful years	내용년수의 계산
computation period	산정기간
computation procedure	계산절차
computed price	계산가격
computer aided design (CAD)	캐드
computer aided manufacture (CAM)	컴퓨터지원생산
computer assisted animation	컴퓨터 애니메이션
computer assisted execution system	자동 딜링 거래 시스템
computer personnel	컴퓨터 요원
computer supported cooperation work	컴퓨터 지원협조작업
computerization	컴퓨터화

conative judgement	능동적 판결
concealment	고지의무위반
concentrated investment	집중투자
concentrated marketing strategy	집중 마케팅 전략
concentrated merchandising	집중 머천다이징
concentration	집중
concentration effect	집중효과
concentration of enterprise	기업집중
concentric diversification	동심원적 다각화
concept formation	개념형성
concept of conservatism	보수주의 회계
concept of historical cost	원가주의 회계
concept statement	컨셉 설명서
concept testing	컨셉 테스팅
conceptual framework	개념구조
concern	이해관계
concerned	당핵의
concerns interested	관계회사
concerted activity	공동행위
concerted intervention	협조개입
concession	수수료
concession contract	컨세션 컨트렉트
concession hunter	이권(利權)을 쫓는 자
concessionaire	판매점
concessions for nonresident	비거주자에 대한 감면
conciliation	조정
conclusion	결론
conclusion drawing	결론의
conclusion of a contract	계약체결
conclusive presumption	결정적 추정
concord	화해
concurrent cause	병존 원인

concurrent insurance	동위 보험
concurrent jurisdiction	경합관할권
concurrent lease	병존 임차권
concurrent liens	동순위선취특권
concurrent negligence	경합과실
concurrent policies	동위계약
concurrent promises	동시이행의 약속
concurrent test	동시조사 테스트
concurrent writs	복수영장
condemn	공용수용하다
condemnation	유죄선고
condemnation of land	토지의 수용
condensed account form	요약계정식
condensed balance sheet	요약대차대조표
condensed income statement	요약손익계산서
condensed report form	요약보고식
condition	조건
condition collateral	부대조건
condition express	명시조건
condition implied	묵시조건
condition of average	비례전보조항
condition precedent	정지조건
conditional	조건부의
conditional acceptance	조건부 인수
conditional approval	조건부 승인
conditional contract	조건부 계약
conditional distribution	조건부 분포
conditional liquidity	조건부 유동성
conditional loan	조건부 융자
conditional regression analysis	조건부 회귀분석
conditional sales	조건부 매매
conditional sales agreement	정형적으로 정해진 약관

conditional sales floater 대금미불상품포괄보험
conditional subsidy from the national treasury 조건부 국고보조금
conditions for payment 지급조건
conditions of issuance 발행조건
conditions of sale 경매조건
condolence money 조위금
condor type spread transaction 컨더 스프레드 거래
confederacy 공모
conference 협의
Conference of Ministers and Governors 선진국재무장관중앙은행총재회의
Conference of Non-Aligned Nations 비동맹제국회의
Conference on International Economic Cooperation 국제경제협력회의
Conference on Security and Cooperation in Europe 유럽안전보장협력회의
confession 유죄의 자백
confession of judgment 판결 승인
confidence 신임
confidence coefficient 신뢰계수
confidence game 대금을 치르지 않고 주문해온 상품을 차지하거나 그것을 싸게 전매하여 대금을 챙기는 사기
confidence interval confidence coefficient 신뢰구간 신뢰계수
confidence value 신뢰가치
confidential operation 은밀 작용
confidential relation 신뢰관계
confidentiality 기밀성
confidentiality agreement 비밀유지계약
confidentiality of information 수비의무

configuration management	구성관리
confirmed letter of credit	확인신용장
confirmation	확인
confirmation letter	확인장
confirmation note	확인통지서
confirmation request	확인 청구
confirmed letter of credit	확인제 신용장
confirming bank	확인은행
confirming charge	신용장확인수수료
confirming house	컨퍼밍 하우스
confiscation	몰수
conflict of interest	이해의 충돌
conflict of laws	법률의 저촉
conformity	적합성
confounded variable	경로변수
confrontation	대심
confusion	혼동
conglomerate	콩글로머레이트
conglomerate merchandising	콩글로머레이트 머천다이징
conjunctive model	지배모델
connivance	묵인
consecutive dividend	안정배당
consecutive quarters	연속 사분기
consensual contract	낙성계약
consensus	일치
consensus on earnings estimate	수익예측의 컨센서스
consent	동의
consent dividend	간주배당
consent judgment	동의판결
consequential damage	간접손해
consequential loss insurance	사업중단보험
conservatism	보수성

conservator	후견인
conservator bond	재산관리인 보증
considerable rise	급증
consideration	대가, 약인
consideration clause	약인조항
consignee	화물수취인
consignment	위탁판매적송품
consignment contract	위탁계약
consignment fee	위탁수수료
consignment goods	위탁품
consignment guarantee money	위탁증거금
consignment invoice	위탁품 송장
consignment ledger	위탁품 원장
consignment of tax liability	납세위탁
consignment of tax payment	납세위탁
consignment sale	위탁판매
consignment sales and purchases	위탁판매
consignment sales contract	위탁판매계약
consignor	위탁인
consilium	변론기일
consistency	일관성
consistency of auditor	감사원의 일관성
consolation money	위자료
console	조작탁자
consolidate	통합하다
consolidated	연결의
consolidated account	연결계정
consolidated annuities	연결공채
consolidated balance sheet	연결대차대조표
consolidated delivery system	혼재배송시스템
consolidated financial statements	연결재무제표
consolidated financial statistics	연결재무통계

consolidated goodwill	합병시 영업권
consolidated income	연결이익
consolidated income statement	연결손익계산표
consolidated income tax	종합소득세
consolidated net loss	연결순손실
consolidated profit and loss statement	연결손익계산서
consolidated quotation system	통합기배치정보시스템
consolidated sales	연결매상
consolidated stock ticker	통합주식 티커
consolidated surplus	연결잉여금
consolidated tape	통합테이프
consolidated tax return system	그룹과세
consolidated working capital	연결운전자금
consolidation	신설합병, 재무제표의 연결
consolidation excess	연결초과액
consolidation group	연결집단
consolidation ledger	연결원장
consolidation loan	콘솔리데이션 론
consolidation of corporations	회사의 신규합병
consolidation of mortgages	양도저당의 합병
consolidation of public loans	공채정리
consolidation of stocks	주식의 병합
consolidation pattern	조정패턴
consolidation policy	연결방침
consolidation take-over	흡수합병
Consols	콘솔 공채
consortium	국채모집인수단, 컨설티엄
consortium bank	컨설티엄 은행
conspiracy	공동모의
constant capital	불변자본
constant claims amount distribution	항상손해액분포

constant continuously compounded 일정의 연결복리
constant cost 고정비
constant divisor 항상제수(恒常除數)
constant dollar net income 안정가치에 수정한 순이익
constant dollar plan 정액법
constant dollars 안정가치
constant elasticity of variance model 정탄성 분산모형
constant expenses 고정비
constant model 일정형 모형
constant percentage method 정률법
constant power purchasing accounting 안정구매력회계
constant purchasing power 안정구매력
constant risk 불변리스크
constant risk tolerance 불변리스크 허용도
constant sum scale 정화척도
constant-dollar accounting 안정가치회계
constant-dollar profit 안정가치이익
constant-growth rate model 정률성장모형
constant-growth rate valuation model 정률성장평가모형
constituent 선거권자
constitutional right 헌법상의 권리
constructed price 추정가격
construction 해석
construction account 건설비계정
construction bond 건설국채
construction claim 건설 크레임
construction contracts 청부계약
construction cost 건축비
construction expenditure 건설지출
construction in process account 건설가계정
construction of completion 완성공사고

construction revenue	공사수입
Construction Standard Law	건축기준법
construction subsidy	건설조성금
construction work	건설공사
construction work account receivable	공사미수금
construction work revenue	건설공사수입
constructive	추정의
constructive bonus	인정상여
constructive conversion	법정구령
constructive delivery	의제의 인도
constructive dividends	간주배당
constructive eviction	의제추립
constructive notice	추정악의
constructive receipt	인정수입
constructive service	간접송달
constructive taxable year	간주사업연도
constructive total loss	해석전손, 추정전손
constructive trust	법정신탁
consuetude	습관
consul	영사
consular courts	영사재판소
consular invoice	영사송장
consulting sales	컨설팅 세일
consumables	소모품
consumer advertisement	소비자광고
consumer behavior	소비자 행동
consumer behavior analysis	소비자 행동 분석
consumer choice	소비자 선택
consumer credit	소비자 신용
consumer credit company	신용판매회사
consumer credit control law	소비자신용규제법
consumer credit life insurance	소비자 신용생명보험

consumer credit rate	소비자 금리
consumer demand	실수요
consumer education	소비자 교육
consumer electronics	가전
consumer expenditure	소비자 지출
consumer exploitation	소비자 개척
consumer finance company	소비자 금융회사
consumer leasing	소비자 리스
consumer loan	소비자 금융
consumer movement	소비자 운동
consumer perception	소비자 지각
consumer premises equipment	고객 단말
consumer price index	소비자 물가지수
consumer relations	소비자 관계
consumer sector stock	소비자 관련주
consumer spending	소비자 지출
consumer testing	소비자 테스트
consumer thought variable	소비자 사고변수
consumer's behavior	소비자 행동
consumer's cooperative society	소비생활협동조합
consumer's credit file	개인신용정보
consumer's union	소비자단체
consumerism	소비자주의
consumers' durables	내구소비재
consumers group insurance	소비자단체 생명보험
consumption demand	소비수요
consumption entry	소비세신고
consumption function	소비함수
consumption lag	소비재고
consumption multiplier	소비승수
consumption quota	소비할당
consumption tax	소비세

consumption transfer tax	소비양여세
consumption trend	소비동향
consumption values	소비가치
contagion hypothesis	컨테이젼 가설
containerization	컨테이너리제이션
contamination damages	오염 손해
contango	지급유예금, 이연금리
contemplation of bankruptcy	파산예기
contemporaneous reserve accounting	동시적립방식
contempt	모욕
content provider	컨텐츠 제공자
content-certified mail	내용증명우편
contentious	서로 경쟁하다
contestable period	가쟁기간
Continental Depositary Receipts	컨티넨셜 예탁증서
continental form of closing the ledger	대륙식 원장마감수속
contingency	우발사상
contingency freight	불확정 운송임
contingency fund	위험준비금
contingency insurance	우연손실보험
contingency loading	안전할증
contingency reserve	비상위험준비금
contingency risk	우발적 위험
contingency theory	콘틴젼시 이론
contingent	파생적인
contingent annuity	부정연금
contingent assets	우발자산
contingent beneficiary	차순위 보험금 수취인
contingent business interruption insurance	미필영업중단보험
contingent charge	우발비용
contingent claim	파생상품

contingent commission	이익수수료
contingent estate	불확정 재산권
contingent fee	성공보수
contingent fund	우발자금
contingent interest	부정이자
contingent liabilities	우발채무
contingent liability policy	미필배상책임보험
contingent loss	우발손실
contingent order	일정가격차에 의한 조합주문
contingent outlay	임시비
contingent profit	우발이익
contingent reserve	우발채무적립금
contingent transaction	우발거래
continuance	재판의 속행
continuation	계속
continuation clause	계속약관
continuation pattern	보합패턴
continued expenses	계속비
continuing account	계속계정
continuing contract	계속계약
continuing education	계속교육
continuing expenditure	계속비
continuing guaranty	무기한 보증
continuing operations	계속사업
continuous annuity	연속생명연금
continuous audit	계속회계감사
continuous buying and selling	계속적 매매
continuous compound interest rate	연속복리
continuous compounding calculation	연속복리계산
continuous disclosure	계속개시
continuous dividend	연속배당
continuous inventory	계속재고

continuous manufacturing 연속생산
continuous market 계속시장, 연속거래시장
continuous policy 계속적 예정 보험계약
continuous probability distribution 연속확률분포
continuous reinsurance cover 재보험특약
continuous sampling 연속추출
continuous time 연속시간
continuous trading 연속매매
continuous variable 연속변수
contra 상대
contra account 대조계정
contra broker 상대 브로커
contra entry 상대기입
contra-cyclical 반순환적인
contraband 수입금지품
contraband of export 수출금지제품
contraband of import 수입금지제품
contract 계약
contract balance 계약잔액
contract bond 계약보증
contract charge 계약수수료
contract curve 계약곡선
contract deposit paid 계약선급금
contract deposit received 계약선수금
contract entered into by mutual consensus 낙성계약
contract for service 역무계약
contract in bulk 일괄계약
contract in kind 요물계약
contract market 계약시장
contract money 계약금
contract month 약정월

contract notice	약정통지
contract of merger	합병계약서
contract position	계약옵션
contract price	협정가격
contract rate system	계약운임제
contract ratio	계약률
contract review	계약내용확인
contract salvage	계약구조
contract salvage charges	계약구조료
contract size	계약규모
contract slip	매매확인서
contract specification	계약수단서
contract system	청부제도
contract term	계약기간
contract terms	계약조건
contract type	계약형
contract type accumulative investment plan	계약형 계속투자 플랜
contract type investment trust	계약형 투자신탁
contract uberrimae fidei theory	선의계약설
contract work	청부공사
contract work account receivable	청부공사미수금
contract work system	청부제도
contracted interest rate	약정금리
contracted out	적용제외
contracted price	약정가격
contracted rate	약정이율
contracting out	하청에 내다, 연금의 적용제외
contracting party	계약당사자
contractor	공사청부인
contractor' all risks insurance	건설공사보험
contractors' contingent liability insurance	건설청부업자 미필배상책임보험

contractors' equipment floater	건설청부업자 기계기구포괄보험
contractors' insurance policy	공사청부 보험증권
contractors' liability insurance	건설청부업자 책임보험
contractual accumulation plan	이익누적형 투신
contractual documents	계약서
contractual liability	계약책임
contractual liability policy	계약배상책임보험
contractual vertical marketing	계약형 수직전 마케팅
contractual wage	협정임금
contrarian	역발상 투자가
contrary opinion	반대의견
contravention	위반하다
contributed stock	출자자본
contributed surplus	주식발행초과금
contribution	출자금, 분담금
contribution deduction	기부금 공제
contribution in aid of construction	공사부담금
contribution margin	공헌이익
contribution margin form	공헌이익식
contribution plan	갹출제도
contribution system	보험료 분담제
contribution to welfare facilities	복리시설부담액
contributions to affiliated company	관계회사출자금
contributories	출자의무자
contributory annuity	갹출제 연금
contributory infringement	기여침해
contributory margin	공헌이익
contributory negligence	조성과실
contributory plan	보험료 분담제
contributory shares of estate	기여분
contributory sickness fund	갹출식 질병보험
contributory value	공동해손부담가액

control account	통괄계정
control limit	관리한계
control market	지배시장
control measure	억제조치
control. mechanism	관리기구
control of inflation	인플레이션 억제
control procedure	관리수준
control stock	지배주
controllable expenses	관리가능원가
controlled account	피통괄계정
controlled company	피지배회사
controlled currency	관리통화
controlled discretion	법규재량
controlled foreign corporation	관리된 외국기업
controlled preferred stock	보증우선주
controller	회계검사관
controlling account	통괄계정
controlling company	지배회사
controlling inflation	인플레이션 억제
controlling interest	경영지배권
contumacy	명령불복종
convenience	편의
convenience financial statements	외국편의적 재무제표
convenience goods	편의품
convenience of tax collection	징세상의 편의
convenience shelf registration	편의일괄등록
convenience translation	외국편의적 환산
convenience yield	컨비니언스 일드
conveniences	설비
convention expense	회의비
convention for the avoidance of double taxation	이중과세방지조약

Convention on International Civil Aviation 국제민간항공조약
Convention on International Combined Transport 국제복합운송조약
Convention on the Settlement of Investment Disputed between States and Nationals of Other States 국가와 타국가국민 사이 투자분쟁 해결에 관한 조약
conventional commodity market 전통적 상품시장
conventional loan 컨벤셔널 론
conventional marketing channel 전통적 마케팅 경로
conventional mortgage loan 통상형 모기지론
conventional tariff 협정관세
conventional undamaged value 협정무손상가액
converge 수렴하다
convergence analysis 수속분석
convergent fluctuation 수렴성의 변동
convergent marketing 수렴형 마케팅
converse preference 역특혜
conversion 구령, 환산
conversion at market price 시가전환
conversion at par 액면전환
conversion conditions 전환조건
conversion cost 가공비
conversion cost system 공정별 종합원가계산
conversion discount 전환 디스카운트
conversion factor 변환계수
conversion into cash 환가처분
conversion into cash of seized property 차압재산의 환가
conversion issue 차환발행
conversion of items in foreign currencies 외화표시계정항목의 환산

conversion parity 전환비율
conversion period 전환정구기간
conversion premium 전환프레임
conversion price 전환가격
conversion price formula 전환가격방식
conversion privilege 보험종류 변경청구권
conversion ratio 전환비율
conversion to gold 금태환
conversion value 전환가치
convertible 가변보험
convertible bond 전환사채
convertible bonds with option 옵션부 전환사채
convertible contract 중도절제계약
convertible currency 태환통화
convertible mortgage 전환모기지
convertible note 태환지폐
convertible preferred stock 전환우선주
convertible ratio 교환비율
convertible reserve 태환준비
convertible securities 전환증권
convertible stock 전환주식
convertible term insurance 가변정기보험
convexity 컨벡시티
conveyance of estate 재산양도
conveyancer 부동산양도취급인
conveyer system 흐름작업방식
conviction 유죄의 결정
convincing proof 확신적 입증
cooking of a book 장부를 속이다
cooling time 냉각기간
cooling-off 클링 오프
cooperation between industry and academic organizations 산학협동

cooperative association	협동조합
cooperative association on indirect taxes	간접세협력단체
cooperative bank	신용조합
cooperative business association	사업협동조합
cooperative marketing	공동판매
cooperative society	협동조합
coordinate system	좌표계
coordinated cut	협조이윤 하락
coordinated intervention	협조개입
coordination of bond issues	기채조사
coparcenary	상속재산공유
coproduction agreement	공동생산계약
copyright	저작권
core	중핵
core business division	주력부문
core competence	핵심역량
core holding	코아 홀딩
core market	중핵시장
core stock	코아 스톡
core-fringe model	코아 프린지 모델
corn hog cycle	콘 호그 순환
corner lot	각지
cornering	매점
corporate accounting	기업회계
corporate accounting principles	기업회계원칙
corporate action	회사행위
corporate alliance	기업연합
corporate average tax rate	평균법인세율
corporate banking	코퍼레이트 뱅킹
corporate body	법인단체
corporate bond	사채

corporate card 법인카드
corporate charter 인가장
corporate citizenship 기업시민성
corporate color 코퍼레이트 컬러
corporate communication 코퍼레이트 커뮤니케이션
corporate culture 기업문화
corporate customer 법인고객
corporate debenture 사채
corporate deposit 법인예금
corporate domain 기업도메인
corporate equivalent yield 사채환산이율
corporate executive 회사중역
corporate finance 사업금융
corporate franchise 회사특권
corporate governance 지배 조직
corporate identity 코퍼레이트 아이덴티티(CI)
corporate image 기업이미지
corporate imperialism 기업제국주의
corporate income 법인소득
corporate income tax rate 법인소득세율
corporate income taxes expenses 법인소득세 비용
corporate juridical person 사단법인
corporate management 기업경영
corporate mission 기업의 사명
corporate name 상호
corporate pension 기업연금
corporate profile 기업 프로필
corporate raider 수취회사, 시장교란회사
corporate reorganization 회사소생
corporate resolution 감독회사결의
corporate right 법인권
corporate ripoff 기업약탈

corporate savings 법인저축
corporate seal 회사인
corporate securities 사채
corporate separation 회사분할
corporate shareholder 법인주주
corporate strategy 기업전략
corporate suretyship 법인보증인
corporate tax 법인세
corporate tax system 법인세제도
corporate treasurer 기업재무담당자
corporate trust 법인신탁
corporate vitality 기업활력
corporation 법인
corporation aggregate 집합 법인
corporation amalgamated 피합병 법인
corporation bond 사채
corporation card 법인카드
corporation ceased to exist after merger 합병에 의해 소멸하는 회사
corporation filing a blue return 청색신고법인
corporation finance 회사금융
corporation for profit 영리법인
corporation free from taxation 비과세법인
corporation in need of reorganization 소생회사
corporation in public interest 공익법인
corporation in the course of liquidation 청산중인 법인
corporation levy 법인세할 주민세
corporation liable to taxation 납세의무있는 법인
Corporation of Lloyd's 로이즈 조합
corporation of public utility 공익법인

corporation profit tax	법인이득세
corporation reorganization law	회사소생법
corporation report	회사 레포트
corporation sector	기업부문
corporation tax credit	법인세 공제
corporation type	회사형
corporation type investment trust	회사형 투자신탁
corporation under liquidation	청산수속중인 법인
corporation's own stock	자사 주
corporeal hereditament	유체상속부동산
corpus	원본
corpus delicti	죄의 주체
corrected probability	수정제확률
correction	경정, 조정
correction of errors	오류의 정정
correction of prior periods	전기수정항목
corrective action	시정조치
corrective advertising	사죄광고
corrective market	정정상장
corrective selling	정정판매
correlation	상관관계
correlation analysis	상관분석
correlation coefficient	상관계수
correlation diagram	상관도
correlation matrix	상관행렬
correlation of return	수익률의 상관관계
correlation industry	관련산업
correlation table	상관표
correlative adjustment	대응의 조정
correspondent account	대리계좌, 상대계정, 대조계정
correspondent agreement	코레스펀던트 계약
correspondent bank	코레스펀던트 은행

correspondent financial institution	거리금융기관
correspondent relation	코레스펀던트 관계
corresponding account	중매계정
corresponding deposit	중매예금
corresponding period of last year	전년동기
corroborate	보강하다
corroborating evidence	보강증거
corruption	오직
corruption bribery	부패 수뢰
corruption of blood	혈통오손
cosmocorp	세계기업
cost	원가
cost absorption	원가흡수
cost account	원가계정
cost accounting	원가계산
cost accounting by department	부문별 원가계산
cost accounting by product	제품별 원가계산
cost accounting period	원가계산기간
cost acconting standards	원가계산기준
cost accounting system	원가계산제도
cost analysis	원가분석
cost and expenses	원가 또는 비용
cost and freight	운임포함
cost and insurance	보험료포함가격
cost at the margin	한계비용
cost basis	원가주의
cost behavior	비용동향
cost card	원가계산서
cost center	코스트 센터
cost classification	비용분류
cost consciousness	원가의식
cost control	원가관리

cost depletion 감모상각비
cost depletion method 취득잔고비례법
cost distribution 원가배분
cost effective 비용효율의 좋음
cost effectiveness analysis 비용 대 효과분석
cost element 원가요소
cost finding 원가감정
cost flow assumption 재고자산의 평가방법
cost for development 개발비
cost for judicial proceedings 소송절차비용
cost function 비용함수
cost improvement cost 경비개선비용
cost, insurance and freight 운임・보험료 포함
cost ledger 원가원장
cost matching income principle 비용수익대응의 원칙
cost method 원가법
cost method of depletion 감모상각의 원가법
cost of arbitration 중재비용
cost of assets 자산의 취득원가
cost of capital 자본비용
cost of carry 자산소유비용
cost of conformity 적합의 비용
cost of construction 공사비
cost of disposal 처분비용
cost of finished goods 제품원가
cost of goods purchased 매입원가
cost of goods sold 매출원가
cost of issuing stocks 주식발행비용
cost of living index 생활비 지수
cost of maintenance 유지비
cost of manufactured goods 제조원가
cost of processing 가공비

cost of product 제품원가
cost of production budget 제조비 예산
cost of products sold 매각원가
cost of raising funds 자금조달비용
cost of repairs 수선비
cost of reproduction 재생산원가
cost of sales 판매원가
cost of short-term funds 단기자금조달비용
cost of tax collection 징세비용
cost of temporary repair 가수선비
cost of transferred properties 양도자산의 취득비
cost of work performed 기성원가
cost or market whichever is lower basis 저가주의
cost overrun 예산초과
cost per thousand 시청자 천명당 광고비
cost performance 코스트 퍼포먼스
cost plus 코스트 플러스
cost plus fixed fee contract 원가가산확정이익보장계약
cost plus method 원가준비법
cost price 매입가격
cost principle 원가주의, 원가기준
cost rate 원가율
cost recovery 원가의 회수
cost reduction 원가 인하
cost report 제조원가 보고서
cost savings 원가절약
cost sheet 원가계산표
cost standard 원가표준
cost statement 원가계산표
cost system 원가계산 제도
cost trade-off 코스트 트레이드 오프

cost unit	원가계산단위
cost value	원가가치
cost variance	원가차이
cost, insurance	운임, 보험료 포함
cost-benefit analysis	비용·편익분석
cost-of-living index	생활비 지수
cost-or-less principle	원가이하주의
cost-plus contract	실비정산계약
cost-push inflation	비용인상 인플레이션
cost-reduction programs	원가절감계획
cost-reimbursable contract	비용상환계약
cost-volume-profit analysis	비용·조업도·이익분석
costing	원가계산
costing period	원가계산 기간
costing unit	원가계산 단위
costs bond	소송비용 보증증권
cosurety	공동보증인
cotenancy	부동산의 공동보유
council	평의회
Council of Europe	구주회의
council of managing directors	상무회
Council of the Bar	법연변호사평의회
council on alcoholic beverages	주류심의회
counselor	법률고문
count	항목, 총계
count out	정족수를 채우지 않아도 인정하고 유회하다
counter cyclical	반순환적
counter cyclical policy	반순환정책
counter deed	반대증서
counter guarantee	담보보증
counter purchase	담보수입

counter trade	카운터 트레이드, 구상무역
counter value	대가
counter-affidavit	반대선서공술서
counter-plea	반대항변
counter-security	역담보
counterclaim	반소
countercyclical advertising	역주기광고
counterdeed	반대증서
counterfeit	위조
counterfeit card	위조카드
countermand	취소하다
countermeasure	대책
counteroffer	반대청약
counterpart	상대물
counterparty	카운터 파티
counterrolls	공동장부
countersign	부서
countersignature	연서
countervailing duty	상계관세
countervailing power	대항력
counting	감정
country damage	원지손해
country exposure	카운트리 엑스포우저
country having deficit in capital transaction	자본수출국
country limit	컨트리 리미트
country risk	컨트리 리스크
country risk assessment	컨트리리스크 평가
county borough	특별시
coupon	이찰
coupon advertisement	쿠폰광고
coupon bank debenture	이자부금융채

coupon bond	이자증권부 채권
coupon income	쿠폰수입
coupon off	이찰 락
coupon on	이찰 부
coupon pass	쿠폰패스
coupon payment	이자지급
coupon payment date	이자지급기일
coupon plan	쿠폰방식
coupon rate	쿠폰레이트
coupon sale	쿠폰세일
coupon swap	쿠폰스왑
coupon-only currency swap	쿠폰안의 통화스왑
courier service	쿠리어 서비스
court	재판소
court above	상소재판소
court below	원재판소
court clerk	재판소 서기관
court for the trial of impeachments	탄핵재판소
Court of Admiralty	해사재판소
court of appeal	공소재판소
court of bankruptcy	파산재판소
court of equity	에퀴티 재판소
court of first instance	제1심 재판소
court of general sessions	형사 제1 재판소
court of justiciary	형사 상급 재판소
court of nisi prius	민사 제1심 재판소
court of probate	검인재판소
court of request	소액채권재판소
court-hand	법정서체
covariance	공분산
covariance analysis	공분산 분석
covenance	관용

covenant	특약조항, 약인
covenant for title	권한담보조항
covenant of seisin	권리담보조항
covenants	계약, 날인증서
cover	보험에 의한 담보
cover bid	커버 비드
cover dealing	커버 딜링
cover note	커버 노트
cover the loss	손실을 묻다
coverage	담보범위
covered call	커버드 콜
covered call option	커버드 콜 옵션
covered interest arbitrage	커버된 이자재정거래
covered option	커버드 옵션
covered position	커버드 포지션
covered quarter	피보험기
covered warrant	커버드 워런트
covering	커버
covering entry	자동분류기입
covering of a deficit	적자보전
craft	동업조합
crash	폭락
crawling peg	크로우링 페그
crawling peg system	단계적 평가 변동제
craze for speculation	투기열
cream skimming	좋은 곳 차지
creaming merchandise	최유망상품
creation	창립
creation of utility	효용의 창조
creative strategy	창조적 전략
credibility	신용도
credit	대방, 채권, 신용

credit accommodation	신용공여
credit account	내번계정
credit against corporation tax	법인세의 공제
credit against tax	세액공제
credit agreement	여신계약
credit among corporations	기업간 신용
credit analysis	여신분석
credit and suretyship insurance	신용 또는 보증보험
credit association	신용조합
credit authorization terminal	신용조회단말
credit availability	크레디트 능력
credit balance	대변잔액, 예금잔액
credit bill	신용어음
credit business	여신업무
credit buying	기한부 어음구매
credit capability	신용력
credit card	신용카드
credit card burglary insurance	카드도난보험
credit card business	신용카드 업무
credit card company	신용카드 회사
credit cards issued by the agent	대행카드
credit ceiling	신용한도
credit ceiling application system	대출한도액전용제도
credit control	여신관리
credit conversion factor	신용환산계수
credit creation	신용창조
credit crisis	신용공황
credit crunch	신용규제, 신용제한
credit customer	외상판매거래처
credit ease	신용완화
credit economy	신용경제
credit exposure management	여신관리

credit facility	신용능력
credit for dividend	배당공제
credit for foreign taxes	외국세액공제
credit for handicapped person	장애자 공제
credit for income tax	소득세액의 공제
credit guarantee	신용보증
credit guarantee corporation	신용보증협회
credit history	신용역사
credit inquiry	신용조회
credit insurance	신용보험
credit investigation	신용조사
credit life insurance	신용생명보험
credit limit	신용한도
credit line	신용한도
credit line system	신용라인 시스템
credit loan	신용대출
credit losses	대손
credit margin	신용증거금
credit memorandum	대출방법 메모
credit money	신용화폐
credit note	대변전표
credit past due date	기일도래원본
credit policy	크레디트 폴리시
credit price	외상판매가격
credit purchase	외상
credit quality	신용도
credit rating	신용등급을 매김
credit ratio	신용비율
credit rationing	신용제한
credit records	신용정보
credit reference	신용조회
credit risk	신용위험

credit sales	외상으로 파는 것 또는 그 대금
credit sales accounts	수취계정
credit slip	입금표
credit spread	신용격차
credit squeeze	금융절약
credit standing	신용상태
credit standing condition	신용상태
credit structure	신용구조
credit swap	크레디트 스왑
credit system	외상제도
credit terms	외상조건
credit tranche	크레디트 트란시
credit union	신용조합
credit union exchange	신용조합 환
credit watch system	크레디트 워치 시스템
credit worthiness	신용력
creditable amount of foreign taxes	외국세액의 공제한도액
creditor	채권자
creditor account	대변계정
creditor bank	대출은행
creditor country	채권국
creditor group insurance	단체신용생명보험
creditor side	대변
creditor's equity to tolal assets	부채비율
creditor's meeting	채권자 회의
creditor's voluntary winding-up	채권자에 의한 임의청산
creditors ledger	외상매입처원장
creditworthy	신용력 있는
creep back upwards	조금씩 조금씩 높아지는 경향이 있는
creeping	신고없이
creeping expropriation	슬그머니 수용
creeping inflation	크립핑 인플레이션

creeping nationalization	조금씩 국유화하는 것
crime bond	범죄보증증권
crime insurance	범죄보험
crime of interference with execution of official duty	공무집행방해죄
crimen falsi	위조죄
criminal action	형사소송
criminal information	약식 기소장
criminal investigation	강제조사
criminal investigation system	사찰제도
criminal of tax evasion	탈세범
criminal proceedings	형사소송수속
criminal record	범죄력
crisis	공황
crisis at maturity	일괄 반제리스크
crisis rate	위기 레이트
criteria	규준
criteria rights	기준설정권
critical function	비판적 기능
critical mass	임계질량
critical mass of reward	보수 한계량
critical path method	크리티컬 패스 매소드
critical point	임계치
critical-path accounting	크리티컬 패스 회계
criticality hazard	임계위험
corp	수확고
corp basis	수확기준
crop insurance	수확물 보호
cross	크로스 상업
cross action	반대소송
cross arbitration	크로스 재정
cross claim	강제소송 참가

cross correlation	교차 상관
cross culture	크로스 컬쳐, 이문화
cross currency swap	통화간 재무교환거래(홍정)
cross debt	상대채무
cross default	크로스 디폴트
cross default clause	크로스 디폴트 조항
cross elasticity	교차탄력성
cross entry	대체기입
cross examination	반대심문
cross hedge	교차 헷지
cross impact analysis	크로스 임팩트 분석
cross liabilities basis	교차책임주의
cross license	특허권 교환
cross license contract	크로스 라이선스 계약
cross margin	크로스 마진
cross offer	교차신청
cross order	교차주문
cross rate	크로스 레이트
cross reference list	상호참조표
cross sectional analysis	타기업비교
cross slip	입금전표
cross subsidization	내부 상호보조
cross tabulation	크로스 집계표
cross trading	교차 거래
cross-appeal	반대상소
cross-boarder transactions	크로스보더 거래, 국경간 거래
cross-cultural analysis	이문화 비교분석
cross-currency interest rate swap	크로스 커런시 금리 스왑
cross-default clause	크로스 디폴트 조항
cross-demand	반대청구
cross-examination	반대심문
cross-hauling	상호수송교류

cross-holding	보합(시세변동이 없음)
cross-sectional analysis	횡단면 분석
cross-sectional data	횡단면 데이터
cross-sectional valuation approach	크로스 섹션 평가 어프로치
crossed check	횡선수표
crossed market	역전시장
crossing for the purpose of financing	금융크로스
cross-licensing	크로스라이선싱
crowd	브로커 중개
crowd trading	크라우드 거래
crowding out	크라우딩 아웃, 구축
crowding out effect	구축효과
crown event	관이벤트
crown jewel	중요부문
crown law	형법
CRT projection display	CRT 투사 디스플레이
crude oil futures option	원유 선물 옵션
crunch	재정핍박
crystallization	부동담보의 결정
cuff quote	추량호가
culpa	과실
culpa concurrens	경합과실
culpability	유책성
culpable	과실하다
cultural assimilation	문화융합
cultural change	문화 변용
cultural influence	문화 영향
cultural synergy	문화 시너지
cultural values	문화적 가치관
cum call	납입부
cum coupon	이찰부
cum dividend	배당부

cum new 신주부
cum right 신주인수권의 권리부
cum warrant 컴 워런트
cumulative amount of depreciation 감가상각누계액
cumulative deficit 누적적자
cumulative dividend 누적배당
cumulative experience 누적 경험
cumulative fiscal deficit 국가예산누적적자
cumulative index 누적지수
cumulative legacy 누적적 유증
cumulative liability 누적 책임
cumulative limit 누적 한도액 기준
cumulative limitation 누적적 제한
cumulative method 누가법
cumulative offenses 반복범죄
cumulative preferred stock 누적우선주
cumulative surplus 누적흑자
cumulative taxation 누적과세
cumulative voting 누적투표
Curacao Depositary Receipts 큐라소 예탁증서
curator 후견인
curb dealings 장외거래
curb market 장외시장
curia 재판소
currency 통화
currency alignment 통화조정
currency and demand deposits 현금 및 예금통화
currency appreciation 통화가치상승
currency basket 통화 바스켓
currency cocktail 통화 칵테일
currency commodity 통화상품
currency conversion 통화환산

currency conversion bond	커런시 컨버젼 채
currency convertible in fact	사실상 교환가능 통화
currency crisis	통화위기
currency deflation	통화 디플레
currency deposit	통화성 예금
currency depreciation	통화가치하락
currency devaluation	통화절하
currency fluctuation	통화변동
currency futures	통화선물
currency futures price movement	통화선물가치동향
currency futures trading	통화선물거래
currency hedging	환 헷지
currency in circulation	유통통화
currency indemnity	통화보상
currency inflation	통화인플레
currency movement	환동향
currency note	정부통화
currency option trading	통화옵션거래
currency principle	통화주의
currency swap	통화스왑
currency swap bond	통화스왑채
currency system	통화체계
currency translation	통화 확산
currency translation adjustments	외화환산 조정액
currency unit	통화단위
currency upvaluation	통화절상
currency value	통화가치
current	경상, 당좌의
current account	당좌계정
current account balance	경상수지
current account check	당좌수표
current annuity	현재 유효한 연금

current arrangement	유동성배열법
current assets	유동자산
current balance	경상수지
current budget	경상예산
current cost	현재원가
current cost accounting	취득원가주의 회계
current cost method	시가방식
current cost/constant dollar accounting	시가주의 안정가치 회계
current cost/nominal dollar accounting	시가주의 명목가치 회계
current coupon	기간지표
current credit accounts with agencies	대리점 대여
current deposit	당좌예금
current disbursement approach	부과방식
current dollar	경상달러
current expenditure	경상지출
current expenses	경상비용
current fiscal year	현회계년도
current fund	당좌자금, 유동자금, 운영자금
current income	당기이익
current insurance	현재유효한 보험
current insured status	당좌수급자격
current interest rate	현행이자율
current investment	단기투자
current level of stock price	현재의 주가수준
current liabilities	유동부채
current market value	현행시장가액
current market yield spread	실세시장 이익회전범위
current maturities of long-term debt	장기부채의 반제액
current maturity	당기만기부분
current money	유통화폐

current operating performance basis	당기업적주의
current operating performance income statement	당기업적주의에 따른 손익계산서
current operating performance theory	당기업적주의
current payment	경상지불
current period	당기
current premium value	현행 프리미엄
current price	시가
current ratio	유동비율
current replacement cost	재취득가격
current risks	책임보험 리스크
current service pension	현재 근무연금
current taxable year	당기
current taxes	당기세액
current term net income	당기순익
current term net loss	당기순손실
current term net profit	당기순이익
current term net profit or loss	당기순손익
current term settlement	당기결산
current transaction	경상거래
current transfer	경상이전
current value	현재가치
current value accounting	시가회계
current year	당기
current yield	직접이율
current-asset cycle	유동자산 회전기간
current-assumption whole life insurance	커런트 어썸프션 종신보험
current-first order	유동성 배열
current-outlay cost	당기지출원액
curtailment of expenditure	경비삭감
curtailment of operation	조업단축

curtate expectation of life	단순평균여명
curve steepening	커브의 경사화
curving trend line	비직선적 트랜드라인
cushion bond	쿠션채
custodial account	보관계정
custodian	주식보관인
custodian bank	보관은행
custodian's agent	행사명의대리인
custody	보관
custody fee	보관료
custom	관습법
custom fee	세관수수료
custom index	커스텀 인덱스
custom of merchant	상관습
custom-house	세관
customary losses	통상손해
customary practice	관행
customary tenure	관습상의 보유
customary tenure estates	관습상의 보유권
customer holdover effect	고객이연효과
customer market	고객시장
customer mix	고객믹스
customer oriented	고객지향
customer preference	고객선호
customer rationalization	고객의 합리성
customer relations	고객관계
customer repos	커스터머 레포
customer research	고객조사
customer transaction	고객단가
customer's account	매출처계정
customer's agreement and consent	취인약낙서
customer's loan	신용거래대출

customer's order	고객의 주문
customer's satisfaction	고객만족도
customers' deposits	예탁보증금
customers' ledger	외상판매대금 원장
customers' liabilities on guaranties	보증채무담보
customers mobilizing power	고객동원력
customized performance standards	커스텀 퍼포먼스 스탠다드
customs autonomy	관세 자주권
customs debenture	여세증명서
customs duty refund system	관세환급제도
customs duty tariff	관세
customs house	세관
customs invoice	통관용 송장
customs of merchant	상관습법
customs procedures	통관수속
customs tariff table	관세율표
customs union	관세동맹
cutoff date	마감일
cutting	할인
cyan magenta yellow black	인쇄 프로세스 컬러
cybernetics	사이버네틱스
customs union	관세동맹
cycle	주기
cycle of fashion	유행주기
cycle stock	운전재고
cyclical depression	순환불황
cyclical fluctuation	순환적 변동
cyclical growth	순환적 성장
cyclical stock	순환주

≪ D ≫

daily account	일계표
daily balance	일일잔액, 일일결산
daily bordereau	인수일보
daily chart	일족차트
daily diminishing clause	일차 체감약관
daily interest for arrearage	연체일보
daily pro-rata return of premium	일할반환보험료
daily rate	일보
daily trial balance	일계표, 일일시산표
daily workers insurance	일일고용 노무자 건강보험
daimyo bond	다이묘우 본드
damage	손해
damage insurance	손해보험
damageability	역(이)손성
damaged property	피해자산
damaged value	손상가액
damages	손해배상액
damnum sine injuria	배상청구가 인정될 수 없는 손해
dangers of navigation	해상위험
data broadcasting	데이터방송
data processing business	데이터 가공업무
data reduction	데이터 정리
data retrieval	데이터 검색
data transmission	데이터 통신, 데이터 전송
date	기일
date of enforcement	시행일
date of execution	집행기일

date of record	기준일
date proved by notary	확정일부
dated date	이자기산일
dating backward	후일부의
dating forward	선일부의
daughter company	자회사
dawn raid	긴급구입
day duty allowance	일직료
day for paying taxes	납세기일
day loan	익일물대금
day order	당일에 유효한 주문
day trading	일일계획장사
day-to-day management	항상적 운영
daylight trading	일일계획장사
days after sight	일람후~일불
days in arrears	연체일수
days of grace	지불유예기간
days to run	할인일수
days worked abroad	국외근무일수
de bone esse	잠정적 효력을 지니다
de bonis asportatis	동산의 불법수거
de bonis non	승계유산관리
de facto	사실상
de jure	법률상
de novo	다시 처음부터
de novo entry	신규진입
de son tort	무권한의
dead corner	사각
dead cross	데드 크로스
dead freight	공하운임
dead loan	대손
dead stock	불량재고

dead weight loss of customs duty 관세의 사중손실
deadline for filing 신고마감기일
deal between speculators 사수전
dealer financing 딜러금융
dealer loan 딜러 론
dealer market 딜러 시장
dealer paper 딜러 페이퍼
dealer's bond 소매업자 보증증권
dealer's fee 딜러 수수료
dealer's option 딜러 옵션
dealer's position 딜러 포지션
dealers' market 업자간 상장
dealing 자기매매
dealing for money 현금거래
dealing market 딜링상장(相場)
dealing risk 딜링 리스크
dealings 거래고
dean 학부장, 학장
dear money policy 고금리정책
death duty 상속세
death from natural causes 자연사
death rate 사망률
debenture 채권
debenture assignment 사채권양도
debenture bond 사채권
debenture convertible at par 액면전환사채
debenture interest 사채이자
debenture redemption 사채상환
debenture stock 무상환사채
debenture trust 사채권신탁
debenture with lump-sum payment at maturity 이자일시불 이부금융채

debenture-issuing expenses	사채발행비
debentures account	사채권계정
debit	차변, 잡아당겨 쓰러뜨리다
debit account	차변계정
debit advice	차기통지서
debit authorization	인낙승인
debit balance	차변잔액
debit card	지급카드
debit memorandum	차변메모
debit note	차변표
debit note for premium	보험금청구서
debit side	차변
debit slip	지불전표
debit system	데빗 시스템
debt	채무, 부채
debt account	차입금계정
debt accumulation	누적채무
debt assumption	채무인수
debt bond swap	채무의 채권화
debt ceiling	차입한도액
debt collection	채권회수
debt collector	회수업자
debt cross	뎃 크로스
debt discount and expenses	사채발행차금
debt exposure	대출리스크
debt finance	차입에 의한 자금조달
debt for collection	징수채무
debt in foreign currency	외화표시채무
debt in U.S. dollar	달러표시채무
debt instrument	채무수단
debt leverage	채무 레버리지
debt loan	차입금

debt management policy	공채관리정책
debt maturity	부채기간
debt pooling	채무일괄조정
debt ratio	부채비율
debt reduction	채무소멸
debt relief	채무면제
debt rescheduling	채무조정
debt retirement	채무반제
debt securities	채무증권
debt service	미불금
debt service ratio	채무반제비율
debt servicing	이자의 지급
debt warrant	뎃 워런트 채
debt-credit transaction	대차거래
debt-equity ratio	부채・자본비율
debt-equity swap	대외채무의 주식화
debtor	채무자
debtor account	차변계정
debtor and creditor accounts	대차계정
debtor and estate	채무자와 파산재단
debtor balance	차변잔고
debtor bank	차변은행
debtor country	채무국
debtor in possession	점유채무자
debtor side	차변
debtor's bond	채무자보증증서
debtor's deposit	채무자예금
debts and credits	채권채무
debugging	디버깅
decapitalization	디캐피털라이제이션
decay rate	고객상실률
decelerating trend	감속경향

deceleration	둔화
decentralization	집중배제, 분권
decentralized	분산구입
decentralized channel	분산경로
decentralized management	분권관리
decentralized responsibility	분산책임
decision effectiveness	결정의 유효성
decision making	의사결정
decision making unit	의사결정단위
decision of a general meeting of stockholders	주주총회의 결의
decision of a reorganization scheme	재건계획의 결정
decision of the general meeting	총회의 결정
decision on request for reinvestigation	이의결정
decision room	의사결정 룸
decision support system	의사결정지원 시스템
decision technology	결정기술
decision variable	결정변수
deckholder	데크홀더
declaration	신고, 배당발표
declaration against interest	이익에 반하는 공술(진술)
Declaration and Decisions on International investment and Multinational Enterprises	국제투자, 다국적기업에 관한 선언 및 결정
declaration form	신고용지
declaration of bankruptcy	파산선고
declaration of change of land category	지목변환계
declaration of import	수입신고
declaration of income	소득신고
declaration nonpayment	지급거절선언

declaration policy	통지보험
declaratory	확인하다
declaratory decree	확인결정
declaratory judgment	선언적 판결
declaratory part of law	법률의 선언적 부분
declaratory statute	선명적 법률
declaratory stipulation	선언규정
declared back reinsurance	시세회복 재보험
declared capital	공시자본
declared profit	계상이익
declination	인수사절
decline	하락하다
decline in prices of inventories	재고자산의 평가하락
declining balance depreciation	정률감가상각방법
declining balance method	정률법
declining industry	사양산업
decode	해독
decrease in book value	장부가격의 감소
decrease of capital	감자
decrease of income tax	소득세의 감액
decreased receipts	감수
decreasing rate	저하율
decreasing term insurance	체감정기보험
decree	판결
decree of distribution	배분판결
decree of insolvency	지불불능판결
decree of nullity	무효판결
decrement	실질적 가치의 하락
dedi et concessi	권원담보문서
dedicated bond portfolio	채권의 데디케이티드 포트폴리오
deductible	공제면책금액
deductible amount for donation	기부금의 손금산입한도액
deductible clause	공제조항

deductible coverage	공제면책 조항부 담보방식
deductible expenses	손금
deductible franchise	공제면책 타협
deductible liabilities	공제되어야 할 채무
deductible reserve	손금산입할 수 있는 충당금
deduction	공제
deduction for casualty losses	난손공제
deduction for contributions	기부금공제
deduction for damage insurance	손해보험공제
deduction for dependents	부양공제
deduction for dividends	배당공제
deduction for donation	기부금공제
deduction for employment income	급여소득공제
deduction for family employees	전종자 공제
deduction for foreign taxes	외국세액손금산입
deduction for housing savings	주택저축 공제
deduction for insurance proceeds	보험금 공제
deduction for life insurance premiums	생명보험료 공제
deduction for medical expenses	의료비 공제
deduction for old-age person	노년자 공제
deduction for physically handicapped person	장애자 공제
deduction for public pension	공적연금 공제
deduction for retirement income	퇴직소득 공제
deduction for small enterprise mutual aid premiums	소규모 기업공제 외상공제
deduction for social insurance premiums	회사보험료 공제
deduction for spouse	배우자 공제
deduction for tax reduction	감면세액의 공제
deduction for widow	과부 공제
deduction for working student	근로학생 공제

deduction from property	유형고정자산으로부터의 공제
deduction limit applicable to donation	기부금 손금산입한도액
deduction of entertainment expenses	교제비의 공제
deduction of estimated expenses	개산 경비공제
deduction of interest on borrowed fund	부채이자공제
deduction of liabilities	채무공제
deductions from income	소득공제
deductions from working capital	운전자본의 감소
deductive method	연역법
deed	(날인)증서
deed of arrangement	채무정리증서
deed of conveyance	양도증서
deed of incorporation	주식회사 설립증서
deed of title	권리증서
deed of trust	신탁증서
deed poll	평형날인 계약서
deemed accounting period	가정사업연도
deemed bounty	가정교부금
deemed dividend	가정배당
deemed donations	가정기부금
deemed inherited property	가정상속재산
deemed request for reconsideration	가정심사청구
deemed transfer	가정양도
deemer clause	가정가능규정
deep bid	딥 비드
deep discount	대폭의 할인
deep discount bond	딥 디스카운트 채
deep earth natural gas	심층천연가스
deep in the money	딥 인더 머니
deep pocket	유복한
deep rock doctrine	딥 로크 주의

deep-rooted inflation	만성적 인플레이션
defacto standard	사실상 표준
defalcation	위탁금 착복
defamation	명예훼손
default interest	연체이자
default loss compensation reserve	위약손실보상준비금
default of obligation	채무불이행
default risk	채무불이행 리스크
default risk premium	채무불이행 위험 프리미엄
defaulter	불이행자
defeasance	채무계약해제
defeasance clause	해제조항
defease	해제하다
defeased	기한전
defeasible	무효로 할 수 있다.
defeasible fee	소멸조항당 소유권
defeasible interest	소멸시켜 파는 피보험이익
defeasible title	취소당해 파는 권원
defective	불완전한
defective check	부정수표
defective goods	공손품
defective random variables	불완전 확률변수
defective title	하자있는 권원
defective work	공손품
defendant	피고
defendant bond	피고보험증권
defendemus	하자담보문언
defense	항변
defense association	소송비용 상호보험조합
defense bond	방위채
defense insurance	응소보험
defense of the dollar	달러방위

defense right of attachment	검색의 항변권
defensive allegation	응소주장
defensive investment	방위적 투자
defensive purchase	방위매입
defensive securities	방위적 증권
defensive stock	방위주
deferment	연기
deferment of investment	투자연기
deferment of payment	연납
deferment of taxation	과세보류
deferred	(변동없이) 그대로 있음, 미수
deferred account	이연계정
deferred and accrued accounts	경과계정
deferred annuity	거치연금
deferred assets	이연자산
deferred bond	(변동없이) 그대로 있는 채권
deferred charge	이연비용
deferred charge account	이연비용계정
deferred charge before amortization	상각전의 이연자산
deferred charges	이연비용
deferred compensation	이연보수비용
deferred credit	이연대변항목, 이연수익
deferred debit	이연차변항목
deferred delibery	거치된 납품
deferred depreciation	이연상각
deferred expenditure	이연지출
deferred expenses	이연비용, 선급비용
deferred income	이연수익, 선수수익
deferred income tax liability	이연법인세 채무
deferred income taxes	이연법인세
deferred interest	선수이자
deferred item	이연항목

deferred liabilities	이연부채
deferred life annuity	(변동없이) 그대로 있는 종신연금
deferred payment	후불, 연불
deferred payment basis	연불기준
deferred payment conditional sales	연불조건부 판매, 할부 조건부 판매
deferred payment credit	후일불 신용장
deferred payment note	연기불입채권
deferred payment of income tax	소득세의 연납
deferred payment sales	연불조건부 판매
deferred premium	미수보험료
deferred rebate	보험료의 연려
deferred rebate system	운임연려제
deferred repairs	이연수선비
deferred revenue	선수수익
deferred savings	(변동없이) 그대로 있는 저금
deferred share	후배주, 배당거치주
deferred swap	디퍼드 스왑
deferred tax	이연세금
deficiency	결손
deficiency account	결손계정
deficiency bill	일시차입어음
deficiency guarantee	부족액 보증
deficit	적자
deficit account	결손금계정
deficit disposition statement	결손금처리계산서
deficit finance	적자 재정
deficit financing	적자융자
deficit for the current term	당기결손금
deficit of fiscal balance	재정적자
deficit reconciliation statement	결손금처리계산서
deficit statement	결손금계산서
deficit-covering bond	적자국채

deficit-covering finance 적자금융
defined benefit plan 확정급부형 연금플랜
defined contribution plan 확정지출형 연금플랜
definite bordereau 확정 보더루
definite declaration 확정통지
definite policy 확정보험증권
definite premium 확정보험료
definite settlement of accounts 확정결산
definition 정의
definitive bond 정식본권
definitive policy 확정보험증권
definitive sentence 종국판결
deflation 디플레이션
deflation caused by yen appreciation 엔고 디플레이션
deflation expectation 디플레이션 기대
deflation gap 디플레이션 갭
defl.ation policy 디플레이션 정책
deflationary effect 디플레이션 효과
deflationary gap 디플레이션 갭
deflationary period 디플레이션 기간
deflationary pressure 디플레이션 압력
deflator 디플레이터
deforceor 불법점유자
deforciant 화해양도인
defrayal 지출
defunct company 말소회사
degree 등급
degree of accuracy 정도(정밀도)
degree of concentration 집중도
degree of concentration of control 지배집중도
degree of confidence 신뢰도
degree of consanguinity 친등

degree of dependence	의존도
degree of dependence upon exports	수출의존도
degree of dependence upon imports	수입의존도
degree of financial leverage	재무면의 증익효과도
degree of freedom	자유도
degree of monopoly	자유도
degree of operating leverage	경영면의 증익효과도
degressive cost	체감원가
deindustrialization	산업의 공동화
del credere agent	델 크레더 에이전트
del credere commission	지급수수료
delay	연체
delay claims	지연 클레임
delay of evacuation	명도의 지체
delayed interest	지연이자
delayed payment	연납
delaying settlement	연기결제
delegate	위임하다
delegation	권한부여
delegation of authority	권한위임
deletion of exclusion	면책사항의 삭제
delict	불법행위
delictum	유책성
delinking	이탈
delinquency	체납
delinquency tax	연체세
delinquent charge	지연손해금
delinquent tax	체납세
delinquent taxpayer	체납자
delisting	상장폐지
deliverable issue	수도적격상표
deliverance	발표

delivered	인도완료
delivered at frontier	국경인도
delivered at frontier price	국경인도가격
delivered duty paid	관세지급인도(DDP)
delivered duty unpaid	관세미지급인도(DDU)
delivered ex quay	부두인도(DEQ)
delivered ex ship	착선인도(DES)
delivered money due to merger	합병교부금
delivered price	인도가격
delivered stock due to merger	합병교부주식
delivery	수도(인도)
delivery against payment	지불인도
delivery basis	인도기준
delivery bond	교부국채
delivery date	결제일
delivery expenses	발송비
delivery month	한월
delivery of articles	물품납부
delivery of dividends	배당의 지불
delivery of government bond	교부국채
delivery of long-term contract work	장기공사의 인도
delivery of subsidies	보조금의 교부
delivery of substitute property	환지처분
delivery order	화물인도지시서
delivery price	수도(인도) 가격
delivery settlement	인도결제
delivery system by calendar month	역월도제
delivery versus payment	지불인도
delivery with option	옵션인도
delivery-certified mail	배달증명우편
Delphi method	델파이 법
Delphi process	델파이 과정

delta	델타
delta hedge	델타 헷지
delta neutral hedge	델타 뉴트롤 헷지
delta value	델타 가치
demand	수요, 독촉
demand account	요구불계정
demand analysis	수요분석
demand and supply	수급
demand bill	일람불어음
demand changes	수요변화
demand creation	수요창조
demand curve	수요곡선
demand debt	요구불 채무
demand deficiency	수요부족
demand deposits	통지예금
demand draft	일람불어음, 송금수표
demand elasticity	수요탄력성
demand for capital	자본수요
demand for fund	자금수요
demand for money	화폐수요
demand for tax payment	납부의 독촉
demand forecast	수요예측
demand function	수요함수
demand function for money	화폐수요함수
demand in reconvention	반송
demand index	수요지수
demand line	신용
demand loan	당좌대부
demand note	요구불어음
demand pull inflation	수요견인 인플레이션
demand season	수요기
demand stimulation	수요자극

demand to hold securities	증권보유의 수요
demand-and-supply balance	수급균형
demandant	원고
demesne	점유
demises	지소
demographic factors	인구통계적 요인
demographic statistics	인구통계
demolition	철거
demolition expenses	철거비, 해체비
demonetization of gold	금폐화
demonstration	실증
demonstration effect	데몬스트레이션 효과, 전시효과
demonstrative legacy	지시적 유증
demotion	강등, 격하
demurrage	체선료
demurrer	방소항변
demurrer book	쟁점기록
demurrer to evidence	이의
denial	부인
denization	국적부여
denominated in each currency	각국 통화표시
denominated in foreign currency	외화 표시
denominated in U.S. dollar	달러 표시
denominated in yen	엔화 표시
denomination	권면, 액면금액 평가절하
denomination related stocks	데노미네이션 관련주
denotative meanings	외면적 의미
dental insurance	치과치료보험
depackaging	디패킹
Department of Commerce	상무성
Department of State	국무성
Department of Trade and Industry	무역산업성

Department of Treasury	재무성
department store floater	백화점 포괄보험
department store sales	백화점 매상고
department variance on overhead	부문 간접비 차이
departmental burden	부문 부담비
departmental charge	부문비
departmental cost	부문원가
departmental costing	부문별 원가계산
departmental cost accounting	부문별 원가계산
departmental expenses	부문비
departmental expenses budget	부문비 예산
departmental overhead	부문 간접비
departmental process cost system	공정별 총합원가계산
departmental profit	부문별 이익
departure	일탈
dependence	의존
dependence effect	의존효과
dependency	종속
dependent	부양가족
dependent allowance	가족수당
dependent family member	부양가족
dependent variable	종족변수
depletable	감가 가능한
depleted cost	감가상각후 원가
depletion	감가상각
depletion allowance	감가저당
depletion assets	감가자산
deponent	선서진술자
depose	진술하다
deposit	예탁금
deposit account	예금계정
deposit administration	예탁관리

deposit administration fund	예탁관리기금
deposit and saving	예적금
deposit at financial institutions	금융기관기금
deposit at notice	통지예금
deposit certificate	예금증서
deposit company	기탁회사
deposit diary	예금기입장
deposit due to bank	은행예탁금
deposit for public auction	경매보증금
deposit for tax	납세준비예금
deposit from employees	종업원예탁금
deposit in a fictitious name	가공명의예금
deposit in trust	신탁예금
deposit insurance system	예금보험제도
deposit interest rate	예금금리
deposit law	공탁법
deposit ledger	예금원장
deposit loan	예금대부
deposit minus checks and bills on hand	실세예금
deposit money	예금통화
deposit of nondebtor	비채무자예금
deposit of public money	공금예금
deposit of title-deeds	권리서기탁
deposit office	공탁소
deposit on a net basis	실세예금
deposit payoff	예금정산불 방식
deposit premium	예탁보험료
deposit rate	예금이율
deposit received	보증금
deposit share	예금 쉐어
deposit slip	예금전표

deposit taking business	수신업무
deposit to be relet to a third party	도입예금
deposit transfer	예금대체방식
deposit window	예금창구
deposit with landlord	보증금
deposit with other bank	타행예금
deposit-to-loan ratio	예금대부비율
depositary	예탁인
depositary assets	예탁자산
depositary bank	예탁은행
depositary institution	예금수입금융기관
depositary receipts	예탁증서
Depositary Receipts of Singapore	싱가폴 예탁증서
depositary shares	예탁주식
depositary trust company	주권 대체기관
deposited article	공탁물
deposited money	예탁금
deposited securities	예탁유가증권
deposition	증언기록
depositor	공탁자
depositor protection	예금자 보호
depositor's forgery bond	예금자 위조 보증증권
depository preferred stock	예탁우선주
deposits and savings	예저금
deposits in current account	당좌예금
deposits of securities on contracts	보증차입 유가증권
deposits on contract	예탁보증금
deposits on long-term leases	장기임대계약 위탁금
deposits paid on construction work	공사선급금
deposits paid to trade creditors	구입전 지불대금
deposits received for guarantees	예탁보증금
deposits with public utility corporations	공익사업회사 예탁금

depot theory 디폿 이론
depreciable 감가상각 가능한
depreciable assets 감가상각자산
depreciable cost 감가상각원가
depreciable limit 상각한도액
depreciable property 상각자산
depreciable property for nonbusiness 비영업용 상각자산
depreciable property used in business 영업용 상각자산
depreciated cost 감가상각후 원가
depreciated original cost 감가상각후 원시원가
depreciated value 감가상각후 가액
depreciation 감가상각
depreciation account 상각계정
depreciation accounting 감가상각회계
depreciation adequacy 감가상각타당성
depreciation allowance 감가상각저당
depreciation and amortization 상각
depreciation assets 상각자산
depreciation base 감가상각 기초액
depreciation burden 감가상각 부담
depreciation by depreciation rate 감가율에 의한 상각
depreciation expense 감가상각비
depreciation fund 감가상각기금
depreciation in excess of the limit 초과상각
depreciation insurance 신가보험
depreciation method 감가상각법
depreciation of building 건물감가상각
depreciation of currency 통화가치의 절하
depreciation of deposit by inflation 예금의 실질적 가치하락
depreciation of ship costs 선가상각
depreciation of time value 시간가치의 감가
depreciation on obsolete assets 진부화 자산의 상각

depreciation on property 자산의 감가상각
depreciation period 감가상각년수
depreciation rate 감가상각률
depreciation reserve 감가상각충당금
depreciation reserve ratio 감가상각 충당금 비율
depreciation unit 감가상각단위
depression 불황
depression of business 불경기
depth interview 심층면접
depth of exposure 노출강도
deputy 대리
deputy governor 부총재
depyramidding 디피라미딩 과정
derailment 탈선
derecognition 인식종료
deregulated interest rate 자유금리
deregulated interest rate product 자유금리상품
deregulation 규제완화
deregulation of financial and capital market 금융・자본시장의 규제완화
dereliction 유기
derivative deposit 파생적 예금
derivative income 파생적 취득
derivative pass-through securities market 파생 패스 스루 증권시장
derivative product 파생상품
derivative security 파생증권
derivative suit 파생소송
derivative transaction 파생거래
derived demand 간접수요, 파생수요
derived function 도함수
derived income 파생소득

derogatory-clause	실효약관
descendant	직계비속
descending	하강
descending curve	디센딩 커브
descending tops	디센딩 톱스
descending triangle	디센딩 트라이앵글
descending triangle pattern	하강 트라이앵글
description of business	영업과목
descriptive data	기술 데이터
descriptive financial statement	설명부 재무제표
descriptive function	기술적 기능
descriptive labeling	기술적 표시
descriptive statistics	기술적 통계
desertion	포기
design change	설계변경
design control	설계관리
design fee	의장료
design law	의장법
design qualification	설계인정
design review	설계심사
design right	의장권
design verification	설계검증
designated account	지정계좌
designated city	지정도시
designated currency	지정통화
designated deposit	지정예금
designated exchange	지정거래소
designated net	지명 넷
designated nominee	지정명의인
designated statistics	지정통계
designated stock	지정상표
designation for transfer	납입지정

designation of accounting period 사업연도의 지정
designation of place for tax payment 납세지 지정
designs 의장
desired profit 목표이익
desk top music 데스크 탑 뮤직
desk top publishing 데스크 탑 퍼블리싱
desk top video 데스크 탑 비디오
desperate debt 대손
destination 행선지, 도착지
destocking 비축철거
destruction of environment 환경파괴
destructive disposition 파괴처분
detachable warrant 분리가능 근거
detached employees 파견사원
detailed account form 세목계정식
detailed audit report 장문식 감사보고서
detailed check 정밀조사
detailed enforcement regulations 시행세칙
detailed statement 내역서
deteriorate 침체
deteriorated assets 열화자산
deterioration 악화
determination 부동산권 만료
determination by estimate 추계에 의한 결정
determination coefficient 결정계수
determination of dividend 배당의 결정
determining the necessary adjustments 수정사항의 결정
deterministic model 확정적 모형
detinue 동산반환청구소송
devaluation 절하
develop and import scheme 개발수입

developer	개발업자
development assistance	해외원조
development cost	개발비
development cost of residential site	택지조성비
development expenses	개발비
development fund	개발자금
development gap	개발격차
development of route	루트 개발
deviating company	요율산정기관하 참가회사
deviation	특별요율의 적용, 편차
deviation permit	규격외 허가
device	장치
devise	유증
devisee	수유자
devisor	유증자
diagnostic process	진단과정
diagonal spread	다이아고널 스프레드
dial telephone line	다이얼 회선
Dialog Information Services	다이얼로그 정보 서비스
diamond formation	다이아몬드형 구조
diamond semiconductor	다이아몬드 반도체
DIC color	딕 컬러
dichotomous question	이분질문법
dichotomous variable	이치변수
dichotomy	이분법
dichroic mirror	다이크로익 미러
difference	차액
difference among issues	상품간 격차
difference by renewal	갱신차액
difference from exchange of property	교환차액
difference in yield	이자격차
differences	차액

different account	계좌상위
differential cost	차액원가
differential of return	수익률교차
differential payoff	차별이득
differential rate	차별적 요율
differentiation	차별화
differentiation strategy	차별화 전략
diffusion	보급
diffusion index	경기동향지수
diffusion model	보급모형
diffusion of risks	위험분산
diffusion process	보급과정
diffusion rate	보급률
digest	포함시키다
diggings	채굴료
digital audio workstation	디지털 오디오 워크스테이션
digital compact cassette	디지털 컴팩트 카세트
digital picking	디지털 픽킹
digital picture effect	디지털 영화효과
digital signal processor	디지털 시그널 프로세서
digital video interactive	디지털 비디오 인터액티브
dilapidations	손모료
dilatory	연기적
dilatory plea	천연(지연)적 항변
diligence	주의
dilution	희석화
dimension	차원
dimensionality	차원성
diminishing balance depreciation	정률상각
diminishing balance method	지연원가법
diorama	디오라마
dip	일시급락, 후퇴

direct attack	직접공격
direct broadcasting	위성방송
direct capital	직접자본
direct channel	직판경로
direct claim of claimant	피해자 직접청구
direct costing	직접원가계산
direct deal	직거래
direct dealing	직접환거래
direct department	직접 부문
direct department cost	부문개별비
direct deposit	직접예금
direct evidence	직접증거
direct examination	직접심문
direct exchange arbitrage	직접환재정
direct expense	직접경비
direct financing	직접금융
direct financing lease	직접금융형 리스
direct foreign tax credit	외국세액의 직접공제
direct insurance	원수보험
direct insurer	원수보험자
direct interest	직접적인 이해관계
direct investment	직접투자
direct inward investment	대내 직접투자
direct issue paper	직접판매 페이퍼
direct labor	직접노동
direct labor cost	직접노무비
direct liabilities	확정부채
direct loan	직접금융
direct material cost	직접재료비
direct method	직접법
direct method of depreciation	직접상각
direct national tax	직접국세

direct or equity investment	직접투자
direct overhead	직접경비
direct paper	다이렉트 페이퍼
direct participation program	직접참가 프로그램
direct payment	완전변제
direct placement	직접모집
direct premium	원수보험료
direct premium tax	원수보험료세
direct presentation	직접표시
direct pricing	직접채산법
direct rated deposit administration contract	직접참가예탁관리계약
direct tax	직접세
direct tax credit	세액 직접공제
direct valuation	직접평가
direct writing premium	원수보험료
direct writing system	직불모집제도
direct yield	직접이율
directed verdict	지도평결
direction	지도
directional index	방향성 지수
directional movement	방향성
directive	통달
director	임원
director's retirement allowance	임원퇴직급여금
director's salaries and remuneration	임원보수
Directory of Social Change	사회변화 디렉토리
directors and officers liability insurance	회사임원배상책임보험
directory statute	지시적 법률
directory trust	지시신탁
dirty float	더티 플로트

dirty shares	오염주식
disability	고도장애
disability annuity	고도장애연금
disability benefits	고도장애급부
disability benefits insurance	고도장애급부보험
disability income insurance	직업불능 소득보상보험
disability insurance	소득보상보험
disablement benefit	장애보상
disabling statutes	재산이전금지법
disagreement	부동의
disappointing	실망시키는
disappointing export	수출의 부조
disbar	박탈하다
disbursement	지출금
disbursement book	현금지출장
disbursement cycle	지출환경
disbursement slip	출금전표
disbursements	직무집행비용
disbursements insurance	선비보험
disbursing agent	지불대리인
discarded equipment	폐잔설비
discharge	잘라버림, 면책
discharge in bankruptcy	파산취소
discharge of debts	채무면제
discharge of delinquent tax	연체세 면제
discharge of repayment	상환면제
disclaim report	의견거절보고서
disclaimer	면책문언
disclaimer clause	발주자면책조항
disclaims	의견거절
disclosing function	공시기능
disclosure	개시, 정보공시

disclosure in accounts	재무제표 개시
Disclosure Incorporated	기업정보공개서비스회사
disclosure of terms and conditions of loans	대출조건의 명시
disclosure philosophy	개시의 원칙
disclosure system	정보공시제도
disconfirmation of expectations	기대의 배반효과
discontinuance	철회
discontinuance of business	폐업
discontinued operations	폐지부문
discount	현재가치에 환원하다, 디스카운트
discount bank	할인은행
discount bank debenture	할인금융채
discount bond	할인채
discount broker	디스카운트 브로커, 할인전문 브로커
discount charge	할인료
discount commission	할인수수료
discount earned	수취할인료
discount factor	할인계수
discount function	할인함수
discount government bond	할인국채
discount house	할인상사
discount issue	할인발행
discount ledger	할인어음원장
discount market	할인시장
discount on banker's acceptances	은행인수어음할인
discount on bill	어음할인
discount on bills sold on condition of repurchase	매입조건부 매각어음할인
discount on bond premium	사채발행차금
discount on note	어음할인율
discount policy	할인정책

discount rate	할인율
discount rate cut	공정비율인하
discount rate policy	공정비율조작
discount register	할인어음기입장
discount structure	할인구조
discount window	할인창구
discount yield	할인이율
discounted bill	할인어음
discounted cash flow	할인수익
discounters	수수료 할인업자
discounting	할인
discounting of a bill	어음할인
discounts on bills bought	매입어음 할인표
discounts on bonds payable	사채할인 발행차금
discovery	개시
discovery basis	디스커버리 베이시스
discovery bond	디스커버리 본드
discovery period	발견기간
discredit	신용하지 않다
discrepancy	차이
discrepancy of assortment	상품진열 불일치
discrepant information	어긋난 정보
discrete time	이산시간형
discrete variable	이산변수
descretion	자유재량
discretional act	재량행위
discretionary account	매매일임계정
discretionary account transaction	매매일임계정거래
discretionary expenses	임의비용
discretionary loan	재량대출
discretionary order	일임주문
discretionary trust	일임신탁

discriminating duty	차별관세
discrimination	차별적 취급, 차별대우
discrimination test	직별테스트
discriminative price	차별가격
discriminative tariff	차별세율
diseconomies of scale	규모의 비경제성
disequilibrating capital flows	교활적 자본이동
disequilibrium	불균형
disequilibrium growth	불균형성장
disfranchise	공권을 박탈하다
disguised act	속임수행위
dishonesty loss	불성실손해
dishonor	인수거절
dishonored bill	부도어음
dishonored check	부도수표
disinflation	디스인플레이션
disinterested	이해관계가 없다
disinterested party	이해관계가 없는 사람
disinterested witness	이해관계가 없는 증인
disintermediation	탈중개
disinvestment	부의 투자
disjunctive allegation	택일적 신립
dismissal	각하(받아들이지 않고 물리침)
dismissal notice	해고통지
dismissal without prejudice	각하
disorderly conduct	치안문란행위
disparity	불평형
dispatch	파견하다
dispatch money	조출료
dispensation	적용면제
displaced diffusion model	확산변환 모델
displacement effect	치환효과

display advertising	디스플레이 광고
disposable income	가처분소득
disposable personal income	개인 가처분소득
disposable profit	가처분이익
disposal	처분
disposal of fixed assets	고정자산처분
disposal price	처분가격
disposal value	처분가치
disposing capacity	재산처분능력
disposition	처분
disposition by public sale	공매처분
disposition by suspension of bank credit	은행거래정지
disposition by suspension of business	거래정지처분
disposition for failure to pay	체납처분
disposition of assets	자산의 처분
disposition of cost variance	원가차액조정
disposition of failure to pay income tax in advance	예정납세액 체납처분
disposition of net income	순익처분
dispossession	불법점유
dispute	분쟁
disqualify	자격을 상실하여 가로채다
disregard of tax rule	세법무시
disruption claims	저해
disseise	부동산의 점유를 빼앗다
disseisin	점유침탈
dissent	반대하다
dissenting opinion	반대의견
dissolution	해산
dissolution of corporation	법인의 해산

distance clause 공지조항
distance concept 거리개념
distance learning 원격교육
distrain 유치하다
distrainor 차압인
distress 차압
distress carrier 인수전문보험회사
distress infinite 무기한 차압
distress merchandise 투매품
distress sale 차압물건매각
distress selling 투매
distribution 배분
distribution channel 유통경로
distribution channel selection 유통경로선택
distribution cost 판매비
distribution cost analysis 유통비분석
distribution industry 유통업체
distribution logistics 유통 로지스틱스
distribution mix 유통 믹스
distribution of local allocation tax 지방교부세 교부금
distribution of net profit 이익처분
distribution of overhead cost 간접비 배분
distribution of profits 이익배당
distribution of property 재산배분
distribution of residual property 잔여재산배분
distribution of stocks 주식공포
distribution of surplus 이익금 처분
distribution productivity 물류생산성
distribution rate of overhead cost 간접비 배부율
distribution ratio 구성비율
distribution revolution 유통혁명
distribution structure 유통기구

distribution tax 배부세
district attorney 지방검사
district registry 지방등록소
districts 관할구
disutility 부의 효용
divasa 판정
divergence 괴리
divergence indicator 괴리지표
divergence threshold 괴리한도
divergent marketing 분산형 마케팅
diverse exercise of voting right 의결권의 불통일행사
diversification 분산화, 다각화
diversification of risks 리스크 분산
diversification strategy 다각화 전략
diversified company 다각화 기업
diversified investment 분산투자
diversified management 다각경영
diversified portfolio on stock investment 분산주식투자 포트폴리오
diversified type common stock fund 분산형 보통주 펀드
diversified type investment company 분산형 투자회사
diversified type portfolio 분산형 포트폴리오
diversify 분산하다
diversion charge 양륙지변경료
diversion of water 용수
diversionary pricing 양동적 가격설정
diversity antenna 다이버시티 안테나
divestiture barrier 철퇴장벽
divestment 철수
divided account 분할계좌
dividend 배당
dividend account 배당계정

dividend addition	보험금액증가
dividend credit	배당공제
dividend cut	감배
dividend declared	배당의결
dividend decrease	감배
dividend discount method	배당환원방식
dividend discount model	배당환원 모형
dividend discount rate	배당할인율
dividend distribution	배당
dividend earned	수입배당금
dividend equalization fund	배당평균기금(적립금)
dividend equalization reserve	배당평균적립금
dividend excluded from income	수취배당금익금불산입
dividend exclusion	배당공제
dividend extra	특별배당
dividend flow	배당 플로우
dividend for the second half	후기배당
dividend from capital	자본배당
dividend from stocks owned	주식소유에 걸리는 배당
dividend in arrears	연체배당금
dividend income	배당소득
dividend increase	증배
dividend off	배당락
dividend on	배당부
dividend on common stock	보통주 배당
dividend on dummy stock	명의배당
dividend on interest	이자배당
dividend on preferred stock	우선주배당
dividend on stock	주식배당
dividend option	배당선택
dividend payable	미지급배당금, 배당금
dividend payment	배당지불

dividend payout ratio	배당성향
dividend per share	주낭 배낭금
dividend policy	배당정책
dividend preferred stock	배당우선주식
dividend rate	배당률
dividend receivable	미수배당
dividend received	수취배당금
dividend reinvestment plan	배당재투자계획
dividend repatriation	배당송금
dividend reserve	배당준비적립금
dividend stock	배당주
dividend to policyholders	계약자배당
dividend yield	배당이율
dividend-paid deduction method	배당손금법
dividend-paying stock	유배당 주식
divisible claim	가능채권
divisible contract	가분계약
divisible obligation	가분채권
divisible surplus	배당가능잉여금
division	사업부
division of markets	시장분할
division of succession	분할상속제
division system	사업부제
divisional breakdown	부문별 손익
divisional management	부문경영진
divisional sales	부문별 매출
divisional sales breakdown	부문별 매출내역
divisional structure	부문구조
divisionalized company	사업부제 회사
dockage	도크사용료
docket	심리예정표
doctrine of discovered peril	발견위험의 원칙

doctrine of domicile	주소지법주의
doctrine of immunity	면책주의
doctrine of liability without fault	무과실책임주의
document	서류
document against acceptance	인수양도
document control	문서관리
document of seizure	차압서
document of title	권리증권
documentary bill	화환어음
documentary clean credit	클린화환신용장
documentary credit	화환신용장
documentary draft	화환어음
documentary evidence	증거서류
documentary letter of credit	화환어음신용장
documentary stamp tax	인지세
documentation	문서화
documented discount note	신용장보증부 할인어음
documented procedure	수순서
documents for opening a U.S. dollar account	달러계좌개설서류
Dodge Line	돗지 라인
dog and pony show	신상품설명회
doing business	영업행위
doli capax	책임 능력
doli incapax	책임 무능력
dollar account	달러 계정
dollar average method	달러 평균법
dollar bloc	달러 블록
dollar call option	달러 콜 옵션
dollar convertible bond	달러표시 전환사채
dollar cost averaging	코스트 평균투자법
dollar crisis	달러위기

dollar merchandise budgeting	상품예산편성
dollar overhung	과잉달러
dollar parity	달러평가
dollar preference	달러선호
dollar price	채권가격
dollar put option	달러 풋 옵션
dollar sales volume quota	판매할당
dollar shift	달러 시프트
dollar support	달러 방위
dollar-weighted rate of return	달러가중수익률
dollar-weighted return	달러가중수익
domain	활동영역
domestic corporation	내국법인
domestic currency	자국통화
domestic demand	내수
domestic demand expansion	내수확대
domestic demand oriented industry	내수산업
domestic demand related stock	내수관련주
domestic demand stimulation	내수진흥
domestic equilibrium	국내평형
domestic expenditure	국내지출
domestic goods	국산품
domestic institutional investor	국내 기관투자가
domestic investment	국내투자
domestic loan system	국내 론 방식
domestic operations	국내사업
domestic satellite communication	국내위성통신
domestic source	국내원천
domestic source income	국내원천소득
domestic sourcing	국내조달
domestic value added	국내부가가치
domicile	어음지불장소

domiciled bill	지급지 지정어음
dominant estate	요역지
dominant firm	지배적 기업
dominate the market	시장을 점하다
dominated strategy	우위적 전략
domino effect	도미노 효과
donated property	증여재산
donated stock	증여주
donated surplus	증여잉여금
donation	증여
donation due to death	사인증여
donation tax	증여세
donation to designated organization	지정기부금
donator	기증자
done	계약성립
donee	수증자
donor	증여자
door-to-door sales	방문판매
dormant account	휴지계정
dormant balance	휴지잔고
dormant motive	수면적 동기
dormant partnership	익명조합
dots per inch	도트 퍼 인치
double account interests	춤추는 이자
double accounting	복식회계
double attachment	이중차압
double barreled	이중보험의
double bottom	이심저, 이중바닥
double check	재감
double counting	이중설계
double crossover	더블 크로스오버
double dated	이중만기

double declining balance method	배액 정률법
double decremental table	이중탈퇴잔존표
double dipping	이중이익의
double distribution	이중분배
double endowment insurance	만기배액 지불 양로보험
double exemption bond	이중면제채
double indemnity	보험금의 배액지불
double insurance	중복보험
double jeopardy	이중의 위험
double liability	이중부채
double name paper	복명어음
double option	더블 옵션
double peak	더블피크
double price	이중가격
double sampling	이중추출법
double seizure	이중차압
double settlement	삼영업일 인도
double soucing	더블 소싱
double tariff	이중세율제
double taxation	이중과세
double taxation agreement	이중과세(회피)협정
double truck	좌우양면 광고
double-digit recurring profit growth	두자리수 이익증가기조
double-entry bookkeeping	복식부기
double-up	더블 업
doubtful account	불량채권
doubtful loan	불량대출
Dow Jones Average	다우 존스 평균
Dow Theory	다우 이론
Dow-Jones Commodity Index	다우 존스식 상품지수
download	다운로드
down payment	선지급금

down spread	하방경사
down trend	다운 트렌드
down under bond	호달러 유로채
down-and-out option	다운 앤드 아웃 옵션
downfall	하락
downhill course	하강선
downside elasticity	하방탄력성
downside potential	가치하락여지
downside risk	가치하락불안
downsizing	다운사이징
downstairs merger	역호흡합병
downswing phase	하강국면
downtick	하락국면
downturn	악화, 하강
downward movement	시세가 하락세임
downward phase of the business cycle	하강국면
downward revision	하방수정
downward revision on business results	업적전망의 하방수정
downward rigidity of price	가격의 하방경직성
draft	환어음, 어음
draft at sight	일람불어음
draft authority	소손해의 심정 · 지불권한
draft bill of exchange	환어음
dragon curve	드래곤 곡선
drainage district	배수사업지구
dramatic surge	큰장사
draw	발행하다
draw down	자금인출
drawback	관세환급, 환급
drawback allowance	환급세급부
drawee	수취인
drawer	발행인

drawer of bill	어음발행인
drawing	발행
drawing bank	발행은행
drawing of bill	어음발행
drawing right	인출권
drawn bill	발행어음
drifting management	표류관리
drifting mix	표류 믹스
driver's liability policy	운전자 책임보험
drop	하강
drop below per	액면조각
drop-lock bond	드롭-록 채
dry weight	건중량
dual banking system	이중은행제도
dual capacity	이중자격
dual character of investment	투자의 이중성
dual closed-end fund	듀얼 클로즈드-엔드 펀드
dual convertible bonds	이중 전환사채
dual currency	이중통화
dual currency bond	이중통화표시 채권
dual economy	이중경제
dual exchange market	이중환시장제
dual fund	이중 펀드
dual interest policy	이중금리정책
dual listing	이중상장
dual merchandising	복합 머천다이징
dual option	이중 옵션
dual pricing	이중가격표시
dual purpose	이중목적
dual rate corporation tax system	이중기준세율법인세제도
dual rate system	이중운임제
dual sourcing	이중 조달

dual structure	이중구조
dual tariff	이중관세
dual trading	이중감정거래
dualism	이중성
duality	이중성
dubbing	더빙
due and deferred premiums	미수보험료
due bill	금전채무인증서
due bill check	차용증서수표
due date	만기일
due date coming basis	회수기한 도래기준
due date for payment	지불기한
due date for tax payment	납기한
due date of bills	어음의 만기
due date of filing return	신고기한
due date of payment	불입일(납부일)
due date of property tax payment	고정자산 세납기
due date of the tax return	신고기한
due diligence	정사
Due Diligence (DD)	상당의 주의
due from foreign banks	외국지점예탁
due on sale	매각시 반제
due process of law	적법수속
due to foreign banks	외국지점예탁
dues	요금
dull	기승부
dumbbell portfolio	덤블 포트폴리오
dummy company	가상회사
dummy stock	명의주
dump	손해를 각오하고 처분하다
dumping	덤핑
duopoly	이사독점

duplex system	이중계약주의
duplicate	부의
duplicate policy	두통의 보험증권
duplicate taxation	이중과세
duplicate tenor	등본
duplicity	범죄복합
durable consumer goods	내구소비재
durable years	내용년수
duration	계속기간
duration method	존속법
duration of bond	채권의 존속
duration of guaranty	보증기간
duration of insurance	보험기간
duration of risk	위험기간
duration of risk clause	보험기간 조항
duration-matching	듀레이션 매칭
duration-weighted yield	듀레이션 가중이율
Durbin-Watson ratio	더빈-왓슨 비율
Dutch auction	역경매
dutiable goods	유세품
dutiable value	과세가격
duties	공과
duty contingency	미필수입세
duty exemption	면세
duty free	면세의
duty free imports	면세수입품
duty of care	주의의무
duty of disclosure	고지의무
duty of support	부양의무
duty to sue and labor	손해방지의무
duty-paid	납세제
dwelling house	주거

dwelling risk	주택물건
dyad customer	한조(한 팀)의 고객
dyadic communication	쌍방적 커뮤니케이션
dynamic analysis	동태분석
dynamic data exchange	다이나믹 데이터 교환
dynamic hedge scheme	다이나믹 방지계획
dynamic input-output analysis	동학적 산업연관분석
dynamic marketing	동태적 마케팅
dynamic model	동태 모델
dynamic multiplier	동학 승수
dynamic programming	다이나믹 프로그래밍
Dynamic Random Access Memory	D-램
dynamic range	동태적 범위
dynamic risk	동태적 위험
dynamic strategies	다이나믹 전략
dysfunction	역기능

≪ E ≫

each way	수수료 각자 지불
early adopters	초기채용자
early exercise	기한전 행사
early majority	초기 추종자
early ownership mortgage loan	조기상환제 모기지론
early redemption option	조기상환옵션
early redemption	조기상환
early repayment	조기상환제
early warning system	조기경보시스템
earmarked tax	목적세
earmuff problem	일방적 설명상황
earn out	잉여이익을 분배하다
earn-out right	잉여수익수취권
earned basis	실수기준
earned income	가득소득
earned income allowance	근로소득공제
earned income tax	근로소득세
earned premium	경과보험료
earned reinsurance premium	경과재보험
earned surplus	이익잉여금
earned surplus reserve	이익준비금
earned surplus statement	이익잉여금 계산금
earnest money	계약증거금
earnest money received	받은 계약금
earning assets	수익자산
earning per share	주당 순이익
earning power	수익력

earning rate	수익률
earning statement	손익계산서
earning tax	수익세
earnings	수익
earnings before extraordinary items	특별손익전 이익
earnings before interest and taxes	금리세전이익
earnings before tax	세전이익
earnings coverage ratios	부담이익배율
earnings forecast	수익전망
earnings from continuing operations	계속사업부문 이익
earnings growth	수익증가
earnings growth rate	수익성장률
earnings growth ratio per share	한 주당 수익성장률
earnings model	수익모형
earnings on equity	자기자본이익률
earnings per share of common stock	보통주식 주당 순이익
earnings performance	업적
earnings retained in business	이익잉여금
earnings retention rate	수익유보율
earnings stability	수익안정성
earnings yield	이율
earthquake clause	지진위험담보 특별약관
earthquake insurance	지진보험
ease	반락
ease off	시세가 떨어지다
easement	지역권
easement appurtenant	부속지역권
easement holder	지역권자
easement in gross	대인적 지역권
easier	약세
easing	완화
East African Community	동아프리카 공동체

East Asia Economic Caucus 동아시아 경제협의체
eastern account 분할인수
easy 저리(低利)
easy payment 분할지급
eat inde sine die 즉시 석방
eavesdropping 도청
EC Code of Conduct for Companies with Subsidiaries, Branches or Representation in South Africa 남아프리카 자회사, 지점, 대리점을 가진 기업에 관한 EU 행동규범
EC directives EC 이사회의령 · EC 지침서
EC joint floating system EU 공동시스템
echo effect 반향효과
echo principle 반향원리
eclectic theory 절충이론
eco-system 메아리 시스템
ecological factor 생태적 요인
ecology 생태학
econometric analysis 계량분석
econometric model 계량경제모형
economic activity 경제활동
economic activity stimulating measure 경제활동 자극책
economic aid 경제원조
Economic and Development Review Committee 경제개발검토위원회
Economic and Social Commission for Asia and the Pacific 아시아 · 태평양 경제사회위원회
Economic and Social Council of the United Nations 국제연맹 경제사회이사회
economic assistance 경제협력
economic barometer 경제지표
economic benefits 경제적 편익

economic big power 경제대국
economic bloc 경제권
economic blockade 경제봉쇄
economic center 경제센터
economic channeling 경제적 집중
economic channeling of liability 경제적 책임집중
economic circles 경제계
Economic Commission for Africa 국제연맹 아프리카 경제이사회
Economic Commission for Asia and the Far East 아시아 극동 경제위원회
Economic Commission for Europe 유럽경제위원회
economic conditions 경제상황
economic consequence 경제적 귀결(귀착)
economic continuity 경제적 연속성
economic cooperation 경제협력
economic cooperation amongst developing countries (ECDC) 개발도상국 경제협력
economic cost 경제원가
economic crisis 경제공황
economic cycle 경기순환
Economic Deliberation Council 경제심의회
economic double taxation 경제적 이중과세
economic dualism 이중경제구조
economic earnings 경제적 이익
economic earnings beta 경제적 이익 베타가치
economic emulation stage 경제적 모방단계
economic engineering 경제성 공학
economic ethics 경제윤리
economic figure 경제지표
economic fluctuation 경기변동
economic forecast 경제예측
economic friction 경제마찰

economic function	경제기능
economic goods	경제재
economic growth	경제성장
economic growth model	경제성장모형
economic growth policy	경제성장정책
economic growth rate	경제성장률
economic index	경제지수
economic indicator	경제지표
economic integration	경제통합
economic interaction	경제적 상호작용
economic interpretation	경제적 관찰방법
economic life	경제생활
economic malaise	경제질병
economic man	경제인
economic maturity	경제적 성숙
economic model	경제모델
economic nationalism	경제민족주의
economic number effect	경제지표효과
economic obsolescence	경제적 진부화
economic order	경제질서
economic organization	경제조직
economic outlook	경제예측
economic philosophy	경제철학
economic plan	경제계획
economic policy	경제정책
economic prediction	경제예측
economic priority	경제우선
economic progress	경제진보
economic prospect	경제전망
economic quality	경제적 품질
economic recession	경제후퇴
economic sovereignty	경제주권

economic recovery	경기회복
economic reform	경제개혁
economic regime	경제체제
economic risk	경제적 리스크
economic sanction	경제 제재
economic science	경제과학
economic security	경제안전보장
economic slump	경기후퇴
economic statistics	경제통계
economic structural adjustment	경제구조조정
Economic Summit	선진국수뇌회의
economic system	경제체재
economic table	경제표
economic tide	경제흐름
economic union	경제동맹
economic unit	경제주체
economic utility	경제효용
economic viability	경제활력
economic war	경제전쟁
economic waste	경제적 낭비
economic white paper	경제백서
economies of scale	규모의 경제성
economies of scope	범위의 경제성
edge	우위
Edge Act Corporation (EAC)	에지법회사
edge up	소폭상승
edict	포고
education expense	교육비
educational endowment	학자보험
educational level	교육수준
edutainment	에듀테인먼트
effect	효과

effect of correction	수정 등의 효과
effect of discount	할인효과
effect of exchange rate changes	환 환산수정
effect of limiting risk	위험한정효과
effect of message	메시지 효과
effect of rescission	계약해제의 효과
effective address	실효어드레스
effective aggregate tax rate	총합효과세율
effective buying income	실질구매소득
effective competition	유효경쟁
effective date	발효일
effective demand	유효수요
effective exchange rate	실효환 상장
effective interest rate	실효금리
effective life	유효기간
effective price	유효가격
effective rate	실세율
effective rate of discount	실제할인율
effective rate of protection	실효보호율
effective tariff	실효세율
effective volatility	유효변동폭
effective yield	실효이율
effectiveness of diversified investment	분산투자의 효과성
effects	인적재산
effects principles	효과원칙
efficiency audit	능률감사
efficiency management	능률관리
efficiency of measuring	측정효율
efficiency variance	능률차이
efficient cause	주원인
efficient frontier	효율프론티어

efficient market	효율적 시장
efficient market hypothesis	효율적 시장가설
efficient portfolio	효과적 포트폴리오
efficient statistics	유효통계
efficient-scale facility	유효적 규모
effluxion of time	기간만료
either way market	쌍방향시장
ejectment	부동산 회복소송
"ejusdem generis" doctrine	동종제한의 원칙
elapsed years	경과년수
elastic demand	탄력적 수요
elastic limit system	탄력제한제도
elastic tariff	탄력관세
elasticities approach	탄력성 어프로치
elasticity index	탄력성 지수
elasticity of advertising	광고탄력성
elasticity of demand	수요의 탄력성
elasticity of distribution	유통탄력성
elasticity of expectations	기대탄력성
elasticity of price	가격탄력성
elasticity of substitution	대체탄력성
elasticity of supply	공급의 탄력성
elasticity of the balance of payments	국제수지탄력성
elasticity optimism	탄력성 낙관주의
elasticity pessimism	탄력성 비관주의
elbow	급각도의 이론곡선
elder title	선권원
electric access member	시스템으로 입회장에 접속가능한 회원
electric power expense	전력비
electricity and gas tax	전기가스세
electricity tax	전기세
electronic banking	전자금융

electronic book	전자책
electronic data gathering analysis and retrieval system	EDGAR 시스템
electronic filing system	전자충전 시스템
electronic fund transfer	전신송금
electronic library	전자도서관
electronic mail	전자메일
electronic media	전자적 매체
electronic money	전자화폐
electronic order transfer system	전자주문전달 시스템
electronic publishing	전자출판
electronic video recording	녹화
elegit	토지강제관리영장
element of control	관리요소
element of cost	원가요소
elementary cost accounting	요소별 원가계산
elementary unit	기본단위
eligibility	적격성
eligibility requirements	적격조건
eligible	유자격
eligible bill	할인적격수형
eligible investment	적격투자
eligible security	적격담보
elimination of cause	원인의 제거
elimination of intercompany indebtedness	사회상호간 대차소거
elimination of intercompany ownership	사회상호간 지분소거
elimination of intercompany profits	사회상호간 이익소거
elisors	배심선정관
elite card	엘리트 카드
Elliot Wave Theory	엘리엇 웨이브 이론

emancipation	해방
embargo	수출입의 금지
embezzlement	횡령
emergency amortization	긴급상환
emergency duty	긴급관세
emergency funds	임시비
emergency legislation	긴급입법
emergency loan	긴급융자
emergency tariff	긴급관세
emergency warning system	긴급경보방송
emergent financial disposition	재정상 긴급처분
emerging industry	첨단업계
emerging market	신흥시장
emerging technology	선단(첨단) 기술
Emigration and Immigration Central Order	출입국관리령
eminent domain	재산권 수용권
empirical analysis	실증적 분석
empirical approach	경험적 접근
empirical demand curve	경제적 수요곡선
empirical study	실증연구
employed assets	운용자산
employee	종업원
employee bonus	상여
employee compensation	미지급급여
employee deposits	종업원예금
employee discount	종업원 할인
employee evaluation	인사고과
employee pension benefit plan	종업원 연금제도
Employee Retirement Income Security Act	ERISA 법
employee stock ownership plan	종업원 지주제도

employee stock purchase plan 종업원 주식구입 계획
employee welfare benefit plan 종업원 복지급부제도
employees bonus and allowance 종업원 급여수당
employees' deposits 종업원 예금
employees' own conveniences 종업원 자기사정
employees' pension fund 종업원 연금기금 적립금
employees' relief fund 종업원 상부상조 기금
employees' retirement allowance 고용자 퇴직급여금
employees' retirement benefit 퇴직급여 충당금
employees union 종업원 조합
employer 사용자(고용자)
employer's liability insurance 사용자 배상책임보험
employment 고용
employment adjustment 고용조정
employment at will 기간을 정하지 않은 고용계약
employment cost 인건비
employment income 급여소득
employment income deduction 급여소득공제
employment income earner 급여소득자
employment income exemption 급여소득공제
employment index 고용지수
employment market 고용시장
employment multiplier 고용승수
employment producers 고용수속
employment service 직업안정소
emptor 매(買)수인
empty nest 부부세대
empty set 공집합
emulation 대항
emulative product 경쟁제품
enabling statute 수권법(권한부여)
enacting clause 제정조항

enactment	판정
encashment	환가
enclave economy	도약경제
enclosure	포위
encode	부합화하다
encroachment	권리의 불법확장
encumbrance	토지부담
encumbrancer	토지부담의 권리자
end of the fiscal year	연도말
end of the month	월말
end of the year	기말
end run	앤드 런
end-user	최종수요자
ending balance	기말잔고
endogenous change	내생변화
endogenous variable	내생변수
endorsed	배서되다
endorsed bill	배서어음
endorsed bills exchanged between two parties	돌림어음
endorsed bond	배서채권
endorsed note	배서어음
endorsee	피배서인
endorsement	배서
endorsement fee	배서수수료
endorsement for option contract	옵션계약의 배서
endorsement for transfer	배서양도
endorsement in blank	백지식 배서
endorsement to order	지시식 배서
endorsement to transfer	양도배서
endorsers	배서인
endowment insurance	양로보험

endowments	기금
energy risk	에너지 위험
energy sector stock	에너지 주
enforce	강제하다
enforceable	강행가능
enforced vacation	강제퇴거
enforcement	시행
enforcement law	시행법
enforcement order	시행령
enforcement regulations	시행규칙
enforcement right	실행권
enfranchisement	특허부여
engagement	약정, 책무
English auction	영국식 경매
English form of balance sheet	영국식 대차대조표
engrossing	정식으로 다 씀
enhance	가격을 높이다, 제고하다
Enhanced Graphics Adapter	EGA
enjoin	임명하다
enlarged European Communities	확대 EC
enquiry	대면, 대조
enrollment	등기
ensuing account	차기계정
ensure	확실시하다
enter	기입하다
enter in an account-book	기장하다
enter wrongly	오기하다
entering short	어음금 징수기입
enterprise	사업
enterprise accounting	기업회계
enterprise approach	기업체에서의 위험평가
enterprise cost	기업원가

enterprise economy 기업경제
enterprise mortgage 기업담보권
enterprise tax 사업세
enterprise tax on corporation 법인사업세
entertainment and social expenses 교제비
entertainment expenses not qualifying for deduction 손금불산입 교제비
entire agreement clause 완전합의조항
entire day 만기일 계산
entire tenancy 단독보유
entitle 권리를 주다
entitlement 권리의 확보
entity 실체
entity accounting 실체회계
entity theory 법인이론
entrance fee 입회금
entrance to Korea 입국
entrant 신규참가업자
entrepreneurial orientation 기업가 의향
entrepreneurship 기업가정신
entropy 일률화, 무변화
entrust of collection 징수의 촉탁(위촉)
entrusted business commission 위탁업무 수수료
entry 기입
entry age cost method 가입연령방식
entry market 참가시장
entry of judgment 판결등록
entry under homestead laws 등기
entry value 입장가액
enumerate 열거하다
envelope curve 포락곡선
environment assessment 환경평가

environmental change	환경변화
environmental diagnosis	환경진단
environmental impairment liability insurance	환경오염 배상책임보험
environmental pollution	환경공해
environmental refugee	환경난민
environmental risk	환경위험
environmental variable	환경변수
epistemological criteria	인식론적 기준
equal annual premium	평균연불보험료
equal credit opportunity	신용향유의 기회균등
equal employment opportunities	고용기회 균등
equal footing	대등한 지위
equal installment repayment method	원본균등지급방식
equal interval sampling method	등간격 추출법
equal monthly payments with interest	원리균등반제
equal payment method	원리균등지급방식
equal protection of the laws	법의 평등한 보호
equal weighted portfolio	등금액 포트폴리오
equal-annual-payment method	연간 정액지급법
equal-weighted average	균등가중평균
equaled time of payment	평균지급기일, 균등지급기일
equalization fund	평형준비금
equalization of tax burden	세부담의 평준화
equalization of tax collection	징세의 공평
equalization of tax payment	납세의 공평
equalization reserve	평준화 준비금
equalizer	이퀄라이저
equalizing divergences	격차균등화
equalizing dividends	배당평균준비금
equally divided	균분
equation of exchange	교환방정식

equilibrium basis	적정베이스
equilibrium economies	균형경제학
equilibrium price	균형가격
equilibrium rate of exchange	균형환상장
equilibrium rate of interest	균형이자율
equipment	설비
equipment control	설비관리
equipment fund	설비자금
equipment trust	설비신탁
equipment trust certificate	동산신탁증서
equitable mortgage	형평법상의 모기지
equities insurance	변액보험
equity	주식, 형평법, 지분
equity at book value	자기자본부가
equity at market value	자기자본시가
equity capital	자기자본
equity capital ratio to fixed assets	고정자산자기자본율
equity capital ratio to long-term capital	장기부채자기자본율
equity capital ratio to long-term liabilities	장기부채 자기자본율
equity capital ratio to total debt	총부채 자기자본율
equity finance	에쿼티 파이낸스
equity financing	주식에 의한 자금조달
equity fund	출자금
equity growth rate	자기자본 성장률
equity in earnings	소득에 대한 지분
equity instruments	출자계약
equity investment	주식투자
equity investor	주식투자가
equity kicker	조건부 주식구입권
equity margin	주식마진

equity method	지분법
equity note	주식채
equity participant	출자자
equity participation	자본참가
equity products	주식상품
equity purchase accounting	지분법
equity purchases by institutions	기관구매
equity ratio	자기자본비율
equity receiver	회사갱생수속관리인
equity risk premium	주식위험프리미엄
equity securities	소유주식
equity securities dealer	주식딜러
equity share	지분주식
equity stake	주식의 지분
equity warrant	주식의 보증
equity weighting	주식조입률
equivalence	등가
equivalence relationship	등가관계
equivalent bond yield	채권상응이율
equivalent coefficient	등가계수
equivalent exchange	등가교환
equivalent level annual dividend	균등평준연차배상
era of high interest rate	고금리시대
erasure	소거
erection insurance	조직보험
erection work	설치공사
ergonomics	인간공학
erode	감소하다
erosion in purchasing power	구매력의 침식
erosion rate	실질적인 가치하락 비율
erratic	불안정한
erratic fluctuation	(물가 등의) 오르내림이 심함

error of prediction	예측오차
errors and omissions excepted	오차탈루 제외
errors in calculation	틀린 계산
errors in posting	전기상의 잘못
errors or omissions	오차 누락
escalator clause	에스컬레이터 조항
escapable cost	회피가능원가
cscape clause	면책조항
escape sequence	에스케이프 시퀀스
escheat	부동산 복귀
escrow	조건부 날인증서
escrow account	에스크로우 계정
escrow agreement	에스크로우 계약
escrow and trust agreement	에스크로우 신탁계약
escrow credit	에스크로우 신용장
escrow receipt depository	에스크로우 보관증서예탁
essential condition	필수조건
established surplus	확정잉여금
establishing a lease	차지권의 설정
establishment	사업소, 설정
establishment expenses	사업소비
establishment of corporation	법인의 설립
establishment of hypothec	저당권의 설정
establishment of leasehold	차지권의 설정
establishment of tax liability	납세의무의 확정
establishment of the right of pledge	질권설정
estate	재산
estate accounting	유산회계
estate agent	부동산업자
estate contract	부동산 계약
estate duty	상속세
estate income	유산소득

estate planning 자산계획
estate upon condition 조건부 부동산권
estate upon limitation 제한부 부동산권
estimate 추계
estimate of budget requests 추정요구
estimate of sales 예상매출액
estimated appropriation 경비예산
estimated balance sheet 견적대차대조표
estimated cost 추정원가
estimated cost accounting 견적원가계산
estimated cost accounting system 견적원가계산제도
estimated cost of construction work 견적공사원가
estimated expenses 견적비용
estimated future income taxes 조연(이월)소득과세채무
estimated holding period return 예상보유기간수익률
estimated liabilities 추정부채
estimated mining period 채굴예정년수
estimated profit 견적이익
estimated profit and loss statement 견적손익계산서
estimated tax 견적세액
estimated tax prepayment 예정납세
estimated uncollectable amount 징수불능예상액
estimated usable period 사용가능기간
estimated useful life 견적내용년수
estimated value 평가가격
estimating-cost system 견적원가제도
estimation 견적
estoppel 금반언(禁反言)
estoppel principle 반언금지원칙
estovers 필요물
ethernet 이더넷
Ethical Investment Research and Information Services (EIRIS) 윤리적 투자조사

ethics	윤리
ethnocentric	자기민족중심의
ethnocentrism	자기민족중심주의
etiquette of the profession	변호사 도덕
eurobank	유로뱅크
Eurobond	유로채, 유로본드
eurocredit	유로크레디트
Eurobond market	유로채 시장
Euroclear	유로크리어
Eurocommercial paper	유로콤마샬페이퍼
Eurocredit market	유로대부시장
Eurocurrency	유로통화
Eurocurrency banking market	유로금융시장
Eurocurrency market	유로커렌시시장
Eurocurrency syndicated loan market	유로신디케이트론시장
Eurodollar	유로달러
Eurodollar deposit	유로달러예금
Eurodollar depositary interest futures	유로달러예금금리선물
Eurodollar futures option	유로달러선물옵션
Eurodollar market	유로자금시장
Eurodollar time deposit	유로달러정기예금
Euroline	유로라인
Euromark futures	유로마르크선물
Euromarket	유로시장
Euromoney	유로머니
Euronote	중기유로채
European Atomic Energy Community	유럽원자력 공동체
European Central Bank	유럽중앙은행
European Coal and Steel Community	유럽석탄철강공동체
European Communities	유럽공동체
European Community (EU)	구주공동체
European Composite Unit (EURCO)	유럽복수통화단위

European Currency Market 유럽통화시장
European Currency Unit (ECU) 유럽통화단위
European Depositary Receipts 유럽예탁증권
European Economic Area 유럽경제지역
European Economic Community 유럽경제공동체
European Economic Interest Grouping 유럽경제이익단체
European Free Trade Association 유럽자유무역연합
European Investment Bank 유럽투자은행
European Investment Trust 유럽투자신탁기관
European Monetary Agreement 유럽통화협정
European Monetary Cooperation Fund 유럽통화협정기금
European Monetary Fund 유럽통화기금
European Monetary System (EMS) 유럽통화제도
European Monetary Unit (EMU) 유럽통화단위
European option 유럽옵션
European Options Exchange 유럽옵션거래소
European Parliament 유럽의회
European Patent Convention (EPC) 유럽특허조약
European Payment Union 유럽지불동맹
European term 유럽방식
European Trade Union Confederation (ETUC) 유럽노동조합연맹
European type 유럽타입
European Union (EU) 유럽연합
European unit of account 유럽계산단위
Europound bond 유로파운드채
Eurosyndicate loan 유로신디케이트 론
Eurotrack 유로트랙
Euroyen 유로엔
Euroyen bond for resident 거주자 유로엔채
Euroyen bond issue 유로엔채발행

Euroyen interest rate	유로엔 금리
Euroyen market	유로엔 시장
evacuation	명도(내어줌)
evade	도피하다
evaluation method of investment	투자 평가 방법
evaluation of importance	중요성의 평가
evaluation of market mechanism	시장기구의 평가
evaluation of solvency	지급능력평가
evasion of tax	탈세
even basis swap	이븐 베이시스 스왑
even keel	금융정책에 변화가 없는 상태
even lot	단위주
evening up	전매·환매를 끝마쳐 거래관계를 완료함
event insured against	보험사고
event of default	기한의 이익·손실 사유
event subsequent to balance sheet date	대차대조표일후의 발생상황
events	사상
evergreen credit	계속적 신용공여
eviction	쫓아냄
eviction order	퇴거명령
evidence	증거
evidenced document	증빙서류
evidences of indebtedness	채무증서
evidentiary facts	증거사실
evil practice	악용
ex contractu	계약상의
ex dock(or ex pier, or ex quay)	부두인도
executive judgment	경영자진단
ex facto	행위에 기초하다
ex factory (or ex warehouse, ex plantation)	공장인도

ex gratia 은혜로서
ex gratia payment 임의급부
ex post facto 사후
ex proprio motu 임의로
ex works 공장도
ex-allotment 신주락
ex-ante analysis 사전분석
ex-coupon 이찰락
ex-dividend 배당락
ex-dividend date 배당낙일
ex-interest 이자하락
ex-interest bond 이자하락 채권
ex-interest period 이자하락 기간
ex-new 권리하락
ex-post alpha value 사후알파가치
ex-post analysis 사후분석
ex-post assessment 사후적인 평가
ex-post characteristic line 사후특성선
ex-post investment 사후적 투자
ex-post saving 사후적 저축
ex-rights of capital increase 증자권리락
exaction 불법보수청구죄
exaggerated advertisement 과대광고
exaggerated final return 과대신고
examination 심사
examination and decision 심사재결
examination by reference 조사
examination in chief 주심문
examination of entrance qualification 입회심사
examination of loan application 대출심사
examination of witness 증인심문
examined copy 대조한 등본

examiner	국세조사관
except for	제외하고는
excepted perils	면책위험
excepted risks	제외위험
exception	제외사항
exception clause	면책조항
exception principle	예외의 원칙
exception rate	예외운임
exception to amortization of deferred charge	이연자산의 상각의 특례
exception to depreciation deduction	감가상각의 특례
exceptional rates of tax	예외적 세율
exceptional tax treatment	세무상의 특례
exceptions clause	면책약관
excess	소손해면책
excess and deficiency	과부족
excess capacity	과잉설비, 과잉능력
excess cash	여유자금
excess demand	초과수요
excess disbursement	초과지불
excess franchise	공제면책보합
excess general average	초과공공해손
excess income	초과소득
excess insurance	초과보험
excess legal liability policy	법정책임액초과보상책임보험
excess liabilities clause	초과책임담보약관
excess line	초과액
excess line reinsurance	초과액재보험
excess liquidity	과잉유동성
excess margin	초과증거금
excess margin account	잉여마진계정
excess mortality	초과사망률

excess of loss	초과손해액
excess of loss ratio reinsurance	초과손해율재보험
excess of loss reinsurance	초과손해재보험
excess of loss treaty reinsurance	초과손해액특약재보험
excess payment	초과지불
excess profitability	초과이윤
excess profits	초과이윤
excess profits credit	초과이윤공제
excess profits tax	초과이득
excess receipt over contract price	가증금
excess reinsurance	초과액 재보험
excess reserves	과잉준비
excess supply	초과공급
excessive competition	과당경쟁
excessive consumption	과잉소비
excessive depreciation deduction	초과상각
excessive lending	과잉융자
excessive liquidity	과잉유동성
excessive profit	부당이득
excessive savings	과잉저축
excessive seizure	초과차압
excessive stocks	과잉주
excessive trading	과잉거래
exchange	환, 거래소
exchange acquisition	거래소 수매
exchange arbitrage	환재정거래
exchange arbitrage transaction	환재정거래
exchange at night	야간교환
exchange bank	환은행
exchange bill payable	병환
exchange bought	매입환
exchange broker	환 브로커

exchange business	환업무
exchange cambiste	외환딜러
exchange check for money	금전의 인환권
exchange clause	환문구
exchange clearing	환결제청산
exchange clearing agreement	환청산협력
exchange contract	환예약
exchange contract with option	선택권부 환예약
exchange control	환관리
exchange cover	커버거래
exchange cover rate	출합상장
exchange dealer	환딜러
exchange dealing	환거래
exchange distribution	환소분배
exchange dumping	환덤핑
exchange efficiency	교환효율
exchange equalization account	환평형 계정
exchange equalization fund	환평형 기금
exchange equalization operation	환평형 조작
exchange fluctuation	환 변동
exchange for collection	징수환
exchange for means of foreign payment	대외지불을 위한 환
exchange for physical program	프로그램 매매
exchange forward contract	선물환예약
exchange fund cover	자금조정거래
exchange fund cover or operation	환자금조정거래
exchange funds operation	자금조작
exchange gain	환차익
exchange gain from the won appreciation	원고차익
exchange gain or loss	환환산차손익
exchange intervention	환개입

exchange law	거래소법
exchange link	외국환의 링크
exchange loss	환차손
exchange loss and profit	환차손익
exchange manipulation	환조작
exchange marrige profit	환결합이익
exchange marry	환결합
exchange member	거래소 회원
exchange of equivalents	등가교환
exchange of notes	교환공문
exchange of property	자산의 교환
exchange offer	주식취득신청
exchange operation	환조작
exchange parity	환평가
exchange position	환포지션
exchange premium	환프리미엄
exchange profit	환차익
exchange quotation	대고객 환율
exchange rate	환율
exchange rate at break-even point	손익분기환율
exchange rate in favor of won	원고
exchange rate in foreign currency	외화표시환율
exchange reservation	환예약
exchange risk	환리스크
exchange risk cover	환위험조정조작
exchange risk insurance	환변동보험
exchange settlement	환결제
exchange sold	매도환
exchange speculation	환투기
exchange stabilization fund	환안정기금
exchange tax	거래소특별세
exchange ticket	주문집행확인서

exchange traded option	상장옵션
exchange transactions	거래소 거래
exchequer bills	영국대장증시
excise duty	물품세
exclude	제외하다, 면책하다
excluded perils	면책위험
exclusion	제외, 면책
exclusion from expenses	손실금불산입
exclusion from expenses of corporation tax	법인세액 손실금불산입
exclusion from gross revenue	이익금부산입
exclusion from taxation	비과세
exclusion of loss	손실제외
exclusion of profit accrued from valuation profit	평가익의 익금산입
exclusion of refund from gross revenue	환부금의 환금부산입
exclusion of subrogation	대위구상권행사의 폐지
exclusive agent	독점대리점
exclusive channel	패쇄채널
exclusive dealing	경쟁품취급금지계약
exclusive distributorship	독점판매권
exclusive jurisdiction	전속관할권
exclusive privilege/right	독점권
exclusive selling agency	독점 판매대리점
exclusive use	전용
exclusive-occupation house	전용주택
exculpatory clause	면책조항
excusable	면책당하다
excuse	변명, 면책사유
executed	기이행
executed contract of sale	완성매매계약

execution	체결, 이력
execution creditor	집행채권자
execution of order	주문의 집행
execution organ	실행기관
executive committee	집행위원회
executive compensation option	임원보장을 위한 옵션
executive measure	집행처분
executive officer	집행관
executive pension	경영관리자 연금
executive power	집행권
executive proceedings	집행수속
executive salaries	임원보수
executor	집행자
executor be son tort	무권임원집행자
executory contract	미확정의 계약
executory interest	장래권
exemplification	인증등본
exempt corporation	비과세법인
exempt from taxation	면세
exempt gift	비과세 증여
exempt income	비과세 소득
exempt private company	면제사기업
exempt property	비과세 재산
exempt securities	면제증권
exempt stock exchange	등록면제거래소
exempted securities	적용제외증권
exemption	비과세
exemption agreement	면책약정
exemption and deduction from income	소득공제
exemption clause	면책조항
exemption for aged person	노년자 공제

exemption for dependents	부양공제
exemption for handicapped person	장애자 공제
exemption for spouse	배우자 공제
exemption for working student	근로학생 공제
exemption from payment of premium	보험료 지불 면제
exemption from return of subsidy	보조금 반환 면제
exemption from taxation	면세
exemption method	외국소득면제방식
exemption point	면세점
exemptions	차압금지채권
exercise	권리행사
exercise date	만기일
exercise limit	권리행사가 인정되어 있는 거래량
exercise of security right	담보권의 행사
exercise price	행사가격
exhaustion	소모
exhibit	증거서류, 첨부서류
EX-IM Bank	수출입은행
existential proposition	존재명제
existing assets	기존자산
existing debt	기존채무
existing preferential duties	기존특혜
exit barrier	철퇴장벽
exit bond	졸업채
exit value	퇴장가액
exogenous change	외생변화
exogenous demand	외생수요
exogenous variables	외생변수
exoneration	면책
exorbitant profit	법외의 이익
exotic derivatives	외래(이그조틱) 파생상품

expand mode	확장모드
expansion of a new market	신시장의 개척
expansion of currency	통화팽창
expansionary budget	적극예산
expansive economy	확대경제
expatriate	해외파견 사원
expatriate investment	회외파견자투자
expatriate management	해외주재관리자
expatriate management quota	해외주재관리자 할당
expectancy theory	기대이론
expectancy-value model	예측치 모형
expectant heir	기대상속인
expectation	기대
expectation function	기대함수
expectation gap	기대의 갭
expectation hypothesis	기대가설
expectation of life	평균여명
expectation theory	기대이론
expected demand	기대수요
expected earnings	기대수익
expected earnings growth rate	기대이익성장률
expected holding-period rate of return	기대보유기간 이익률
expected income	예정수입
expected life	견적내용연수
expected mortality rate	예정사망률
expected profit	기대이윤
expected return ratio of loan trust	대부신탁예상배당률
expected satisfaction	기대만족
expected total rate of return	기대총수익률
expected value	기대치
expected value theory	기대치이론

expected volatility	예상변동률
expected yield-to-maturity	기대만기이율
expendable fund	지출가능자금
expenditure	지출
expenditure curtailment	지출삭감
expenditure for public bond	공채비
expenditure for public works	공공사업비
expenditure on capital accounts	자본계정지출
expenditure on unemployment benefit	실업보험지출
expenditure rate	지출률
expenditure tax	지출세
expenditure unaccounted for	용도가 불명확한 지출
expense analysis book	경비내역원장
expense arising from outside-manufacture	외주가공비
expense distribution	비용배부
expense item	비목
expense ledger	경비원장
expenses	비용
expenses budget	경비예산
expenses for education and culture	교양비
expenses incurred for having the user remove	이전료
expenses incurred for maintaining household	가사관련비
expenses incurred for opening of business	개업비
expenses incurred for the transfer	양도비용
expenses of bringing up children	양육비
expenses of entering port	입항비용
expenses paid-in advance	미경과비용

expenses quota	경비할당
experience assumptions	기초율
experience curve	경험곡선
experience effects	경험효과
experience grading and rating schedule	경험분류요율표
experience rating	경험요율
experience table	경험표
experimental and research expense	시험연구비
experimental and research expense tax credit	시험연구비 세액공제
experimental effect	실험효과
experimental manufacturing cost	시험제작비
expiration	만료
expiration date	만기일
expiration date of the credit card	카드유효기간
expiration file	만기파일
expiration notice	만기통지
expiration of obligation	채무소멸
expired card	기한만료카드
expired cost	소멸가치
expiry	기한만료
explanatory note	주석(註釋)
explanatory variable	설명변수
explicit cost	명시적 비용
exploitation	착취
exploitation of new resources	신자원의 개발
exponential distribution	지수분포
exponential function	지수함수
exponential growth	지수적 성장
export account	외환당좌계좌
Export Administration Act	수출관리법

export advance 수출전 대출
export advance loan 수출전 대출금융
export advanced account 수출전 대출계정
export and import price index 수출입 물가지수
export and import statistics 외국무역통계
export bill 수출어음
export bounty 수출장려금
export broker 수출중개인
export commission representative 수출대리점
export credit 수출신용
export credit insurance 수출신용보험
Export Credits Guarantee Department (ECGD) 수출신용보증국
export declaration 수출신고
export dependence 수출의존도
export distributor 수출업자
export drive 수출드라이브
export duties 수출세
export exemption 수출면세
export factoring 수출채권매취
export financing 수출금융
export function 수출함수
Export Import Bank (Ex-Im Bank) 수출입은행
export in terms of won 원건 수출
export insurance 수출보험
export license 수출승인증
export management company 수출업자
export merchant 수출상인
export on consignment 위탁판매수출
export platform 수출플랫폼
export price index 수출물가지수
export processing 수출가공지구

export profitability	수출의 수익성
export supplier credit	수출업자 신용
export tax	수출세
export to an overseas territory	이출
export-import bank	수출입은행
export-import control	수출입규제
exporting trade terms	수출거래조건
exposure	(상품의) 진열
exposure draft	공개초안
exposure frequency	노출빈도
exposure hazard	연소위험
exposure to risk	위험부담
express	명시
express condition	명시조건
express contract	명시계약
express trust	명시신탁
express warranty	명시담보
expropriation	공용징수, 수용
expropriation loss	접수에 의한 손실
expropriation of land	토지수용
extel card	익스텔카드
Extel Information Service	익스텔 정보서비스
extended benefit	확장급부
extended bill	연기어음
extended coupon	조연이찰
extended cover clause	연장담보약관
extended coverage	확장담보특약
extended definition television	클리어비젼 방송
extended fund facility	확대신용공여제도
extended insurance	확장보험
extended slot	확장슬롯
extended term insurance	연장정기보험

extendible debt security	연장가능 채권
sxtendible maturity	연장가능 만기
extensible swap	신장성 있는 교환
extension	확장, 신장
extension effect	기간효과
extension of due date	납기한의 연장
extension of loan	융자의 실행
extension of the maturity	상환연장
extension of time claims	연장 클레임
extension of time for completion	공기의 연장
extension of time to file	지출의 연장
extensive channel	해방형 채널
extent	재산평가
extent of audit	감사의 범위
extenuation	경감
external audit	외부감사
external auditor	외부감사인
external bond	외국사채
external consistency	외부정합성
external economy	외부경제
external equilibrium	대외균형
external evidence	외적증거
external failure	외부실패
external financing	외부금융
external forces	외압
external hazard	외부위험
external information	외부정보
external intangible loss	외부의 무형손실
external liabilities	외부부채
external loan	외채
external purchasing power of money	화폐의 대외가치
external quality assurance	외부품질보증

external quality audit 외부품질감사
external reserves 외화준비
external resources 외부자원
external restraint 외부적 제약
external transaction 외부거래
external transactions account 해외거래계정
external user 사외이용자
externality 외부성
extinction 소멸
extinctive prescription 소멸시효
extinguishment of hypothec 저당권의 소멸
extinguishment of property 자산의 멸실
extinguishment of the right of rescission 해제권의 소멸
extortion 강요
extra 별도계정
extra charges 부대비용
extra cost 추가비용
extra depreciation 할증상각
extra dividend 특별배당
extra expenditure 임시비
extra expense insurance 임시비용 보험
extra item 이상항목
extra premium 할증보험료
extra risk 추가위험
extra wage 할증임금
extra work claims 여분공사 클레임
extra-judicial 재판의
extradition 본국송환
extramural 구역의
extraneous evidence 외부증거
extraneous risk 부가위험

extraordinary average	비상해손
extraordinary depreciation	특별상각
extraordinary expenses	임시비
extraordinary gain	특별이익
extraordinary income	임시소득
extraordinary items	특별손익항목
extraordinary loss	특별손실
extraordinary profit and loss	특별손익
extraordinary repairs	임시수선비
extraordinary resolution	임시결의
extrapolation	외삽법
extraterritoriality	치외법권
exterritoriality on tax laws	면세특권
extrinsic evidence	외부증거
eye camera	아이카메라
eye catcher	아이캐처

≪ f ≫

fabless	제조부문을 기다리지 않는 개발 메이커
fabricating cost	제조원가
face	액면
face amount	액면금액
face amount certificate company	액면증서회사
face of instrument	증서의 방면
face of note	할부가격
face value	액면가
facilitating functions	보조기능
facilitation	조성사례금
facilities	설비
facility of payment clause	지불경의조항
Fackler's formula	Fackler's 공식
fact	사실
fact book	사실책
fact finding	사실조사
fact in issue	주요사실
factor	재료, 요인
factor analysis	요인분석
factor comparison system	주요비교법
factor endowment	유소부존
factor loadings matrix	인자부하행렬
factor mobility	요소이동성
factor return	요소수익률
factor's lien	채권매수업자 유치권
factorage	중개상 수수료

factoring	채권매수, 팩토링, 수금대리
factors of production	생산요소
factory	공장
factory account	공장계정
factory accounting	공장회계
factory bookkeeping	공장부기
factory burden	제조간접비
factory cost	제조원가
factory cost report	제조원가보고서
factory expenses	제조경비
factory expenses variance	경비차액
factory furniture	공장집기(비품)
factory furnitures and fixtures	공장집기와 비품
factory ledger	제조원장
factory ledger account	제조원장계정
factory mutual insurance	공장주 상호보험
factory overhead	제조간접비
factory risk	공장물건
factory supplies	공장용 소모품
facultative reinsurance	임의재보험
facultative reinsurance agreement	임의재보험 협정
faculty theory of taxation	지급능력 과세설
fad	일시적인 유행
fade in	페이드 인
fade out	페이드 아웃
fade-out formula	페이드 아웃 방식
fade-out polices	페이드 아웃 정책
fade-out policy	외자비율 삭감정책
faded	하방수정되다
fail	상환이 실행되지 않다
fail position	불이행 포지션
failing company	파탄기업

failing of record	기록부 제출
failure	불이행
failure mode	고장 모드
failure of consideration	약인의 감실
faint action	무력소송
fair	적정
fair and equitable	공정과 형평
fair average quality	평균 품질
fair leasehold value	차지권의 가격
fair market value	공정시장가격, 시가
fair market value system	공정시장 가격제도
fair price	공정가격
fair trade bureau	공정거래국
Fair Trade Commission	공정거래위원회
Fair Trading Act	공정거래법
fair value	공정가치
fair value accounting	시가주의 회계
fair wage	적정임금
fairness	공평성
fairness doctrine	공정원칙
fairy and impartially	공평하게
fall	하강, 기한도래
fall due	지급기일이 되다
fall of building clause	건물붕괴약관
fall of gold standard	금본위제도 붕괴
falling in price	가격하락
falling in stock price	주가하락
falling interest rate	금리하락
falling market	하락기조의 시장
false declaration	허위신고
false demonstration	오류표시
false imprisonment	불법감금

false missing	위장분실
false personation	성명사기
false pretense	착취죄
false representation	허위표시
false return	허위신고
false statement	허위진술
false trade description	허위상품표시
false verdict	부당평결
family allowance	가족수당
family bookkeeping	가계부
family brand	통일 브랜드
family characteristics	가족특성
family corporation	동족회사
family estate	가독(그 집의 상속인)
family fund	가족펀드
family income and expenditure survey	가계조사
family insurance	가족보험
family medical expense policy	가정의료비보험
family member	친족
family partnership	동족조합
family personal accident policy	가족상해보험
family saving survey	저축동향조사
family taxation of assets income	자산소득의 세대합산 과세
family-register	호적
Fan theory	팬 이론
fancy stocks	터무니없는 물량
Fannie Mae	연방저당공사
fare	운임
farm accounting	농업회계
farming of taxes	조세징수청부
fashion forecasting	유행예측

fault	과실
fault tree analysis	고장 트리 분석
favorable	순조
favorable balance of overall	종합수지흑자
favorable balance of payments	국제수지 흑자
favorable balance of trade	무역수지흑자
favorable balance on current account	경상수지 흑자
favorable cash flows	바람직한 현금흐름
favorable factor	호재
favorable leverage effect	바른 증익효과
favorable news	호재
fear	경계
feasance	행위
feasibility study	타당성 조사
Fed watcher	페드 윷처
Federal Advisory Committee	연방자문위원회
Federal Bankruptcy Act	연방파산법
federal chartering	연방허가제(회사설립)
Federal Communication Commission	연방통신위원회
federal credit agency	연방금융기관
federal decentralization	연방적 분권제
Federal Deposit Insurance Corporation	연방예금보험공사
federal fund market	연방자금시장
federal fund rate	연방기금금리
Federal Home Loan Bank	연방주택대부은행
Federal Home Loan Bank Board	연방주택대부은행이사회
Federal Home Loan Bank System	연방주택대부은행제도
Federal Home Loan Mortgage Corporation	연방주택금융저당금고
federal income tax	연방소득세
Federal Intermediate Credit Bank	연방중개신용은행

Federal Land Bank	연방토지은행
Federal National Mortgage Association	연방저당금고
Federal Open Market Commission	연방공개시장위원회
Federal Reserve Bank	연방준비은행
Federal Reserve Bank of New York	뉴욕연방준비은행
Federal Reserve Board	연방준비제도이사회
Federal Reserve District	연방준비지구
Federal Trade Commission (FTC)	연방거래위원회
fee	보수
fee business	수수료 장사
fee for legal advice	법률상담료
fee simple	단순부동산권
feed	원재료를 보내다
feed consumption	원료소비량
feedback	피드백
feedback information	피드백 정보
feeder factory	피더 공장
fees and permits	면허료
fellow	정회원
fellowship grant	연구보조금, 장학금
fence sitter	투자판단을 하지 못하는 사람
feneration	고리대
fertility rate	출생률
feverish market	열광시장
fiber to the home	가정내 광케이블
Fibonacci sequence	피보나치수열
fiction	법률상의 의제
fictional theory of corporation	법인의제설
fictitious	가공
fictitious assets	의제자산
fictitious capital	의제자본

fictitious demand	가수요
fictitious dividend	가배당
fictitious name deposit	가공명의 예금
fictitious price	터무니없는 가격
fictitious profit	가공이익
fictitious sales slip	가공매출전표
fidelity contract	신용계약
fidelity guarantee insurance	신원신용보험
fidelity insurance	신용보험
fidelity rebate system	운임할려제, (수령액 중 몇 할을) 되돌려 줌
fiduciary	수탁자
fiduciary accounting	신탁회계
fiduciary bond	수탁자보증증권
fiduciary contract	신탁계약
fiduciary duty	신임의무
fiduciary estate	신탁재산
fiduciary issue	(무담보)신용발행
fiduciary power	신탁권한
fiduciary relation	신뢰관계
fiduciary responsibility	수탁자 책임
field	매초상수
field audit	실지감사, 현장감사
field examinations	임점검사
field inspection	현장감사
field inspector	현장감사인
field test	실지검사
field underwriter	외무직원
field-work audit standards	감사실시준비
file allocation table	화일할당표
file and use	제출후 사용제
file and use system	보험요율 제출제
file compression	파일압축

file income tax return	소득액을 신고하다
filiation	인지
filing final return of merger	합병확정신고
filing of claims	채권제출
filing return	신고
fill-ins	보충발주
fill-or-kill order	즉시 또는 취소주문
filling up of a deficit	적자보전
film sensitivity	필름감도
final	종국
final audit	기말감사
final balance	기말잔액
final balance method	최종잔고방식
final beneficiary	최종수익자
final call	최종분담금
final claim	본 클레임
final declaration	확정신고
final demand	최종수요
final depreciable limit	상각가능한도액
final maturity	만기
final notice of claim	확정손해배상청구통지서
final pay type	최종급료형
final payment	확정신고에 의한 납부
final products	최종생산물
final prospectus	최종목론견서
final rate of return	최종수익률
final return	확정신고
final return in the case of loss	손실신청서
final return of liquidation	청산확정신고서
final return of merger	합병확정신고서
final settlement of accounts	확정된 결산
final tax return	확정신고

final transaction date	최종거래일
final value	종가
final verification	최종검증
final yield	최종이율
final yield on investment	최종투자이율
finally settled financial statements	최종적으로 확정된 재무제표
finance	금융
finance bill	정부단기증권
finance capital	금융자본
finance charge	금융비용
finance company	금융회사
finance for deficit	적자금융
finance for prepaid installment sales	선지급식 할부판매금융
finance law	재정법
finance lease	대부(貸付)
Finance Ministry note	대장성 증권
Finance Ministry Ordinance	대장성 법령
finance paper	금융어음
finance receivable	대출채권
finance receivables as collateral	채권담보
financial accounting	재무회계
financial accounting standards for business enterprise	기업회계기준
financial accounts	재무제표
financial activities	금융활동
financial advisor	재무고문
financial affairs	재무
financial agreement	금융협정
financial aid	금융원조
financial analysis	재무분석
Financial Analysts Federation	전미 애널리스트협회 연합회
financial appraisal	재무평가

financial assets	금융자산
financial assets and liabilities account	금융자산부채잔고표
financial audit	재무감사
financial balance	재무밸런스
financial books	회계장부
financial buyer	재무적인 구매자
financial capital	금융자본
financial center	금융중심지
financial charges	금융비용
financial claim	금융채권
financial clique	재벌
financial collapse	금융붕괴
financial condition	재무상태
financial considerations	재무상 배려
financial cost	재무비용
financial crisis	금융위기
financial damages	금전상의 손실
financial decision	금융면에서의 결단
financial deficit	자금부족
financial democracy	재정민주주의
financial difficulty	금융난
financial documents	계산서류
financial engineering	재테크
financial environment	금융환경
financial expenses	금융비용
financial facilities	금융서비스
financial forward contract	금융선도계약
financial futures	금융선물
financial futures contract	금융선물계약
financial futures instrument	금융선물상품
financial futures market	금융선물시장
financial futures option	금융선물옵션

financial futures transaction	금융선물거래
financial guarantee	자력보증
Financial Guaranty Insurance Company	금융보증보험회사
financial highlights	경리개요, 재무요점
financial innovation	금융혁신
financial institution	금융기관
financial institution for agriculture forestry and fisheries	농림어업금융기관
financial institution for foreign exchange	외국환금융기관
financial institutions for long-term credit	장기신용금융기관
financial institutions for small business	중소기업금융기관
financial instrument	금융상품
financial intermediaries or brokers	금융중개기관
financial item	금융항목
financial lease	금융리스
financial leverage	재무 레버리지
financial leverage effect	재무상의 증익효과
financial leverage ratio	재무 레버리지 비율
financial liability	금융부채
financial liberalization	금융의 자유화
financial liberalization policy	금융자유화정책
financial management	재무관리
financial market	금융시장
financial market analysis	금융시장 분석
financial model	금융모델
Financial News index option	파이낸셜 뉴스 지수 옵션
financial obligation	금융채무
financial operations	금융업

financial option contract	금융옵션계약
financial option market	금융옵션시장
financial panic	금융공황
financial planner	파이낸셜 플래너, 재무 설계사
financial planning	재무계획
financial policy	금융정책
financial position	재정상태
financial position statement	대차대조표
financial product	금융상품
financial profit	금융수익
financial ratio	재무비율
financial regulation	금융규제
financial report	유가증권보고서
financial reporting accounting	재무보고회계
financial reports	재무보고서
financial research center	금융연구소
financial resources	재원
financial retrenchment	경비절감
financial revenue	재무수익
financial review	재무개황
financial revolution	금융혁명
financial sector stocks	금융주
financial service	금융서비스
financial slack	금융상 불경기
financial standing	재정상태
financial statement analysis	제무제표 분석
financial statement audit	재무제표 감사
financial statements	재무제표
financial statistics	금융통계
financial status	재정상태
financial strain and stress	금융긴박
financial strength	재무의 건전성

financial structure	재무구조
financial surplus or deficit	자금과부족
financial system	금융제도
Financial Times International Business Yearbook	FT 국제비즈니스 연감
financial transaction	금융거래
financial year	회계년도
financier	출자자
financing	자금조달
financing activities	재무활동
financing adjustment law	자금조정법
financing bill	금융어음
financing burden	금융부담
financing charge	금융비용
financing corporation	금융회사
financing for carrying unsold inventories	체화금융
financing for deficit-covering	적자융자
financing for sales by installment payment	월부판매금융
financing for stocks	주식자금조달
financing from broker's own capital	자기융자
financing method	자금조달수단
financing regulation	융자준칙
financing regulation law	자금조정법
financing vehicle	금융수단
finder	화인더
finding of fact	사실인정
fine	벌금
finished artwork	완전원고
finished goods	완제품
finished goods on hand	수지제품

finished product verification	완제품의 검증
finished products	완제품
finished products account	제품계정
finished products inventory	제품재고
finished products on hand	제품재고
finite difference	유한 차분
finiteness	유한성
Fire and Marine Insurance Rating Association of Japan	손해보험요율 산정회
fire and other casualty insurance premiums deduction	손해보험공제
fire clause	화재보험약관
fire company	화재보험회사
fire damage	화재손해
fire insurance	화재보험
fire insurance on dwelling houses	주택화재보험
fire insurance policy	화재보험증권
fire insurance premium	화재보험료
fire insurance proceeds	화재보험금
fire loss	화재손실
fire loss suspense account	화재손실 미결산계정
fire mutual insurance	화재상호보험
fire peril	화재보험
fire wall	방화벽
fire-insurance for mortgagee interest	채권보전화재보험
firm	사업법인, 견고
firm banking	펌 뱅킹
firm bid	확정매도 호가
firm commitment	확약, 완액인수
firm commitment underwriting	매취인수
firm contract	확정계약
firm offer	확정가격제시

firm order	확정주문
firm price	확정가격
firm quote	확약가격
firm tone of the U.S. dollar	달러고 기조
firmer	강보합
firmer tone	강함
first blush	한번 봄
first board	전장참석
first call date	제1회 도중상환일
first check	초감
first cost	준비원가
first coupon date	제1회 이자 지불일
first demand bond	즉시지급보증서(공사채)
first exchange	제1권
first generation on-line system	제1차 온라인
first instance	제1심
first mortgage	제1저당
first mortgage bond	제1순위 저당권부사채
first preferred stock	제1 우선주식
first purchaser	최초의 취득자
first risk policy	제1차 손해보험
first section market	1부 상장
first session of the month	발회
first surplus treaty	제1차 초과액특약
First World	제1 세계
first year commission	초연도 수수료
first-dollar coverage	무공제 담보방식
first-in first-out method	선입선출법
first-loss insurance	실손전보
fisc	국고
fiscal agent	재무대리인
fiscal agent agreement	재무대리인 계약

fiscal agent for treasury fund	국고재무대리인
fiscal and monetary policy	재정금융정책
fiscal balance	재정수지
fiscal drug	재정팽창의 제동
fiscal expenditure	재정지출
fiscal illusion	재정착상
fiscal inflation	재정인플레이션
fiscal inflexibility	재정경직화
fiscal investment	재정투자
fiscal investment and loan	재정투·융자
fiscal outlook	재정전망
fiscal period	회계기간
fiscal policy	재정정책
fiscal privileges of diplomat	외교관과세특권
fiscal reform	재정개각
fiscal target	재정목표
fiscal tightness	재정의 핍박
fiscal year	회계연도
Fisher effect	피셔 효과
fishing right	어업권
fit	적성치
fitness for purpose	목적적합성
fitness for use	사양적합성
fittings	부속품
five-and-dime store	균일가격점
fixed amount method	정액법
fixed amount minimum payment	최저한 지불의무액
fixed amount taxation	정액과세
fixed annuity	정액연금
fixed arrangement	고정성배열법
fixed asset ledger	고정자산대장
fixed asset ratio	고장자산비율

fixed asset tax	고정자산세
fixed asset to net worth ratio	고정비율
fixed asset turnover ratio	고정자산회전율
fixed assets	고정자산
fixed capital	고정자본
fixed capital investment	고정자본투자
fixed charge	특정담보
fixed collateral	근저당
fixed costs and expenses	고정비
fixed coupon bond	확정이표채
fixed date	확정일부
fixed date delivery	확정일 인도
fixed debt	고정차입금
fixed deposit	정기예금
fixed difference	확정차액
fixed dollar security	고정달러증권
fixed exchange rate	고정환 상장(시세)
fixed exchange rate system	고정환 상장제도
fixed expenses	고정비용
fixed fee	정률보수
fixed gain	확정이익
fixed general tariff	고정세율
fixed income	고정수입
fixed income market	고정채시장, 채권시장
fixed income security	고정금리증권
fixed installment	정액상각
fixed installment method	정액법
fixed interest	확정이자
fixed interest security	확정이자증권
fixed interest-bearing bond	확정이자채권
fixed investment	확정자본투자
fixed liabilities	고정부채

fixed liquidity reserve requirements	고정적 유동비율제도
fixed loan	고정대부금
fixed mortgage	근저당권
fixed obligations	확정채무
fixed overhead	고정비
fixed parity system	고정평가제
fixed penalty bond	정액채무보증증권
fixed percentage depreciation	정률감가상각법
fixed percentage method	감가정률법
fixed percentage on unexpired cost method	정률법
fixed position	정위치
fixed price	일정가격
fixed property	부동산
fixed rate	고정금리
fixed ratio	고정비율
fixed return securities	고정이자증권
fixed salary	고정급
fixed tax rate	고정세율
fixed term policies	확정일불(日佛)보험
fixed trust	확정신탁
fixed unit trust	고정단위형 투자신탁
fixed wages	고정급
fixed-asset schedule	고정자산명세표
fixed-charge coverage ratio	고정비율부담배율
fixed-date delivery	확정일양도
fixed-first type	고정성배열
fixed-income benchmark	확정이자증권
fixed-income target	확정이자타겟
fixed-percentage on declining balance method	정률법
fixed-rate assets	고정금리자산

fixed-rate bond	확정이자채
fixed-rate liability	고정금리부채
fixed-rate payer	고정금리지불인
fixing	고정
fixtures	비품
flag of convenience vessel	편의치적선
flat	곡물 최종인도가격
flat commission	균일수수료
flat curve	균일곡선
flat deductible	정액공제면책비율
flat exchange contract	플랫 환예약
flat growth	같은 증가율(성장률)
flat market	불경기의 시장
flat rate	균일요율
flat yield	직리
flattening of the yield curve	이자곡선의 평판화
flea market	벼룩시장
fleet insured	플릿 계약자
fleet retention	보험그룹에 의한 보유액
flexible mortgage	근저당
flexible tariff	신축세율
flexible time	근무시간연동제
flexible-premium variable life insurance	변액 유니버셜 보험
flier	전단, 등귀(오름)
flight to quality	질로의 도피
flip-flop FRN	플립플랍 변동금리부채권
flip-over clause	flip-over조항
float	미결제수표
floater	부동증권, 포괄보험증권
floating assets	유동자산
floating basis	유동베이시스

floating capital	유동자본
floating charge	유동담보
floating debt	유동채무
floating exchange rate	변동환율
floating exchange rate system	변동환율제
floating interest rate	변동이율
floating interest rate account with ceiling	변동상한금리 계정
floating liability	유동부채
floating lien	유동 담보권
floating policy	포괄예정보험계약
floating prime rate	신장연동형 우대금리
floating property	포괄재산
floating rate	변동금리
floating rate bond	변동이자채권
floating rate certificate of deposit	변동금리 CD
floating rate index	변동금리표시
floating rate lending	변동금리대출
floating rate mortgage	변동이자 모기지
floating rate note	변동이자채
floating rate of interest	가변금리
floating rate payer	변동금리지불인
floating stock	부동주
floating supply	부동적 공급, 재고량
floating system	변동제
floor	하한, 입회장
floor broker	(증권거래소의) 거래회원, 거래중개인, 거래원
floor issue	입회장 명칭
floor of the court	당사자석
floor price	저가치
floor rate	하한금리

floor representative	증권업자의 대리인으로서 거래를 담당하는 직원
floor trader	(증권거래소의) 거래회원
flooring debt	일시차입금
flotation	증권발행
flotation of external loan	외채모집
flotation of government bond	공채발행
flotation of loan	기채(국가나 회사 등이 채권을 발행함)
flow chart	흐름도, 생산공정도
flow of fund account	자금순환계정
flow of funds analysis	자금순환분석
flower bond	플라워본드
fluctuate	변동하다
fluctuating and extraordinary income	변동소득에 따른 임시소득
fluctuating income	변동소득
fluctuation clause	변동조항
fluctuation limit	시세폭 제한
fluctuation of stock prices	주가시세변동
fluctuations in prices of raw materials	원료가격변동
flyer	전단
focus strategy	집중전략
'follow the leader' theory	'선도자 추종' 이론
follow-up advertisement	사후광고
follow-up selling	추격팔기
following underwriter	보험업자
font	폰트
food bill	식량증권
foot	합계하다
foot note	각주
footing	계산대조
footloose investment	입지조건무제약투자

for sale 매물
forbearance 자제
force majeure 불가항력
force majeure clasuse 불가항력 조항
force of discount 할인력
force of interest 이자력
forced auction 강제경매
forced conversion 강제적 전환
forced liquidation 강제청산
forced sale 강제매각
forced saving 강제저축
forced transfer 강제이전
forced-sale value 강제처분가치
forcible disposition 강제처분
forcible entry 불법침입
forcible execution 강제집행
forcible provisions 강행규정
forcing methods 촉성법
forecast by the econometric model 계량모형예측
forecast for market tendency 시장관
forecast of sales 예상매출고
forecasting model 예측모형
foreclosure 저당권 집행
foreclosure under power of sale 사법처분에 의하지 않은 매각
foregift 권리금
forehand rent 전불지대
foreign 외국, 예외적
foreign access zone 수입촉진지역
foreign adjustment clause 외국청산약관
foreign affiliate 외국계 기업
foreign agents accounts 외국대리점 계정
foreign attachment 채권차압

foreign banks in Korea	재한외국계은행
foreign bill	외국어음
foreign bill of exchange	외국환 어음
foreign bond	외국채권
foreign branch-our account	외국지점 발송계정
foreign branch-their account	외국지점 피발송계정
foreign buying	외국인매수
foreign capital	외자
foreign capital consumer finance company	외자계 소비자 금융
foreign capital inducement	외자 흡수
foreign capital intake	외자유치
foreign competition	국제경쟁
foreign content	외국 컨텐츠
foreign corporation	외국법인
foreign corporation company	외국기업
foreign corporation tax	외국법인세
foreign corporation tax credit	외국법인세액공제
foreign corrupt practices	외국 부패 방지
foreign currency	외자
foreign currency account	외화계정
foreign currency bill receivable	외화징수외국환
foreign currency bond	외화채권
foreign currency deposit	외화예금
foreign currency deposit account	외화예금계정
foreign currency deposit with exchange bank	외화예탁
foreign currency futures	외국통화선물
foreign currency futures contracts	외국통화 선물계약
foreign currency holdings	외화보유고
foreign currency inflow	외화유입
foreign currency reserves	외화준비

foreign currency securities	외화증권
foreign currency series securities	외화표시증권
foreign currency statements	외화표시재무제표
foreign currency transactions	외화거래
foreign currency translation gain or loss	환차손
foreign currency-denominated bond	외화건채
foreign debt	외채
Foreign Direct Investment (FDI)	해외직접투자
foreign environment	국제환경
foreign exchange	외국환
foreign exchange accounts	외국환 계정
foreign exchange allocation system	외화할당제
foreign exchange bank	외국환 은행
foreign exchange bill	외국환어음
foreign exchange bills bought	매입외국환
foreign exchange broker	외국환 브로커
foreign exchange budget	외화예산
foreign exchange centralization system	외화집중제도
foreign exchange contract	외국환 예약
foreign exchange control	외국환 관리
foreign exchange conversion rate	외국환 환산율
foreign exchange conversion table	외국환 환산표
foreign exchange fund bill	외국환 자금증권
foreign exchange futures	외국환 선물
foreign exchange gains and losses	외국환 차손익
foreign exchange law	외환법
foreign exchange market	외국환시장
foreign exchange market intervention	외국환시장개입
foreign exchange market operation	외국환시장조작
foreign exchange operation	외국환 조작
foreign exchange position	외국환 포지션

foreign exchange position sheet	외국환 포지션 시트
foreign exchange rate	환율
foreign exchange reserves	외화준비금
foreign exchange risk	외환위험
foreign exchange speculation	외국환투기
foreign freight forwarder	국제운송화물취급업자
foreign geographic areas	해외지역별
foreign income tax	외국소득세
foreign insurer	외국보험세
foreign investment	해외투자
Foreign Investment Law	외자법
foreign investment regulations	외국자본 규정
foreign investors	외국인투자자
foreign involvement	외국 인볼브먼트
foreign judgment	외국의 판결
foreign juridical person	외국법인
foreign jurisdiction	영토외 관할권
foreign loan	외채
foreign means of payment	대외지불수단
foreign money bill	외화어음
foreign operations	해외사업
foreign portfolio investment	대외무역기구
foreign reserves	외화준비금
foreign securities company	외국증권회사
foreign service allowance	국외근무수당
foreign source income	국외원천소득
foreign stock holding ratio	외국인이 가지고 있는 주식비율
foreign stocks unlisted	외국비상장주
foreign subsidiary	해외 자회사
foreign subsidiary corporation	외국자회사
foreign tax	외국세액
foreign tax credit	외국세액 공제

foreign tax credit method 외국세액 공제방법
foreign tax credit system 외국세액 공제제도
foreign tax deductible as expenses 손금산입외국세
foreign tax exemption method 외국세액면제방식
foreign trade finance 무역금융
foreign trade multiplier 외국무역승수
Foreign Trade Organization (FTO) 대외무역기구
foreign trade policy 무역정책
foreign trade statistics 무역통계
foreign transactions 외국거래
foreigner's investment 외인투자
foreigin-related transaction 국외 관련자 거래
controlled transaction
forejudge 권리를 박탈하다
foreman 감독자
forensic medicine 법의학
forerunner stock 선구주
forest fire insurance 삼림화재보험
forestall 통행방해
forestalling the market 시장방해
forestry income 산림소득
forestry income deduction 산림소득의 특별공제
forex club 전문외환딜러의 사적인 사교기구
forfeit 위약금
forfeited share 실권주
forfeiting 수출대금인수
forfeiture 몰수
forfeiture clause 실권약관
forfeiture of bail 보석금손실
forged bill 위조어음
forged cards 변조카드
forged check 위조수표

forged note	위조지폐
forged securities policy	유가증권 위조보험
forged stock	위조 주권
forgery	문서위조
forgery insurance	위조보험
forgery insuring clause	위조담보약관
forgiveness of debt	채무면제
forgiveness of repayment	상환면제
form	형식
form of action	소송방식
form of bid	입찰서
form required by law	법률을 요구하는 형식
formal	형식적
formal capitalization of reserves	자본을 끌어들임
formal contract	정식계약
formal lawsuits	본소
formal model	형식모형
formal plan annuity	공식연금
formalities of incorporation	설립수속
formation expenses	창업비
formation of concept	개념형성
former adjudication	전의 판결
forms control	장표관리
forms of enterprise	기업형태
formula	공식
formula additions	정식이월액
formula fund	포뮬러주식펀드
formula investing	포뮬러플랜에 따른 증권투자
formula plan	포뮬러플랜
forswear	강하게 부인하다
forthwith	신속히
fortuitous event	우연적인 사고

fortuity	우연성
forum	재판소
forum origins	출생지 재판소
forward agreement	선도거래
forward bargain	선지급환 매매
forward commitment	대부예약
forward contract	선도계약
forward delivery	선지급
forward deposit	선지급예금
forward difference	전방차분
forward discount	선물 디스카운트
forward discount of U.S. dollar	달러의 선물 디스카운트
forward exchange	선지급환
forward exchange contract	선물환 예약
forward exchange market hedge	선물환시장 헷지
forward exchange rate	선물환율
forward exchange transaction	선물환 거래
forward integration	선방통합
forward interest rate	장래이자율
forward linkages	전방관련
forward margin	선물마진
forward market	선물시장
forward operation	선물환 거래
forward position	선물환 지대
forward premium	선물환 프리미엄
forward price	선지급가격
forward quotation	선물환율
forward rate	선지급금리
forward rate agreement	금리선불거래
forward rate spread	선물환 스프레드
forward settlement	선지급결제
forward swap	선도스왑

forward transaction	선불거래
forward vertical integration	전방수직통합
forward-backward integration	전·후방통합
forward-forward rate	선-선 rate
forwarder	운송업자
forwarding charges	운송료
forwarding merchant	운송취급인
fossil fuel	화석연료
foul B/L	고장 선하증권
foul bill	고장어음
foundation	재단, 창설
foundation collateral	재단저당
founder	창립자
founder's profit	창업자 이익
fourth market	기관투자가간 시장
fractal	프랙탈
fraction of a day	1일 1부
fractional figure	단수
fractional interest	단수이자
fractional order	단주(端株; 거래단위에 미달하는 주식) 주문
fractional year	1년으로 채우지 않는 해
fragmentation	세분화
fragmented industry	다수난전업계
frame editing	코마촬영
frame relay	프레임릴레이(랜들을 연결하는 고속통신 기술의 하나)
frame translation	프레임 수변환
franchise	소손해 면책비율
franchise clause	면책비율조항
franchise group insurance	개별계약단체조항
franchise selling	특약판매

franchise tax 특허세
franchised retail store 프랜차이즈 가맹점
franchising 프랜차이즈 계약
franco 반입인도가격
franco delivered 반입인도
frank 무료배달우편
fraternal benefit society 공제조합
fraternal insurance 공제보험
fraud 부정수단, 사기
fraudulent act 부정행위
fraudulent bankruptcy 사기파산
fraudulent cards 부정카드
fraudulent conveyance 사기양도
fraudulent creditor 사기채권자
fraudulent gains 부정이득
fraudulent misrepresentation 사기표시
fraudulent transfer 사기적 양도
Freddie Mac 프레디 맥
free alongside ship 선측양도
Free Alongside Ship (FAS) 선측인도
free article 면세품
free carrier 운송인 양도
free dial 통화료 수신자부담 서비스
free economy 자유경제
free enterprise system 자유기업제도
free equity 프리 이쿼티
free float 자유변동
free floating exchange rates system 자유변동환율제
free form deformation 자유형상변형법
free form modeling 자유형상모델링
free from all averages but to cover salvage charges 전손에 의한 구조비 부담

free from capture and seizure clause 포획불부담조항
free from particular average 단독해손부담보, 분손부담보
free goods 면세품
free list 무세품표
free of damage absolutely 물적분손절 대불담보
free of premium 보험료의 지불면제
free of taxation 면세
free offer 자유 오퍼
free on board 본선양도
Free On Board (FOB) 본선인도
free paper 구독료 무료신문
free payment 임의수도
free payment system 자유반제(반납) 시스템
free port 자유항(무역)
free processing zone 자유가공구
free rate 자유요율
free reserves 자유준비
free riding 무임승차
free share 자유주
free surplus 자유잉여금
free trade zone 자유무역지대
Free Trade Zone (FTZ) 자유무역지대(역)
free yen account 자유엔계정
free yen deposit 자유엔예금
free-price 자유가격
free-ride period 우대조치기간
free-standing company 프리 스탠딩 기업, 독점기업
free-standing store 독립점포
freedom from incumbrance 무담보
freedom of association 결사의 자유
freedom of expression 표현의 자유
freedom of movement 이전의 자유

freedom of speech	언론의 자유
freedom of the press	출판의 자유
freedom of the sea	해양의 자유
freehold	자유토지보유권
freight	화물
freight and cartage outward	발송운임
freight collect	수취인이 지불함
freight contingency	미필운송임
freight earnings	화물수입
freight insurance	운임보험
freight inward	구입운임
freight out	판매운임
freight prepaid	운임선불
freight pro-rata	할당운송임
freight rates	화물운임
freight receipts	운임수입
freight tariff	화물운임
freight to collect	운임후불
freight usance	운임 유산스
freight-in	구매운임
freight-out	판매운임
frequency curve	도수곡선
frequency distribution	도수분포
frequency modulation	FM
frequency modulation oscillator	FM음원
frequency of risk	위험발생률
fresh pursuit	즉시추급(추궁, 추적)
fresh water damage	담수에 젖음
frictional unemployment	마찰적 실업
friendly society	우애조합
fringe benefits	부가급부(급부; 채무를 이행하는 행위)
fringe market	주변시장

frivolity	쓸데없는 (헛된) 사용
frivolous answer	불성실한 답변
front end computer	전치컴퓨터
front end processor	전치계산기
front loaded	먼저 쓰러짐
front running	먼저 뜀
front-end fee	선불금
front-foot rule	전회(지난번) 규칙
frontage	간구(전면의 폭), 인접지
frontier tax	국경세
fronting	프론팅
fronting business	프론팅 비즈니스
fronting loan	프론팅 론
frozen account	동결계정
frozen assets	동결자산
frozen credit	변동없는 채권
frozen stock	팔고 남음
fruit	수익
frustration	계약목적의 달성불능
fuel account	연료계정
fuel and light prices	광열비
fuel expenses	연료비
fugitive from justice	도망범인
fulfillment of a contract	계약이행
full age	성년
full capacity output	완전이용산출량
full cash refund annuity	완전즉시상환식 연금
full compensation	충분한 보상
full cost	전부원가
full cost principle	풀 코스트 원칙
full costing	전부원가계산
full disclosure	완전개시

full employment 완전고용
full employment policy 완전고용정책
full hedge 완전 헷지
full insurance 전액보험
full legal tender 완전법화
full payment 전액지불
full pension 완전연금
full preliminary term reserve 초년정기식 채무준비금
full proof 완전증명
full repayment before maturity 조기완제
full service middlemen 완전서비스형 중간업자
full value insurance 전부보험
full year 평년도
full year business result 본결산
full-bodied money 완전화폐
full-faith-and-credit debt 신의 · 신용채무
full-paid capital stock 전액납부제주식
full-scale local production 현지 일관생산
fully depreciated 감가상각완결
fully diluted 희석완결(종료)
fully insured status 완전수급자금
fully owned subsidiary 전액출자의 자회사
fully paid-up 전액납부
function 기능
function of group 집단기능
functional accounting 기능별 회계
functional analysis 기능분석
functional approach 기능적 어프로치
functional currency 기능통화
functional currency method 기능통화법
functional depreciation 기능적 감가
functional effect 기능적 효과

functional organization	기능별 조직
functional pricing	기능적산법
functional responsibility	직무상의 책임
functional specialization	기능적 전문화
functional statement	기능별 계산서
functionalized organization	기능별 조직
functions of marketing	마케팅 기능
functus officio	임무종료
fund	기금, 자금, 펀드
fund absorption	자금흡수력
fund account	기금계정
fund accounting	기금회계
fund and trust	기금과 신탁
fund balance sheet	기금대차대조표
fund cost	기금조달비용
fund for operation of foreign exchange	외국환 운영기금
fund management	자금운용
fund management method	자금운용수단
fund manager	펀드매니저
fund obligation	자금부채
fund of funds	자금중의 자금
fund position	자금포지션
fund raising business	자금조달업무
fund raising capacity	자금조달력
fund settlement	자금결제
fund shortage	자금부족
fund statement	자금운용표
fund surplus	자금잉여금
fund swap	자금관련 스왑
fund transfer	자금이전
fund transfer service	자금대체서비스
fund's mission	연금기금의 사명

fundamental analysis	기초 분석
fundamental directives of income tax	소속세 기본통달
fundamental disequilibrium	기초적 불균형
fundamental financial approach	기초적 금융상품 어프로치
fundamental rights	기본적 권리
fundamental rules	기준적 규칙
fundamental scientific research	기초연구
fundamental tax	기간세
fundamental theorem	기초정리
fundamentalist	경제기초조건 중시파
fundamentals	경제기초조건
fundamentals deterioration	기초적인 악화
funded debt	1년 이상의 채권발행에 의한 차입금
funding	자금조달
funding agency	연금기금적립기관
funding cost	조달비용
funding gap	자금부족
funding instrument	연금기금적립계약
funding method	적립방식
funding policy	차환정책
funds for purchase	매입자금
funds from operations	영업수입
fungibility	대체가능성
fungible	대용가능하다
fungible goods	대체가능물
fungible securities	대체가능증권
funnel	집중시키다
furnishings	비품
furniture and fixture	가구집기
furniture and household goods	가재도구
further advance	재대부

further consideration	심리속행
further directions	속행
further maintenance of the action	소송속행
fusion process	융합과도
future cash flows	미래현금흐름
future cost	미래원가
future service benefits	장래근무연금
future service credits	장래의 근무실적
future service pension	장래근무연금
future specific risk	장래의 고유리스크
future value	장래가치
futures	선물
futures commission merchant	선물중개업자
futures contract	선물계약
futures dealer	선물딜러
futures margin	선물마진
futures market	선물시장
futures option	선물옵션
futures option market	선물옵션시장
futures price	선물가격
futures product	선물상품
futures quotation	선물상장
futures rate	선물 레이트
futures trading	선물거래
fuzzy theory	퍼지이론

≪ G ≫

gag order	함구명령
gage	담보
gain	수익
gaining	강보합
gains	상승폭
gains from appreciation of securities	유가증권평가익
gains from exchange of properties	교환차익
gains from forgiveness of debt	채무면제권
gains from revaluation of fixed assets	고정자산 평가익
gains from sale of fixed assets	고정자산매각익
gains from stock retirement	감자차익
gains from the transfer of property	자산의 양도익
gains of sales	매출증가
gains on bond retirement	사채상환차금
gains on insurance claim	보험차익
galley proof	갤리 인쇄
galloping inflation	악성인플레이션
game plan	작전계획
gamma	감마
gamma correction	감마 보정
gamma exposure	감마 노출
Gantt chart	갠트차트
gap	괴리, 차액
gap analysis	갭분석
gap management technology	갭법
garnishee	제3채무자
garnisher	채권차압인

garnishment	채권차압통고
gas and water expenses	가스수도비
gas tax	가스세
gasoline tax	휘발유세
gather steam	활황
gavel	지대, 조세, 연공
gazette	관보
gearing	기어링
gearing effect	기어링 효과
general account	일반회계
general account expenditure	일반회계세출
General Accounting Office	회계검사원
general accounting principles	일반회계원칙
general administrative and selling expenses	일반관리비에 따른 판매비
general administrative expenses budget	일반관리비 예산
general advertising	전국광고
general agency system	총대리점 제도
general agent	총대리점
general agreement	일반협정
General Agreement on Tariffs and Trade (GATT)	관세와 무역에 관한 일반협정
General Agreement to Borrow	일반차입결의
general and administrative expenses	일반관리비
general audit	일반감사
general audit standards	감사기준
general authority	포괄적 권한
general average	공동해손
general average balance	공동해손청산고
general average bond	공동해선 맹약서
general average contribution	공동해손 분담액

general average expenditure	공동해손비용
general average sacrifice	공동해손 희생손해
general balance sheet	일반대차대조표
general binded-debt fund	일반공채자금
general building scheme	일반주택지 분양계획
general business	일반사업
general cargo	일반화물
general cash	일반현금
general closing	통상결산
general condition of contract	보통계약약관
general conditions and terms of the contract	일반조건서
general corporate assets	일반회사 자산
general corporate bond	회사채
general corporate revenues and expenses	회사수지
general credit	일반신용
general crossed check	일반횡선수표
general election	총선거
general expenses	일반경비
general fixed-assets fund	일반고정자산자금
general fund	일반자금
general government section	일반정부부문
general index	총합지수
general indirect cost	일반간접비
general insurance	손해 전종목 보험
general insurance clausel	보통보험 약관
general insurance law	보험법
general inventory	재산목록
general journal	보통 분개장
general ledger	총계정원장
general ledger account	총계정원장 계정

general letter of credit	매입은행 무지정 신용장
general liability insurance	일반배상책임보험
general management	총괄 경영층
general market	일반시장
general means of payment	일반적 지불수단
general meeting of shareholders	주주총회
general meeting of substitutional members	사원총대회
general merchandise	잡화
general mortgage	일반저당
general mortgage bond	일반 부동산 담보부 채권
general obligation bond	일반재원채
general operating expenses	일반경영활동비
general overhead	일반간접비
general partner	무한책임사원
general partnership	무한책임 파트너쉽
general place of tax payment	원칙적 납세지
general price level	일반물가수준
general price-level accounting	일반물가수준회계
general profit and loss account	손익계정
general property tax	일반재산세
general provisions	총칙
general provisions of budget	예산총칙
general reserve	별도 적립금
general risk	보통 물건
general security agreement	일반담보계약
general survey	전반검사
general tax	보통세
general tax reduction	일반감세
general taxation	종합과세
general terms and conditions of trade	일반무역조건
general words	일반문언

general-obligation bonds 일반공채
general-purpose financial statements 일반목적 재부제표
generally accepted accounting principle 일반공정타당과 인정되는 회계기준
generate favorable cash flows 바람직한 현금흐름을 산출하다
generating function 생성함수
genetic strategy 포괄적 전략
genetic algorithm 유전적 알고리즘
geocentric 세계지향
geocentrism 세계지향
geographical price differential 지역적 가격차
geographical pricing 지역별 가격제
geometric average 기하평균
geometric model 형상모형
German Bearer Certificate 독일 무기증명서
getting ashore 매입약정만 하고 아직 결재되지 않은 주식
ghosting 방해전파
Gibson paradox Gibson 역설
gift 증여
gift advertisement 기프트 광고
gift causa mortis 사인증여
gift during life 생전증여
gift enterprise 추첨분배법
gift in kind 물품에 의한 증여
gift tax 증여설
gift tax credit 상속세 공제
gift tickets account 상품권 감정
giga byte 기가바이트
giga chip 기가 칩
gilt-edged bond 금록채권
gilt-edged securities 금록증권
Ginnie Mae 전미저당금융금고의 별칭
giving quotation 지불감정건 상장

glamor stock	매력주
global bearer certificate	글로벌부기명예탁증권
global bond	글로벌 본드
global chess	글로벌 체스
global company	글로벌 기업
global corporation	세계기업
global efficiency	글로벌효율성
global industrial systems constellation (GISC)	글로벌 산업시스템 컨설레이션
global industry	지구규모산업
global market	세계적인 시장
global marketing	글로벌 마케팅
global matrix organization	글로벌 매트릭스 조직
global portfolio	글로벌 포트폴리오
global R&D	글로벌 연구개발
global reforms	포괄적 개혁
global scanning	글로벌환경평가조사
global strategy	글로벌전략
global trading	글로벌 트레이딩
globalization	국제화
GNMA debenture	미국정부주택저당 금고증권
gnome	금언
gnomes of Zurich	국제금융시장
GNP deflator	GNP 디플레이터
go on selling	판매
goal conflict	목표적 충돌
goal congruence	목표의 일치
goal variable	목표변수
going concern	계속기업
going concern value	계속기업가치
going long	혼동구매
going private	기업의 비공개화

going public 주식공개화
going short 혼동판매
going value 계속기업가치
gold and foreign exchange reserves 외화준비금
gold and silver bimetallism 금은복본위제도
gold bond 금채권
gold bullion futures contract 금선물계약
gold bullion standard 금자금본위제
gold center 금센터
gold clause 금약관
gold coin standard 금화본위제
gold exchange reserve 금환준비
gold exchange standard 금환본위제
gold fixing 금매매 기준가격 결정
gold futures option 금선물 옵션
gold holdings 금보유고
gold parity 금평가
gold points 금현송점
gold pool 금 풀
gold purchase warrant 금매입 워런트
gold rush 골드 러쉬
gold standard 금본위제
gold sterilization policy 금불태화정책
gold tranche 골드트란시
golden cross 골든크로스
golden hand cuffs 특별우대조치
golden parachute 황금낙하산
golden rule 황금률
golden section 황금분할
golfers' insurance 골퍼스 보험
Gonzalez Amendment 곤잘레스 수정법
good 유효한

good and collectible	회수확실한
good and lawful men	유자격자
good behavior	선행
good consideration	선량약인
good debt	회수확실한 임금
good delivery	적격수수
good faith	성실
good merchantable quality	판매적성품질
good money	사용가능자금
good news	호재
good offices of banking facilities	금융기관의 알선
good result return	호성적 리턴
good risk	우량물건
good this month order	당월까지 유효한 주문
good value	자금화 자금
good yield	호이자
good-until-canceled orders	취소까지 유효한 주문
goods	재화
goods account	상품계정
goods and chattels	인적재산
goods and products	상품 또는 제품
goods carried over	이월상품
goods earnings	화물수입
goods for sale	판매용 상품
goods in process	과정품
goods in process ledger	과정품원장
goods in transit	미착품
goods left	팔고 남음
goods on approval	시송품
goods on consignment-in	수탁품
goods on hands	수중의 재고품
goods returned to vendor	반환품

goods sold on credit 길에서 판 상품
goods to arrive 미착품
goodswill 영업권, 난염
governing clause 준거법조항
governing law 준거법
government account 정부계정
government accounting 관청회계
government agency 정부계기관
government agency bond 정부계기관 채권
government agency securities 정부기관 증권
government bond 국채
government bond book-entry system 국채대체결제제도
government bond for tax reduction 감세국채
government bond for the purpose of public works 건설국채
government bond in foreign currency 외화국채
government bonds and corporate debentures 공사채
government bonds in domestic currency 내국화국채
government bookkeeping 관청부기
government broker 정부브로커
government compensation bond 교대공채
government credit 정부차관
government current surplus 정부경영임대
government debt 공채
government enterprise 정부기업
government expenditure 정부지출
government financial agency 정부금융기관
government financial corporation 국고
government fund transactions 국고수지
government fund transactions with the public 국고대 민간 수지

government guaranteed bond	정부보증채
Government National Mortgage Association	정부저당금고
Government National Mortgage Association debenture	GNMA채
government note	정부지폐
government obligation	정부보증채
government ordinance	정부조례
government purchases	정부구입
government related deposit	정보관계예금
government saving	정부저축
government securities	정부증권
government subsidy for capital expenditure	건설조성금
government to government trade	정부간 무역
government trade	정부무역
government transaction	정부거래
government transfers	정부이전수지
governor	총재
grab	불법손실
grace of payment	지불유예
grace period	거치기간, 유예기간
gradation	계조
grade	등급
grade description system	분류법
graded commission	등급별 수수료
graded expense	단계적 경비
graded fariff	차등세율
grading function	등급가능
grading transaction	등급거래
gradual devaluation	서서히 절하
graduated payment mortgage	고정금리건 저당

graduated tax	누진세
graduated taxation	누진과세
graduation clause	졸업조항
grain market	곡물시장
grand bill of sale	선박양도증서
grand distress	전부차압
grand jury	대배심
grand strategy	총합전략
grand total	총계
grandfather clause	조부조항
grandfather provision	기득권 조항
grant	허인가
grant back provision	그랜트 백 규정
grant element	증여등가비율
grant in aid	조성금
granting credit	신용공여
grantor	양여자(양도자)
graphical user interface	GUI
grassroot entry	그래스루트 진입
gratis appearance	임의지출
gratis dictum	임의의 진술
gratuitous bailment	무상기탁
gratuitous contract	무상계약
gratuitous use of property	무상의 재산사용
gravure printing	그라비어 인쇄
gray market	발행전 유통시장
great depression	대공황
greater fool theory	큰바보 이론
green buck	미달러 지폐
green card	소액저축 등 이용자 카드
green card system	그린카드 제도
green field	미개발 지역의
green goods	위조지폐

green mail	그린 메일
green marketing	그린 마케팅
green shoe clause	그린 슈 조항
Greenfield investment	그린필드 투자
Gresham's law	그레샴의 법칙
grievance committee	고정처리위원회
grievance machinery	고정처리기관
gripsack general agent	출장총대리점
gross amount	총액
gross amount principle	총액주의
gross assets	총자산
gross base	총액베이스
gross billing	광고회사의 총매출
gross book value	총장부가격
gross capital	총자본
gross cost	총원가
gross cost of merchandise sold	총매출원가
gross demand	총수요
gross domestic capital formation	국내총자본형성
gross domestic product	국내총생산
gross earnings	총수익
gross error	과실
gross expenditure	총지출
gross fund position	총자금포지션
gross gain	총수익
gross income	총소득
gross income of corporation	법인의 익금
gross investment	총투자
gross loss	총손실
gross loss on sales	매출총손실
gross margin	매출총이익
gross margin ratio	매출총이익률

gross merchandise margin 총상품매매차익
gross national expenditure 국민총지출
gross national product 국민총생산
gross national wealth 국민총자산
gross negligence 중과실
gross operating spread 총영업이폭
gross profit 총이익
gross profit analysis 총이익분석
gross profit margin rate 총이익률
gross profit method 총이익법
gross profit on sales 매출 총이익
gross profit percentage 총이익률
gross profit ratio 총이익률
gross profit test 총이익테스트
gross profits 총이익금
gross purchase 매입 이익 총액
gross rating point 도달률
gross revenue 총수입
gross sales 총매출액
gross sound value 총정품가액
gross spread 인수모집수수료
gross trading volume 총거래금액
gross transaction 총거래
gross up method 그로스 업 방식
gross-profit ratio 매상총이익률
ground coverage 지상위험부담
ground of action 소송원가
ground price 공장원가
ground-making expenses 토지조성비
groundage 정박료
grounded 승양
grounding clause 승양조항

grounds for disbarment	변호사 자격 박탈 이유
group accident insurance	단체상해보험
group annuity	단체연금
group annuity insurance	단체연금보험
group annuity insurance contract	단체연금보험계약
group auction	격탁매매
Group B states	B 그룹 국
group behavior	집단행동
group buying	공동매입
group conformity	집단적합
group cost system	등급별 원가계산
group credit insurance	단체신용보험
group credit life insurance	단체신용생명보험
Group D states	D 그룹 국
group deferred annuity contract	단체거치연금계약
group deposit administration contract	단체예탁관리계약
group depreciation	조별상각
group dynamics	집단역학
group endowment insurance	단체양로보험
group financial statement	기업집단 재무제표
group health insurance	단체건강보험
group insurance	단체보험
group interview	집단면접
group life insurance	집단생명보험
group marketing	균일가치
group medical expense insurance	단체의료비보험
group method	조별법
group mortgage insurance	단체 모기지보상생명보험
group norm	집단규범
Group of 77 (G-77)	77개 그룹
group pension	단체연금
group permanent insurance	단체종신보험

group permanent insurance contract 단체장기보험계약
group pressure 집단입력
group representative 보험담당자
group retention 단체보유액
group special mobile communication 이동체 통신
group term insurance 단체정기보험
group variable annuity 단체변액연금
Grouped etudes des experts comptables de la CEE 유럽경제공동체회계학
group speciale mobile 유럽이동통신규격
groupware 그룹웨어
growing at a moderate speed 적당히 신장하다
growing currency 성장통화
growth of industrial structure 생산구조고도화
growth potential 성장성
growth rate 성장률
growth stock 성장주
growing strategy 성장전략
growing vector matrix 성장벡터 매트릭스
guarantee 보증
guarantee by endorsement 이서보증
guarantee capital 보증자본
guarantee charge 보증료
guarantee deposits 보증금
guarantee in favor of the primary guarantor 이보증
guarantee insurance 보증보험
guarantee loan 보증론
guarantee money 보증금
guarantee of repayment 차입반제 보증
guaranteed bond 보증사채
guaranteed continuous policy 계속보증계약

guaranteed cost contract	비용보증계약
guaranteed deferred annuity	보증거치연금
guaranteed dividend	확정배당
guaranteed freight	보증연채
guaranteed immediate annuity	보증즉시연금
guaranteed income contract	보증부 투자계획
guaranteed insurability rider	무진사 증액권 특약
guaranteed insurance trust	보증보험신탁
guaranteed interest contract	이용보증계약
guaranteed investment contract	보증투자계약
guaranteed minimum life annuity	최저보증부종신연금
guaranteed securities	보증증권
guaranteed spread	보증 스프레드
guaranteed stock	보증주
guarantor	보증인
guarantor bank	보증은행
guarantor's right of indemnity	구상권
guaranty	보증계약
guaranty insurance	손해보험계약
guaranty money	보증금
guaranty money deposited	차입보증금
guaranty of liabilities	채무보증
guardian ad litem	후견인
guardianship	후견
guessed mean	반평균
guessing	억측
guidance	지침
guideline	가이드라인
guild	동업조합
guilty	유죄
Gulf Cooperation Council	만안협력회의
gun jumping	정보공개전의 증권거래

≪ H ≫

habeas corpus	신병제출영장
habit	관행
habit persistence hypothesis	관습가설
haggling price	깎은 가격
Hague Protocol	헤이그 의정서
hair cut	이발
halation	할레이션
half tax	후생보험
half tone	그물에 걸림
half-finished goods	반제품
half-yearly	반년의
hammering the market	물량 쏟아붓기
hand-to-mouth buying	당장의 매입
handle	거래총액
handling expenses	취급비
happening subsequent to balance sheet date	대차대조표일후의 발생사항
harbor dues	입항세
harbor currency	교환가능통화
harbor disk	하드 디스크
harbor labor	중노동
hard currency	하드커런시
harden	절약하다
harmless error	무해의 오류
harmonization policies	협조정책
harvesting strategy	수확전략
haulege	운반비

Havana Charter	하바나 헌장
hazard	위험
head	주석
head and shoulder	머리 어깨
head book	주요장부
head hunter	헤드헌터, 인재스카우트 담당자
head money	인두세
head office	본점
head office account	본사계정
head tax	인두세
heading	항목
health care obligation	의료급부채무
health examination	건강진단
health insurance	건강보험
health insurance premium	건강보험료
healthy revenue growth	순조로운 수입성장
healthy trend	고수준
hearsay evidence	전문증언
heating	뜸이 들다
heavy	연조(시세가 하락하는 경향임)
heavy additional charge imposed	중가산금
heavy additional tax	중가산세
heavy electrical stocks	중전
heavy market	하락세 시장
heavy penalty tax	중가산세
heavy taxation	중세
heavy users	고관여자
heckscher-Ohlin theorem	헥셔오린 이론
hedge	위험분산기법
hedge account representation letter	헷지 감정대행서
hedge clause	면책조항
hedge fund	헷지 펀드

hedge operation　헷지 조작
hedge ratio　헷지 비율
hedge trading　헷지 거래
hedge transaction　헷지 거래
hedged bond　헷지드채
hedger　헷져
hedging　연계보험
hedging cost　헷지 비용
hedging function　헷지 기능
hedging on commodity futures　상품선물거래의 헤징
hedging on option　헷징의 옵션
hegemony　주도권
heir　상속인
heir apparent　법정상속인
heir collateral　방계상속인
heir general　통상상속인
heir of the body　직계상속인
heir presumptive　추정상속인
heir-looms　법정상속동산
held to maturity　상환기한까지 보유
hell or high water clause　헬 오어 하이 워터 조항
hello effect　헬로우 효과
help　보조
hereditaments　재산부동산
heritage　상속부동산
hertz-gap　하쯔 갭
heterogeneous competition　이질적 경쟁
heterogeneous demand　이질수요
heterogeneous market　이질시장
heterogeneous oligopoly　이질과점
hidden assets stock　자산주 포함
hidden line elimination　은선처리

hidden profit distributions	숨은처분이익
hidden reserve	은닉적립금, 비밀적립금
hierarchical theory	계층이론
high	고가치
high assay model	광고매체 선택모형
high context	고맥락
high cost	고원가
high definition television	HD 텔레비젼
high degree of positive correlation	고도의 정(+)의 상관관계
high density	고밀도
high grade investment	유리한 투자
high income brackets	다액납세자
high income trust security	고액신탁증권
high interest rate	고금리
high interest rate policy	고금리정책
high justice	재판권한
high level of business activity	고수준의 경기
high mortality	높은 사망률
high possibility	높은 공채
high price	고가
high rise	급등
high seas	공해
high taxpayers	다액납세자
high yield bond	고이자채
high-coupon bond	하이-쿠폰 채
high-interest-bearing debenture	고이자부 사채
high-leveraged	효과가 높다
high-low method	고저법
high-priced stock	높게 매겨진 주식
high-risk high-return	고위험고수익
high-tech stock	하이-테크 주식
higher interest rates application system	고율적용제도

higher order goods	고차재
higher quotation	높은 가치
highway by prescription	시효에 의한 공로
highway by user	사용자에 의한 공로
hire purchase	할부구입
hire purchase agreement	매입선택권부 물품 사용계약
histogram method	히스토그램법
historical cost	취득원가
historical cost basis	취득원가 기준
historical cost/nominal dollar accounting	취득원가주의 명목가치회계
historical earnings	과거의 실적
historical trading range	과거의 가격움직임폭
historical volatility	역사적 변동성
historical yield	누적이자
historical-cost financial statements	취득원가주의의 재무제표
historical-dependent derivative	경로의존형 파생상품
hit	확실한 손실, 달성하다
hit the bottom	최저수준까지 하락하다
hitting the ceiling	천정을 쏘다
hive off	하도급에 내다
hoarding	매점
hold	보유하다
hold harmless agreement	면책특약
hold off buying	매입을 하지 않고 관망하다
hold point	홀드 포인트
holder	소지인
holder for value	유상소지인
holder in bad faith	악의의 제3자
holder in due course	선의의 제3자
holder in good faith	선의의 소지인
holder of record	주주명부상의 주주

holding company 지주회사
holding gain or loss 보유손익
holding high 고보합
holding of assets 자산의 보유
holding period return 보유기간수익률
holding period value-relative 보유기간 상대가치
holding ratio for a company's stock 주식보유율
holding the market 시장점유
holdings 지분
hole sort card 가장자리 구멍 카드
holism 전체론
hologram 홀로그램
holograph 자필증서
holography 홀로그래피
home banking 홈뱅킹
home country control 원적국주의, 본점 감독주의
home currency 자국통화
home currency bill bought 방화매입 외국환
home equity loan 가계자금대출
home improvement loan 증개축론
home mortgage 주택 저당
home port 선적항
home production 국내생산
home rule 자치
home service 내지근무
home service agent 지구외무원
home service life insurance 간이생명보험
home state 본거주
homestead 가산
homegeneity 동질성
homegeneous competition 동질적 경쟁
homegeneous market 동질시장

homegeneous security group	동종증권의 그룹
homologation	확인
honor	보증
honor policy	명예 보험증권
honorable agreement	명예계약
honorarium	사찰금
hook damage	갈고리 손해
hooked	매입이 늘어짐
horizon analysis	투자계획기간분석
horizon return	소유기간이자
horizontal	수평적
horizontal acquisition	수평적 대우
horizontal analysis	수평분석
horizontal angle of view	수평 재각
horizontal audit	수평적 감사
horizontal buy	수평매수
horizontal competition	수평적 경쟁
horizontal concurrence	수평적 협력
horizontal diversification	수평적 다각화
horizontal expansion	수평적 확장
horizontal integration	수평형 통합
horizontal international specialization	수평적 국제분업
horizontal market	수평적 시장
horizontal merger	수평합병
horizontal organization	횡단적 조직
horizontal specialization	수평분업
horizontal split	수평분단
horizontal spread	수평적 스프레드
horizontal trade	수평적 무역
hospital expense insurance	입원비 보험
host country	수용국
hostile possession	적대적 점유

hot issue	인기증권
hot money	국제단기부동자금, 핫머니
hot money market	핫머니 시장
hot pursuit	긴급출입
hours worked	가동시간
hours-of-service method	사용시간비열법
house agency	하우스 에이전시
house bill	하우스 빌
house breaking	주거침입죄
house duty	가옥세
house farmer	건물전대인
house margin rule	증거금 내부규제
house media	자가매체
house organ	사내보
house rent received	수취가
house-rent income	대가료
house-rent law	차가법
household	가계
household consumption expenditure	가계소비지출
household expenses	가계비
household goods	가재도구
household sector	가계부문
household taxation	세대과세
householder's comprehensive insurance	주택종합보험
housekeeping expenses	가계비
housing allowance	주거수당
housing credit	주택신용
housing expenses	주거비
housing loan	주택금융
housing loan corporation	주택금융회사
housing permits	주택착공허가건수

housing renewal program	굴림방식
housing savings tax credit	주택저축공제
housing starts	주택건축착공수
hub	허브
hull insurance	선박보험
human assessment	휴먼어세스먼트
human engineering	인간공학
human interface	휴먼 인터페이스
human life value	인간의 생명가치
human relations	인적관계
human resources accounting	인적자원 회계
human resources development	인재개발
humped	혹이 있다
humped curve	수익률곡선형태
hung up	매입이 늘어짐
hunters' insurance	헌터보험
hurdle rate	최저목표수익율
hush-money	구지(口止)료
hybrid	혼합
hybrid cap	혼합캡
hybrid model	혼합형
hybrid securities	복합증권
hybrid stocks	혼합주식
hybrid trust	혼합신탁
hygiene factor	위생요인
hyper inflation	초인플레이션
hyphenation	하이퍼네이션
hypothecate	저당권을 설정하다
hypothecated assets	담보자산
hypothecation agreement	담보차입동의서

≪ I ≫

I-S curve · L-M curve	IS곡선 · LM곡선
ID code	ID 코드
idea advertising	의견광고
ideal standard cost	이상표준가격
identifiable assets	인식
identification	식별
identification card	신분증명서
identified cost method	개별법
identity	동일성
identity matrix	단위행렬
idle assets	유휴자산
idle balance	유휴잔고
idle capacity cost	제조업도원가
idle cash	잉여의 현금
idle cost	부동비
idle equipment	유휴설비
idle facilities	유휴시설
idle money	갈곳이 정해지지 않은 자금
idle plant	유휴설비
idle properties	유휴자산
idle time	유휴시간
IFAC International Federation of Accountants	국제회계사연맹
IFPMA Code IFPMA	국제의약품제조업협회
ignorance	무지
ignore	받아들이지 않고 물리치다

ILEF-Instituto Latinoamericano de Estudios Transnacionales 라틴아메리카 다국적기업연구소
illegal 불법의
illegal act 위법행위
illegality 불법
illiquid 비유동적
image advertising 이미지 광고
image board 이미지 보드
image formation 이미지 형성
image maker 이미지 메이커
image profile 이미지 프로필
image research 이미지 조사
image setter 이미지 셋터
image strategy 이미지 전략
imaginary demand 가수요
imbalance 불균형
imbalance of orders 주문의 불균형
imbedded 편입되어 있는
Committee on International Investment and Multinational Enterprises (IME Committee) 국제투자 및 다국적기업위원회
IMF loan IMF 차관
IMF per value IMF 평가
imitation 모조품
imitative price 추수가격
immaterial capital 무형자본
immaterial evidence 중요하지 않은 근거
immaterial issue 중요하지 않은 쟁점
immaterial property 무형재산
immediacy 즉시적 유동성
immediate annuity 즉시개시연금
immediate cause 직근원인

immediate descent 직접상담
immediate liquidity 당면의 유동성
immediate order 지급주문
immediate participation guarantee contract 직접참가방식 단체연금계약
immediately available fund 즉시 이용가능한 자금
immovable property 부동산
immovables account 부동산 계정
immunity 면허
immunity of witness 증언의무의 면허특권
immunization 면역화
immunization fund 면역기금
impact claims 파급효과 클레임
impact loan 임팩트 론
impact printer 임팩트 프린터
impairment of contract 계약상의 권리침해
impartial taxation 과세의 공평
impeachement 탄핵
impeachement of witness 증인의 탄핵
imperfect competition 불완전 경쟁
imperfect competition market 불완전경쟁시장
imperfect obligation 불완전의무
imperfect trust 불완전신탁
imperialism 제국주의
impersonal deduction 물적공제
impersonal exclusion from taxation 물적과세제외
impersonal security 대물담보
impersonal tax 물세
impertinent 무관세의
impignoration 질입
impignorative contract 질입계약
implead 소추하다, 기소하다

implication 추단
implicit call price 내재적 콜 가격
implicit cost 비명시적 비용
implicit deflator 비명시적 가격변동지수
implicit interest 내포금리
implied 묵시적인
implied condition 묵시조건
implied contract 준계약
implied forward rates 묵시적 선도금리
implied license 묵시허용
implied need 묵시적 수요
implied repo rate 묵시적 회수비율
implied trust 묵시신탁
implied undertaking 묵시의 약속
implied volatility 묵시적 변동성
implied warranty 묵시담보
import bill 수입어음
import control 수입무역관리
import duties tariff 수입세표
import duty 수입세
import finance 수입금융
import financing system 수입대금 대부제도
import for manufacturing 이입
import function 수입함수
import license 수입승인증
import on consignment 위탁판매수입
import permit 수입허가
import price index 수입물가지수
import quota 수입할당
import restriction 수입규제
import settlement bill system 수입결제어음제도
import substitute 수입대체

import substitution 수입대체제
import surcharge 수입과징금
import tax 수입세
import tax system 임퓨테이션 세금제도
import usance 수입 유산스
important factor 중요한 요소
importation of foreign capital 외자수입
imported inflation 수입 인플레이션
imposition 과세
imposition of income tax 소득세의 과세
impossibility of performance 미행불능
impossible contract 불능한 계약
impost 수입세
impound 몰수되다
impressment 징발
imprest 선불금
imprest cash 선도자금
imprest cash fund 소구전불금
imprest fund 정액전도자금
imprest money 징발포상금
imprest system 정액전도제
imprimatur 간행허가
imprisonment 구금
improvement 개량
improvement expense 개량비
improvement of the property 자산의 개량
improvement partner 개량특허
improvidence 재산관리상의 태만
impulse buying 충동구매
impulse goods 충동구매상품
impunity 면제
imputation 귀속계속

imputation method	귀속계속법
impute	귀속시키다
imputed cost	귀속원가, 부가가치
imputed income	귀속소득
imputed interest	귀속이자
imputed negligence	귀책과실
imputed price	귀속가격
imputed value	귀속가치
in concert	공동으로
in extenso	완전하게
in fee	단순부동산권으로
in good faith	성실히
in good standing	우량하다
in gross	인적
in kind	동종의
in lieu	대신
in line whth	연동해서
in number	건수 레벨로
in pais	법적수속을 밟지 않고
in person	자신이
in real terms	실질적으로
in rem	대물적
in return	담보로써
in se	그 자체
in session	개연품
in specie	정화의, 특정의
in terms of revenue	수익면에서
in the near term	눈앞
in uptrend	상승경향이 있다.
in-and-out trading	회전매매
in-basket method	인-바스켓 방법
in-charge accountant	주임회계사

in-cycle work	기계운전시 작업
in-house exchange	행내교환
in-house product	자사제품
in-house training	기업내 교육
in-port duty	항만세
in-process inspection	공도내 관리
in-sourcing	인소싱
inactive	부상의, 한산
inactive account	비활동계좌
inactive bond	비인기채권
inactive market	한산시장
inadequate capital	과소자본
inadmissible	허용할 수 없다.
inadmitted assets	부승인 자산
inalienable rights	부가양의 친리
inaugural meeting	창립총회
incentive	장려
incentive effect	장려효과
incentive fee	성공보수
incentive stock option	자사주 저가격 구입권
incentive wage system	능률급
incidence of taxation	조세부담
incidental	부수적
incidental appeal	부대소송
incidental condition	부대조건
incidental expenses	부대비용
incidental gains	부대적 수입
incidental increase payment	일부증액반제
incidental suit	부대소송
including tax	세금이 포함됨
inclusion in expenses	손금산입
inclusion in gross revenue	익금산입

income	이익
income account	손익계정
income accrued from domestic sources	국내원천소득
income accrued from foreign sources	외국원천소득
income after tax audit	조사후 소득
income and expenditure liquidation	수지방정식
income and expenses	손익
income approach	소득접근법
income at liquidation	청산소득
income before employee bonus	상여전 소득
income before income taxes	세전 이익
income bond	배당사채
income bracket	소득층
income by coupon re-investment	쿠폰재투자수입
income deposit	소득예금
income derived from business	사업으로부터 생기는 소득
income distribution	소득분포
income earned	가득이익
income effect	소득효과
income effect of exchange adjustments	환조정의 소득효과
income elasticity	소득탄력성
income endowment	연금부보험
income enhancer	소득제고 인자
income from appreciation of assets	재산평가익
income from assets	자산소득
income from continuing operations	계속사업부문의 이익
income from discharge of indebtedness	채무면제익
income from discountinued operations	폐지부문으로부터의 이익
income from real estate	부동산 수입
income from transfer of securities	유가증권의 양도소득
income from trust deposits	금전신탁이익
income fund	소득펀드

income gain	배당소득
income in advance	선수수익
income indemnity insurance	소득보상보험
income inflation	소득인플레이션
income leveling	이익의 평준화
income leveling off	소득의 평준화
income policy	소득정책
income realization	이익실현
income received but unearned	이월수익
income redistribution effect	소득재분배효과
income return	소득신고
income return blank	소득신고 용지
income share	채산주
income share note	이익분배채
income statement	손익계산서
income statement account	손익계산서 계정
income statement approach	손익계산서 어프로치
income statement audit	손익계산서 감사
income statement principles	손익계산서 원칙
income statement ratio	손익계산서 비율
income stock	자산주
income summary	손익
income tax	소득세
income tax allocations	소득과세의 배분
income tax credit	소득세 공제
income tax law	소득세법
income tax prepayment system	예정납세제도
income tax rapid calculation table	소득세의 속산표
income tax rate	소득세율
income tax return	소득세신고
income tax return form	소득세신고서
income tax self-assessed	신고납세액

income tax withheld at source	원천공제소득세
income taxes payable	미지급법인세, 미지급소득세
income terms of trade	소득교역조건
income-consumption curve	소득소비곡선
income-generating effect	소득창출효과
incompetency	금치산
incomplete transaction	미완료 거래
inconvertible bank note	불환은행권
inconvertible paper money	불환지폐
incorporated company	회사
incorporated school	학교법인
incorporation	법인설립
incorporation procedures	회사설립수속
incorporator	발기인
incorporeal chattel	무체동산
incorporeal property	무체재산
incoterms	인코텀즈
incoterms, 1953-International Commercial Terms	국제회계기준위원회
increase and decrease method	증감법
increase in capital at the market price	주식의 시가발행
increase in capital stock	증자
increase in cost of working insurance	임시비용보험
increase of revenue	증수
increase of sales	매출증가
increased income tax	증가소득세
increased tax	증세
increased value insurance	증가가치보험
increasing annuity	체증연금
increasing domestic demand	연수확대
increasing term life insurance	체증정기보험
increasing whole life insurance	체증종신보험

increasing working capital	증가운전자본
increment card	증가카드
incremental analysis	증분분석
incremental cost	증분원가
incremental rate of return	증분수익률
incremental return	증가수익
incumbrance	토지에 대한 부담
indebtedness	채무
indebtedness of affiliates	관계회사채권
indefeasible	파기할 수 없는
indemnification	변상
indemnify	보상의 약속을 하다
indemnities	배당금
indemnity	면책
indemnity agreement	보증위탁계약
indemnity allowance	보상금
indemnity reinsurance	전보재보험
indent	수매위탁서
indenture	계약서
indenture trustee	계약서 수탁인
independence of auditor	감사원의 독립성
independent accountant	독립회계사
independent agency	독립기관
independent audit	독립감사
independent contract	독립계약
independent contractor	첨부인
independent intermediary	독립소개자
independent liability method	독립책임액 비례주의
independent marketing organization	독립판매조직
independent tax	독립세
independent variable	독립변수
index	지수

index arbitrager 지수재정거래자
index bond 인덱스 채권
index clause 지수약관
index clause insurance 지수보험
index fund 인덱스 펀드
index holding 지수보유
index linked bond 지수연계채권
index new value insurance 지수신가보험
index number by aggregative method 총화법지수
index number of production 생산지수
index number technique 지수법
index of net terms of trade 순교역조건지수
index of productivity 생산성지수
index of retail price 소매물가지수
index of trade 무역지수
index option 인덱스 옵션
index participation 인덱스 참가
index risk 지수리스크
index-number trend series 경향지수
indexation 지수화
indexes of producers' shipments 생산자출하지수
indicated market 참고상장시장
indication 기배치, 표시, 지침가격
indication method 인디케이션 방식
indicative price 기배치
indicator 지표
indices of urban land prices 전국시가지가격지수
indictment 기송
indifference curve 무차별곡선
indigenization 토착화
indirect deposit 간접예금

indirect evidence	간접증거
indirect exchange arbitrage	간접재정
indirect expenses	간접비
indirect financing	간접금융
indirect foreign tax credit	간접외국세액공제
indirect guarantee	간접보증
indirect incidental expenses	간접적 부수비용
indirect investment	간접투자
indirect inward investment	대내간접투자
indirect issue	간접발행
indirect labor cost	간접노무비
indirect liability	간접부채
indirect material cost	간접재료비
indirect method	간접법
indirect method of depreciation	간접상각
indirect presentation	간접표시
indirect production	간접생산
indirect sales	간접매매
indirect securities	간접증권
indirect tax	간접세
indirect trade	간접무역
indirect wage	간접임금
indirect yield	간접이자
individual annuity	개인연금
individual bond	개별보증증권
individual dealing system	개별매매방식
individual depreciation	개별상각
individual exclusion	개인공제
individual fidelity bond	개별신원보증증권
individual firm	개별기업
individual health insurance	개인건강보험
individual income tax	개인소득세

individual inhabitant tax	개인주민세
individual insurance	개별보험
individual investor	일반투자가
individual policy pension trust	개별보험연금계획
individual production	개별생산
individual proprietor	자영업자
individual retirement account	개인퇴직계정
individual separate account	단일고객분리계정
individual stockholder	개인주주
individual taxation	개별과세
individual underwriter	개인보험업자
individual useful life	개별내용연수
individual variable annuity	개인변액연금
indivisible credit	불가분채권
indorsed note	배서어음
indorsement	배서
indoser	배서인
induced investment	유발투자
inducement	유인
inducement to invest	투자유인
induciae	적하처분 기간
inductive statistical model	귀납적 통계모델
indulgence	지불유예
industrial accounting	공업회계
industrial advertisement	산업광고
industrial bookkeeping	공업부기
industrial capital	산업자본
industrial classification	산업분류
industrial complex	산업단지
industrial composition	산업구조
industrial cooperation method	산업협력방식
industrial corporation	사업법인

industrial debenture	사업채
industrial design	공업디자인
industrial development bond	산업개발채권
industrial dispute	노동쟁의
industrial distribution	산업재 유통
industrial dynamics	산업동력학
industrial engineering	생산공학
industrial espionage	산업 스파이
industrial estate	공업단지
industrial factory foundation	공업재단
industrial foundation	공업재단
industrial free zone	산업자유지역
industrial fund	산업자금
industrial insurance	간이보험
industrial law	노동법
industrial life insurance	간이생명보험
industrial loan	사업대부
industrial new design	실용신안
industrial organization	산업조직
industrial organization theory	산업조직론
industrial origin of net national product	산업별 국민순생산
industrial pension	기업연금
industrial policy	산업정책
industrial production	공업생산
industrial production index	광공업생산지수
industrial proprietorship	산업재산권
industrial publication	산업출판물
industrial rationalization	산업합리화
industrial revenue bond	특정재원채
industrial right	공업소유권
industrial risk	공장물건
industrial stock	공업주

industrial structure 산업구조
industrial structure policy 산업구조정책
industrial-accident reserve 산업사고 준비금
industrialized countries 공업국
industry 사업
industry association 업계단체
industry average 업계평균
industry beta value 산업의 베타가치
industry concentration 산업집중
industry effect 산업효과
industry information 산업정보
industry protection 산업보호
industry segments 업계
industry specialist 산업스페셜리스트
industry standard 업계기준
industry weighting ratio 업종별 조입률
ineligible 비적격한
ineligible bill 비적격채
inescapable cost 회피불능비
inevitable accident 불가도적 사고
infamous crime 파렴치죄
infamous punishment 불명예로운 형벌
infamy 명예박탈
infant 미성년자
inference 추리
inference engine 추리엔진
inferior character 하부문자
infirmative 경감할 듯한
inflation 인플레이션
inflation accounting 인플레이션 회계
inflation caused by won depreciation 원저 인플레이션
inflation differential 인플레이션 격자

inflation gap	인플레이션 갭
inflation led by import	수입 인플레이션
inflation-sensitivity factor	인플레이션 감응도
inflationary demand curve	인플레 수요곡선
inflationary expectation	인플레 기대
inflationary money supply	인플레 머니
inflationary supply curve	인플레 공급곡선
inflow of foreign capital	외자유입
influence the market trend	시장동향을 좌우하다
influx	유입
influx of foreign capital	외자유입
informal group	비공식집단
informal imperialism	비공식 제국주의
informal investigation	양식조사
informal organization	비공식조직
informal plan annuity	비공식연금
informal proceeding	간이수속
informal sector	비공식부문
information disclosure	정보공개
information home electronics	정보가전
information input	정보입력
information network system	고도정보통신시스템
information output	정보출력
information processing facility	정보처리설비
information provider	정보제공자
information ratio	정보비율
information revolution	정보혁명
information society	정보화 사회
information sources on beta value	베타가치의 정보원
information system	정보시스템
information system business	정보시스템 사업
information utility	정보효용

information value	정보가치
information vendors	정보벤더
information-motivated trader	정보동기에 의한 거래자
information-motivated transaction	정보동기에 의한 매매
informed consent	설명에 기초한 승낙
infostructure	정보기반구조
infringement	권리침해
infringement of copyright	판권침해
infringement of ownership	소유권침해
infringement of patent right	특허권 침해
infringement of trade-mark	상표권 침해
ingredient labeling	성분표시
ingress	출입
inhabitant tax	주민세
inherent defect	고유하자
inherent hazard	고유위험
inherit	법정상속하다
inheritance	상속
inheritance of bequest	유산상속
inheritance tax	상속세
inheritance tax on undivided bequest	미분할유산의 상속세
inheritance tax paid in kind	상속세 현물납
inherited property	상속재산
inheritor	상속인
initial	기초
initial balance	기초재고, 기초잔액
initial capital	기초자본
initial cost	원가
initial cost of business	개업비
initial date in reckoning	기산일
initial delivery	당초인도
initial depreciation	초기상각

initial down payment	내입금
initial establishment	당초설정
initial expenses	창업비
initial goods in process	기초설비금
initial installment	납입금
initial inventories	기초재고자산
initial listing requirement	상장기준
initial margin	기본증거금
initial margin requirement	당초증거금률
initial measurements	당초측정
initial par value	제1차 평가
initial payment	납입금
Initial Public Offering (IPO)	주식신규공개
initial reserve	최초준비금
initial special depreciation	초년도 특별상각
initial work in process account	기초준비계정
initiation fee	입회금
injunction	보전처분
inland bill	국내어음
inland bill of exchange	국내환어음
Inland Revenue	영국내 국세입청
innocent misrepresentation	섭의의 부실표시
innocent purchaser	섭의의 매주
innovation	혁신, 개정
innovation competition	혁신적 경쟁
innovation efficiency	혁신적 효율
innovator group	혁신자 집단
input coefficient	투입계수
input variable	투입변수
input-output analysis	투입산출분석
input-output table	투입산출표
inquiry agency	신용조사기관

inquiry for the balances 잔고조회
inquisition 심문
inquisitor 검증관
inscribed bond 기명채권
inscribed stock certificate 기명주권
insecurity clause 유저당약관
insert 광고물
insert editing 광고물편집
inside build-up 책임준비금 증가액
inside information 내부정보
inside the room 장내
insider trading 내부자 거래
insolvency 재무초과
insolvency of debtors 채무자의 지급불능
insolvent corporation 지급불능회사
insolvent debtor 파산자
inspection 검사
inspection certificate 검사증명서
inspection of corporate record 회사기록의 검사
inspection of documents 문서의 열람
inspection of property 재산의 검사
inspection report 검사보고서
inspection status 검사상태
installation 거부
installation work 거부공사
installment 할부
installment basis 할부기준
installment credit 할부채권
installment method 할부기준
installment payment 할부지급금
installment plan 할부
installment purchase 할부구매

installment receivable 할부외상금
installment sale 할부판매
installment savings 정기적금
installment settlement 분할지불
installment time deposit 적립정기예금
installments receivable 할부미수입금
instance 제기, 신청
instanter 즉시
Institute cargo clauses 협회화물약관
Institute clauses 협회약관
Institute of Chartered Financial Analyst 미국공인증권애널리스트협회
Institute of Internal Auditors 아메리카 내부감사인 협회
Institute of London Underwriters 런던보험업자협회
institutes 협회, 학회
institution 기관, 제도
institution buying 법인수매
institution of law suits 소송
institutional advertisement 기업광고
institutional advertising 제도광고
institutional analysis 제도적 분석
institutional arbitration 기관중재
institutional buying 기관매입
institutional decentralization 유통기관의 분산화
institutional delivery 대체결제
institutional investors 기관투자가
institutional investors' index option 기관투자가지수옵션
institutional school 제도학파
institutional selling 기관판매
institutional stock purchase 기관매입
institutional stockholder 법인주주
institutionalized saving 제도적 저축
instore merchandising 상품화 전략

instruction	지시
instruction to bidders	입찰자에의 지시서
instrument	상품
instrument trust	사후적 신탁
instrument for buying operation	매입대상채권
insubordination	발항
insufficient funds	잔고부족
insurable interest	피보험이익
insurable interest in property	물상피보험이익
insurable risk	보험대상이 되는 리스크
insurable value	보험가액
insurance	보험
insurance accounting	보험회계
Insurance Accounting and Statistical Association	보험회계통계협회
insurance activities	보험업무
insurance against death	사망보험
insurance amount	보험금액
Insurance Board	보험청
insurance broker	보험브로커
insurance broker's liability insurance	보험브로커 책임보험
Insurance Brokers Registration Council	보험브로커등록평의회
insurance business	보험업
insurance carrier	보험업자
insurance cartel	보험 카르텔
insurance claims	미수보험금
insurance claims unsettled	미결산보험금
insurance clause	보험약관
insurance collector	보험집금원
insurance companies blanket bond	보험회사포괄보증증권
insurance company	보험회사

insurance contract law 보험계약법
insurance control 보험통제
Insurance Council 보험심의회
insurance expense 보험료
insurance expense exhibit 보험경비명세서
insurance group 보험그룹
insurance law 보험감독법
insurance management 보험관리
insurance market 보험시장
insurance of medical expenses 의료비용보험
insurance of substandard lives 표준하체보험계약
insurance on mortagee's interest 저당보험
insurance payable at death 사망보험
insurance policy 보험증권
insurance pool 보험 풀
insurance premium 보험료
insurance premium deduction 보험료공제
insurance prepaid 선불보험
insurance principle 보험원리
insurance product firm 보험상품취급업자
insurance proposal form 보험계약신청서
insurance scheme 보험형연금
insurance science 보험학
insurance syndicate 보험 신디케이트
insurance tax 보험세
insurance to value 전부보험
insurance value 보험가액
insurance with bonus 특별배당금부보험
insurance with medical examination 진사보험
insurance with settlement options 선택권부 보험
insurance without medical examination 무진사보험

insured	피보험자
insured amount	보험금액
insured event	보험사고
insured peril	피보험 위험
ensured plan	보험형 연금
insurer	보험자
intaglio	요판
intake of foreign capital	외자도입
intake value	구입가격
intangible assets	무형자산
intangible capital	무형자본
intangible depreciable assets	무형감가상각자산
intangible depreciable property	무형상각자산
intangible effects	무형의 효과
intangible fixed assets	무형고정재산
intangible property	무형자산
intangibles	무형고정자산
integer programming	정수계획법
integral prat	중요한 부분
Integrated Circuit card	IC 카드
integrated organization	총합적 조직
integrated production	일괄생산
integrated services digital broadcasting	총합디지털 방송
integration	통산
integration of business	사업총합
intellectual property right	지적 소유권
intelligent building	인텔리전트 빌딩
intelligent encoding	지적부호화
intelligent manufacturing system	IMS, 지식제조 시스템
intelligent network	인텔리전트 네트워크
intemperance	음주벽, 폭음
intendant	감독관

intendment of law	법의 진의
intensive distribution	개방적 판로
intensive investment	집중투자
intention	의의
intention of concept	개념의 내포
intention to purchase	구입의 의의
intentional	고의의
inter industry analysis	산업연관분석
inter-bank	은행간의
inter-bank deposit	은행간의 예금
inter-bank exchange transaction	인터뱅크 환거래
inter-bank market	인터뱅크 시장
inter-bank rate	은행간 상장
inter-enterprise credit	기업간 신용
inter-imperialist competition	제국주의간 경쟁
inter-industry-relations table	산업연관표
inter-market spread	시장간 스프레드
inter-market trading system	시장간 거래시스템
inter-office account	본지점 계정
inter-office exchange adjustment account	환고환산차금
inter-office rate	본지점 상장
inter-period tax allocation	연도간 세배분
interaction	쌍방향성
interaction approach	상호작용
interactive	쌍방향
interactive television	쌍방향 TV
inter-affiliate trade	계열기업간 거래
interbank loan	인터뱅크 론
interbank rate	인터뱅크 상장
interbranch account	지점상호계정
interbranch loss	지점상호간 손실

interbranch profit	지점상호간 이익
interchangeability	호환성
intercommon	상호입회하다
intercompany account	회사간 계정
intercompany elimination	회사간 제거
intercompany loss	회사상호간 손실
intercompany profit	회사간 이익
intercompany transfer variance	내부환차익
interconnection	상호접속
interdepartment account	부문간 계정
interdepartmental profit	내부환 이익
interdiction	금치산
interdisciplinary	학제
interest	지분, 이해관계, 이권
interest advance	선불이자
interest after the maturity	기한후 이자
interest arbitrage	금리제정
interest arrears	지연이자
interest bearing	이자부
interest bearing issuance	유리발행
interest bill	이자어음
interest burden	이자부담
interest cap trading	금리 캡 거래
interest capitalization method	원가방식
interest claims	이자클레임
interest cost	이자비용
interest cover	이자비용
interest coverage ratio	금리부담률
interest differential	금리차
interest during construction	건설이자
interest earned	수취이자
interest equalization tax	금리평형설

interest for arrears 지연이자
interest for delay 연체이자
interest for delinquency 연체이자
interest futures 금리선물
interest in arrears 연체이자
interest included 원리합계
interest income 이자소득
interest incurred during construction 건설이자
interest method 이자법
interest on bond 사채이자
interest on borrowed 차입금이자
interest on borrowed fund 부채이자
interest on call loans 콜 론 이자
interest on call money 콜 머니 이자
interest on deposit 예금금리
interest on external bond 외채이자
interest on foreign currency deposits 외화예금이자
interest on government bond 공채이자
interest on government securities 국채이자
interest on guaranty capital 기금이자
interest on interest 손이자
interest on loans and discount 대출금이자
interest on loans on bills 어음대부이자
interest on loans rebated 대부금이자 할인
interest on overdrafts for export bills 환당 좌대이자
interest on postal savings 우편예금이자
interest on public bond 공채이자
interest on refund 환부가산금
interest on savings deposit 저금금리
interest on securities 유가증권이자
interest option transaction 금리옵션거래
interest parity 금리평가

interest payable	미지급이자
interest payment	이자지급
interest payment method	이자지급 방법
interest payments on foreign debt	대외채무이자지급
interest per annum	연리
interest policy	금리정책
interest prepaid	전수이자
interest rate	금리
interest rate abroad	해외금리
interest rate arbitrage	금리재정
interest rate arbitrage transaction	금리재정거래
interest rate change	이자율변화
interest rate collar	금리 컬러
interest rate control	금리조작
interest rate differential	금리차
interest rate floor	금리 최저한도
interest rate fluctuation	금리변동
interest rate futures	금리선물
interest rate futures contracts	금리선물계약
interest rate futures option trading	금리선물옵션
interest rate minded	금리 마인드
interest rate movement	금리동향
interest rate on borrowing	차입금 금리
interest rate on inter-bank deposit	은행간 예금금리
interest rate on loans	대출금리
interest rate on loans secured by time deposit	정기예금담보대출금리
interest rate on the Eurocurrency market	유로금리
interest rate on time deposit	정기예금금리
interest rate option	금리옵션
interest rate parity	이자율평가

interest rate raise 금리 상승
interest rate risk 금리 리스크
interest rate sensitive items 금리감응항목
interest sensitive products 금리민감형 상품
interest rate sensitive stock 금리 민감주
interest rate spread 금리 감응도
interest rate swap 금리 스왑
interest rate parity theory 이자평가이론
interest receivable 수취이자
interest receivable on bank deposits 미수은행 예금이자
interest received 수취이자
interest sensitivity of the pension surplus 연금잉여의 금리감응도
interest skimming 금리 분리
interest spread 금리차
interest surplus 이자차익
interest swap 금리 스왑
interest rate parity theory 이자율평가이론
interest swap bond 금리 스왑 채
interest tax 이자세
interest tax on delayed payment 연납에 드는 이자세
interest-bearing bank debenture 이자부 금융
interest-bearing bond 이자부채
interest-bearing debt 이자부 부담
interest-bearing security 이자부 증권
interested party 이해관계자
interference with trade 영업방해
interfirm analysis 기업간 분석
interim 거짓의
interim account 중간계정
interim audit 기중감사
interim call 중간분담금 불입청구서

interim closing	중간결산
interim dividend	중간배당
interim financial statements	중간재무제표
interim interest payment	중간지불이자
interim loan	연결융자
interim measure	경과조치
interim meeting	중간회의
interim premium adjustment	예납보험료의 잠정조정
interim receipt	가영수증
interim report	중간보고
interim return form	중간신고서
interim sales	중간매출
interim statement	중간계산서
interim tax return	중간신고
interlace	인터레이스
interlineation	행간기입
interlocking	연동
interlocking directorates	임원겸임
interlocking directors	겸임중역
interlocking stockholding	주식보합
interlocutory	중간의
interlocutory judgment	중간판결
intermarket	시장간
intermarket trading system	시장간 거래제도
intermediary	중개자
intermediary bank	중개은행
intermediary trade	삼국간 무역
intermediate accounting	중급회계학
intermediate lag	중간 래그
intermediate market	중간시장
intermediate target	운영목표
intermediate tariff	중간세율

intermediate technology	중간기술
intermediate term market outlook	중기예상
intermediating financial institution	금융중개기관
intern	억류하다
internal allocation	내부할당
internal analysis	내부분석
internal audit	내부감사
internal audit report	내부감사보고서
internal audit standard	내부감사기준
internal audit system	내부감사제도
internal auditing	내부감사
internal auditor	내부감사인
internal business analysis	내부경영분석
internal check	내부견제
internal check system	내부견제제도
internal consistency	내부정합성
internal control	내부통제
internal debt	내부 채무
internal evidence	내부증거
internal exposure hazard	내부 연소위험
internal factor	내부 요인
internal financing	내부 금융
internal information	내부 정보, 내부 자료
internal investment management	자가운용
internal labor market	내부 노동시장
internal liability	내부 부채
internal operation	내부운용
internal price	내부가격
internal rate of return	내부 수익률
internal reporting	내부보고
internal reporting system	내부보고제도
internal reserve	내부유보금

internal revenue bond	소득세지불 보증증권
Internal Revenue Code	미국 내국 세입법
Internal Revenue Code Section 482	미국 내국 세입법 제482조
Internal Revenue Service	미국 내국 세입청
internal rule	사내규정
internal structure	내부구조
internal tax	내국세
internal transaction	내부거래
internal transfer profit	사내 환이익
internalization theory	내부화이론
internalized order	내부화 주문
international accounting	국제기업회계
international accounting standards	국제회계기준
International Accounting Standards Committee (IASC)	국제회계기준위원회
international agency bond	국제기관정권
international agreed specialization	합의적 국제분업
International Air Transport Association	국제항공운송협회
international asset management	국제자산운용
International Atomic Energy Agency	국제원자력 기관
international auditing firms	국제감사법인
international balance of payment	국제수지
international bank for economic cooperation	국제경제협력은행
international bank for investment	국제투자은행
International Bank for Reconstruction and Development (IBRD)	국제부흥개발
international banking facility	국제은행업무
International Banking Facility (IBF)	국제은행업무기관
international banking operation	국제은행업무
international bond	국제본드

international broking	국제 중개업
international comparison	국제 비교
international capital	국제 자본
international capital market	국제 자본이동
international capital movement	국제 자본이동
international cartel	국제 카르텔
International Center for Settlement of Investment Disputes	국제 투자분쟁해결센터
International Chamber of Commerce (ICC)	국제상업회의소
International Chamber of Shipping	국제해운회의소
International Civil Aviation Organization	국제민간항공기관
International Committee for Accounting Co-operation	국제회계협조위원회
international commodity agreement	국제상품협정
International Confederation of Free Trade Unions (ICFTU)	국제자유무역노동조합연합
International Congress of Actuaries	국제 보험수리사 회의
International Convention for the Protection of Industrial Property	산업소권보호에 관한 국제조약
international corporation/firm	국제기업
International Court of Justice (ICJ)	국제사법재판소
International Criminal Police Organization	국제형사경찰기구
international currency	국제통화
international currency system	국제통화제도
international custom	국제관습법
International Depositary Receipts	국제예탁증서
International Development Association (IDA)	국제개발협회
international distribution	국제유통

international diversified investment 국제분산투자
international division 국제사업부
international division of labor 국제분업
international double taxation 국제 이중과세
international economics 국제경제학
International Energy Agency 국제 에너지 기관
international exchange 국제환
International Federation of Accountants (IFA) 국제회계사연맹
International Federation of Stock Exchanges 국제증권거래소연합
international finance 국제금융
International Finance Corporation (IFC) 국제금융공사
international financial institution 국제금융기관
international financial market 국제금융시장
international financial system 국제금융제도
international firm 국제기업
international fisher effect 국제 피셔효과
international fund 국제자금
International Fund for Agricultural Development 국제농업개발기금
international indebtedness 국제대차
international interest-spread 내외금리차
international investment 국제투자
international investment bank 국제투자은행
international investment trust 국제투자신탁
International Labor Organization (ILO) 국제노동기관
international law 국제법
International Law Association 국제법협회
international lease 국제 리스
international liquidity 국제유동성
international long-tern capital movement 국제장기자본이동

international managed currency system	국제관리통화제도
International Marine Satellite Telecommunication Organization	국제해사위성통신기구
International Maritime Organization	국제해사기관
international market	국제시장
international market price	국제시장가격
international marketing	국제마케팅
international marketing research	국제시장조사
international merchandise	국제상품
international monetary exchanges	국제금융거래소
International Monetary Fund (IMF)	국제통화기금
international monetary turmoil	국제통화불안
international money management	국제적 금융관리
international money market	국제금융시장
International Money Market of Chicago	시카고 국제통화시장
international movements of funds	국제자금이동
International Multinational Directory	국제다국적기업총람
international normals	국제 표준
International Olympic Committee	국제올림픽위원회
International Organization of Consumer's Unions	국제소비자기구
International Organization of Employers	국제경영자단체연맹
International Organization of Journalists	국제저널리스트 기구
International Organization of Securities Commissions	국제증권위원회기구
International Organization of Consumer Unions (IOCU)	국제소비자연맹
International Organization of Employer (IOE)	국제경영자단체연맹

International Peace Bureau	국제평화사무국
international portfolio	국제 포트폴리오
international portfolio diversification	국제분산투자
international production	국제생산
international public law	국제공법
international recognized standard	국제기준
International Red Cross	국제적십자
international relations	국제관계
International Resources Bank	국제자원은행
international securities	국제증권
International Securities Clearing Corporation	국제결제기관
international settlement	국제결제
international settlement currency	국제결제통화
international short-term capital transaction	국제단기자본거래
international short-term money market	국제단기금융시장
International Social Security Association	국제사회보험협회
international spread of risk	국제적 위험분산
International Standardization Organization	국제표준화기구
international stock	국제주권
international subcontracting	국제하도급
International Swap Dealers Association	국제교환딜러협회
international syndicate	국제기업조합
international tax law	국제조세법
International Telecommunication Satellite Consortium	인텔셋(ITSC)
International Telecommunication Union	국제전기통신연합

International Trade Commission 국제무역위원회
International Trade Secretariats (ITS) 국제노동조합연맹
international transaction currency 국제거래통화
international underwriting group 국제인수단
International Union Aviation Insurers 국제항공보험연합
International Union of Credit and Investment Insurers 국제수출신용보험기관
International Union of Marine Insurance 국제해상보험연합
international unit 국제단위
internationalization 국제화
interperiod income tax allocation 조직간 시스템
interpersonal perception 소득과세의 기간상호 배분
interpersonal perception 대인지각
interpleader 권리자 확인
interpolation 보간법
interpretation clause 해석조항
interpretation of cash flows 캐쉬 플로우의 견해
interregional analysis 지역연관분석
interrogation 취조
interruption effect 방해 효과
interruption of business 영업정지
interruption of prescription 시효의 중단
intersegment sales 사업구분간 매출
interstate commerce 주제통상
Interstate Commerce Commission 주제통상위원회
intertype competition 이업종간 경쟁
interunit pricing 부문간 대체가격의 결정
interunit transfer 부문간 대체
intervene 소송에 참가하다
intervening variable 중개변수
intervention 개입

intervention against market	역풍개입
intervention by selling dollars	날러판매 개입
intervention currency	개입 통화
intervention following market	역풍 개입
intervention level	개입수준
intervention operation	개입조작
intervention point	개인점
intervention purchase	개입매수
intervention rate	개입금리
intra vires	권한내에서
intra-contract spread	상품간 스프레드
intra-day high and low	일중고저치
intra-firm trade	기업내 무역
intra-group trade	기업그룹내 무역
intracompany transfer	내부대체
intracompany transfer price	내부대체가격
intrafirm analysis	기업내 분석
intramarginal intervention	허용변동 국내개입
intramarket	시장내
intraperiod income tax	소득과세의 기간내 배분
intraperiod tax allocation	세금의 기간내 배분
intrapreneuring	사내 기업
intraventure	사내 벤처
intrinsic deposit	본원적 예금
intrinsic value	본원적 가치
introduced stock	공개주
introducing	중계
introductory period	주문중계업자
introduction	도입부
introductory period	도입기
intrusion	불법점유
invalid card	무효카드

invalid coupon	무효이표
invention	발명
inventories of merchandise and supplies	저장품
inventor's certificate	발명자증
inventory	재고자산
inventory adjustment	재고조정
inventory assets	재고자산
inventory audit	재고자산감사
inventory capital	재고자본
inventory carrying cost	보관비
inventory certificate	재고증명서
inventory change	재고변동
inventory control	재고조사
inventory cycles	재고순환
inventory financing	재고금융
inventory investment	재고투자
inventory loss	재고손실
inventory method	재고자산계산법
inventory model	재고모형
inventory of security	담보목록
inventory profit	재고자산이익
inventory recession	재고리세션
inventory reserve	재고자산평가충당금
inventory sheet	재고표
inventory shipments ratio	재고율
inventory tag	재고표
inventory turnover	재고자산회전율
inventory unit	재고단위
inventory valuation	재고자산평가
inventory valuation adjustment	재고평가조정
inventory valuation method	재고자산평가방법

inventory valuation reserves	재고자산평가충당금
inventory value	재고평가액
inventory variation	재고자산증감
inventory-sales ratio	재고율
inventoryless system	무재고방식
inverse demand pattern	역수요 패턴
inverse floater	역 부동증권
inverse matrix	역행렬
inverse matrix table	역행렬표
inverse yield	역이자
invest in Britain bureau (IBB)	대영투자국
invested assets	운용자산
invested capital	투하자본
investigation of cause	원인조사
investigator	국제사찰관
investing activities	투자활동
investing public	대중투자가
investment	출자
investment abroad	해외투자
investment account	투자계정부문
investment advisor	투자고문
investment advisory industry	투자고문업계
investment advisory law	투자고문법
investment analysis	투자분석
investment and loan	투자융자
investment bank	투자은행
Investment Banking Financing Company	투자은행금융기관
investment boom	투자경기
investment buying	투자매수
investment by foreign investors	외국인 투자
investment climate	투자환경
investment club	투자클럽
investment center	투자센터

investment committee	투자위원회
investment company	두사회사
investment counselor	투자카운셀러
investment credit	투자공제
investment criteria	투자척도
investment currency	투자통화
investment curve	투자곡선
investment decision	투자결정
investment demand	투자수요
investment dollar	투자달러
investment environment	투자환경
investment expenditure	투자지출
investment expense	투자경비
investment flexibility	투자유연성
investment function	투자함수
investment function of profit principle type	이윤원리형 투자함수
investment fund	투자신탁
investment grade	투자적격
investment grade corporate	투자대상기업
investment horizon	소유기간
investment in affiliates	관계회사출자금
investment in capital	출자금
investment in kind	현물출자
investment in money	현금출자
investment in plant and machinery	설비투자
investment in securities	투자유가증권
investment in stocks	주식투자
investment income	투자소득
investment information sources	투자정보원
investment ledger	유가증권원장
investment letter	투자목적확인서
investment management company	투자고문회사

investment manager	투자매니저
investment market	투자시장
investment multiplier	투자승수
investment objectives	투자목표
investment of life insurance fund	생보자금투자
investment opportunities	투자기회
investment outlet	투자대상
investment overseas	해외투자
investment period	투자기관
investment philosophy	투자철학
investment policy	투자정책
investment profit	자기계정매수익
investment program	투자계획
investment propensity	투자성향
investment protection treaty	투자보호조약
investment purchased register	유가증권매입기입장
investment result	투자성과
investment return	이자
investment securities	투자유가증권
investment security	투자증권
investment selection summary	투자선택의 개괄
investment skeleton	기대외의 증권
investment sold register	유가증권매각기입장
investment stock	투자주
investment strategy	투자전략
investment tax credit	투자세액공제
investment trust	투자신탁
investment trust management company	투자신탁위탁회사
investment trust on securities	증권투자신탁
investment value	투자가치
investment year method	투자연도별 방식
investor	출자자

Investor Relations (IR)	인베스트 릴레이션
investors relations	투자자관계
invisible assets	무형자산
invisible hand	보이지 않는 손
invisible trade	무역외
invisible trade balance	무역외 수지
invitation	유인
invitation telex	권유 텔렉스
invoice	송장, 청구서
invoice book	결산장
invoice method	송장방식
invoice-book inward	상품결산장
invoice-book outward	상품송금장
involuntary	자발적이지 않다
involuntary bankruptcy	강제파산
involuntary conversion	강제교환
involuntary exchange	강제처분
involuntary insolvency	강제지급불능
involuntary transfer	강제적 양도
involuntary unemployment	비자발적 실업
involvement	관여
inward investment	대내투자
inwards reinsurance	수재보험
ipso facto	사실상
ipso jure	법률상
irrational tax	악세
irrecoverable cost	회수불능원가
irredeemable bond	불상환채
irregular installment payment	불평등지불
irregular practices	부정행위
irrelevant	관련성 없다
irreparable injury	회복불능의 침해

irretrievable deprivation	전망없는 상실
irrevocable	철회하지 않다
irrevocable letter of credit	취소불능신용장
irrevocable license	취소할수 없는 허가
irrigation right	수이권
issuance of bond	채권발행
issue	쟁점, 발행하다, 상표
issue at face value	액면발행
issue at intermediate price	중간발행
issue at market price	시가발행
issue at per	액면발행
issue by tender	입찰발행
issue management	문제처리방법
issue market	발행시장
issue of bond	기채
issue of public bonds	공공채발행
issue on fact	사실문제에 대한 쟁점
issue price	매출가격
issue standards	적채기준
issue tax	발행세
issue terms	발행조건
issue used in the average	평균주가채용상표
issue value	발행가격
issue capital stock	발행제주식자본금
issue shares	발행제주식
issuer	발행회사
issuer's cost	발행자비용
issues paper	토의보고서
issues to shareholders	주주할당
issuing bank	발행은행
issuing corporation	발행회사
issuing house	발행상사

item	항목
item depreciation	개별상각
item in transit	미달항목
item of account	계정항목
item parameter	항목특성가치
itemization	내역
itemized account	사역계정, 명세계정
itemized bill	명세서
itemized deduction	내역공제
items of business	영업종목
items of payment	지불항목
items of tax	세목

≪ J ≫

J curve effect	J 커브 효과
jacket	일반문언
Jane's Major Companies of Europe	유럽기업연감
Japanese Industrial Standards	JIS 규격
Japanese management	일본적 경영
jeopardy	위험
job	직무
job contents	업무내역
job cost	개별원가
job cost system	개별원가계산 제도
job description	직책
job enlargement	직무확대
job enrichment	직무충실
job evaluation	직무평가
job lot	소액거래
job order	작업지도서
job order cost system	개별원가계산법
job order costing	개별원가계산
job rotation	직무순환
job slip	작업전표
job specification	직무명세
job ticket	작업표
jobber	도매상인
jobber's turn	도매상의 시세폭
jobbing	회전상업
joinder	합병
joinder of cause of action	소송원인의 합병

joinder of offenses	범죄의 합병
joinder of parties	당사자의 합병
joinder of protests	합병심리
joint	공동의
joint account	공통계정
joint advertisement	공동광고
joint agreement	연합협약
joint and several	연대
joint and several bond	연대증서
joint and several guarantee	연대보증
joint and several liability	연대책임
joint and several obligation	연대채무
joint and several obligation of tax payment	연대납입책임
joint audit	공동감사
joint beneficiary	공동수취인
joint bond	합동채무
joint cost	결합비용
joint currency float	공동변동환율
joint development	공동개발
joint enterprise cooperative	기업조합
joint financing	공동융자
joint float	공동설립
joint floating exchange rate	공동변동환율
joint guarantee	공동보증
joint insureds	공동피보험자
joint investment	합병
joint labor management conference	노사협의
joint liability	공동책임
joint life annuity	연생연금
joint life insurance	연생생명보험
joint marketing	공동판매

joint obligation	합유채무
joint ownership	공유
Joint Photographic Expert Group	제이페크(JPEG)
joint probability	동시확률
joint product	연산품
joint project	공동사업
joint return	공동신고
joint right	합유
joint sales	공동판매
joint stock company	주식회사
joint surety	연대보증인
joint tenancy	합유부동산권
joint tenant	공동보유
joint trust	합동연용신탁
joint venture	조인트 벤처, 합작
joint-floating market system	공동변동상장
journal	분개장, 일기장
journal entry	분개장기입
journal ledger	분개장원장
journal slip	분개전표
journal voucher	분개전표
journalizing	분개
judge	판사
judge's chambers	판사실
judging	심사
judgment	판결
judgment creditor	판결채권자
judgment debtor	판결채무자
judgment in rem	대물판결
judgment nil dicit	무소답에 의한 결석판결
judgment nisi	가판결
judgment of definite liabilities	채무확정의 판결

judgment of exclusion on shareholders' rights	주권의 제권판결
judgment on merits	사실의 판결
judgment on the verdict	평결에 기초한 판결
judgment record	판결기록
judgment set-off	판결채권의 상쇄
judicature acts	재판소득
judicial bond	법정보증
judicial confession	재판상의 자유
judicial convention	재판상의 협정
judicial costs	재판비용
judicial economy	소송경제
judicial judgment	가법심의
judicial legislation	재판에 의한 입법
judicial notice	재판소당연의 확지
judicial power	사법권
judicial proceedings	사법수속
judicial sale	사법상의 매각
judicial valuation	법정평가
"Jumbo" clause	거액위험약관
jumbo risk	거대위험
jump process	점프 과도
jumping juvenile	자동증액소아보험
junior accountant	회계사보
junior bond	후순위채권
junior creditor	후순위채권자
junior director	청년중역
junior execution	수발집행
junior issue	하위증권
junior mortgage	후순위 저당
junior securities	열후증권
junior security	후순위담보

junior subordinated	하위열후
junk bond	정크본드
jurat	묶은 구절
juridical person	법인
juridical person for public interest	공익법인
juridical person in a public law	특수법인
juridical personality	법인격
jurisdiction	관할
jurisdictional defect	관할차이
jurisprudence	법률학
juristic act	법률행위
juror	배심원
jury	배심
jury box	배심원석
jury trial	배심원재판
jus in rem	대물권
just compensation	정당한 보상
just-in-time system	적시시스템
justice	재판관
justifiable act	정당행위
justifiable reason to apply	적용하는 적당한 의무
justification	정당화
juvenile comprehensive insurance	어린이종합보험

≪ K ≫

keep the books	장부에 기입하다
keep-out price	저지가격
keep-well agreement	건전성 유지계약
Keogh Plan	자영업자퇴직연금
key account	주요고객
key currency	기축통화
key executive insurance	경영자보험
key factor	주요인
key industry	기간산업
key reversal day	성장의 대전환일
key station	키 스테이션, 중앙국
keymoney	권리금, 보증금
keynesian	케인즈 학파
keynesian revolution	케인즈 혁명
keystone bond funds	키스톤 채권펀드
kick back	킥 백
killing	큰 벌이, 대성공
kilo bit	킬로 비트
kilo byte	킬로 바이트
kind of income	소득의 종류
Kingston Regime	킹스톤 체제
kinked demand curve	굴절수요곡선
Kitchen cycles	키친 순환
kite	융통어음
knock out	담합경매
knock-down product	넉다운 제품
knock-on effect	파급효과

knock-out option 정지조건부 옵션
knockdown price 작은 가격
knowledge engineering 지식공학
knowledge intensive industry 지식집약산업
Kondratieff wave 콘드라티에프의 파(派)

≪ l ≫

labeled price	매가
labor account	임금회계
labor agreement	노동협약
labor audit	노무감사
labor coefficient	노동계수
labor cost	노임
labor credit associations	노동금고
labor income	노동소득
labor laws	노동법
labor legislation	노동입법
labor management	노동관리
labor market	노동시장
labor & material payment bond	임금하청대금지급
labor productivity	노동생산성
labor rate standard	임률표준
labor rate variance	임률차이
labor regulations	노동법규
labor relative share	노동분배율
labor saving investment	노동력 절약투자
labor share	노동분배율
labor time variance	노동시간차이
labor trouble	노동분쟁
labor turnover	노동자이동
labor union group insurance	노동조합단체보험
labor variance	노무비차이
laborage	공임
laboratory test	실험실조사

lacuna	공백
Laffer curve	래퍼곡선
lag	늦추다, 늦게하다
lag analysis	지연분석
lag effect	지연효과
lag indicator	지행지수
laggard	지행주
lagging	래기지
lagging series	지행계열
laid down cost	도착원가
laissez-faire	자유방임
lame duck	레임 덕
land	토지
land and building	토지건물
land category	지목
land charges	토지부담
land cost	용지비
land development tax	택지개발세
land expropriation	토지수용
land expropriation right	토지수용권
land for residence	주택용토지
land for sale in lots	분양지
land improvement	토지개량
land improvement enterprise	토지개량사업
land improvement expenses	토지개량비
land ledger	토지대장
land lot	토지
land lot without construction	경지
land ownership	토지소유
land purchase for specified business	특정사업의 용지매수
land reform	토지개량
land registration	토지등기

land registry	토지등기소
land tax	토지세
land tax register book	토지과세대장
land taxation	토지세제
land-tenant	토지소유자
land tenure	토지보유
land-value tax	토지가격세
Lange-Gibbons code	랜지-기본스 강령
landed estate	지소
landed property	토지
landed proprietor	토지소유자
landing tax	입국세
landlord	지주
landlord's contingent liability policy	지주미필배상책임보험
landlord's liability policy	지주배상보험
lapping	(외상매출금 따위를) 돌리는 것
laps	집행
lapse	보험계약의 실효
lapse of the leasehold	차지권의 기간경과
lapse ratio	실효율
lapsed days	경과일수
lapsed share	실효주
lapsed time	경과시간
lapsing schedule of fixed assets	고정자산증감명세표
large amount deposit interest	거액예금금리
large amount time deposit	거액정기
large amount transaction	거액거래
large credit	고액채권
large depreciable property	대규모 상각자산
large institutional investors	대규모 기관투자가
large investment bank	대투자은행
large order	거액주문

large risks	거대리스크
large scale retail store law	대점법
large-capital stock	대형주
large-scale bond issue	채권의 대량발행
large-scale retailer	대규모 소매업자
Laspeyres formula	라스파이레스 방식
last close	전일종가
last cost method	최종구입원가법
last heir	최종상속인
last price	종가
last purchase method	최종구입원가법
last quotation	막장(또는 그때의 시세)
last resort	마지막 요청
last resort lender	최종 대부자
last survivor annuity	최종생존자 연금
last trading day	최종거래일
last-in first-out basis	후입선출기준
late payment charge	지연손해금
late presentation	제시의 지연
late shipment	선적지연
latent assets	비밀적립금
latent call option	잠재적 콜 옵션
latent demand	잠재수요
latent equity holdings	보유주의 포함
latent loss	보유손실
latent return	보유수익
latent unemployment	잠재실업
latent variable	잠재변수
latent warrant	잠재보증
lateral diversification	수평형 다각화
lateral thinking	수평사고
Latin American Integration Association	라틴아메리카통합연합

Latin American Working Group	라틴아메리카 자유무역연합
latter half	하반기
latter half of the year	후기
lattice approach	격자법
launch date	발행개시일
launching	기채, 모집발표
laundered money	세탁자금
law change	법률변경
law enforced territory	법시행지
law firm	법무법인
law for foreign securities company	외국증권업법
law of a maximum interest rate	이자제한법
law of combined and uneven development	결합 및 불균형 발전 법칙
law of commerce	상법
law of diminishing return	수익체감의 법칙
law of exception	예외원칙
law of increasing public expenditures	경비팽창의 원칙
law of indifference	무차별의 법칙
law of large numbers	대수의 법칙
law of nations	국제법
law of nature	자연법
law of obligations	채권법
law of ship's flag	기국법
law of subscription	출자법
law of substitution	대체법률
law of succession	상속법
law of the forum	법정지법
Law of the Sea Treaty	국제연합해양법조항
law office	법률사무소
law on bills	어음법
law reports	판례집

law school	법학 대학원
law with expiration date	시한입법
lawful	적법의
lawful age	성년
laws of realty	물건법
lawsuits	소송
lawyer	변호사
lawyer's fee	변호사료
lawyer's liability	변호사책임
lawyer's liability insurance	변호사배상책임보험
lay	초심자의, 비전문가의
lay off	노동자의 해고
lay underwriter	비전문 보험업자
lay-days	양육기간
lay-up	간단한 거래
lay-up refund	휴항에 따른 보험료
lead	재촉하다
lead auditor	주임감사원
lead manager	주간사
leader merchandising	미끼상품전략
leader of long side	매입당사자
leader of short side	매출당사자
leaders	인기종목
leading and lagging	리딩 앤 래깅
leading case	지도적 판례
leading counsel	주임변호인
leading index of business conditions	경기선행지수
leading indicator	경기선행지수
leading questions	유도심문
leading series	선행계열
leading share	인기주
leading underwriter	주도보험자

leads and lags	리즈 앤 래그즈
leak of kow-how	노하우 누수
lean production method	저이익 생산방식
leap	대폭증
learning curve	학습곡선
lease	임차권
lease bond	임대보증증권
lease contract bond	임대차계약 보험증 증권
lease in perpetuity	영구차지권
lease of land	차지증
lease of premises	토지건물임차계약
lease of property	자산임대
lease period	임차기간
lease tenant right	차지권
lease-holder	차지인
leased land	임차지
leasehold	차지권을 부여하는 계약
leasehold estate	임차부동산
leasehold interest insurance	임차권보험
leaseholder	차지권자
leasing business	임차업무
leasing company	임차회사
leasing contract	임차계약
least less developed countries	후발발전도상국
least-squares method	최소자승법
leave order	지정가주문예탁
ledger	원장
ledger account	원장회계(계정)
ledger assets	원장자산
ledger balance	원장잔고
ledger clerk	원장계원
leder folio	원장 페이지수

ledger transfer	원장대체
left-hand	자산남보의
legacy	유산
legacy duty	유산세
legal	적법의
legal ability person	능력자
legal adviser	법률고문
legal aid services	법률상담
legal benefit	법정급부
legal capacity	행위능력
legal capital	법정자본
legal channeling of liability	법률상의 책임집중제도
legal contract	적법계약
legal cost	소송비용
legal counsel	법률상담
legal department	법무부
legal document	법률서류
legal durable years	법정내용년수
legal duty	법률상의 의무
legal earned surplus reserve	법정이익준비금
legal entity	법적 실체
legal evidence	법률상의 근거
legal exemption from income tax	기초공제
legal fee	변호사 보수
legal fiction	가정
legal guardian	법정후견인
legal heir	장남(호주의 지위)
legal interest	법정이자(이율)
legal investment	투자적격대상
legal jeopardy	법적위험
legal lending limit	법정대출한도틀
legal liability	법정책임

legal liability insurance	법정책임보험
legal lien	선취특권
legal liquidation	법적정리
legal mortgage	보통법상의 저당권
legal notice	적법한 통지
legal opinion	변호사의견서
legal organ	정당한 권한을 지닌 기관
legal person	법인
legal portion of legacy	법정상속분
legal possession	법률상의 점유
legal presumption	법률상의 추정
legal procedure	재판수속
legal process	합법적 수속
legal rate	법정이율
legal rate of interest	법정금리
legal relations	법률관계
legal representative	법정대리인
legal reserve	법정준비금
legal reserve life insurance company	법정준비금적립 생명보험회사
legal subrogation	법정대위
legal tax cut	감세
legal tender	법정통화
legal term	법정기한
legal title	보통법상의 소유권
legal valuation	법정평가
legal valuation method of inventory	법정재고정리평가법
legal welfare expense	법정복리비
legally secured portion of succession	유류분
legatee	유산상속인
leges non scriptae	불문법
leges scriptae	성문법
legislative act	입법기관제정립법

legislative action	법적 조치
leisure expenditures	여가지출
leisure industries	레저산업
lender bank	대출은행
lender's preference	대부자 선호
lender's risk	대부자 위험
lending	대부
lending a street name	명의를 빌려줌
lending loss	대손(외상값이나 빚을 떼임)
lending operation	대출업무
lending policy	대출정책
lending rate	대출금리
lending securities	대증권
lending stock	대주
lending terms	대출조건
lending window	대부창구
length of service	재직기한
Leontief's paradox	레온티에프 역설
less than carload	소액취급
lessee	임차인
lesser evil	문제가 적은 제도
lessor	임대인
lessor owner	출자자
letter form	자체
letter of allotment	할당장
letter of attorney	위임장
letter of award	낙찰결정서
letter of confirmation of collateral	담보차입증
letter of credit	신용장
letter of credit confirming bank	신용장확인은행
letter of credit margin money	신용장개설보증금
letter of guarantee	보증장

letter of indemnification	보상계약서
letter of indemnity	손해보전계약서
letter of intent	합의확인서
letter of license	지급기일
letter of subrogation	권리이전증
letter of undertaking	각서
letter securities	비등록사모채
letter stock	매각제한주식
lettered rule	문자규칙
letters patent	특허증
letting out	계약체결
level	수준
level net premium	평균순보험료
level of consumption	소비수준
level of employment	고용수준
level of income	소득수준
level of interest rate	금리수준
level of significance	유의수준
level of society	사회수준
level of transaction	거래수준
level pay floating rate note	정액지급변동금리부채권
level payment	원리균등분할변제
level premium	평준보험료
level premium insurance	평준보험료식 보험
level premium normal cost on entry age	가입연령식 평준표준보험료
leveling of income	이익의 평준화
leverage	자금효율
leverage effect	레버리지 효과
leverage factor	레버리지 계수
leverage factor ratio	레버리지 비
leveraged buyout	레버리지드 바이아웃

leveraged holding 레버리지드 홀딩
leveraged lease 레버리지드 리스
leveraged option 레버리지드 옵션
leveraged position 레버리지드 포지션
leveraged recapitalization 레버리지드 리케피탈리재이션
leveraged stock 레버리지드 증권
leviable property 집행재산
levy 과세
Levy Group 레비 그룹
levy in kind 물납세
levy of attachment 재산차압
lex loci delictus 범죄지법
lex loci rei sita 소재지법
Lexis's principle 렉시스 원리
liabilities account 부채회계
liabilities and capital 부채 및 자본
liabilities exceeding assets 채무초과
liabilities for guarantee 보증채무
liabilities for guarantee against repairs 수선보증담보금
liabilities off the book 부외부채
liabilities on guaranties 보증채무
liability 채무, 책임
liability insurance 손해배상책임보험
liability management 부채관리
liability of estimated amount 견적에 의한 채무
liability reserve 책임준비금
liability reserves 부채성 담보금
liability side 부채측
liability swap 채무교환
liability with interest 유이자 부채
liaison office 주재원 사무소

libel	문서비훼
libel liability insurance	명예훼손배상책임보험
libelant	원고
liberalization of capital transactions	자본거래자유화
liberalization of exchange control	환전자유화
liberalization of interest rate	금리자유화
liberalization of trade	무역자유화
liberate	보석자 인도영장
liberty of contract	계약자유의 원칙
license	허가
license fees	면허료
license insurance	면허보험
license tax	면허세
licensed tax accountant	세무사
licensing agreement	라이선스 계약
licensing system	면허제
lie in grant	증서이전이 가능하다
lien	선취특권
lien of partners	조합원 선취특권
lien theory	선취특권이론
lienor	선취특권자
life annuity	종신연금
life annuity certain and continuous	보증기한이 있는 연금
life annuity due	초기지불연금
life annuity fund	생명연금적립금
life annuity insurance	종신연금보험
life annuity payable in arrears	기말지불생명연금
life annuity with no refund	무상환 종신연금
life insurance	생명보험
life insurance company	생명보험회사
life insurance credit	생명보험료 공제
life insurance medicine	생명보험의학

life insurance policy	생명보험증권
life insurance premium	생명보험료
life insurance premiums deduction	생명보험료 공제
life insurance trust	생명보험신탁
life reinsurance	생명보험의 재보험
life table	생명표
life tenant	영구차지인
life time policy	종신보험증권
life-interest	일생동안의 권리
life-long education	생애교육
life-to-call	전기상환까지의 거치기간
LIFO adaptation of retail method	후입선출매가환원법
LIFO reserve	후입선출법담보금
lifting charges	취급수수료
lifting of gold embargo	금수출해금
light and fuel expenses	광열비
light mortality	낮은 사망률
light oil delivery tax	경유인수세
light vehicle tax	경자동차세
lighting model	광원모델
like goods	동종상품
limit calculation	지정값 계정법
limit deviation	한계치
limit high	증시의 폭등을 억제하는 장치
limit low	증시의 폭락을 억제하는 장치
limit of age	가입연령범위
limit of cession	출재한도액
limit of cover	인수한도액
limit of credit	신용한도 손해보전
limit of indemnity	한도액
limit of liability	배상책임한도액
limit of overdrawn account	과진한도

limit of retention	보유한도액
limit on foreign investor's holdings of stocks	외국인 보유주식제한
limit order	지정가 주문
limit to credit reserve for bad debts	매손담보회계조입한도액
limitation of actions	출소기한
limitation on benefits provision	조세조약상 은전방지 조항
limitation on dividend	배당제한
limitation on interlocking	업무겸업제한
limitation on issue principle	쟁점주의
limitation on proprietary right of land	상지
limitational factor	제한적 요소
limitations of price theory	가격이론의 한계
limited annuity	유한연금
limited audit	한정감사
limited branching	특정지역지점설치
limited company	유한책임회사
limited convertibility	제한부 교환성
limited damages	확정손해배상액
limited distribution	한정적 판로
limited guarantee	제한적 보증
limited income method	소득원천세
limited legal tender	제한법화
limited liability	유한책임
limited obligation bond	특정재원채
limited partnership	유한책임조합
limited payment life policy	단기불입생명보험
limited policies	제한적 보험
limited premium payment	유한불입
limited private company	유한회사
limited tax liability	제한납세의무
limited tax rate	제한세율

limited-life assets	유한내용연수자산
limited factor	한정요인
line card	계약자 카드
line feed	(컴퓨터) 개행(改行)
line guide	인수한도표
line of business	영업과목
line of credit	대출예약틀
line organization	라인조직
line production	직선생산
line space	행간
lineal warranty	승계담보
linear accelerator	선형가속도계수
linear combination	선형결합
linear discriminant analysis	선형판별분석
linear discriminant function	선형판별함수
linear programming	선형계획법
linear regression	선형회귀
link financing	링크 금융
linked bond	링크채(연결채)
linked long term	가격변동에 따른 생명보험
liquid assets	유동자산
liquid capital	유동자본
liquid crystal display	액정 디스플레이
liquid deposit	유동성 예금
liquid part	유동부분
liquid ratio	유동비율
liquid reserve	유동성준비금
liquid stock	유통상표(종목)
liquid yield option note	해약옵션부 채권
liquid-asset hypothesis	유동자산가설
liquidate	현금화하다
liquidated account	확정회계

liquidated company	청산회사
liquidated damages	손해배상금
liquidated debt	확정채무
liquidating dividend	청산배당
liquidating partner	청산인
liquidation	청산
liquidation accounts	청산회계
liquidation affairs	청산사무
liquidation balance sheet	청산대차대조표
liquidation by compromise	계약을 해소하다
liquidation dividend	청산배당
liquidation final return	청산확정신고
liquidation income	청산소득
liquidation income from dissolution	해산에 의한 청산소득
liquidation matter	청산사무
liquidation of claim	채권변제
liquidation of duties	관세사정
liquidation of special bad debts	채권상각특별회계철회
liquidation of speculative accounts	가격정리
liquidation office	청산사무소
liquidation preference	청산우선권
liquidation price	청산값
liquidation proceedings	청산수속
liquidation profit and loss	청산손익
liquidation tax	청산소득세
liquidation value	청산가치
liquidator	청산인
liquidity	유동성
liquidity creation	유동성 창출
liquidity differential	유동성 격차
liquidity dilemma	유동성 딜레마
liquidity diversification	유동성 분산

liquidity effect	유동성 효과
liquidity index	유동지수
liquidity management	유동성 관리
liquidity of the banking system	은행 유동성
liquidity position	유동성 포지션
liquidity preference theory	유동성 선호이론
liquidity premium	유동성 프리미엄
liquidity ratio	유동성 비율
liquidity risk	유동성 위험
liquidity scarcity	유동성의 부족
liquidity trap	유동성 함정
liquidity-driven issue	유동성 상장주
liquidity-driven market	유동성 지향상장
liquidity-motivated transactions	유동성동기에 의한 매매
liquor tax	주세
lis pendens	계속중의 소송
list of members	회원명부
list of property	재산목록
list of shareholders	주주명부
list quotation	상장표
listed bond market	상장채권시장
listed company	상장회사
listed futures	상장선물
listed issue	상장종목
listed option	상장옵션
listed product	상장상품
listed securities	상장증권
listed stock	상장주
listing	상장
listing agent	상장대리인
listing requirements	상장심사기준
listing standard	상장기준

litigant 소송당사자
litigation 소송추행
litigation bond 소송보증증권
litigation expense insurance 소송비용보험
litigation officer 송무관
litigious right 계쟁권리
little guy 소액투자가
living 생계
living cost 생계비
living trust 생전신탁
Lloyd's broker 로이드 중개인
Lloyd's survey report 로이드 검사인보고서
Lloyd's surveyor 로이드 검사인
Lloyd's underwriter 로이드 보험자
load 판매수수료
load up 값에 의존함
loading 부가보험료
loading charges 본선인도비용
loading for expense 경비부가보험료
loading profit 비차익
loading surplus 부가익
loan 융자
loan account 대부회계
loan agreement 금전대차계약
loan application 융자신청
loan association 금융조합
loan business on real property 부동산 대부업
loan capital 차입자본
loan claims 대부채권
loan extension 차관공여
loan for carrying unsold inventory 체화융자
loan for consumption 소비대부

loan for education	교육대부
loan for exchange	교환대차
loan from banks	은행차입
loan insurance	대부금보험
loan interest rate	대출이율
loan ledger	대부원장
loan limit	융자한도
loan loss	대손
loan of subscription payment funds	불입융자대부
loan on bill	어음대부
loan on deeds	증서대부
loan on personal guarantee	보증대부
loan on real property	부동산대부
loan on security	담보대부
loan participation	대부지분참가
loan payable	차입금
loan rate	대출금리
loan receivable in securities	대부유가증권
loan received	차관형수
loan restrictions	융자규제
loan sales	대부채권매매
loan secured by deposit	예금담보대부
loan secured by government bonds or corporate debentures	공사채담보대부
loan secured by real estate	부동산저당대부금
loan secured by securities	유가증권담보대부금
loan shark	고리대
loan society	금융조합
loan spread	대부 스프레드
loan stock	대주
loan subparticipation	대출채권분매
loan to affiliated companies	계열융자
loan to financial institutions	금융기관 대부금

loan to subsidiary	자회사 대부금
loan transaction	대차거래
loan trust	대부신탁
loan value	대부한도
loan value method	대부가치법
loan with third party's guarantee	보증부대부
loan without interest	무이자대부
loan-deposit ratio	예대율
loanable fund	대부자금
loanable fund theory	대부자금이론
loanable resources	대부자금
loanable value	거는 것(가치창출을 도모하기 위해)
loans and bills discounted	대부금
loans and bills discounted accounts	대부금회계
loans and discounts by industry	업종별대출통계
lobbying	원외운동
lobbying contract	원외계약
lobster trap	랍스터 트랩
local	현지, 지방
local allocation tax	지방분여세
local area network	기업내 고속정보통신망
local authorities	지방자치단체
local autonomy	지방자치
local bond	지방채
local competition	지역경쟁
local content	로컬 콘텐트
local content ratio	현지조달률
local court	지방재판소
local credit	로컬 크레디트
local currency	현지통화
local custom	지방관습
local expenditure	지방비

local finance bureau	재무국
local government	지방자치단체
local government bond	지방채
local grant tax	지방교부세
local incorporation	현지법인
local law	지역법
local media	지방광고매체
local national	로컬 내셔널
local production factory	현지생산공장
local public entity	지방자치단체
local public finance	지방재정
local road tax	지방도로세
local sourcing	현지조달
local stock exchange	지방증권거래소
local tax	지방세
local transfer tax	지방양도세
local transport expenses	교통비
local value added	현지부가가치
localization	현지화
locals	로컬스
location	소재지
location clause	집적손해제한약관
location of industry	산업입지
location of loss or damage	손실발생지
location policy	입지정책
location specific advantages	입지특수적 우위
location theory	입지론
lock-in	확정
lock-up option	록업 옵션
lock-up period	록업 기간
locked market	동결시장
loco price	현장인도가격

locomotive theory	기관차론
locus sigilli	날인개소
logarithmic calculation	대수(로그) 계산
logarithmic spiral	로그스파이럴, 로그 나선
logistic function	로지스틱스 계수
lognormal distribution	대수(로그) 정규분포
lollipop tactic	롤리팝 전술
Lombard Street	롬바드 거리
Lome Convention	로메협정
London clearing banks	런던어음교환소가맹은행
London Club	런던클럽
London Depositary Receipts	런던예탁증서
London Inter-bank Bid Rate	런던은행간 수취인 금리
London Inter-Bank Offered Rate	런던은행간 출자인 금리
London refinance	런던 리파이넌스
long	매입(자)
long account	사는 값
long and medium-term interest rate	중장기 금리
long butterfly spread transaction	롱 버터플라이 스프레드 거래
long calendar spread transaction	롱 카렌더 스프레드 거래
long call	롱콜
long condor	롱 콘도르
long coupon	롱 쿠폰
long exchange	장기환
long hedge	매입(자) 헷지
long hedging	시세가 오를 것을 예상하고 사둠
long list/short list	롱 리스트/숏 리스트
long position	매입(자) 포지션
long position risk	매입(자) 위험
long put	롱풋
long service allowance	근속수당
long-term postponement of credit	채권보류

long treasury bond 장기미국재무성증권
long waves 장기파동
long-dated bill 장기어음
long-dated forwards 장기선도거래
long-form report 장문식보고서
long-run equilibrium 장기균형
long-term accounts payable in foreign currency 장기외화시세채무
long-term accounts receivable in foreign currency 장기외화시세채권
long-term bill 장기어음
long-term bond 장기채
long-term borrowing 장기차입금
long-term business 장기사업
long-term buying 장기매입
long-term capital 장기자본
long-term capital balance 장기자본수지
long-term capital gains 장기양도소득
long-term capital transaction 장기자본거래
long-term comprehensive insurance 장기종합보험
long-term contract 장기청부공사
long-term credit 장기신용
long-term debt 장기채무
long-term debt assumed 장기채무증가
long-term finance 장기금융
long-term forward exchange agreement 장기환예약
long-term fund 장기자금
long-term government bond 장기국채
long-term interest rate 장기금리
long-term investment 장기투자
long-term loan payable 장기차입금

long-term loan receivable 장기대부금
long-term money market 장기금융시장
long-term national bond of England 영국장기국채
long-term prime rate 장기 프라임 레이트
long-term solvency 장기지급능력
long-term suspended claims 장기보류채권
long-term wage agreement 장기임금협정
long term lease 장기임대차계약
long term yield 장기이율
look-back option 룩 백옵션
loop 루프
loose leaf book 루즈 리프식 장부
lord chief justice 수석 재판관
Lorenz curve 로렌츠 곡선
losers game 패자게임
loss 손실
loss adjustment 손해사정
loss and gain 손익
loss and gain account 손익회계
loss and gain statement 손익계산서
loss carryback 조연손실
loss cut 손절
loss due to spoiled work 공손비
loss expense 손해조사비
loss experience 손해경험
loss factor 손해팩터
loss for the current term 당기손실금
loss frequency 손해발생률
loss from bad debts 대손손실
loss from capital reduction 감자차손
loss from putting on reserve for deferred income tax 압축담보금조입손

loss function 손실함수
loss leader 값이 많이 떨어진 종목(상품)
loss making operations 적자경영
loss of income benefit 소득상실급부
loss of productivity claims 생산성상실크레임
loss of profits insurance 이익보험
loss of work 작업손실
loss on assets 자산손실
loss on foreign exchange 외국환차손
loss on property abandoned 자산폐기손
loss on property destroyed 자산상실비
loss on property revaluation 자산평가손
loss on retirement of fixed assets 제거손실
loss on sale of fixed assets 고정자산매각론
loss on sale on real estate 부동산 매각손
loss on securities sold 유가증권매각손
loss payable clause 제3자 지불약관
loss portfolio 로스 포트폴리오
loss ratio 손해율
loss reserve 지급준비금
loss retention 보유손해액
loss statistics 손해통계
loss-making division 불채산부문
losses ejusdem generis 동종위험에 따른 손해
losses on insurance claims 보험금차손
lost card 분실카드
lost instrument bond 분실증권보증증권
lot 거래시세
lot consolidation 조각주(단주)정리
lot sampling 랏 추출
lot-money 경매수수료
lottingout 분양

Louvre accord	루브르 합의
low capital intensive industry	자본집약성이 낮은 산업
low context	저맥락
low earth orbit	저고도궤도
low earth orbit communication	저궤도통신
low grade stocks	하위주
low growth	저성장
low income countries	저소득국
low input sustainable	저투입자속형의
low interest loan	저금리대부
low price	싼 가격
low risk stocks	안전성이 높은 주식
low-context culture	저맥락 문화
low-cost strategy	저비용전략
low-dividend stock	저배당 주식
low-involvement purchases	저관여형 구매
low-par issue	저액면주식
lower closing quotation	내림세의 막장
lower end of the market	저가격시장
lower in quotation	낮은 차액
lower limit rate	하한상장
lower price	낮은 가격
lower order goods	저차재
lower-of-cost-or-market method	저가법
lower-priced stock	하위주식
lowering of interest rate	금리인하
lowest taxable limit	과세최저한
loyalty rebate	특약리베이트
lucrative capital	관리자본
luminance	휘도
luminance signal	휘도신호
lump sum settlement	럼섬해결

lump-sum contract	정액청부계약
lump-sum freight	총괄운임
lump-sum payment	일괄지불
lump-sum payment of dividends at maturity	수익만기지불
lump-sum pension	일시은급
lump-sum purchase	일괄구입
lump-sum settlement	보험금 일괄지불
luxury tax	사치세
lying down	계약이행거절

≪ m ≫

M2+CD Statistics	M2+CD 통계
Maastricht Treaty	마스트리히 조약
machine bookkeeping	기계부기
machine plate	쇄판
machine tool	기계공구
machine-hour rate	기계시간율
machine-hour rate method	기계시간율 배부법
machinery	기계
machinery and equipment	기계장치
machinery and tool	기기
machinery insurance	기계보험
macroeconomic	거시경제적
macroeconomic factor	거시 경제요인
macroeconomic model	거시 경제모형
macrofunction	매크로 기능
macrohedge	매크로 헷지
macroview	대세관
magistrate	하급판사
magnet optical disk	MO 디스크
magnet store	핵점포
mail confirmation	메일 컨퍼메이션
mail credit	메일 크레디트
mail credit facility	메일 크레디트 팩실리티
mail days	우편수
mail exchange bill	문서환
mail transfer	우편환

mail transfer payable	송금환
mail-order	통신판매
mail-order loan	메일대부
mailing cost	우송료
main account	주요회계
main bank	메인 뱅크(주거래 은행)
main books	주요장부
main budget	본예산
main customer	주요거래
main income earner	주요소득자
main materials	주요원재료
main office	주요사무소
maintainability	보전성
maintained markup	실현치인액
maintenance	유지
maintenance and repairs	수선비
maintenance bond	하자보수보증증권
maintenance call	추가증거금
maintenance clause	부양약관
maintenance cost	유지비
maintenance department	영선과
maintenance expense	유지비, 계약유지비
maintenance fee	관리비
maintenance funds	유지자금
maintenance lease	메인테넌스 리스
maintenance margins	유지증거금
maintenance of books and records	장부서류의 정리보존
maintenance of capital	자본유지
maintenance of competence	능력의 유지
maintenance of financial capital	화폐 자본유지
maintenance of membership	조합원 자격유지
maintenance of physical capital	실제 자본유지

maintenance reserve 유지준비금
major 큰손(거물)
major bottom 대강
major casualties 주요사고
major cycles 주순환
major economic power 경제대국
major hospitalization insurance 고액입원비보험
Major Import Agreement 주요수입화물료율협정
major industry 주요산업
major market index 메이저 마켓지수
major medical expense insurance 고액치료비 보험
major move 메이저 무브
major multinational grain firms 곡물 메이저
major order 대량수주
major peak 최고시세
major product 주제품
major raw materials 주요원재료
major relationship bank 주력은행
major stockholders 주요주주
major trend 주요 트렌드
majority 다수
majority control 과반수지배
majority-owned forign affiliate 과반수소유해외계열사
majority-owned subsidiary 과반수소유자회사
make a downward revision 하향수정하다
make good 배상하다
make two-sided markets 쌍방이 값을 매김
make up 되돌리다
make-ready time 단취시간
make-up 할부
maker 작성자
making up of a deficit 적자보전

mala fides	악의
malefactor	유죄로 인정된 사람
malice	범의(범죄를 자행한 의도)
malicious act	악의적 행위
malicious arrest	부당한 체포
malicious damage clause	악의적 손해담보약관
malign neglect	유해한 태만
malpractice	의료과오, 부당행위
malpractice coverage	과실담보
malpractice insurance	전문직 과실책임보험
malversation	공금사취
man-power development	능력개발
man-to-man system	대인비교법
managed crawling peg	관리 크로링 펙
managed currency	관리통화
managed currency system	관리통화제도
managed float	관리변동환율
managed floating rate system	관리프로팅
managed fund	합동운용펀드
managed liabilities	관리채무
managed price	관리가격
managed trade	관리무역
management	관리자
management accounting	관리회계
management agreement	경영위탁계약
management area	관리영역
management audit	경영감사
management business of investment	투자신탁위탁업무
management buyout	매니지먼트 바이아웃
management by objective	목표관리
management capacity	관리능력
management company	투자신탁위탁회사

management concept	관리이념
management consultant	경영컨설턴트
management consulting	기업집단
management contract	매니지먼트 컨트랙트
management cycle	매니지먼트 사이클
management effect	관리효과
management fee	간사수수료
management function	관리직능
management group	인수간사단
management hierarchy	관리계층
management information system	경영정보시스템
management labor relations	노사관계
management of collateral	담보관리
management of indirect cost	간접부문합리화
management of juristic act	법무처리
management of property	재산관리
management of supply	공급관리
management participation	경영참가
management participation right	경영참가권
management philosophy	경영이념
management plan	경영계획
management principles	관리원칙
management resources	경영자원
management responsibility	경영자책임
management review	경영감사
management service for bill for collection	징수어음관리서비스
management simulation	매니지먼트 시뮬레이션
management strategy	경영전략
management supervisor	감독관
management through figures	계수관리
management tool	관리수단

manager	간사
manager's contribution	매니저의 기여도
manager-client relations	투자관리자와 고객의 관계
managerial resources	경영자원
managers	간사단
managing bank	간사은행
managing committee	경영위원회
managing underwriter	간사증권
mandate	맨데이트
mandate on remission	환송명령
mandatory	위임통치국
mandatory clause	필수조건
mandatory control	법적 규제
mandatory control program	강제관리계획
mandatory injunction	명령적 차지명령
mandatory redemption	강제상환
mandatory securities valuation reserve	법정유가증권평가준비금
mandatory sinking fund requirement	강제적 감채기금조항
mandatory valuation reserve	법정평가손적립금
manifest	적하목록
manifesto	선언
manipulation	조작
manipulation of stock price	주가조작
manipulation of the market	가격조작
manner of amortization	상환방법
manpower accounting	인적회계
manpower plan	인원계획
manual manipulator	매뉴얼 매니플래이터
manufacture order	제조 지도서
manufactured goods	제품
manufactured imports	제품수입

manufacturer's risks	제조자 위험
manufacturing accounting	공업회계
manufacturing bookkeeping	공업부기
manufacturing burden	제조간접비
manufacturing cost accounting	제조원가계산
manufacturing department	제조부문
manufacturing expenses	제조경비
manufacturing expenses budget	제조간접비예산
manufacturing expenses ledger	제조간접비원장
manufacturing license	제조허가
manufacturing process	제조공정
manufacturing statement	제조원가보고서
manufacturing taxation	제조과세
manufacturing-retailer alliance	제판동맹
maquiladora	마기라도라 멕시코 자유무역지역의 변형
margin	위탁증여금, 차금
margin account	증거금 회계, 신용거래구좌
margin buying	신용을 삼
margin call	추가증거금
margin collateral	신용거래위탁보증금
margin debt	증거금 부채
margin deficiency	증거금 부족
margin money	유지증거금
margin money system	증거금 제도
margin of safety	안전여력
margin of solvency	지불여력
margin on commodity futures	상품선물거래의 증거금
margin rate	증거금률
margin rations	이익폭률
margin required method	필요증거금법
margin requirements	위탁보증금률
margin trading	신용거래

margin transaction 증거금거래
marginal analysis 한계분석
marginal balance 한계이익
marginal capital coefficient 한계자본계수
marginal capital expenditure 한계자본지출
marginal clauses 난외약관
marginal condition 한계조건
marginal cost 한계비용
marginal cost curve 한계비용곡선
marginal cost of production 한계생산비
marginal costing 한계원가계산
marginal credit 한계신용
marginal deduction system 한계공제제도
marginal effect 한계효과
marginal efficiency 한계효율
marginal factor 한계요소
marginal income statement 한계손익계산
marginal loan-deposit ratio 한계예대율
marginal net suitability 한계도매값 적합도
marginal principle 한계원리
marginal production 한계생산
marginal productivity 한계생산성
marginal profit 한계이익
marginal profit ratio 한계이익률
marginal propensity to consume 한계소비성향
marginal propensity to import 한계수입성향
marginal propensity to save 한계저축성향
marginal rate of return 한계수익률
marginal ratio 한계비율
marginal returns 한계수익
marginal revenue 한계수입
marginal rise 미증(조금 오름)

marginal seal 사인(사용하지 않아버린 인장 따위)
marginal tax rate 한계세율
marginal theory 한계이론
marginal unit cost 한계단위원가
marginal utility 한계효용
marginal value 한계가치
marginal value curve 한계가치곡선
margins of solvency 지급여력
marine adventure 항해사업
marine and transport insurance 해상 및 운송보험
marine cargo insurance 화물해상보험
marine cargo policy 화물해상보험증권
marine casualty 해난
marine clasuse 해상보험조항
marine hull insurance 선박해상보험
marine insurance 해상보험
marine insurance account 해상보험회계
marine insurance policy 해상보험증권
marine perils 해상위험
marine protest 해난보고서
marine surveyor 해사검사관
marine transportation 해운
mariner 해원
maritime 해사의
maritime association 해사협회
maritime belt 영해
maritime court 해사재판소
maritime hypothecation 해사저당
maritime law 해사법
maritime lien 해사선취특권
maritime perils 해상위험
maritime traffic 해운

mark bond	마르크채
mark down	가격인하
mark to market	일일결제
mark to the market	시가평가
mark up	가격인상
mark-on required	필요가격 인상액
marked cheques	기호 수표
marker risk	시장위험
market	시장, 상장
market analysis	시장분석
market area	시장지역
market basket contract	마켓바스켓 방식
market basket trading	시장바스켓 거래
market beta	시장베타
market capitalization	시가총액
market claim	시장 크레임
market conduct	시장행동
market control	시장지배
market crash	상장하락
market creating effect	시장창조효과
market cycle	시장주기
market demand	시장수요
market demand curve	시장수요곡선
market demand function	시장수요함수
market development	시장개발
market dynamics	시장역학
market economy	시장경제
market economy model	시장경제모델
market efficiency	시장의 효율성
market equilibrium	시장균형
market equilibrium curve	시장균형곡선
market expansion effect	시장확장효과

market expectation 시장예측
market extinction 시장소멸
market failure 시장의 실패
market hours 입회시간
market impact 시장으로의 영향
market in hand contract 판매조건부 계약
market index 시장지수
market information center 시황정보센터
market interest rate 시중금리
market leaders 시장주도주
market maker 마켓메이커
market making condition 값이 결정되어 거래가 이루어지는 상황
market making function 값이 결정되어 거래가 이루어지는 기능
market manipulation 상장조종
market maturity 시장성숙
market mechanism 시장기구
market method 시가법
market milking 시장을 조종하다
market momentum 시장의 기세
market multiple 시장배율
market multiple method 상랑주가 비교법
market niche strategy 틈새시장 전략
market on close 종가지정 주문
market opening 시장개방
market order without limit 과정주문
market out clause 마켓 아웃 조항
market overt 공개시장
market overview 시장개황
market penetration 시장침투
market portfolio 시장포트폴리오
market potential 시장잠재력
market prediction 시장예측

market price	시장가격
market price basis	시가주의
market of risk	위험부담시장가격
market price of stock	주가
market principle	시장원리
market psychology	시장심리
market quotation	시장시세
market rate	시장상장
market rate of interest	시장이자율
market recovery	시황회복
market report	시황보고
market research	시장조사
market rhythm	시장기조
market risk	가격시장 위험
market sector	시장섹터
market segment	시장구분
market segmentation	마켓 세그멘테이션, 시장 분할
market sensitivity	시장감응도
market sentiment	시장동향(정서, 경향)
market share	시장점유율
market stabilization	시장안정조작
market standing	시장내 지위
market structure	시장구조
market survey	시장조사
market timing	마켓 타이밍
market timing assessment	시장 타이밍 평가
market transaction	거래
market valuation	시장평가
market value	시장가격, 시가
market value basis	시가주의
market value clause	시장가격약관
market value method	시가법

market value of inventory	재고정리자산의 시가
market value of weighted index	시장가치가중평균지수
market yield	시장이율
market-if-touched order	마켓-이프-터치 오더
market-on-close order	마켓-온-클로즈 오더
market-oriented	시장지향형
marketability	시장성
marketable debt securities	시장성이 있는 채권
marketable securities	시장성증권
marketable title	매매에 적합한 권리
marketing	마케팅
marketing agreement	판매협정
marketing channel	판매경로
marketing channel selection	마케팅경로선정
marketing control	마케팅 통제
marketing control system	마케팅 통제시스템
marketing cost	판매비
marketing cost accounting	마케팅 원가계산
marketing cost analysis	마케팅 원가분석
marketing decision	마케팅 결정
marketing decision support system	마케팅의사결정지원시스템
marketing decision variable	마케팅 결정변수
marketing environment	마케팅 환경
marketing expense	판매비
marketing force	마케팅 요인
marketing function	마케팅 기능
marketing intermediary	마케팅 중개업자
marketing monopoly	마케팅 독점
marketing opportunity	마케팅 기회
marketing organization	마케팅 조직
marketing performance	마케팅 성과
marketing phenomena	마케팅 현상

marketing practices	마케팅 관행
marketing relativism	마케팅 상대주의
marketing research company	시장조사회사
marketing research control	시장조사계약
marketing risk	마케팅 위험
marketing stimuli	마케팅 자극
marketing structure	마케팅 구조
marketing tactics	마케팅 전술
marketing theory	마케팅 이론
markup cancellation	가격인상정정
markup pricing	가격인상법
markup reduction planning	가격인하계획
marry	매리
marrying transaction of securities company	증권매리
marshal	집행관
marshaling assets	재산순위결정
marshaling securities	담보권 행사의 순위결정
Marshall curve	마샬 곡선
Marshallian demand curve	마샬적 수요곡선
masking	매스킹
mass consumption society	대중소비사회
mass culture	대중문화
mass distribution	대량유통
mass media	매스 미디어
mass merchandiser	매스 머천다이저
mass merchandising strategy	매스 머천다이징 전략
mass production	대량생산
mass risks	대중위험
mass sales	대량추장판매
mass society	대중사회
mass transportation	대량수송

master letter of credit	원신용장
master plan	기본계획
master policy	일괄증권
match	일치시키다
match making	균형(이 잡힘)
matched book	매매의 일치
matched maturities	기간일치
matched order	공모매매
matching	대응
matching costs and revenues	비용수익의 대응
matching ratio	조회 적합률
matching swap	대응 스왑
matching transaction	대응 거래
mate's receipt	본선수취증, 본선화물수취증
material	원료, 재료
material allegation	중요주장
material alternation	중요변조
material control	재료관리
material cost	재료비
material cost budget	재료비 예산
material damage	물적손해
material evidence	중요증거
material fact	중요사실
material for repair	수리용 재료
material in process	제작재료비
material misrepresentation	중대하게 되는 부실표시
material price variance	재료소비가격차이
material quantity variance	재료수량차이
material requirement program	자재소요량계획
material variance	실질적 차이
materiality	중요성
materiality principle	중요성 원칙

materials budget 재료예산
materials department 자재부
materials distribution sheet 재료분개장
materials for investigation 조사자료
materials in storage 저장원 재료
materials inventory 재료재고조사 많음
materials ledger 재료원장
materials on hand 재고재료
materials price standard 재료표준가격
materials purchased 재료구입조사
materials purchased report 원재료 구입보고서
materials received report 원재료 수입보고서
materials requirements planning 자재요청계획
materials returned report 원재료 반환표
materials specification 재료시방서(示方書), 재료사양서
materials usage curve 자재사용곡선
materials variance 재료비 차액
maternity benefit 출산급부
maternity insurance 임신출산보험
mathematical economics 수리경제학
mathematical expectation 수학적 기대치
mathematical model 수학적 모형
mathematical program 수리계획법
mathematical reserve 수리적 책임준비금
mathematical statistics 수리통계학
matrimonial domicile 혼인상의 주소
matrimony 호인상태
matrix 행렬
matrix algebra 행렬 대수
matrix multiplier 행렬 승수
matrix organization 매트릭스 조직
matter 기초사실

matter in deed	증서사항
matter in issue	쟁점사항
matter of record	기록사항
mature	기간이 임박하다
mature company	성숙기업
mature economy	성숙경제
mature phase	성숙단계
mature plans	성숙한 플랜
mature product strategy	성숙제품전략
matured bill	만기어음
matured bond	만기채권
matured liability	만기채권
maturing liability	만기에 다다른 채무
maturity	만기
maturity basis	만기일 시세
maturity date	만기일
maturity distribution range	만기분포차
maturity gap exposure	운용과 조달기간의 갭
maturity list	만기일표
maturity repayment	만기상환금
maturity stripping	머츄어리티 스트리핑
maturity structure	만기일 구성
maturity value	상환가액
maturity-designated time deposit	기일지정 정기예금
maultichannel access radio system	MCA 무선
maverick risk	이단자 위험
maximal collateral	근저당
maximin criterion	맥시민 기준
maximization	최대화
maxims	법률격언
maximum and minimum tariff system	최고최저세율제

maximum demand 최대수요
maximum effort plan 최대노력계획
maximum inventory 최대재고량
maximum limit for interest rate 부리최고한도
maximum limit of fluctuation 스탑가격
maximum limit of overdraft 대월극도액
maximum limit system 최고발행액 제한제도
maximum loan value 대출한도액
maximum operating stock 최대운전재고량
maximum possible loss 발생가능최고손해액
maximum price change limit 시세차 제한
maximum probable loss 최고손해액
maximum retention 최고보유액
maximum special depreciation allowance 특별상환한도액
maxmil rate 맥스밀 레이트
mayhem 신체상해
McCarthy's Information Service 맥커시 정보 서비스
mean absolute deviation 평균절대편차
mean absolute error 평균절대오차
mean curve 평균곡선
mean deviation 평균편차
mean difference 평균차
mean price 중간값
mean reversion 평균회귀
mean reverting 평균재귀
mean reverting process 평균회귀과정
mean squared error 평균자승오차
mean sum insured 평균보험금액
mean test 수입조사
mean time between failures 평균고장간격
mean time to repair 평균수리시간

mean value	중간값
mean for hedging	헷지수단
mean of foreign payment	대외지불수단
measure for monetary ease	금융완화조치
measure of association	속성상관
measure of central tendency	대표값
measure of dispersion	산문도
measure of indemnity	손해보전의 한도
measure of investment	투자척도
measure of productivity	생산성 측정
measure of return	수익률 측도
measure of risk	위험측도
measure of value	가치적도
measurement contract	측정계약
measurement control	측정관리
measurement of attitude	유효성
measurement of effectiveness	유효성 측정
measuring effectiveness	계측유효성
measuring results	계측결과
mecena	메세나
mechanical efficiency	기계효율
mechanical recorder method	기계장치기록방식
mechanical trading	기계화거래
mechanism	기구
mechanization method	기계화 방식
mechanized accounting	기계화 회계
mechatronics	메카트로닉스
media	매체
media advertising	매체광고
media control	매체지배
media decision	매체결정
media effect	매체효과

media mix	매체믹스
media selection model	미디어선택모형
median	중위수
mediate descent	간접상속
mediate powers	부수권한
Medicaid	연방의료부조제도
medical assistance	의료보조금
medical certificate	의사진단서
medical corporation	의료법인
medical credit	의료비 공제
medical examination	의료심사
medical expense insurance	의료비 보험
medical expenses	의료비
medical expenses deduction	의료비공제
medical jurisprudence	법의학
medical malpractice	의료과오
medical payment coverage	의료비 담보
medical payments insurance	의료지불보험
medical professional liability	의료손해배상책임
medical selection	의료서비스 선택
medical treatment clause	의료신고약관
medical underwriting	의무사정
medicalinsurance	의료보험
medico-actuarial science	의료수리학
medium of capital transfer	자본이전수단
medium-term government bond fund	중기국채펀드
medium-term bond	중기채
medium-term fixed rate government bond	중기이자부국채
medium-term government bond fund	중국펀드
medium-term loan	중기대부
medium-term note	미디엄 텀 노트

medium-term outlook	중기전망
meeting of bond-holders	사채권자 집회
meeting of promoters	발기인회
meeting of representative policy holders	사원총대회
meeting of shareholders	주주총회
mega byte	메가 바이트
mega transport network	메가 트랜스포트 네트워크
megamarketing	메가마케팅
megaselling	메가셀링
melon cutting	고액배당
member bank	회원은행
member banks of the clearing house	어음교환소 회원은행
member firm	회원회사
member organization	회원회사
member's fee	거래소회비
member's store	가맹점
member's voluntary winding-up	주주에 의한 임의청산
membership	회원권
membership business	회원비지니스
membership fee	회비
membership group	소속단체
membership in the capacity of a corporation	회사명의의 회원
memorandum	협정서, 면책보합조항
memorandum decision	이유를 제외시킨 판결
memorandum for offering	모집요강
memorandum goods	시험판매상품
memorandum of alteration	특허에 관한 일부포기서
memorandum of association	기본정관
memorandum of balance sheet audit	대차대조표감사각서
memorandum of protest	거절증서

memorandum price 비망가액
memorandum value 비망가격
memorandum-check 부제시특약수표
memorial dividend 기념배당
memory 기억
mens legislatoris 입법취지
menu approach 메뉴 어프로치
mercantile agency 상사대리
mercantile block insurance 판매업자일괄보험
mercantile credit 기업간 신용
mercantile law 상업법
mercantile paper 상업어음
mercantile partnership 상업조합
mercantile risk 상품위험
merchandise 상품
merchandise account 상품회계
merchandise assortment 물품을 갖춤
merchandise book 상품판매장
merchandise bookkeeping 상업부기
merchandise budget 상품예산
merchandise certificate account 상품권회계
merchandise control 상품관리
merchandise cost 상품원가
merchandise in transit 미달상품
merchandise inventory 상품재고, 재고정리상품
merchandise knowledge 상품지식
merchandise ledger 상품원장
merchandise loss 상품로스
merchandise management 상품관리
merchandise mart 머천다이즈 마트
merchandise of approval floater 시용상품포괄보험
merchandise procurement cost 상품조달원가

merchandise resources 매입처
merchandise turnover ratio 상품회전율
merchandiser 머천다이저
merchandising 머천다이징
merchant bank 머천트 뱅크
merchant banker 투자은행가
merchant fee 가맹점 수수료
merchant guild 상인 길드
merchant insurance 상인 보험
merchant law 상업법
merchant protective bond 상인보호보증증권
merchantable 시장성이 있음
mere jus 점유를 동반하지 않는 권리
merely nominal persons 단순명의인
merger 합병, 혼동
merger and acquisition 인수·합병
merger of guaranty 보증계약의 혼동에 의한 소멸
merger terms 합병조건
Mergers Panel 합병패널
merit goods 가치재
merit increase 성공보수
merit rating 보장요율제
merits 실체
mesne 중간의
message area 단위통화구역
message channel 메시지 경로
message effect 메시지 효과
messenger floater 메신저 일괄보험
meta-communication 메타 커뮤티케이션
metamarketing 메타 마케팅
metalized lithography 금속평판
metes and bounds 토지경계

method	방법
method of bonus allocation	계약자배당방식
method of comparative analysis	비교분석법
method of fixed percentage on cost	정률법
method of policy dividend allocation	계약자 배당방식
method of price of last purchase	최종 매입원가법
methodical approach	계통적 어프로치
methodology	방법론
metromarket	수도권시장
metropolitan	수도의
metropolitan inhabitant tax	도민세
mezzanine bond	열후사채
mezzanine bracket	메자닌 브랙켓
mezzanine debt	메자닌 채무
mezzanine finance	매자닌 파이넨스
mezzanine money	전환사채
Multifiber Arrangement (MFA)	다국적섬유협정
Most-favoured Nation clause (MFN clause)	최혜국 조항
M-form organization	M형조직
microanalysis	마이크로 분석
microbehavioral sales model	마이크로 행동적 판매모형
microcomponent sales model	마이크로 구성요소 판매모형
microhedge	마이크로 헷지
mid-term cancellation	중도해약
middle class	중간층
middle rate	중간값
middle-sized stock	중견주
middleman	중계업자
military government	군정
military jurisdiction courts	군사재판소
milline rate	미들라인 레이트

Million Instruction Per Second	MIPS(100만분의 1초)
Milne's table	밀른 생명표
mind share	마인드 쉐어
mineral product tax	광산세
mineral properties mining right	광업권
mini. max. bond	미니 맥스 채
mini-refunding	미니 리펀딩
minimil rate	미니밀 레이트
minimum age requirement	최저수급연령
minimum capital system	최저자본금제도
minimum cost principle	최소비용원칙
minimum cost rule	원가비교법
minimum denomination on which interest in calculated	부리단위
minimum exempt income	최저면세소득
minimum fluctuation unit	최소변동단위
minimum freight	최저운임
minimum funding standard	최저적립기준
minimum inventory	최저재고
minimum lease payment	최저리스 지불액
minimum lending rate	최저대출율
minimum liability	최소부채
minimum liquidity ratio	최저유동성 비율
minimum margin	최저이폭
minimum margin requirement	최저증거금률
minimum marginal cost	최소한계비용
minimum payment	최저지불액
minimum premium	최저보험료
minimum profit	최소이윤
minimum quantity	최저주문량
minimum rate	최저료율
minimum rate of interest	최저이율

minimum sacrifice	최저의 희생
minimum service requirement	최저의무기간
minimum stock	최저재고
minimum surplus	자본의 최저한도
minimum tax	최저과세
minimum value	최소치
minimum wage	최저임금
minimum wage system	최저임금제도
mining accounting	광업회계
mining concession	채굴권
mining lease	광업임차권
mining license	광업권
mining location	광업권취득
mining partnership	광업조합
mining property	광업자산
mining rent	채광료
mining rights	채굴권
mining royalty	광구사용료
mining tax	광업세
ministerial ordinance	성령
ministerial power	사무적 권능
minor	미성년자
minor account	미성년자 거래계좌
minor cycle	소순환
minor loss	소손해(적은 손해)
minor rally	소폭회복(소규합)
minor service	2류 서비스
minor tax credit	미성년자 공제
minority control	소수지배
minority group	소수파 집단
minority interest	소수주주지분
minority representation	소수대표법

minority shareholders	소수주주
minority shareholders' right	소수주주권
mint par of exchange	법정평가
mint price	주조가격
minus factor	마이너스 요인
minus growth	마이너스 성장
minus tick	마이너스 틱
minus-ceiling	마이너스 실링
minute book	소송기록서
minutes	의사록
misappropriation	착복
misappropriation of funds	부당지출
misappropriation of goods	물품횡령
misbranding	부당표시
miscalculation	계산착오
miscellaneous accounts payable	제미지급금
miscellaneous accounts receivable	제미수금
miscellaneous assets	기타자산
miscellaneous bond	잡종보증증권
miscellaneous expenses	잡비
miscellaneous gains	잡익
miscellaneous income	잡수입
miscellaneous local taxes	잡종세
miscellaneous losses	잡손실
miscellaneous movable articles floater	각종동산포괄보험
miscellaneous receipts	잡수입
miscellaneous revenue	잡수익
misconduct	위반행위
misdemeanor	경죄
misery index	경제불쾌지수
misfeasance	불법행위
misfit return	부적합 리턴

misfit risk 부적합 위험
misfit-portfolio 부적합 포트폴리오
mismatch between assets and liabilities 자산과 부채의 미스매치
mismatch risk 미스매치위험
mismatching 미스매칭
misnomer 인명오기
mispricing 미스프라이싱
misprision 오기
misredemption 오상환
misrepresentation 부실표시
missing the market 시장을 잃어버리는 것
mission 사명
mistake 착오
mistake of fact 사실의 착오
mistake of law 법률착오
mitigation 경감
mitigation of damage 손해경감
mixed 망설임
mixed account 혼합회계
mixed action 혼합소송
mixed assets 혼합자산
mixed contract 혼합계약
mixed economy 혼합경제
mixed gift 혼합증여
mixed insurance 혼합보험
mixed inventory 혼합재고정리
mixed nuisance 혼합불법방해
mixed policy 혼합보험
mixed property 혼합재산
mixed question of law and fact 법률과 사실의 혼합문제
mixed quota-surplus reinsurance 비례・초과액 혼합재보험
mixed reserve 혼합준비금

mixed surplus 혼합잉여금
mixed transaction 혼합거래
mixed trust 믹스트러스트
mixed undertaking 공사혼합기업
mixed variance 혼합차이
multinational corporation (MNC) 다국적기업
multinational enterprise (MNE) 다국적기업
mobile franchise 이동형 프랜차이즈
mobile shop 이동점포
mobility barrier 이동장벽
mobilization 동원
mobilization fee 공작료
mock auction 경매
modal shift 모달 쉬프트
mode 방법, 양식, 표준치
mode of transportation 수송방법
model analysis 모형분석
model of consumer behavior 소비자행동모형
model of diffusion process 보급과정모형
model of response to price 가격반응모형
model safety-responsibility bill 사고방지책임모범법안
model stock plan 모형주식계획
modern portfolio theory 현대 포트폴리오 이론
modern utility theory 근대효용이론
modernization of smaller enterprise 중소기업의 근대화
modernized concession agreement 근대적 이권 협정
modestly-priced 값이 쌈
modification 수정
modified accelerated cost recovery system 수정가속상환법
modified all-inclusive theory 수정포괄주의
modified capitalism 수정자본주의

modified cash refund annuity 수정현금반환부연금
modified duration 수정 듀레이션
modified endowment 수정양로보험계약
modified file and use system 수정율 신고사용제도
modified net premium 수정순보험료
modified pass-through securities 모디파이드 패스 쓰로우 증권
modified preliminary term reserve 수정초년정기식 책임준비금
modified prior approval system 수정율사전승인제도
Modigliani-Miller theory 모딜리아니-밀러 이론
modular fixtures 모듈러 비품
moiety 일부
moment 순간, 시기
momentum oscillator 모멘텀 오실레이터
monetarism 통화주의
monetary aggregate 통화총량
monetary agreement 통화협정
monetary analysis 화폐분석
monetary and financial policy 통화금융정책
monetary approach 머니터리 어프로치
monetary assets 금융자산
monetary authority 통화당국
monetary control 통화관리
monetary crisis 통화위기
monetary ease 금융완화
monetary expansion 금융확대
monetary financial assets 통화성 금융자산
monetary growth 금융확대
monetary growth model 화폐성장모형
monetary illusion 화폐환상
monetary instability 통화불안
monetary interest rate 화폐이자율
monetary items 금전항목

monetary liabilities	금전채무
monetary management	통화관리
monetary policy	금융정책
monetary policy for easing	금융완화정책
monetary reform	통화개혁
monetary reserve	통화준비
monetary restraint policy	금융긴축정책
monetary stability	통화안정
monetary standard	본위제도
monetary standard policy	본위정책
monetary stringency	돈의 융통이 막힘
monetary survey	머니터리 서베이
monetary system	화폐제도
monetary target	머니터리 타겟
monetary tightening	금융긴축
monetary transfer	화폐적 트랜스퍼
monetary union	통화동맹
monetary unit	통화단위
monetization of government bonds	국채의 화폐화
money and securities broad form	금전·유가증권종합보증증권
money appropriated	충당금
money at call	단기융자
money bill	금전법안
money borrowed for short-term	단기차입금
money broker	금융업자
money center bank	머니센터뱅크
money changer	환전상
money claim	금전채권
money demand	금전청구
money deposited	예탁금
money earmarked	충당금
money flow	자금순환

money flow analysis	머니 플로우 분석
money flow table	머니 플로우 표
money game	머니게임
money in bank	예금
money in trust	위탁금
money income	현금수입
money judgment	금전판결
money laundering	자금세탁
money lender	금융업자
money lending business	금전대부업
money manager	자산운용자
money market	단기금융시장
money market account	단기금융화폐
money market broker	단자업자
money market certificate	시장금리연동형 정기예금
money market conditions index	금융시장정세지표
money market data	금융시장 데이터
money market dealer	단자회사
money market deposit account	단기금융시장예금회계
money market fund	단기금융상품투자신탁
money market index	단기금융시장지수
money market instrument	단기금융상품
money market intervention	금융시장으로의 개입
money market management	금융조절
money market preferred stock	머니마켓 우선주
money market rate	시중금리
money market securities	금융시장증권
money market unit trust	머니마켓 유닛 트러스트
money multiplier	통화승수
money of adieu	계약금
money of the world	세계화폐
money order	송금환

money orders and counterfeit paper currency coverage	소환 및 위조지폐손해담보
money paid-in part	선지급금
money paid temporarily	일시금
money position	머니 포지션
money purchase plan	보험료시세연금제도
money rate	금리
money received	입금
money spread	머니 스프레드
money stock	통화증권
money supply	통화공급량
money supply control	머니 서플라이 관리
money trust	금전신탁
money-flow tables	자금순환표
money-lending business	금전대부업
money-making	영리
money-veil theory	화폐베일 이론
monitoring	감시
monitoring of delivery	수수감시
monitoring system and Non-Governmental Organization	감시체제/NGO
monkey letter	몽키레터
mono line	모노라인
mono-purpose credit card	단일목적카드
monochronic	모노크로닉
monography	계산도표
monopolistic competition	독점적 경쟁
monopoly	점유권
monopoly assessment	전매과세
monopoly capital	독점자본
monopoly price	독점가격
monopoly pricing	독점가격의 설정

monopoly profit	전매이익
monopsony	수요독점
monopurpose credit card	단일목적카드
monorate of exchange system	단일환시장제
Monroe Doctrine	몬로주의
montage	몽타주
month order	먼스 오더
month-end	월말
month-end average method	이월평균단가불출법
month-end delivery	월말인도
monthly accounting	월말결산
monthly allotment of depreciable period	감가상각의 월평균계산
monthly average method	월차총평균법
monthly balance sheet	월차대차대조표
monthly chart	월별차트
monthly debit industry	데빗시스템 월부간이보험
monthly debit ordinary	데빗시스템월부보통보험
monthly diminishing clause	월차체감약관
monthly income statement	월차손익계산서
monthly installment	월부
monthly installment sales	월부판매
monthly investment plan	월적립투자계획
monthly payment	매월지불
monthly prorata fraction system	월차안분비례방식
monthly prorata return premium	월부반환보험
monthly report	월보
monthly reversal	먼스리 리버살
monthly statement	월차계산서
monthly statement of account	월계표
monthly trial balance	월차계시표
Moodies Services	무디스 서비스

mook 무크
moral consideration 도덕적 약인
moral hazard 도덕적 해이
moral obligation 자연채무
moral obligation bond 도덕적 지급보증채권
moral risks 모럴 리스크
moral suasion 도의적 설득
moral turpitude 부도덕 행위
morale survey 사기조사
moratorium 지불정지
moratorium period 지불유예기간
moratory interest 손해배상이자
more margin 추증
more or less terms 수량과부족용인조건
morning session 전장
morphing 모핑
mortality 폐기, 소비
mortality curve 사망률 커브
mortality loss 사차손
mortality profit 사차익
mortality table 생명표
mortgage 저당권
mortgage backed bond 저당권 담보채권
mortgage backed securities 저당권 증권
mortgage bank 저당은행
mortgage bond 저당담보부사채
mortgage bond coupon 저당권 사채금리
mortgage clause 저당권 설정약관
mortgage collateral type 저당권 담보형태
mortgage company 저당금융회사
mortgage credit 주택저당 세액공제
Mortgage Credit Association 저당신용조합

mortgage credit bond 저당신용채
mortgage creditor 저당권자
mortgage debenture 저당증서
mortgage debentures trust law 담보부사채신탁법
mortgage debtor 저당권 설정자
mortgage documents 저당증서류
mortgage guarantee insurance 저당보증보험
mortgage insurance 저당보험
mortgage investment trust 담보부투자신탁
mortgage loan 저당대부
mortgage of goods 동산저당권
mortgage of ship 선박저당권
mortgage pass-through certificate 부동산저당 전가증권
mortgage payable 저당차입금
mortgage pool 저당권 풀
mortgage securities 저당증서
mortgage service 저당권 관리
mortgageable chattels 저당이 될만한 동산
mortgagee 저당권자
mortgagees' interest 담보이익
mortgages receivable 담보부대부금
mortgagor 저당권설정자
mortgagor's completion bond 저당권설정자완성 보증증권
mortuary bonus 사망시 배당
most deliverable bond 수수최적채권
most favored nation clause 최혜국조항
most favored nation treatment 최혜국대우
most favored reinsurer clause 최혜재보험자약관
most recent purchase method 최종매입원가법
most seriously affected countries 가장 심각하게 피해를 입은 나라
most-favoured nation (MFN) clause 최혜국 조항
mother fund 마더 펀드

motion 신청, 동의
motion day 신청심리일
motion for directed verdict 지시평결의 신청
motion for judgment 판결신청
motion for new trial 재심리신청
motion model 운동 모형
motion study 동작연구
motion to strike out 삭제신청
motivating factor 동기마련인자
motivation 동기마련
motivation level 동기마련 수준
motivation research 동기조사
motive 동기
motor hull insurance 자동차차량보험
motor insurance 자동차보험
motor third party insurance 자동차배상책임보험
motor vehicle passenger insurance 자동차승객보험
mounting 설치하는 일
movable and immovable assets account 동산부동산 회계
movable band 무버블 밴드
movable property in trust 동산신탁
movables 동산
movables comprehnesive insurance 동산종합보험
move 제안하다
movement of funds 자금이동
movement of price 가격움직임
moving average 이동평균
moving average convergence divergence trading method 이동평균수속분산트레이딩법
moving average cost method 이동평균법
moving average deviations 이동평균치
moving average index 이동평균지수

moving average method	이동평균법
moving average model	이동평균모형
moving averages	이동평균
moving downward	하강
Moving Picture Expert Group	엠펙(MPEG)
moving weighted average method	이동가중평균
multiattribute model	다속성 모형
multibank holding company	복수은행지주회사
multibrand strategy	복수브랜드 전략
multichannel society	고도선택사회
multicurrency bond	다통화 본드
multicurrency clause	통화선택권
multicurrency intervention	복수개입통화
multicurrency loan	멀티커런시 론
multidivisional company	복수사업부기업
multidomestic	멀티도메스틱
multifactor model	복수요인 모형
multifibre Arrangement	다자간 섬유협정
multilateral agreement	다자간 협정
multilateral clearing agreement	다자간 청산협정
Multilateral Investment Guarantee Agency	다수국간 투자보증기관
multilateral netting	다자간넷팅
multilateral trade negotiations	다자간 무역교섭
multilevel marketing system	멀티 상법
multimedia	멀티미디어
multimedia personal computer	멀티미디어 퍼스널 컴퓨터
multinational corporation	다국적 기업
multinational marketing	다국적 마케팅
Multinational Monitor	멀티내셔널 모니터
multinationalim	다자주의
multiperiod model	다기관 모형
multiple answer	복수회답

multiple banking system 복수은행제도
multiple brand entries 복수브랜드 참입
multiple channel 복합경로
multiple choice 다항목 선택법
multiple correlation 다중상관
multiple decremental table 다중탈퇴잔존표
multiple evidence 다원적 증거
multiple line 멀티플 라인
multiple line agent 복수 종목취급 대리인
multiple line policy 멀티플 라인 보험증권
multiple location risk insurance 다수 소재지 물건보험
multiple management 복합경영
multiple maturity deposit 복수만기예금
multiple option funding facilities 멀티플 옵션 펀딩 패실리티
multiple payment credit card 할부카드
multiple perils insurance for cinemas 영화극장 종합보험
multiple purpose bank account 종합계좌
multiple regression analysis 다중회귀분석
multiple step 구분식
multiple sub-nyquist sampling encoding 뮤즈방식
multiple tariff system 복수세제
multiple tax rate 복수세율
multiple-step form 다단계식
multiple-step income statement 구분손익계산서
multiple-step statement 복수구분계산서
multiplication rule 승법규칙
multiplicity of action 소송의 중복
multiplied effect 파급효과
multiplier analysis 승수분석
multiplier effect 승수효과
multiplier theory 승수이론
multiprocessing 통합생산체제

multisectoral analysis 다부문 분석
multisourcing 멀티소싱
multitask 멀티테스크
multivariate analysis 다변량 분석
multiwill 다수자 유언
multiwindow 멀티 윈도우
multo-domestic/strategy 멀티 도메스틱 전략
municipal accounting 관청부기
municipal bond fund 지방공공단체채권펀드
municipal bonds 지방채
municipal by-laws 조례
municipal corporation 지방공공단체
municipal courts 시재판소
municipal futures 지방채선물
municipal law 조례
municipal ordinance 시조례
municipal property tax 고정자산세
municipal securities dealer 공공채 딜러
muniments 권리증
mute 침묵
mutilated check 훼손수표
mutual account 상호계산
mutual adjustment 상호조리
mutual agreement procedure 상호협의
mutual aid 공제
mutual aid contract for retirement allowance 퇴직금공제계약
mutual aid money 공제금
mutual aid organization for specific retirement allowance 특정퇴직금공제단체
mutual aid premiums 공제부금
mutual aid system 공제금제도
mutual association 상호보험조합

mutual benefit association	공제조합
mutual benefit society	상호조합
mutual company	상호회사
mutual condition	상호조건
mutual covenant	상호날인계약
mutual credits	상호대차
mutual debt	상대채무
mutual fund	뮤추얼 펀드
mutual fund redemption value insurance	투자신탁상환가격보증보험
mutual fund underwriters	뮤추얼펀드 인수업자
mutual installment	상호부금
mutual insurance	상호보험
mutual insurance company	상호생명보험회사
mutual insurance society	상호보험조합
mutual offset system	상호결제제도
mutual pension	공제연금
mutual promise	상호약속
mutual reinforcement	상호보강효과
mutual savings bank	상호저축은행
mutual wills	상호유언
mutual-type associations	상호주의적 보험단체
mutualism	상호주의
mutuality of insurance institution	보험제도의 상호성
mutuality of obligation	채무의 상호성
mutuality of remedy	구제의 상호성
mutualization	상호화
mutually exclusive event	상호독립적 일(사건)
myopia	근시안적 사고방식
Mysigma profitability graph	미시그마의 수익그래프
mysterious disappearance	분실

≪ n ≫

nail damage	정(釘)손
nailed down	초저가격 광고상품
naked call	네이키드 콜
naked confession	불완전자백
naked contract	나계약
naked option	네이키드 옵션
naked position	네이키드 포지션
naked warrant	네이키드 워런트
name	상표, 종목
name list	인명부
name of the corporation	상호
name share	기명주
name transfer	명의서환
named bill	기명식 어음
named insured	기명피보험자
named nonowner policy	기명비소유자보험
named peril	특정위험
named peril insurance	열거위험담보보험
named schedule bond	기명식 보증증권
nano-second	나노 초
narrative form	보고 식
narrow	축소하다
narrow based stock index	업종별 주가지수
narrow market	난산시장
narrow market security	품귀주
narrow movement	소폭왕래
narrow range	소폭

narrow seas	해협
narrow spread	소차액
narrowcasting	내로우캐스팅
narrowing of spread	시세변동으로 매매차익금이 적어짐
NASDAQ Composite Index	나스닥 종합주가지수
nation	국가
national balance sheet	국민대차대조표
national bank	국법은행
national bond futures market	국채선물시장
national brand	전국브랜드
national capital	국민자본
national capital account	국민자본회계
national capital sheet	국민자본표
national certification	국민인증
national contact point	각국 연락소
national credit	국가신용
national debt	국가채무
national debt service expenditure	공채비
national economic accounting	국민경제계산
national finance	국가재정
national full line firm	종합증권회사
National Futures Association	전미(全美) 선물협회
national government debts	정부채무
National Health Insurance Law	국민건강보험법
national health insurance tax	국민건강보험세
national income	국민소득
national income accounting	국민소득회계
national income accounts	국민소득회계
national income analysis	국민소득분석
national income distributed	분배국민소득
national income expended	지출국민소득
national income produced	생산국민소득

national income statistics	국민소득통계
national information structure	전미정보기관
national pension	국민연금
national property	국유재산
national registry of technology	기술의 국가 등록
national subsidy	국고보조금
national tariff	국정세율
national tax	국세
national tax procedure law	국세통칙법
national treasury	국고
national treatment	내국민대우
national wealth	국부
national wealth statistics	국부통계
nationalism	민족주의
nationalization	국유화
nationalized reinsurance	국영재보험
natural boundary	자연적 경계
natural business year	자연영업년수
natural capital	자연자본
natural classification	자연발생적 분류
natural disaster relief loans	자연재해 구호자금
natural gas pipeline	천연가스 파이프라인
natural heirs	혈연상속인
natural infancy	유년
natural language system	자연언어체계
natural law	자연법
natural liberty	자연적 자유
natural person	자연인
natural premium	자연보험료
natural presumption	자연적 추정
natural rate of interest	자연이자율
natural rate of unemployment	자연실업률

natural rights	자연권
natural support	자연적 지지
natural year	역년
naturalization	귀화
nature and degree	성질과 정도
nature of business	사업의 종류
navigable	항행가능한
ne exeat	이국금지영장
ne varietur	동일성의 확증
near future	가까운 미래
near maturity	기근
near money	준통화
near the money	니어 더 머니
near time prospect	선견관
near-panic market	공황시장
near-term bond	기근채
nearest month	직근한 월
necessaries	생활필수품
necessary evidence documents	필요한 증거서류
necessary expense	필요경비
necessary household furniture	필수가구
necessary party	필요당사자
necessary tax procedure	필요한 세무수속
necessity	긴급피난
neck line	네크라인
need hierarchy	요구계층
need-satisfaction approach	요구충족 어프로치
needs	니즈
needs test	필요조사
needs theory	인용설
negative adaptation	음성순응
negative assets	소극자산

negative assurance	소극적 보증
negative averments	소극적 주장
negative capital	부채
negative carry	네가티브 캐리
negative clause	담보보유조항
negative confirmation	소극적 확인
negative covenant	경쟁제한 특약
negative duration	부(-)의 듀레이션
negative effect	부(-)의 효과
negative evidence	소극적 증거
negative factor	마이너스 요건
negative film	음화용 필름
negative goodwill	소극신용
negative growth	마이너스 성장
negative income tax	역소득세
negative interest	역금리
negative interest rate spread	역차익
negative leverage effect	부(-)의 레버리지 효과
negative list	네거티브 리스트
negative monetary position	금전채무상태
negative option sales	압부상법
negative plea	소극적 항변
negative pledge clause	담보제한조항
negative pledge pari passu clause	네가티브 플레지 파리 파스 조항
negative prescription	소멸시효
negative property	소멸재산
negative reaction	거절반응
negative reserve	부수책임준비금
negative statute	금지적 법률
negative testimony	소극적 증언
negative valuation accounts	소극적 평가회계
negative yield curve	부(-)의 이율곡선

negligence 과실
negligence clause 면책조항
negligence liability 과실책임
negligible in amount 무시할 수 있는 가격
negotiable 양도가능
negotiable certificate of deposit 양도성 예금증서
negotiable instrument 유통증권
negotiable letter of credit 매입가능신용장
negotiable order of withdrawal account 양도가능환불지도 예금회계
negotiable securities 유가증권
negotiable time certificates of deposits 나우계정(Now Account)
negotiated 상대
negotiated contracts 수의계약
negotiated market 상대매매시장
negotiated price system 교섭가격시스템
negotiated transaction 상대거래
negotiated underwriting 협의인수
negotiating bank 어음매입은행
negotiation 매입
negotiation charge 어음매입수수료
negotiation credit 외국환 매매계약신용
negotiation effect 교섭효과
negotiation for budget draft 부활절충
negotiation on terms and conditions 조건교섭
neighborhood benefits 인접자의
nemine contradicente 전원일치
neo-behaviorism 신행동주의
neo-classical trade theory 신고전학파 무역이론
neo-factor trade theory 신요소무역론
neo-functionalism 신기능주의

neo-imperialism 신제국주의
neo-quantity theory of money 신화폐수량설
neo-technology trade theory 신기술이론
nervous 신경질적인
nervous shock 정신적 충격
net 순
net amount after provision for loss 대손담보금공제후의 금액
net amount principle 순액주의
net asset per share 한주에 해당하는 순자산
net asset value 순자산가치
net asset value per unit 유닛당 순자산
net asset worth per share 주당 순자산
net assets 순자산, 도매값 재산
net assets value 도매값 자산가치
net avails 도매값 수취액
net balance 넷 밸런스
net base 순액베이스
net block flow 넷 블록 플로우
net book value 순 장부가액
net borrowed reserves 순차입준비금
net budget 예산순계
net capital stock 조자본 증권
net carry-over cost 순이월비용
net cash 순 현금
net cash flow 순 현금흐름
net cash inflows 도매값의 현금유입
net changes in each element 과목별 순변동액
net collectible amounts 도매값 회수가능액
net commodity terms of trade 순상품교역조건
net cost 순원가
net creditor country 순 채권국
net current assets 도매값 유동자산

net cycle time 도매값 운전시간
net damaged value 손해시가
net debt 순부채
net deposit 실세예금
net earned surplus forwarded 이월이익 잉여금
net earnings 순이익
net equity assets 도매값 지분자산
net export 순수출
net external assets 대외순자산
net financial income 순금융 수입
net free reserves 순자유준비금
net income 순이익
net income ratio 순이익률
net income to sales 매출순이익
net interest 순이자
net interest cost 순이자비용
net interest income 순수입이자
net investment 순투자
net lease 넷 리스
net level premium reserve 평균순보험료식 책임준비금
net liabilities 순부채
net line 도매값 수중(手中) 금액
net liquidity balance 순유동성 수지
net loss 도매값 손실
net loss carried forward 이월결손금
net make-on 순가격 인상액
net monetary items 도매값 금전항목
net monetary position 순화폐 포지션
net national product 국민순생산
net national welfare 국민복지지표
net of 제외하고
net of reserves 대손담보금공제후 수취채권

net open position 넷 오픈 포지션
net operating cycle 도매값 영업순환일수
net operating earnings 경상순익액
net operating loss 순영업손실
net operating profit 순영업이익
net operation profit 업무순익
net outgo 도매값 지불
net pay 급료
net position 차감위치
net premium 도매값 수입보험료
net premium payable 도매값 지불보험금
net premiums written 도매값 계상보험료
net present value 순현재가치
net price 도매가격
net price index 넷 프라이스 인덱스
net proceeds 도매값 수취액
net production value 도매값 생산고
net profit 순이익
net profit after depreciation 상환후순이익
net profit before corporation tax 법인세공제전순이익
net profit before depreciation 상환전순이익
net profit for the year 당기순이익
net profit margin 매상순이익률
net profit on sales 매출순익
net profit or loss 순손익
net profit or loss account 순손익계산
net profit or loss section 순손익구분
net profit ratio 순익률
net profit to net worth 자기자본이익률
net profit to sales 매출순이익률
net purchase 구매초과, 순매입
net quick assets 순 당좌자산

net realizable value	순 실현가능가격
net receipt	순수입
net return	순환입
net sales	순매출
net saving	순저축
net settlement	차금결제
net short hedging	순매도 헷징
net succession	순상속재산
net supply of industrial funds	산업자금 공급상황
net surplus	순잉여금
net tangible asset ratio to long-term debt	장기부채 순 고정자산
net tangible assets	순 고정자산
net taxable assets	순과세 재산
net trading volume	넷 거래고
net value	순가치
net working capital	순 운전자본
net worth	순 자산
net worth equity	순자산
net worth equity capital	자기자본
net worth method	자산부채 증감법
net worth of collateral	담보여력
net worth tax	부유세
net worth to debts	자본부채비율
net worth to fixed capital	자본고정비율
net yield	순이익
netdown	상계
netting	넷팅
network architecture	네트워크 아키텍처
network broadcast	네트워크 분석
network control unit	네트워크 제어 장치
network of credit	신용네트워크

neural computing	뉴럴 컴퓨팅
neutrality	중립성
neutrality of taxation	조세의 중립성
never-out list	상비상품목록
new	신규
new account	신규계정
new banking law	신은행법
new bond	신규발행채권
new common carrier	뉴 커먼 캐리어
new design	신안
new face bond	신안채
new field	신규분야
new foreign exchange law	신외국환 관리법
new high	신고가(당일 가장 높은 시세)
new industrial revolution	신산업혁명
new international division of labour	신국제분업
New International Economic Order (NIEO)	신국제경제질서
new issue	신규발행
new issue of stocks	신주발행
new listing	신규상장
new loan	신규대출
new low	신저가(당일 가장 낮은 시세)
new media community	뉴 미디어 커뮤니티
new monetary adjustment system	신금융조절
new mortgage	신규 저당권
new order	신규수주
new premium	신규 프리미엄
new print film	차세대 사진필름
new product failures	신제품의 실패
new product introduction	신제품 소개
new product screening	신제품의 선발

new share 신주
new share issuing expense 신주발행비
new share off 신주누락
new social indicators 국민생활지표
new stock issuing expenses 신주발행비
new trial 재심
new type of gold standard 신형의 금본위제
new welfare economics 신후생경제학
New York acceptance credit 뉴욕인수신용장
New York Stock Exchange 뉴욕증권거래소
newly industrialized countries 신흥공업국
Newly Industrializing Countries (NICS) 신흥공업국
newly issued corporate bond 신규발행사채
next closing of account 차기결산
next day fund 익일자본화자금
next friend 가까운 친구
next time 차기
next to kin 근친자
niche 니치, 틈새
niche market 틈새시장
niche strategy 틈새전략
Nielsen research 닐슨조사
nient comprise 해당사실 없음
nient dedire 부인하지 않다
nient le fait 작성부인의 항변
nifty fifty 인기 50종목(상표)
night deposit safe 야간금고
night duty allowance 숙직료
nil dicit 무답변
nine bond rule 나인 본드 룰
no action letter 노 액션 레터

no claim return	무사고로 돌림
no consideration	무약인 항변
no effect	무효
no fault automobile insurance	노 폴트 자동차보험
no franchise clause	면책보합 부적용 약관
no limit order	과정주문
no load fund	노 로드 펀드
no protest	거절증서 불필요
no return rule	노 리턴 룰
no-down	계약금 없이
no-par-value stock	무액면주식
NOB spread	NOB 스프레드
Nobel Foundation	노벨 재단
node	교점, 결절점
node method	노드 방식
noise	소음
noise gate	노이즈 게이트
noise reduction	노이즈 리덕션
nominal account	명목계정
nominal amount	액면가격
nominal assets	명목자산
nominal assured	명목상의 피보험자
nominal capital	명목자본
nominal coupon	표면이율
nominal damages	명목적 손해배상액
nominal exchange rate	명목환율
nominal GNP	명목 GNP
nominal gross deposit	표면예금
nominal income	명목수입
nominal interest rate	표면금리
nominal liabilities	명목부채
nominal partner	명목적 파트너

nominal price quotation	호가(呼價)
nominal profit	명목이익
nominal proxy	무권대리
nominal quotation	명목상 시가
nominal rate	표면금리
nominal rate of discount	명목 할인율
nominal rate of interest	명목 이율
nominal rate of protection	명목 보호율
nominal rate of return	명목 수익률
nominal scale	명의척도
nominal transaction	명목거래
nominal value	액면가격
nominal wage	명목임금
nominal wealth tax	명목적 재산세
nominal yield	명목이율
nominalism	명목주의
nominate	지명하다
nominated subcontractor	지정하청업자
nominee	명의인
nonamortizable securities	일시불 유가증권
nonassessable insurance	비부과식 보험
nonassessable policy	보험료 추징 불필요 증권
nonassumpsit	비인수답변
nonaverage insurance	실손보전계약
nonbank	은행 비은행
nonbank financial institution	비은행 금융기관
nonbasic shareholder of family corporation	비동족 주주
nonboard company	요율산정 기관불참가회사
nonborrowed reserves	비차입 준비금
nonbusiness activity	비사업 활동
nonbusiness expenses	사업외 경비

nonbusiness property	비영업용 자산
noncallable	청구되는 대로 지불되지 않는
noncancellable	해약불가능한
noncancellable insurance	해제할 수 없는 보험계약
noncash assets	비현금자산
noncash investing activities	수지를 동반하지 않는 투자활동
nonclaim	청구해태
noncommercial enterprise	비영리회사
noncommercial insurance	비영리보험
noncommercial trader	비영리적 상인
noncompensatory model	비보정 모형
noncompetitive tender	비경쟁입찰
nonconcealed assets	장부외 자산
nonconcurrency	이위성
nonconcurrent policies	이위계약
nonconforming product	부적합 제품
nonconformity	부적합
noncontinuous policy	보험금액 감소보험
noncontrollable cost	관리불능원가
noncost items	비원가항목
noncumulative dividend	비누적형 배당
noncumulative preferred stock	비누적형 우선주식
noncurrent assets	비유동자산
noncurrent liabilities	장기채무
nondeclarant	미선언자
nondeductible franchise	무공제 면책보합
nondeductible taxes	손실금미처리기입의 조세과금
nondelivery	수도불이행
nondeprecialble	비상환자산
nondetachable warrant	분리불능 근거
non-discrimination rule	무차별원칙
nondiversified investment company	비분산자산형 투자회사

nondividend 무분배
nondraft export 무환수출
nondraft import 무환수입
nonduplication of benefits 이중급부 배제
nondurables 비내구재
nonexclusive 비독점적
nonexpendable fund 사용불능 자금
nonfamily corporation 비동족회사
nonfeasance 불이행
nonfinancial accounts 비금융회계
nonfinancial assets 비금융자산
nonfinancial market 비금융시장
nonfinancial transaction 비금융거래
nonforfeiture act 비몰수법
nonfulfillment of a contract 계약불이행
nonfund transactions 수지를 동반치 않는 거래
nongenuine agreement 이면계약(뒤로하는 계약)
nongovernment bond 민간채
nonhomogeneity 비동질성
noninstallment 비할부
noninterest-bearing bond 비이자부채
noninterest-sensitive item 금리비감응항목
noninvestment cooperative association 비출자조합
nonjoinder 비병합
nonjuridical organization 법인격 없는 조직
nonledger assets 미기장 자산
nonlegal standards 법률로 되어 있지 않은 기준
nonlicensed micropower broadcasting 미약전파방송
nonlife insurance 손해보험
nonlife insurance agent 손해보험대리점
nonlife insurance company 손해보험회사

nonliquid assets	비유동성자산
nonmarket economy	비시장경제
nonmarket risk	비시장성 위험
nonmarket risk sources	비시장성 위험의 원천
nonmarketable securities	비시장성 증권
nonmarking	정가표 붙이는 것의 생략
nonmember firm	비회원증권회사
nonmonetary indirect security	비화폐적 간접증권
nonmonetary items	비금전항목
nonmonetized economy	비화폐적 경제
nonmoney trust	넌머니신탁
nonnegotiable	유동성이 없다
nonnegotiable bill	이서금지어음
nonnegotiable endorsement	이서금지이서
nonnegotiable instrument	비유통증권
nonnegotiable safekeeping receipts	양도불능보호예탁증
nonoperating	영업외의
nonoperating expenditure	영업외 비용
nonoperating expenses	영업외 경비
nonoperating gains and loss	영업외 손익
nonoperating revenue	영업외 수익
nonoperating section	영업외 손익구분
nonopinion report	무한정 감사보고서
nonorder bill	지도금지어음
nonpar stock	무액면주
nonpar-value stock	무액면주식
nonparametric test	비모수 검정
nonparticipating fund	무배당보험자산
nonparticipating preferred stock	비참가우선주식
nonparticipating premium	무배당보험료
nonpayment protest	비지불에 대한 통지
nonpayments	미납

nonperformance	불이행
nonpermanent resident	비영주자
nonpersonal family corporation	비동족의 동족회사
nonpersonnel expenses	물건비
nonpolicy writing agent	비발권대리점
nonprice competition	비가격경쟁
nonprobability sample	비확률 표본
nonprofit corporation	비영리회사
nonprofit foundation	공익법인
nonprofit institution	비영리기관
nonprofit-making activity	공익사업
nonprofit-making business	비영리사업
nonprofit-making company	비영리회사
nonprofit-making organization	비영리조직
nonprogrammed decision	비정형적 의사결정
nonproportional reinsurance	비비례비율 재보험
nonpurpose loan	비특정대부
nonrate earnings assets	비금리자산
nonrate-paying liability	비금리부채
nonrate-sensitive liability	금리비감응부채
nonreciprocal	비상호적
nonreciprocal reinsurance	일방적 재보험
nonrecourse	의지(의뢰)하지 않는
nonrecurrent item	임시의 항목, 비경상 항목
nonrecurring cost	경상외 비용
nonrecurring profit	임시이익
nonrecurring profit and loss	경상외 손익
nonregistered	미등기
nonresident foreign currency account	비거주자 외화 예금계정
nonresident yen account	비거주자 엔 예금계정
nonresident yen deposit	비거주자 엔 예금
nonrisk assets	비위험 자산

nonrisk interest rate 비위험 이자율
nonselling area 비매장면적
nonsettled 미결제
nonsigner 비계약자
nonstochastic model 비확률모형
nonstrategic division 비전략부문
nonsuit 소송의 각하(기각)
nonsystematic risk 비체계적 위험
non-tariff barrier 비관세장벽
nontax payment 세외부담
nontax recepts 세외수입
nontaxable corporation 비과세법인
nontaxable document 비과세문서
nontaxable exchanges of properties 수용환지
nontaxable goods 면제품
nontaxable income 비과세소득
nontaxable interest income 비과세이자소득
nontaxable property 비과세재산
nontaxable receiving 미납세인수
nontaxable savings 비과세저축
nontaxable securities 면세증권
nontaxable transaction 비과세거래
nontaxable-goods for special use 특수용도면세
nontie-up loan 비제휴대부
nontraditional asset class 비전통적인 에셋 클래스
nonuser 비행사
nonvoting stock 무의결권주
noon clause 정오조항
Nordic Council 북구이사회
Nordic Council of Ministers 북구각료회의
Norin Chukin Bank 농림중앙금고
norm 기준

normal and average use hours 통상사용시간
normal asset mix 노말 에셋 믹스
normal auditing procedures 정상적 감사절차
normal balances 정상잔고
normal burden rate 정상배부율
normal cost 정상원가
normal depreciation 정상감가상각
normal distribution 정규분포
normal market 순차액 시장
normal operating cycle 정상영업순환
normal probability curve 정규확률분포곡선
normal probability distribution 정규확률분포
normal procedure 정상절차
normal profit 정상이윤
normal rate of exchange 정상환 상장
normal return 정상이익
normal standard cost 정상표준원가
normal stock 정상재고
normal target allocation 정상표적배부
normal tax 보통세
normalization 표준화
normalized EPS 표준 EPS
normative change 표준적 변화
normative influence 규범적 영향
normative theory 규범론
norms in society 사회규범
norms of behavior 행동규범
North America Free Trade Agreement 북미자유무역협정
North Atlantic Assembly 북대서양회의
North Atlantic Free Trade Area 북대서양자유무역지역
North Atlantic Treaty Organization 북대서양조약기구
North Brent 북해브랜트

north-south problem	남북문제
north-south trade	남북무역
Northampton table	노샘프턴 생명표
nostro	당방국
Nostro account	당방계정
not excessive	값이 비싸서는 안된다
not inadequate	값이 싸서는 안된다
not otherwise provided	별도의 결정이 없는 한
not possessed	점유하고 있지 않았었다
not proven	증거불충분
not unfairly discriminatory	차별적으로 돼서는 안된다.
not yet delivered	미착의
notarial charges	공증료
notarial deed	공정증서
notarial document	공정증서
notary	공증인
notary public liability policy	공증인배상책임보험
note at sight	일람불약속어음
note endorsed	이서양도어음
note for payment of tonnage dues	(선박 · 적하의) 톤세납부착서
note issuance facility	채권발행 보증조건
note of payment	지불통지서
note of protest	거절각서
note payable register	지불어음기입장
note purchase agreement	채무매입계약서
note received discounted	할인어음
note register	어음기입장
notes and accounts payable	지불채무
notes and accounts receivable	수취채무
notes and bills discounted	할인어음
notes and bills endorsed	이서어음
notes and bills payable	지불어음

notes and bills receivable 수취어음
notes endorsed for payment 이서양도어음
notes payable to banks 은행차입금
notes receivable resister 수취어음기입장
note to financial statement 재무제표각주
noteworthy 주목할 가치가 있다
notice 통지
notice deposit 통지예금
notice of abandonment 위임통지
notice of demand to guarantor 납부최고서
notice of determination 결정통지서
notice of lien 선취득권통지
notice of loss and damage 사고통지
notice of redemption 상황통지
notice of seizure 차압통지서
notice to produce 문서제출요구서
notice to quit 예약예고
notification 최고서
notification in writing 문서에 의한 통지
notification of appropriation of refund 환부금 충당통지서
notification of audit 조사사전통지서
notification of claim 구상통고
notification of depreciation method 상환방법신고
notification of incorporation 설립신고
notification of opening of business 개업신고
notification of payment of refund 환부금 지불통지서
notification of tax agent 납세관리인의 신고
notification of tax payment 납세통지서
notification of the taxable year 사업년도의 신고
notification of transfer of place of tax payment 납세지 이동 신고
notification procedure 통고처분
notifying bank 통지은행

noting protest	거절각서작성
notional amount	명목원본
notional certificate	의제증서
notional income	관념상의 소득
notorious possession	공연의 점유
Nottebohm case	노트봄 사례
novelty	신고안품, 신상품
nuclear accident	원자력 사고
nuclear damage	원자력 손해
nuclear energy hazard	원자력 위험
nuclear energy liability insurance	원자력 손해배상 책임보험
nuclear energy property insurance	원자력 재산보험
nuclear installation	원자력 시설
nudge	주의환기
nuisance	불법방해
null and void	무효한
null hypothesis	귀무가설
nullity	무효
number of days' purchases in accounts payable	외상매입채권 회전일수
number of days' sales in inventories	재고정리자산 회전일수
number of days' sales in receivables	매출채권 회전일수
number of machines installed	거치대수
number of scheduled payments	반제회수
number of stocks held	보유주식수
number of stocks issued	발행주식수
number of years elapsed	경과년수
numbered accounts	번호계좌
numberaire	평가기준
numberical integration	수치적분법
numberical rating method	점수사정법
numberical techniques	수치지법

≪ O ≫

oath	선서
object	물건
object cost	요소별 원가
object of taxation	과세물건
object oriented database	목표지향 데이터베이스
object space	목적지
object tax	목적세
objection	이의
objective	요소별의
objective evidence	객관적 증거
objective function	목적함수
objective indicator	객관지표
objective probability	객관적 확률
objective statement	요소별 계산서
objective value	객관적 가치
obligation	채무
obligation fees	부담비
obligation of bookkeeping	기장업무
obligation of contract	계약상의 권리
obligation to disclose	고지의무
obligation to file return	신고의무
obligations incurred	발생채무부담
obligatory insurance	강제보험
obligatory reinsurance	의무재보험
oblige line	오블리지 라인
obligee	채권자

obligor	채무자
obliteration	말소
observation	관찰, 입회
observed depreciation	계상된 감가상각
observed life table	견적내용년수표
observed value	관찰값
obsolescent depreciable property	진부화 상각자산
obsolescing bargain	풍화하는 교섭력
obsolete	사용할 수 없게 되다
obsolete assets	진부화 자산
obsolete property	진부화 자산
obstruction of justice	사법방해
obstruction of navigation	항행방해죄
obtain in advance	가불하다
obtainer of employment income	급여소득자
occasional income	일시소득
occasional income deduction	일시소득의 특별공제
occupancy	자주점유
occupancy terms	점유기간
occupant	점유자
occupation	영업
occupation tax	영업세
occupational accident	직업재해
occupational pension	기업연금
occupational tax	영업면허세
odd date	정형화 이외 거래기간
odd price	단수가격
odd-lot consolidation	단주정리
odd-lot dealer	단주업자
odd-lot shares	단주
odd-lot theory	단주이론
odd-lot transaction	단주거래

OECD Guidelines on Multinational Enterprise　OECD다국적기업가이드라인(행동규범)
of like grade and quality　동등 동질의
off balance　오프 밸런스
off limit　출입금지
off market swap　오프 마켓 스왑
off talk service　오프 토크 통신서비스
off-balance sheet transaction　오프 밸런스 시트 거래
off-board market　장외시장
off-market　오프 마켓
off-setting account　상계계정
offense　범죄
offensive strategy　공격적 전략
offer　신청
offer by subscription　예약공모
offer curve　오퍼 곡선
offer for sale　팔다
offer price　오퍼가격
offer side　오퍼사이드
offered rate　미끼(구실) 레이트
offering　모집
offering circular　모집안내서
offering for sale　매출
offering price　매출가격
office audit　탁상조사
office copy　관제등본
office expense account　영업비 회계
office expenses　사무실 경비
office expenses book　사무실 경비 내역표
office furniture　영업용 집기
office grant　강제이행
office hours　영업시간

office landscape	오피스 계획
office manual	사무규정
office or other fixed place of business	사무실 혹은 일정의 사업소
office overhead	사무실 간접비
office regulation	사내 규정
officer de jure	법률상의 직원
officer's bonus	임원상여
officer's compensation	임원보수
officer's salary	임원급여
officers retiring allowance	임원퇴직금
official assessment	부과과세제도
official check	은행수표
official deposit	공금예금
Official Development-Assistance	정부개발원조
official discount rate	공정할인율
official exchange market	공정시장
official exchange rate	공정환율
official foreign exchange reserves	외환준비금
official information	공보
official inspection	임검
official intervention	공적개입
official invoice	공용 송장
official power	직권
official receiver	관선수익관리인
official reserve transactions balance	공적 결제수지
official retain	영치
official to receive national tax	국세수납관리
offset	상계
offset account	상계 계정
offset error	상계 오류
offset item	상계 항목

offset printing	옵셋 인쇄
offsets	상계
offshoot	자회사
offshore account	역외계정
offshore assembly	옵션형 조립
offshore banking center	오프쇼어 뱅크 센터
offshore banking facility	오프쇼어 은행간 시장
offshore banking unit	오프쇼어 뱅킹 유니트
offshore center	역외센터
offshore finance subsidiary	역외금융자회사
offshore financial centre	역외금융센터
offshore fund	역외펀드
offshore lease	역외리스
offshore market	역외시장
offshore production	해외생산
offshore trade	역외무역
oil concession	석유채굴권
oil money	오일 머니
oil pollution liability insurance	오일 오염 배상책임보험
oil refinery	석유정제업
Oklahoma letter	오클러호마 레터
old account	잔존계정
old age pension	노령연금
old bank act	구은행법
old bond	올드 본드
old person allowance	노년자 공제
old share	구주(舊株)
old-aged pension	노령연금
old-aged, survivor and disability insurance	노령유족방해자연금
oligopolistic competition	과점적 경쟁
oligopolistic control	과점적 지배

oligopolistic economy	과점 경제
oligopolistic interdependence	과점적 상호의존
oligopoly	과점
oligopoly industry	과점산업
oligopoly model	과점모형
oligopoly price	과점가격
oligopoly reaction	과점적 반응
ombudsman	옴부즈맨
omitted dividend	무분배
omnibus account	공동 회계
omnibus clause	합승 조건
on a simple interest basis	단리를 기초로
on account	외상판매
on air test	온 에어 테스트
on balance	온 밸런스
on balance volume	온 밸런스 볼륨
on board notation	선적 이서
on call	청구 순서
on cost	제조비
on demand	요구불
on hook dial	온 훅 다이얼
on or before	기일 또는 기일전에
on our risk	우리 쪽 부담
on passage	운송중
on the books	외상판매장으로
on the job accidents	업무상 사고
on-balance-sheet transaction	온 밸런스 거래
on-line	온라인
on-shore	역내
on-shore market	온 쇼어 마켓
oncost	제경비
one bank holding company	단일은행 지주회사

one day contract 일일계약
on day skipped 하루 영업일을 건너 뛴 뒤에 건네주는 것
one hundred percent income statement 백분율 손익계산서
one name paper 단명어음
one pass scan 선순차방식
one share shareholder 일주 주주
one shot customer 한번 잠깐 들린 손님
one sided hedge 편도 헷지
one way 편도
one year budget principle 예산 단년도 주의
one year rule 일년기준
one's own convenience 자기 형편(상황)
one's own house system 지가제도
one-bank holding company 단일은행 지주회사
one-factor 단일 요인
one-factor model 단일 요인 모형
one-man company 일인회사
one-time rate 단발 요금
one-write policy 원 라이트 증권
onerous contract 유상계약
onerous gift 부담부 증여
ongoing assessment 계속 평가
onomastic 자서(自署)의
onus of proof 입증책임
open 미결산
open account 청산계정
open air market 청공시장
open and current account 교호계산계정
open bid 일반경쟁입찰
open board of broker 공개거래회소
open book 오픈 북

open buying	신규구입
open check	보통수표
open contract	특약이 없는 계약
open corporation	공개회사
open court	공개법정
open cover	오픈 커버, 포괄 보험
open door policies	문호개방정책
open economy	개방경제
open group	개방단체
open house	오픈 하우스
open inflation	개방형 인플레이션
open insurance	포괄 예정보험
open interest	미결제건 값
open interest on buyer's side	구매건 값
open interest on seller's side	판매건 값
open investment trust	오픈형 투자신탁
open ledger	미결산원장
open letter of credit	매입은행 무지정신용장
open market	공개시장
open market operations	공개시장조작
open market quotation	시중가격
open market rate	시중금리
open market selling operation	판매 오퍼레이션
open media framework	오픈 미디어 프레임워크
open money market	공개단기금융시장
open mortgage	개방담보
open mortage clause	단순저당채권자 지불약관
open order	가능한 뒤 주문하는 것
open outcry method	공개경매방식
open plan office	공공사무실
open policy	포괄보험증서
open question	미해결 문제

open rate method	오픈 레이트 방식
open repo	공개시장 조작
open selling	신규판매
open tendering	일반경쟁입찰
open theft	현행 절도죄
open-end	개방식의
open-end bond investment trust	공사채 투자신탁
open-end fund	오픈 엔드형 펀드
open-end investment trust	오픈형 투자신탁
open-end lease	오픈 엔드형 리스
open-end mortgage	개방식 담보
open-end mortgage bond	개방식 담보부(포함) 사채
open-up of money market	금융시장개방
opener	신용장 발행의뢰인
opening balance	기초잔액
opening balance account	기초잔액계정
opening bank	개설은행
opening charge	신용장 발행 수수료
opening commission	발행수수료
opening entry	개시기입
opening inventory	기초재고
opening market	시장개방
opening of branch	지점개설
opening price	신설값
opening price point	최저가격라인
opening quotation	기부가격
opening rate	초기값
opening session	시초값
opening statement	모두 진술
opening tone	개통 음색
opening words	개통 낱말
operand	연계수

operated days 조업일수
operating 영업의
operating accounts 영업계정
operating activities 영업활동
operating assets 운용자산
operating budget 영업예산, 운영예산
operating business 영리기업
operating capital 운전자본
operating characteristics curve 운전특성곡선
operating condition 영업상황
operating cost 운영비용
operating cycle 영업순환
operating cycle rule 영업순환기준
operating earning rate 경영자본이익률
operating efficiency 경영효율
operating expenses 영업경비
operating income 영업수익
operating income to sales 영업이익률
operating lease 오퍼레이팅 리스
operating ledger 영업원장
operating leverage analysis 오퍼레이팅 레버리지 분석
operating leverage effect 영업면에서의 증익효과
operating loss 영업손실
operating margin 영업이익률
operating performance ratios 업적비율
operating profit 영업이익
operating profit and loss 영업손익
operating profit level 영업이익단계
operating profit margin 영업이익률
operating profit on sales 매출대비 영업이익률
operating profit or loss 영업손익
operating rate 조업도

operating ratio	가동률
operating receipt	영업수입
operating report	영업보고
operating reserve	영업준비금
operating results	영업성적
operating revenue	영업수익
operating section	영업손실구분
operating standing	영업상태
operating statement	손익계산서
operating surplus	영업잉여금
operating system	오퍼레이팅 시스템
operating target	조작목표
operation	조업
operation capacity	조업도
operation efficiency	작업능률
operation expenses	작업비
operation in the secondary market	유통시장조작
operation ratio	조업률
operation variance	조업도차이
operational decision	업무적 의사결정
operational efficiency	효율성
operational procedure	실시 절차
operations audit	업무감사
operations for stabilizing the stock market price	주가안정조작
operations research	오퍼레이션 리서치
operative clause	주문
operative words	효력발생문언
opinion	변호사 의견서
opinion of auditors	감사의견서
opinion of independent certified public accountant	감사보고서
opinion survey	의견조사

opportunity analysis	기회분석
opportunity cost	기회비용
opportunity gain	기회이익
opportunity loss	기회손실
opposite accounts	반대계정
opposite party	상대방
oppression	직권남용죄
optical character recognition	광학적 문자인식
optical computing	광 컴퓨팅
optical fiber cable	광 파이버 케이블
optimal condition	최적조건
optimal growth model	최적성장모형
optimal information	최적정보
optimal policy mix	최적 폴리시 믹스
optimal scale	최적규모
optimal strategy index	최적 전략지수
optimal threshold return	적성상하한계수익률
optimization	최적화
optimum advertisement cost	최적광고비
optimum allocation of resources	최적자원배분
optimum currency	최적통화지역
optimum distribution	최적분배
optimum foreign exchange reserves	적정외환준비금
optimum inventory	최적재고량
optimum network	최적네트워크
optimum output	최적생산량
optimum rate of growth	최적성장률
optimum rate of interest	최적이자율
optimum rate of operations	최적조업도
opting-out	오프팅 아웃
option	옵션, 선택권
option bond	옵션부채

option buyer 옵션바이어
option clearing corporation 옵션 청산회사
option combination 풋 콜 조합옵션
option delivery 옵션을 넘기다
option expiration date 옵션의 만기일
option market 옵션시장
option money 특권료
option performance index 옵션 퍼포먼스 지수
option period 선택권 행사 가능기간
option pool 옵션 풀
option position 옵션 포지션
option premier 옵션 프리미어
option pricing model 옵션가격 결정모형
option pricing theory 옵션가격 결정이론
option seller 옵션 판매자
option spreads 옵션 스프레드
option to double 배액감채약관
option transaction 옵션 거래
option warrants 주식매수권 증권
option writer 옵션판매자
optional assessment 원천선택과세
optional calling plan 선택통화요금
optional cancellation 임의해약
optional cargo 양지선택화물
optional court bond 임의재판보증증권
optional perils 선택부보가능위험
optional redemption 임의상환
optional repayment provision 선택적 상환조항
options on stock index futures 주가지수 선물옵션
oral testimony 구두증언
orbital structure 활동범위구조
order and disposition 명목상의 소유

order backlog 수주잔고
order bill of lading 지도인식 선하증권
order book official 오더 북 오피셜
order book tranding 주문부거래
order for attachment of property 전화주문
order for collection 차압명령
order for relief 구제명령
order frequency 주문빈도
order increase 수주증가
order nisi 가명령
order of application 적용순서
order of credit 채권순위
order of filiation 인지명령
order of liquidity 유동성배열법
order of preference 선호순위
order paper 지도식 증권
order stock 수중(手中) 주문
order to outside manufacturer 외주
order to pay 지불명령
order turnaround 주문회송
order volume 수주액
ordering cost 발주비
ordering point 발주점
orderly export marketing 질서있는 수출
orderly marketing agreement 시장질서 유지협정
orders in hand 수주잔고
ordinal scale 순서척도
ordinance 조례
ordinance by local government 조례
ordinary 경상
ordinary agent 생명보험 영업사원
ordinary and normal recurring operations 통상운영

ordinary annual expenditure 경상세출
ordinary annual revenue 경상세입
ordinary bank 보통은행
ordinary bill 보통어음
ordinary care 통상의 주의
ordinary charges 통상비용
ordinary collection 보통징수
ordinary conveyance 통상양도증서
ordinary corporation 보통법인
ordinary corporation income 보통소득
ordinary deposit 일반예금
ordinary depreciation 보통감가상각
ordinary dividend 보통배당
ordinary expenditure 경상비용
ordinary foreign tax credit 통상외국세액공제
ordinary franchise 무공제 면책보합
ordinary general meeting 통상총회
ordinary income 경상수입
ordinary income with recurrent nature 경상소득
ordinary insurance 보통보험
ordinary interest rate 통상이자율
ordinary life insurance 보통생명보험
ordinary local grant tax 보통교부세
ordinary losses 통상손해
ordinary partnership 보통조합
ordinary payment 통상결제
ordinary private company 통상사기업
ordinary profit 경상이익
ordinary profit and loss 경상손익
ordinary remittance 보통송금
ordinary risks of employment 사업상의 통상적인 위험

ordinary share	보통주
ordinary tax	경상세
ordinary temperature	상온
ore-leave	채굴면허
organ	기관지
organic composition of capital	자본의 유기적 구성
organic growth	유기적 성장
organismic model	유기체 모형
organization	창립
organization committee	창립위원
organization development	조직개발
organization expenses amortized	설립상환비
Organization for Asian Economic Cooperation	아시아경제협력기구
Organization for European Economic Cooperation	구주경제협력기구
organization meeting	창립총회
Organization of Arab Petroleum Exporting Countries	아랍석유수출국기구
Organization of Pacific Economic Cooperation	태평양지역경제협력기구
organization office	창립사무소
organizational buyer	조직구매자
organizational change	조직변경
organizational goal	조직목표
organizational strategy	조직전략
organizational structure	조직구조
organizations of primary commodity producers	일차산품생산국기구
organizer	창립자
organizing	조직만들기
original	원본

original capital	원시자본
original cost	취득원가
original cost method	취득원가법
original credit	원신용장
original document	원본
original entry	원시기입
original equipment manufacturing (OEM)	주문자 상표부착 생산
original goods	오리지널 상품
original insurance	원보험
original issue discount	발행시 할인
original jurisdiction	제1심 관할권
original money	본원적 화폐
original package	원포장
original policy	제1통 보험증권
original purchaser	당초 구입자
original rate	원수취 보험료율
original register	원부
originator	발기인
orthogonal	직교
orthogonal factor	직교인자
oscillation theory	진동이론
oscillator	오실래터
OTC company	점두등록기업
other account	타회계
other charges	영업외 비용
other income	잡수익
other insurance clause	타보험조항
other reserve	별도적립금
other revenues	잡수익
our account	당방(우리쪽) 회계
our side	당방(우리쪽)

out line	아웃 라인
out of date	기한경과
out of term	연기폐쇄
out of the money	아웃 어브 더 머니
out town bill	타지역 지불어음
out town check	타지역 지불수표
out town delivery	타지역 운반
out-cycle work	기계휴지시 작업
out-of-court settlement	시담해결
out-of-date check	실효수표
out-of-pocket cost	현금지불비용
out-of-pocket expense	현금지불비
out-of-work pay	실업수당
out-sourcing	아웃소싱
outbuilding	부속건물
ourdoor advertising	옥외광고
outgo	지출
outlaw strike	불법쟁의
outlay	출비
outlay cost	지출원가
outlay expiration	지출비소멸
outlay for advertisement	광고비
outlay tax	간접세
outlet store	아울렛 스토어
outline font	아웃라인 폰트
outlook for consumer spending	소비전망
output	거래총액
output coefficient	산출계수
output cost	제조원가
output method	생산고비례법
output reduction	조업단축
output variable	아웃풋 변수
outright base	무조건 매매(투기매매)

outright forward delivery with option	옵션부 순위인도
outright forward fixed date delivery	순월 확정일 인도
outright forward rate	아웃라이트 선물시세
outright forward rates fixed date	순월 확정일 상장
outright purchase	매절
outright sales	품절
outright transaction	아웃라이트 거래
outside capital	타인자본
outside day	아웃사이드 데이
outside dealing	장외거래
outside environment	외부환경
outside manufacturer	외주업자
outside money	외부화폐
outside premises coverage	구외담보
outside pressure	외압
outside product	외주제품
outside test	외부시험
outsider	장이 다른 것
outsider director	사외중역
outstanding	미지급의
outstanding account	미결제 계정
outstanding amount	발행잔액
outstanding balance	미지급잔액
outstanding balance of issue amount	발행잔고
outstanding balances	잔존원본
outstanding bond	기발사채, 미결채권
outstanding capital	발행제 자본
outstanding capital stock	주식발행액, 사외주식
outstanding contract amount	계약잔고
outstanding debt	미상환부채
outstanding liabilities	미지급부채
outstanding premiums	미수보험료

outstanding principal	잔존원금
outstanding shares	사외주
outstanding title	제3자의 권원
outward freight	발송운임
outward investment	대외투자
over and short account	현금과부족 계정
over drive processor	오버 드라이브 프로세서
over funding	오버 펀딩
over par	오버 파
over time	시간의 경과에 동반하다
over time price of bond	시간의 경과에 동반한 채권가격
over transfer	과잉 불입
over-the-counter currency option	점두통화옵션
over-the-counter market	점두시장
over-the-counter option	점두옵션
over-the-counter stock	점두주
over-the-counter transaction	점두거래
over-the-month delivery	익월수수
overabsorbed burden	간접비 배부초과액
overabsorbed cost	배부초과원가
overabsorption	초과배부
overall balance	종합수지
overall balance of foreign exchange	외환보유고
overall effective tax rate	종합효과세율
overall evaluation method	종합평가법
overall limitation	일괄공제 한도액
overall position	종합보유고
overborrowing	차입초과
overbought market	과매입시장
overbought position	매입 포지션
overbuying	과매입
overcapacity	설비과잉

overcapitalization 과대자본
overcarrying cost 이월비
overcompetition 과당경쟁
overdepreciation 초과상각
overdraft 당좌차월
overdraft economy 차월경제
overdraft facilities 당좌차월계약
overdraft interest 당좌차월이자
overdrafts for export bills 환당좌 대출
overdrawing 차월
overdrawn 대월
overdrawn account 대월회계
overdressing 과도한 분식
overdue 연체의
overdue account 기한경과 계정
overdue bill 기한경과 어음
overdue check 기한경과 수표
overdue interest 연체이자
overdue interest on loan on bills 어음대부연체이자
overdue interest per diem 연체일보
overdue loan 기한경과대부
overdue payment 기일도래채권
overestimate 과대평가
overestimation of goods traded in 하취상품의 과대평가
overestimation of inherited assets 인계자산의 과대평가
overestimation of investment in kind 현물출자의 과대평가
overexberant economy 과열경제
overfunded 자금이 크게 팽창했다
overhauling 수선
overhead 간접비
overhead allocation 제조간접비배부
overhead cost 간접비

overhead cost distribution	간접비 배부
overhead distribution basis	간접비 배부기준
overhead distribution sheet	부분비 계산표
overhead expenses	간접비
overhead rate	간접비 배부율
overhead variance	간접비 차이
overheated economy	과열경제
overheating of business activity	경기과열
overhedge	과대 헷지
overhung	달러 과잉
overindebted person	다액 채무자
overinsuance by double insurance	중복보험
overinsurance	초과보험
overinvestment	과잉투자
overissue	제한외 발행주식
overland freight	육상운송비
overlapping account	중복계정
overlapping debt	중복채무
overlapping time	오버랩핑 타임
overloan	대출초과
overman	조정인
overmonth loan	익월물
overnight	익일반제
overnight delivery	익일인도
overnight money	익일지불대부
overnight rate	오버나잇 레이트
overnight repo	현선거래
overnight transaction	오버나잇 거래
overpaid	과지불의
overpayment	과납
overprivilege	과잉특권
overproduction	생산과잉

overreaching clause	소유권유보조항
overriding commission	특별수수료
overrule	각하
overs and shorts	과부족
overseas affiliated firm	해외관계회사
overseas assets	해외자산
overseas business	해외사업
overseas interest rate	해외금리
overseas interests	대외이권
overseas investment	대외투자
overseas investment loss reserve	해외투자손실준비금
overseas investment report	해외투자보고서
overseas legal reserves	해외법정준비금
overseas liabilities	해외부채
overseas major market	해외주요시장
overseas production capacity	해외생산능력
overseas production ratio	해외생산비율
overseas transaction	해외거래
overseas transactions for technique	기술해외거래
overseas travel accident insurance	해외여행상해보험
overseas travel sickness insurance	해외여행질병보험
overseas traveling expense	해외여행비
overseas undertaking corporation	해외사업법인
overselling	과판매
overshoot	과행(過行)
overshoot method	오버슛 법
oversold	과판매의
oversold position	과판매의
overspeculation	과당투기
overstatement	과대표시
overstatement of taxable income	과대신고
overstock	과잉재고

oversupply	공급과다
overt	공공의
overt act	명백한 행위
overtime allowance	초과작업수당
overtime duties	초과작업
overtime working	초과작업
overtrading	회전상(행위)
overtransfer	과잉불입
overused hours	초과사용시간
overvaluation	과대평가
overvalued	값이 비싼
overvalued futures	값비싼 선물
owing	지불해야함
owing to bank	은행차입
own account	자기회계
own bill	자행인수
own capital	자기자본
own usance	자기수입
own-named cards	자사카드
owned capital	자기자본
owner	소유자
owner control	소유자지배
owner of record	명의상의 주주
owner trustee	오너 트러스티
owner's capital	주주자본
owner's equity	소유자 지분
owner's equity to total assets	자기자본비율
owner's risk	하주위험부담
ownership	소유권
ownership certificate	소유권증
ownership of expiration	만기표소유권
ownership specific advantages	소유특자우위

≪ P ≫

Paasche formula	파쉐방식
Pac-man defense	팩맨 디펜스
pacific blockade	평상시 봉쇄
package automobile policy	자동차 종합보험
package deal	일괄거래
package lease	패키지 리스
package policy	패키지 폴리시
package-deal contract	패키지 딜 계약
packet communication	파켓 통신
packet switching	파켓 교환
packing	짐꾸리기에 사용되는 비용
packing a jury	배심원의 선정을 속이는 일
packing and wrapping expenses	짐꾸리기 비용
packing charge	포장비
packing list	포장명세서
pact	협약
pacta sunt servanda	계약준수
page description language	페이지 기술언어
paid cash book	현금지불장
paid check	지불완료수표
paid-in capital	불입자본
paid-in capital in excess of par	주식불입잉여금
paid-in capital increase	유상증자
paid-in surplus	불입잉여금
paid-up addition	계약자배당에 의한 보험금액의 증가
paid-up capital	지급자본
paid-up insurance	보험료 지급완료 보험

paid-up-policy value	보험료 지급완료 보험금액
painting the tape	가격조작
pair cable	대 케이블
paired comparison	일대비교법
pairing-off	상호기권협정
palletization	팔레티제이션
panel	배심원명부
panel decision	위원회결정
panel doctor	보험의
panel patient	국민보험환자
panel research	패널 조사
panic market	공황시장
panic sale	패닉 세일
panicky selling	난매(亂賣)
pantent pool	특허풀
paper audit	서면감사
paper company	페이퍼 컴퍼니
paper crisis	종이홍수
paper currency	지폐
paper days	구두변론일
paper profit	가공이익
paper-book	소송기록서
paperless trading	페이퍼레스 트레이딩
par	액면
par bond	액면매매사채
par forward	파 포워드
par issue	액면 발행
par price	액면 가격
par value	액면가
par yield	파 일드
par-value capital stock	액면주식
par-value share	액면주식자본금

paradigm	규범
paradox of conceptualization	개념화의 역설
paragraph	항(項)
paralanguage	준언어
parallel import	평행수입
parallel issue	평행기채
parallel loan	파라렐 론
parallel market	파라렐 마켓
parallel money market	병행시장
parallel rate shift	금리의 평행이동
parallel shift	평행이동
parallel transaction	평행거래
parameter	매개변수
parametric design	파라메트릭 디자인
parametric test	모수 검정
paramount right	우월한 권리
para-tariff barrier	준관세장벽
parcel	일필의 토지
parent company	모회사
parent guaranteed	모회사보증부
parent store	본점
parenthetical notes	본체주기
pareto's constant	파레토 정수
pari passu	동순위로
Pariamentarians' code	의회강령
pari-mutuel betting	경마식 도박
Paris Club	파리클럽
Paris Union	파리동맹
parity	평가(平價)
parity account	패리티 계산
parity index	패리티 지수
parity line	패리티 직선

parity of official exchange rate 공정평가
parity quotation 평균상장
parity rate of exchange 환평가
parity value 패리티 가치
parity-grid 패리티 그리드
parking 피난
parliament 국회
parol contract 구두계약
parol license 구두허가
part finished product 반제품
part performance 일부이행
part-owners 공유자
part-timer 부업중개자
partial abandonment 일부 위탁
partial acceptance 일부 인수
partial assignment 일부 양도
partial audit 부분 감사
partial correlation 부분 상관
partial costing 부분 원가계산
partial delivery 일부 수수
partial elasticity 편탄력성
partial legal tender 불완전 법화(法貨)
partial loss 분손
partial payment 내입금(대금의 일부를 지불함)
partial proprietor 부분적 소유자
partial reserve system 일부준비제도
partial shipment 분할선적
partial tax transfer to local government 지방분여세
partially finished goods 반제품
partially finished goods ledger 반제품원장
participant 참가자

participating annuity	이익배당부연금
participating bond	이익참가사채
participating collision	연쇄충돌
participating preferred stock	참가우선주식
participating premium	이익배당부연금
participating stock	이익배당주
participation	참가
participation bank	참가은행
participation certificate	참가증권
participation group	참가집단
participation in seizure	참가차압
participation loan	참가융자
participation method	참가방식
participation preferred stock	참가우선주
particular average	단독해손
particular average warranty	분손약관
particular charges	특별비용
particular loss	분손
particulars	내역
particulars of account	회계명세
parties to lawsuit	소송당사자
partition	공유물 분할
partition of corporation	회사의 분할
partition of the estate	유산분할
partly paid bond	일부지불채권
partner	출자사원
partner shaft	파트너 샤프트
partners	조합원
partnership	조합
partnership assets	조합재산
party	당사자
party insuring	보험계약자

pass book	원장
pass dividend	분배하지 않다
pass on	전가하다
pass-along deal	가격인하거래
pass-through securities	패스 쓰로우 증권
passage	통과
passage of title	소유권 이전
passbook	통장
passbook savings account	통장저축예금계좌
passed dividend	무배당
passenger traffic receipts	여객수입
passengers liability insurance	승객배상책임보험
passengers tax	통행세
passing off	사칭통용
passing ratio	추이율
passive bond	무이자 사채
passive debt	무이자 채무
passive investment management	소극적 투자관리
passive learning	소극적 학습
passive management	소극적 관리
passive strategy	안전형 운용
passive trust	소극 신탁
passive waste	소극적 훼손
password	패스워드
past due interest	연체 이자
past performance	과거 실적
past performance control	과거 실적관리
past service benefit	과거 근무급료
past service credits	과거 근무가산
past service liability	과거 근무채무
past service pension	과거 근무년수
pasteurization	저온감균

patent	특허권
patent ambiguity	명백한 미불명료
patent applied for	특허출원중
patent attorney	특허 변리사
Patent Cooperation Treaty	특허협력조약
patent fee	특허료
patent infringement	특허권 침해
patent law	특허법
patent pending	특허출원중
patent period	특허유효기간
patent revision	특허개정
patent right	특허권
patentability	특허자격
patented article	특허품
patentee	특허권자
patentor	특허권 수여자
path	경로
pattern of consumption	소비패턴
pattern of portfolio return	포트폴리오의 수익패턴
pattern variable	패턴 변수
pauper	빈곤자
pause	조정
pawn	동산 저당물
pawn-shop	전당포
pawnee	질권자
pawnor	동산저당 입수자
Pax Americana	팍스 아메리카나
pay after tax	세금공제 급여
pay by card	카드 결제
pay down	현금지불
pay on application	확인지불
pay pause	임금동결

pay per view	패이 퍼 뷰
pay roll audit	급여 감사
pay television	패이 TV
pay-as-you-go-system	부과방식
pay-back period	회수기간
pay-freeze	임금동결
pay-off	일괄완제(부채따위를 모두 갚음)
pay-off diagram	패이-오프 다이어그램
pay-roll register	임금급여 지불장
pay-through bond	패이 쓰로우 채권
pay-up	추가지불
payable	지불만기의
payable at sight	일람지불
payable on a fixed date	확정일 지불
payable on demand	요구지불
payable register	지불전표 기입장
payable to beared	지참인 지불
payable to holder	소지인 지불식
payable to order	지도인 지불
payables	매입채무
payables to sales ratio	매출채무 비율
payback analysis	자본회수 분석
payback period	회수기간
payday	기불 일
paydown	패이다운
payee	수취인
payer	지불인
paying agent	지불대리인
paying bank	지불은행
paying in slip	임금전표
paying tax	납세
paying & warrant agency agreement	지불 보증 대리인 계약서

paymaster 주계
payment 결세
payment account agreement 지불준비회계계약
payment against acceptance 인수지불
payment against document 증권상환지불
payment at regular fixed times 정시지불
payment at short date 단기지불
payment bond 지불보증 증권
payment book 지불 기입장
payment by beneficiary 수익자 부담금
payment by bill 어음지급
payment by cash 현금지급
payment by installment 분할지급
payment by rough estimate 개산(概算)지급
payment by the result 성과지급
payment for another 대납
payment handling bank 불입취급은행
payment in advance 선금으로
payment in full 전액지급
payment in installments 분할납부
payment in kind 물납
payment in lump sum 일시지급
payment in part 대금의 일부를 미리 지급하는 것
payment in subrogation 대위납부
payment in substitution 대물변제
payment into court 공탁
payment of tax 세금납부
payment of tax in kind 현물납부
payment on account 대금의 일부를 미리 지급하는 것
payment on delivery 물품 인도후 결제
payment order 지불지도
payment periods 반제기간

payment record 지불조서
payment regarded as dividends 간주되어진 배당
payment slip 출금전표
payment statement 지급명세
payment stop 지급정지
payment supra 참가지급
payment system 결제수단
payment terms 지급조건
payment to nonresidents 비거주자의 급여소득
payment-in-kind preferred stock 현물지급 우선주
payoff 급여지급
payoff matrix 이익행렬
payoff pattern 수익패턴
payola 뇌물
payout 배당지급
payout ratio 배당성향
payroll 급여, 임금지급장
payroll deduction 임금공제
payroll deduction type investment trust 급여공제형 투자신탁
payroll savings life insurance 급여적립 생명보험
payroll tax 임금세
peaceable possession 평온한 점유
peak 경기의 절정
pearl harbor file 펄 하버 파일
Pease Bill 피즈법안
peculiar benefits 특수 수익
pecuniary considerations 금전적 보수
pecuniary damage 금전적 손해
pecuniary legacy 금전 유증
pecuniary relation 금전상의 관계
pecuniary transaction 금전거래

pedigree	가계
peer	동년배
pegged exchange	고정환율
pegged exchange rate system	고정환율제도
pegged market	고정율
pegged stock	고정주
pegging	가격의 안정화
pen position	종합 보유고
penal	형사상의
penal action	형사소송
penal interest	위약이자
penal regulations	벌칙
penal servitude	징역
penal statute	형벌법칙
penalty	위약금
penalty against employer and employee	쌍벌규정
penalty and fine	벌과금
penalty on delayed delivery	연체보상금
penalty rate	벌칙금리
penalty tax	가산세
pendency	미정
pendente lite	소송 계속중의
pending	미결의
penetration	삽입, 보급률
penetration chart	시장침투도
penetration price	침투가격
penetration price strategy	침투가격 전략
pennant	페넌트
penny stock	값이 저렴한 주식
pension	연금
pension and life insurance schemes	기업연금 · 기업보험

pension assets 연금자산
pension expense 연금비용
pension financing method 재정방식
pension fund 연금기금
pension fund management 연금기금관리
pension fund spread 연금기금 스프레드
pension fund surplus 연금기금 잉여
pension plan 연금계획
pension scheme 연금제도
pension trust 연금신탁
pensionable age 지급개시연령
pent road 대로
people meter 피플 미터
People's Finance Corporation 국민금융공고
People's Insurance Company of China 중국인민보험공사
peppercorn rent 명의뿐인 지대
per annum 1년씩
per annum rate 년리
per capita 일인당
per capita gross national product 일인당 국민총생산
per capita levy 일인당 세율
per capita rate 일인당 세율
per contra account 대조 회계
per contra noted discounted account 할인어음 회견회계
per diem 일일당
per diem allowance 일당
per diem rate for call loan 콜 일보
per incuriam 부주의에 의해
per procuration 대리로부터
per quod 그것으로부터
per se 본질적으로

per se illegal 그것 자체가 무효
per share data 1주당 수치
per share earning ratio 주가수익률
perceived risk 자각되어진 위험
perceived value 자각되어진 가치
percent distribution 구성비
percent of capacity use 가동률
percentage 수수료
percentage analysis 구성비율
percentage balance sheet 백분율 대차대조표
percentage depletion 비율 감모상각
percentage lease 임대차 수수료
percentage method 백분율법
percentage of capital structure 자본구성비율
percentage of completion basis 공사진행 기준
percentage of credit losses 대손(貸損)율
percentage of debt collection 회수율
percentage of delinquency 연체율
percentage of each classification of assets to total assets 자산구성 비율
percentage of profits available on net worth 자기자본 이익률
percentage of working force 노동비율
percentage on diminishing value plan 정률상각법
percentage statements 백분율 제무제표
percentage table 백분율표
percentage variation method 백분율 변이법
percentage-of-completion method 공사진행 기준
perception 점유하다
perceptual selectivity 지각선택성
perennial tax 영구세

perennial tenant right	영구 소작권
perfect competition	완전 경쟁
perfect obligation	완전 채무
perfect title	완전 권원
perfecting bail	보석완료
perfection standard cost	완전표준원가
perform well	유리하게 전개되다
performance	운용성적
performance analysis	성과분석
performance attribution	퍼포먼스 특성
performance guarantee	계약이행보증
performance requirements	퍼포먼스 요건
performance basis	업무수행기준
performance bond	이행보증증권
performance bond insurance	이행보증보험
performance characteristic	성능특성
performance evaluation	업적평가
performance fund	퍼포먼스 펀드
performance guarantee	이행보증
performance guarantee deposit	이행증거금
performance margin	퍼포먼스 보증금
performance measurement	퍼포먼스의 측도
performance of business	사업수행
performance of obligations of guarantee	보증채무의 이행
performance rating	인사고과
performance-based fee system	퍼포먼스 비례보수체계
peril	위험
peril clause	위험약관
peril point	위험점
perils ejusdem generis	동종위험
perils excepted	면책위험

perils not covered	중성위험
perils of the sea	바다의 고유위험
period	기한
period analysis	기간분석
period call market	정기콜시장
period charge	기간비용
period cost	기간원가
period expense	기간비용
period for tax	납기
period of economic growth	경제의 성장기
period of economic stability	경제의 안정기
period of integration	통합기
period of request for reconsideration	심사청구기간
periodic actual inventory	정기실지재고정리
periodic audit	정기감사
periodic average method	총평균법
periodic balance sheet	기말대차대조표
periodic income	기간이익
periodic inventory	기간재고정리
periodic pension cost	연금의 기간원가
periodic trial balance	기말시산표
periodical accounting	기간계산
periodical deposits	정기적금
periodical return	정기적 수익
periodical transaction	정기적 거래
periodicals	정기간행물
perishable property	소모 재산
perishable tool	소모공구
permanent account	영구 계정, 대차대조표 계정
permanent address	본적
permanent assets	영구자산
permanent auditor	상임감사역

permanent change 항구적 변경
permanent debt 영구공채
permanent difference 영구차이
permanent disability 영구고도장해
permanent employment system 종신고용제
permanent establishment 항구적 시설
permanent exhibit 상설전시
permanent facility 항구적 시설
permanent financing 영구대출
permanent health insurance 종신건강보험
permanent income 항상소득
permanent income hypothesis 항상소득가설
permanent injunction 종국차지명령
permanent liabilities 영구부채
permanent life insurance 종신보험
permanent tenant right 영구소작권
permanent trespass 계속적 침해
permeation of tight money policy 금융긴축의 침투
permissible error 허용오차
permissible loss ratio 허용손해율
permutation 교환
pernor of profits 수익자
perpetual annuity 종신연금
perpetual bond 영구채
perpetual fire insurance policy 영구화재보험증권
perpetual injunction 영구차지명령
perpetual inventory 계속재고정리
perpetual inventory method 계속기록법
perpetual lease 영구차지권
perpetual lessee 영구차지인
perpetual merchandise control 계속적 상품통제
perpetual warrant 영구보증

perpetuating testimony	증거의 증거보전
perpetuity	영구구속
perquisite	임시수입
persistency rate	계속률
person adjudged incompetent	금치산자
person receiving employment income	급여소득자
personable	계약능력자
personal accident insurance	상해보험
personal accident mutual insurance	상해상호보험
personal account	인명회계
personal action	인적소송
personal assets	동산
personal attribute	개인적 특질
personal average tax rate	평균개인세율
personal bankruptcy	개인파산
personal bias	개인적 편향
personal bill	개인 어음
personal checking account	개인당좌계정
personal communication network	개인통신망
personal consumption expenditure	개인소비
personal contact	대인접촉
personal contract	동산계약
personal covenant	인적약관
personal credit	개인신용
personal deposit	개인예금
personal disposable income	개인가처분 소득
personal distress	동산차압
personal dividend income	개인배당소득
personal estate	동산
personal exclusion from taxation	인적과세제외
personal exemption	기초공제
personal expenditure	개인지출

personal expenses	인건비
personal family corporation	동족주의의 동족회사
personal financing	개인대상금융
personal guarantee	개인보증
personal handyphone system	간이휴대전화
personal hereditament	인적상속재산
personal holding company	동족회사
personal identification number	암호번호
personal immunity	개인의 비밀보장권
personal income	개인소득
personal income from property	개인재산소득
personal income tax	개인소득세
personal influence	개인적 영향
personal insurance	개인보험
personal interest income	개인이자소득
personal judgment	인적 판결
personal knowledge	직접 인식
personal ledger	인명원장
personal liability	개인부채
personal liability insurance	개인배상 책임보험
personal liberty	신체의 자유
personal lines statistical plan	가계보험통계계획
personal loan	개인대부
personal media	인적 미디어
personal opinion	자기의견
personal pension	개인연금
personal pension scheme	개인연금제도
personal property	개인재산
personal property floater	가재 포괄보험
personal rental income	개인 임대소득
personal saving	개인저축
personal sector	개인부문

personal security	인적담보
personal service	개인서비스
personal tax	동산세
personal taxation	인적과세
personal valuation	개인적 평가
personality inventory	인물평가법
personality system	퍼스낼리티 체계
personality trait	인격특성
personification theory	의인론
personnel audit	인사감사
personnel division	인사부
personnel floater	개인소유물 포괄보험
personnel inspector	국세청 감찰관
personnel management	인사관리
personnel reshuffle	인사이동
personnel strategy	인사전략
persons in overseas service	해외 근무자
persons in parental authority	친권자
persuasibility	피설득성
petit jury	소배심
petition	청원
petition in bankruptcy	파산신청
petition of right	권리청원
petitioner	신청인
petrobond	원유가격연동형 사채
petrodollar	오일달러
petroleum act	석유업법
petroleum gas tax	석유가스세
petroleum tax	석유세
petty average	소해손
petty cash	소액 현금
petty cash book	소액현금의 출납장

petty cash payment	소액현금지급
petty cash system	소액현금제도
petty current deposit	소액현금예금
petty deposits	소액예금
petty expense analysis book	잡비 내역장
petty expenses	잡비
petty imprest	소액전도금
petty loss and profit	잡손익
petty-sum depreciable property	소액상환자산
petty-sum wasting property	소액감모자산
phantom market	유령시장
phantom shopper	가상매매객
phase change printer	용해형 프린터
phased construction	단계적인 건설
phase-in policy	단계적 이양정책
phases of economic cycle	경기순환의 국면
phatic communication	교감적 언어사용
Philadelphia plan	필라델피아 플랜
philanthropy	자선행위
Phillips curve	필립스 곡선
photo diode	포토 다이오드
photoconductor device	광전도체 장치
photomechanical process	사진제판
phototype setting	사진식자
physical access member	입회장에서 거래 가능한 회원
physical capital	실체자본
physical contingency	물리적 예비비
physical delivery	현실인도
physical depreciation	물리적 감가
physical destruction	실체적 멸실
physical distribution	물류
physical distribution function	물류기능

physical distribution responsibility	물류책임
physical distribution strategy	물류전략
physical inventory	실지재고정리
physical life	물리적 내용년수
physical safety	물적안전성
physical variance	추량차이
physical wear and tear	물리적 감모
physically handicapped person	신체장애자
physically handicapped person allowance	장애자 공제
physician's expense insurance	치료비 보험
physiological drive	생리적 동인
physiological needs	생리적 욕구
pica	파이카
pick up	상향
pick-up of inflation rate	인플레이션율의 상승
pick-up of yield	이율의 개선
picker	소액관련
picketing	픽켓팅
pickup bond	픽업채
pico second	피코 초
pictogram	회화도표
pie chart	분원도
pignorative contract	질권 설정계약
pilot marketing	파일럿 마케팅
pilot plant	파일럿 플랜트
pilot unit	시작기
pilotage	도선(導船) 안내료
pin number	암호번호
pioneering stage	개척단계
pip	핍
piracy	저작권 침해

pit	피트
pit reporter	피트 리포터
pixel	화소
place for tax payment	납세지
place of adjustment	공동해손정산지
place of business	사업소
place of delivery	인도장소
place of fiduciary	수탁취급장소
place of issue	유출지
place of payment	지불지
place of tax payment	납세지
placement	팔다
placement advertisement	인재모집광고
placer claim patent	채광권
placing memorandum	사모요령
plain deal	플래인 딜
plain language	보통어
plain vanilla	플래인 바닐라
plaint	소송신청서
plaintiff	원고
plaintiff legislation	원고보호입법
plaintiffs bond	원고보증
plan	계획
plan assets	연금자산
plan beneficiaries	플랜 가입자
plan documents	연금플랜규정서
plan termination insurance	연금제도종료보험
planned economy	계획경제
planning delivery	계획배송
planning hierarchy	계획계층
planning unit	계획단위
plant	공장

plant account	공장설비회계
plant and equipment	공장설비
plant capacity	생산설비
plant fund	설비자금
plant investment	설비투자
plant ledger	공장설비원장
plantation	대농원
plasma display	플라스마 디스플레이
plastic money	크레디트 카드
plasticity of demand	수요의 유연성
platform	플랫폼
playing cards tax	카드세
playright	흥행권
plaza accord	플라자 합의
plea bargaining	사법거래
plea in abatement	각하항변
plea in bar	소송방지항변
plea of guilty	유죄의 답변
plea side	민사부
plead	변호하다
pleading	변론, 항변
pledge	동산저당, 담보
pledged assets	저당잡힌 자산
pledged security	차입유가증권
pledgee	동산 저당권자
pledgeholder	전당물 수탁자
pledger	질권 설정자
pledgery	보증
pledging	플레징
pledgor	동산을 저당잡힌 사람
plenipotentiary	전권
plottage	토지의 평가

plowing-back	이익의 재투자
plug	짤막한 광고
plum	특별배당
plunger	경솔한 상장사
pluralistic competition	다원적 경쟁
plus-tick	직전 가격보다 높은 가격
point and figure method	포인트 앤 피규어 법
point estimate	점추정
point of indifference	무차별점
Point of Purchase (POP)	구매시점
point of sales	판매시점 정보관리
point scoring	점수기록제
point system	점수법
points	주장의 요점
points reserved	보유논점
poison pills	포이즌 필스
police court	무역형사재판소
policies for promoting competition	경쟁촉진정책
policies for restricting competition	경쟁제한정책
policy	보험증권
policy assignment	정책수단의 할당
policy coordination	정책협조
policy depreciation	정책적 감가상각
policy dividend	계약자 배당금
policy fee	증권발행 수수료
policy formulation	방침책정
policy jacket	보험증권의 본문
policy loan	보험증권 대부
policy mix	폴리시 믹스
policy number	보험증권번호
policy objective	최종목표
policy of the law	공서양속

policy proof of interest	이익보험증권
policy reserve	책임준비금
policy state	정책 포지션
policy summary	계약개요
policy territory	증권적용지역
policy valuation	협정보험가액
policy value	보험증권가액
policy writing agent	보험증권발행대리점
policy year basis	인수년도별 계산
policyholder	보험계약자
policyholder's dividend	보험계약자 배당금
policyholder's reserve	계약자 준비금
policyholder's surplus	계약자 잉여금
political corporation	정치단체
political crime	정치범죄
political office	정치적 관직
political risk	정치리스크
political risk assessment	정치리스크 어세스먼트
political system stability index	정치안정지수
political turmoil	정치적 혼란
poll tax	인두세
pollution control facilities	공해예방시설
pollution control reserve	공해방지준비금
polycentric	현지지향
polycentrism	현지지향
polychronic	폴리크로닉
polynomial-trend	다항식 경향선
pool account	풀 계산
pool of fund approach	자금 풀 법
pool operation	풀 조작
pool reinsurance	풀 재보험
pool treaty	풀 특약

pooled buying	공동구입
pooled common stock account	합동보통주회계
pooled first mortgage	공동제1저당권
pooled income fund	합동수익기금
pooled marketing	공동마케팅
pooled private placement bond account	합동사모채회계
pooled publicly traded bond account	합동공모채회계
pooled real property account	합동부동산회계
pooling arrangement	재보험풀링
pooling contracts	공동계산계약
pooling of interests	지분 풀링
poor laws	구빈법
popular action	민중소송
popular stock	인기종목(상표)
population composition	인구구성
population density	인구밀도
population mortality	국민사망표
populism	포플리즘
port charges	항만료
port dues	입항세
port risks insurance	계선보험
port toll	육양세
portable pension	이동계속년수
portage	운임
portfolio	운용자산
portfolio analysis	포트폴리오 분석
portfolio approach	포트폴리오 수법
portfolio balance approach	포트폴리오 밸런스 어프로치
portfolio bond	포트폴리오 채권
portfolio characteristic line	포트폴리오의 특성선

portfolio engineers	포트폴리오 엔지니어
portfolio investment	자산운용투자, 증권투자
portfolio management	포트폴리오 관리
portfolio method	전자산 합동방식
portfolio mix	포트폴리오 믹스
portfolio monitoring	포트폴리오 모니터링
portfolio of investment trust	투신종목
portfolio optimization	포트폴리오 최적화
portfolio premium	포트폴리오 보험료
portfolio pricing methodology	포트폴리오 가격결정방법
portfolio reinsurance	포트폴리오 재보험
portfolio restructuring	포트폴리오 재편
portfolio revision	포트폴리오 수정
portfolio risk model	포트폴리오 위험모형
portfolio selection	자산선택
portfolio theory	포트폴리오 이론
portfolio view	포트폴리오 견지
position	환보유고
position blanket bond	직무별 포괄 보증증권
position bookkeeping	평형 부기
position delta	포지션 델타
position floating policy	직무별 포괄 신용보험
position gamma	포지션 감마
position instruction	포지션 지도
position media	위치매개
position sheet	운용장
position trader	포지션 트래이더
position trading	포지션 매매
positioning	위치부
positioning analysis	포지셔닝 분석
positive	실정의
positive adjustment policies	적극적 조정정책

positive carry	포지티브 캐리
positive condition	적극조건
positive confirmation	적극적 확인
positive credit file	포지티브 정보
positive figure	흑자
positive film	포지티브 필름
positive financial policy	적극 재정
positive law	실정법
positive leverage effect	정(正)의 레버리지효과
positive marketing	실증적 마케팅
positive monetary position	금전채권의 초과상태
positive prescription	취득시효
positive property	적극 재산
positive yield curve	정(正)의 이윤곡선
positivism	실증주의
possession	점유
possession corporation	속령 기업
possession in deed	현실의 점유
possession in law	법정점유
possession of land	토지점유
possession of property	자산소유
possession utility	소유효용
possessory action	점유소송
possessory interest	단순점유권
possibility	불확정권
post	전기하다
post-audit	사후감사
post-close account	마감후 회계
post-closing entry	마감후 기입
post-closing trial balance	이월계산표
post-decision dissonance	의사결정후의 불협화
post-due bill	기한경과어음

post-entry	추가기입
post-facto	사후의
post-imperialism	포스트제국주의
post-industrial society	탈공업화 사회
post-production	생산후의
post-qualification	사후자격심사
post office annuity	우편연금
post office life insurance	간이생명보험
post to the ledger	원장에 전기하다
postage	우송료
postage paid	우송료 지불완료
postage to be paid on delivery	우송료 선불
postal money order	우편환
postal savings deposit	우체국 저축예금
postal transfer account	대체계좌
postdate	전일(前日) 소인
postdated check	전일소인 수표
posted price	공시가격
posterior analysis	사후분석
posterior probabilities	경험적 확률
posting	전기
postmortem divided	사후배당
postponement	연기
postponement of investment	투자순연(順延)
postponement of payment	지불유예
postponement of tax collection	징수의 유예
postponement of tax payment	연납
postponement benefit	퇴직후 급부
postscript graphic	포스트스크립트 그래픽
postulate of accounting period	회계기간의 공준
postulate of business entity	기업실체의 공준
potential competition	잠재적 경쟁

potential customer	잠재고객
potential demand	잠재수요
potential existence	잠재적 존재
potential injury	잠재적 가해
potential oversupply produced by new issues	증자압박
pound bloc	파운드 블록
pound crisis	파운드 위기
pound sterling commercial paper	영국 파운드 CP
pound sterling currency futrures	영국 파운드 통화선물
pound sterling depositary interest futures	영국 파운드 예금금리 선물
pound sterling time deposit	영국 파운드 정기예금
poundage	집행수수료
poverty line	빈곤선
power	권한
power appendant	부종적 지명권
power curve	검출력 곡선
power expense	전력비
power in gross	독립지명권
power of appointment	지명권
power of attorney	위임장
power of collection	징수권
power of sale	매각권
power structure	권력구조
practicable	실무적으로 가능
practical economy	실전경제
practice	경영하다
practitioner	실무가
pragmatics	실용론
pragmatism	실용주의
prayer	청구취지신청

preacquisition profit	취득일 이전의 유보이익
preamble	서문
preappointed evidences	법이 예정한 증거
preapproach	예비접근
preaudience	우선발언권
preaudit	사전감사
prebid agreement	프레비드 계약
precarious right	불안정의 권리
precaution	주의
precautionary motive	예비적 동기
precedence	우위
precedence rule on tax collection	징수순위
precedent	선례
preceding fiscal year	전년도
preceding page	전엽
preceding taxable year	전사업년수
preceding year	전년
precept	명령
precision	정밀도
preclusive specification	배타적 수단
precognition	증인예비심문
precontract	선계약
precontract assessment	계약전 평가
predate	전일소인으로 하다
predecessor company	피합병회사
predetermined burden rate	예정배부율
predetermined cost	예정원가
predetermined cost system	예정원가계산
predicted cost	예정원가
prediction error	예측오차
prediction of investment return	투자수익의 예측
prediction validity	예측타당성

predictors of default	채무불이행의 예측지표
preemption	우선매입권
preemption entry	선매권의 신청·등록
preemptive right	신주우선적 인수권
preemptory	전단적
preemptory instruction	결정적 지시
preemptory nonsuit	결정적 각하
prefabrication	사전가공
prefectural bond	지방채
prefectural inhabitants tax	지방주민세
prefectural tax	지방세
preference	선호, 우선권
preference dividend	우선배당
preference for interest rate	금리선호
preference income	우선소득
preference of financial assets	금융자산선호
preference segmentation	선호에 의한 세분화
preference share	우선주
preferential	특혜적
preferential creditor	우선채권자
preferential duty	특혜 관세
preferential payment in bankruptcy	파산우선지불
preferential reinsurance	우선재보험
preferential right	우선권
preferential tariff	특혜관세
preferred creditor	우선채권자
preferred dividend	우선배당
preferred dividend coverage ratio	우선배당 부담배율
preferred liability	우선채무
preferred risk	우량물건
preferred stock	우선주
prejudice	권리훼손, 편견

preliminary advice	준비(시험)충고
preliminary audit	예비감사
preliminary balance sheet	예비대차대조표
preliminary bordereau	예정 각서
preliminary claim	예비 클레임
preliminary disclosure of settlement of accounts	결산예비발표
preliminary examination	예비심문
preliminary information	예비정보
preliminary investigation	예비조사
preliminary prospectus	가예견서
preliminary review	예비심사
premature death	조기사망
prematurity redemption	조기상환
premerger notification	사전신고제
premise of a going concern	계속기업을 전제로
premises	서출문언
premises coverage	구내담보
premium	권리금, 보험금
premium adjustment clasuse	보험료 조정조항
premium base	기준보험료
premium bill	보험료 청구서
premium bordereau	보험료 각서
premium condition	프리미엄 상태
premium deposit	특약 재보험 예금
premium discount	보험료를 현장에서 되돌려줌
premium discount for good risks	우량물건 할인
premium due	지급기일이 된 보험료
premium in arrears	미수보험료
premium income	수입보험료
premium issue	프리미엄 발행
premium loan	보험료대체대부

premium on bonds payable 사채할증발행차금
premium on capital stock 주식지불잉여금
premium over conversion value 전환가격을 초과한 금액
premium payment of a retirement annuity 퇴직연금부금
premium pricing strategy 특별가격전략
premium quotation system 프리미엄 매매기준방식
premium sale 경품첨부판매
premium statement 보험료 정산서
premium tax 보험과세
premium trust fund 보험료 신탁기금
premium written 계상보험료
prenegotiation 사전교섭
preopening expenses 창립준비비
preoperating cost and similar deferrals 순연(順延) 자산
prepaid 선불한
prepaid card 선불카드
prepaid expense 선불비용
prepaid freight 선불운임
prepaid income 선불이익
prepaid income taxes 선불법인세
prepaid insurance 선불보험료
prepaid insurance premiums 미경과보험료
prepaid interest 선불이자
prepaid rents on buildings 선불임대료
prepaid salaries and wages 전도 급료 임금
preparatory audit 사전조사
prepay 선지급하다
prepayment 도중상황
prepayment of income tax 예정납세
prepayment of premiums 보험료 일괄 선불

prepayment of tax	조세의 예납
prepayment option	선지급 옵션
prepayment projection	조기상환예상
prepayment risk	조기상환위험
preprint	선인쇄
preproduction cost	생산준비 원가
preproduction grant	산출준비특권부여
prequalification	사전자격심사
presale order	사전판매
prescript	법령
prescription	시효
prescription acquisitive	취득시효
prescription extinctive	소멸시효
present data analysis	현장분석
present of money in token of sympathy	위문금
present price	현재가격
present value	현재가치
present value discounted at compound interest	복리현가
present value method	현가법
present value rate	현가율
present worth	현재가치
presentation	제시
presentation bill	일람지급어음
presentation for acceptance	인수제시
presentation for payment	지급제시
presentation period for payment	지급제시은행
presenting bank	제시은행
presentment	제시
presentment of bill of exchange	환어음의 제시
presents	본증서

preservation	보존
preservative attachment	채권보전
preservative security	보전담보
preservative seizure	보전차압
president	총재
press law	출판법
press release	신문발표
pressure group	압력단체
prestige price	위광가격
presumption	추정
presumption of a real obtainer of income	소득귀속의 추정
presumption of fact	사실상의 추정
presumptive evidence	추정증거
presumptive heir	법정추정 상속인
pretax accounting income	조세차감전 회계이익
pretax income	조세차감전 이익
pretax income to sales	판매세차감전 이익률
prevailing price	일반가격
prevailing value	제조달 가치
prevailing wage	일반임금
preventional cost	예방비용
preventive action	예방처치
preventive justice	예방사법
preventive law	예방법학
preventive maintenance	예방보전
previous close	전일종가
previous illness	조급증
previous indorsements guaranteed	선행이서의 진정증명
previous insurers	선순위보험자
previous term	전기
previous year	전년

price action	가격행동
price adjustment	가격조정
price agreed upon	협정가격
price agreement	가격협정
price analysis	가격분석
price auction	가격입찰
price bargaining	가격교섭
price before tax	세전가격
price book-value ratio	주가순자산 배율
price boost	가격상승
price cartel	가격 카르텔
price cashflow ratio	가격 캐쉬플로 비율
price competition	가격경쟁
price concession	가격양보
price contingency	인플레이션 예비비
price contract	가격계약
price control	가격통제
price cutting	가격인하
price determination	가격결정
price discrimination	가격차별
price divergence	가격이탈
price effect	가격효과
price elasticity	가격탄력성
price elasticity of demand	수요의 가격탄력성
price equalization	가격균등화
price factor	가격계수
price filter	프라이스 필터
price fixing	가격결정
price flexibility	가격의 신축성
price fluctuation	가격변동
price fluctuation reserve	가격변동준비금
price freeze	가격동결

price guaranty	가격보증
price hike	가격인상
price image	가격이미지
price including tax	세금포함 가격
price index	물가지수
price indication method	가격 표시방법
price information	가격정보
price leader	가격선도자
price level	물가수준
price limit	가격폭제한
price limit on commodity futures	상품선물 거래가격폭 제한
price line	가격선
price line of futures price	선물가격곡선
price maker	프라이스 메이커
price margin	가격차익
price mechanism	가격 메커니즘
price mix	가격 믹스
price movement limit	가격폭 제한
price movement of stocks	주가의 움직임
price of corporate bond	사채가격
price of introduced stock	공개가격
price pattern	가격패턴
price priority	가격우선
price protection	가격보호
price pyramid	가격 피라미드
price quotation	매매기준가격
price range	가격폭
price revision	가격개정
price risk	가격위험
price spread	가격의 차이
price stabilization	가격안정
price stabilization policy	물가안정정책

price strategy 가격전략
price structure 가격구조
price supporting 가격안정조작
price system 가격체계
price theory 가격이론
price variation 물가변동
price volatility 가격 볼래틸러티
price war 가격전쟁
price weighted index 평균가격 가중지수
price-support subsidy 가격차 보급금
price-trend on stocks 주가트랜드
price-yield curve 가격 · 이율곡선
prices less tax 세금공제가격
pricing 금리결정, 가격결정
pricing calculation 가격계산
pricing decision 가격결정
pricing model 가격결정모형
pricing strategy 가격결정전략
pricing tool 가격결정도구
prima facie 한번 본 시점에
primage 운임할증
primage duty 수입부가세
primaries 예선
primary account 제1차 회계
primary advance 1차적 부동산 이전행위
primary beneficiary 제1순위 보험금 수취인
primary capital 제1차 자본
primary data 제1차 데이터
primary dealer 프라이머리 딜러
primary deposit 본원적 예금
primary distributions 제1차 분매
primary election 예비선거

primary goods	제1차 산품
primary industry	제1차 산업
primary industry product export	제1차 산품수출
primary liability	제1차 부채
primary market	기채시장
primary materials	원재료
primary mortgage market	저당권의 신규발행시장
primary processed goods	주요가공품
primary regulation notice	기본통달
primary reserve assets	제1차 준비자금
primary securities	직접증권
primary securities market	증권발행시장
primary stimuli	1차 자극
primary user	주 이용자
prime bankers acceptance	일류은행 인수어음
prime bill	우량어음
prime contract	원계약
prime corporate bonds	일류사채
prime cost	수입원가
prime cost method	직접원가 배부법
prime factor	주요인
prime interest rate	프라임 레이트, 우대대출금리
prime name bank	초일류은행
prime paper	우량어음
prime product	주제품
prime rate	프라임 레이트, 우대대출금리
principal	원본, 본인
principal amortization schedule	원본상환방법
principal amount	원금
principal and interest	원리
principal books	주요장부
principal component analysis	주성분분석

principal guaranteed	원본보증
principal paying	주지불
principal paying agent	주지불 대리인
principal payment	원본의 지불
principal place of business	영업상의 본거
principal production order	주요 제조지도서
principal products	주제품
principal sum	기본 보험금액
principal tax	본세
principal of ascertained claim	권리확정주의
principle of balanced budget	건전재정주의
principle of clarity	명료성의 원리
principle of comparative advantage	비교우위의 원리
principle of conservatism	보수주의 원리
principle of consistency	계속성의 원칙
principle of cost allocation	비용배분의 원칙
principle of cross liabilities	교차책임주의
principle of disclosure	공개성의 원칙
principle of effective demand	유효수요의 원리
principle of equilibrium	균형의 원리
principle of equivalence	수지상승의 원칙
principle of gross budget accounting	총액 예산주의
principle of increasing risk	위험 체증의 원리
principle of least effort	최소 노력의 원리
principle of matching	대응의 원칙
principle of materiality	중요성 원칙
principle of need	필요성 원칙
principle of orderly system of bookkeeping	정규부기의 원칙
principle of perennial tax	영구세 주의
principle of place of management and control	관리지배지주의

principle of priority of national tax claim　국세채권우선원칙
principle of priority to first seizure　차압 선착순주의
principle of realization　실현주의의 원칙
principle of single budget　예산단일주의
principle of single liability　단일책임주의
principle of surplus section　잉여금 구분의 원칙
principle of taxation　조세원칙
principle of taxation on actual beneficiary　실질주의
principle of the freedom of contract　계약자유의 원칙
principle of truth　진실성의 원칙
principle of unified accounting　회계단일원칙
principle of valuation　평가원칙
principles of consolidation　연결방침
print media　인쇄매체
printed matter　인쇄물
printing plate　쇄판
prior approval　사전인가제도
prior distribution　사전분포
prior lien　선취유치권
prior lien bond　선취특권채, 우선담보권부 사채
prior period adjustment　전기손익수정
prior preferred stock　제1우선주
prior probability　사전 확률
prior redemption　만기전 상환
prior service cost　과거근무비용
prior taxable year　전사업년도
prior use　우선사용
prior year adjustment items　과년도 손익수정항목
priori probability　선험적 확률
priority　우선성

priority creditor	우선채권자
priority of attachment	우선 차압권
priority of mortgage	저당 우선권
priority of taxes	조세 우선권
priority order of application	충당순위
priority rate of duty	실행관세율
priority reinsurance	우선재보험
prisoner's dilemma	범인딜레마
private account	내회계
private accountant	사적회계사
private automobile policy	자가용 자동차보험
private bill	개인어음
private bond	민간채
private branch exchange	구내교환기
private brand	자가브랜드
private capital	민간자본
private company	비공개기업
private consumption	민간소비
private contract	수의계약
private convertible note	사모전환사채
private corporation	민간회사
private delivery system	자사배송시스템
private enterprise	민영사업
Private Equity Fund (PEF)	사모펀드
private holding company	동족회사
private insurance	자가보험
private insurance company	민영보험회사
private international law	국제사법
private label card	제휴자사카드
private ledger	사용원장
private member	개인회원
private note	사모채

private nuisance	사적불법방해
private offering	사모
private pension	기업연금
private pension plan	기업연금제
private placement	사모발행
private placement bond	연고채
private placement local government bond	연고지방채
private placement securities	사모증권
private placement special bond	연고특별채
private placement straight bond	사모보통사채
private right	사권
private sale	폐쇄매각
private settlement	시담
private subscription	연고모집
private telecommunication network	사설통신회선
private tender	지명입찰
private trust	사익신탁
private undertaking	민간사업
private use	사적사용
privately placed bond	비공모채
privatization	민영화
privilege	특권면책
privilege of conversion	전환특전
privilege tax	영업세
privileged allocation of issuance to stockholders	주주우선 모입
privileged debts	우선지급채권
privileges and immunities	특권 및 면제
privity of contract	계약관계
prize offered for advertisement of the business	사업광고를 위한 상품

pro hac vice	이 경우에 한해서
pro rata distribution clause	보험금액 할당조항
pro rata payment	안분 지불
pro se	자기 자신으로
pro-trade biased growth	순무역편향적 성장
proactive strategy	선행형 전략
probabilistic brand choice	확률론적 브랜드 선택
probabilistic characteristic lines	확률적 특성선
probabilistic forecasting	확률적 예측
probabilistic model	확률론적 모형
probabilistic model of preference	확률론적 선호모형
probability curve	확률곡선
probability distribution	확률분포
probability mass function	확률함수
probability of loss or damage	손해확률
probability sample	확률표본
probable	확률이 높다
probable cause	상당(적합)한 이유
probable dividend	예상배당
probable life	예상내용년수
probable maximum loss	예상최대손해액
probable yield	예상이율
probate	검증
probate bond	검인보증증권
probation	집행유예
problem detection study	문제발견법
problem identification	문제의 선별
procedural audit	수속감사
procedure	소송수속
procedures of tax adjustments	세무조사 수속
proceeding	소송수속
proceeds	수취고, 지불보험금

proceeds account agreement	지불준비회계계약
proceeds from disposals	처분수입
proceeds from external bond issuance	외채발행대금
proceeds from long-term debt	장기차입으로부터의 자금증가
proceeds of life insurance	생명보험금
proceeds of sale	매출액
process	소송수속
process analysis	공적분석
process capacity	공정능력
process color	프로세서 컬러
process control	공정관리
process cost accounting	공정별 원가계산
process cost system	종합 원가계산
process costing	공정별 원가계산
process for the recovery of taxes in arrears	세금체납처분
process innovation	프로세서 이노베이션
process modification	프로세스 변경
process of garnishment	채권수속
process of inspection	검사공정
process parameter	공정파라미터
process production	이관생산
process quality audit	공정품질관리
process specification	공정규정서
process study	공정분석
process variable	프로세스 관리특성
process verbal	조서
processed material	프로세스 관리특성
processing	가공
processing cost	가공비
processing deal trade	가공무역
processing expenses	가공비

processing tax	가공세
proctor	사무변호사
procuration	대리, 위임
procurement	수당
procurement cost	조달비
producer market	생산자 시장
producer price index	생산자 물가지수
producer's cartel	생산국 카르텔
producer's goods	생산재
producer's surplus	생산자 잉여
producing departments cost	제조부문비
product	제품
product assortment	제품구비
product attribute	제품특질
product attribute curve	제품속성곡선
product category	제품 카테고리
product classification	제품분류
product cost accounting	제품별 원가계산
product cycle theory	제품순환론
product deletion	제품삭제
product development	상품개발
product differentiation	상품의 차별화
product diversification	상품의 다양화
product family	제품군
product image	제품 이미지
product improvement	제품개량
product innovation era	상품혁신의 시대
product liability	제조물 배상책임
product liability insurance	제조물 배상책임 보험
product life cycle	제품 라이프 사이클
product maturity	제품 성숙
product mix	제품 믹스

product motive	제품 동기
product planning	제품 계획
product portfolio	제품 포트폴리오
product portfolio management	제품 포트폴리오 매니지먼트
product positioning	제품 포지셔닝
product price	제품가격
product proliferation	제품 증식효과
product quality	제품 품질
product recall	제품 회수
product research	제품 조사
product satisfactions	제품 만족
product sharing agreement	생산분여협정
product space	제품 공간
product warranties	제품 보증
product-in-hand contract	생산조건부계약
product-oriented	생산지향
production	생산고, 연출
production account	생산회계
production base	생산거점
production budget	제조예산
production capital	생산자본
production card	작업표
production control	생산관리
production control system	생산관리시스템
production cost	제조간접비
production department	제조부문
production efficiency variance	제조능률차이
production equipment	제조설비
production expenses	제조경비
production facility	생산설비
production function	생산함수
production goods	생산재

production labor cost	생산노무비
production level	조업도
production loan	프로덕션 론
production method	생산고 비례법
production order	제조지시서
production order cost accounting	개별원가계산
production orientation	생산지향
production permit	생산허가
production process	생산공정
production release	생산개시
production report	제조 보고서
production sharing	생산분배
production sharing agreement	생산분여협정
production stagement	제조보고서
production statistics	제품통계
production upon order	주문생산
productive wages	직접 임금
productivity	생산성
productivity inflation	생산성 격차 인플레이션
productivity measurement	생산성 측정
productivity of capital	자본의 생산성
productivity of labor	노동생산성
productivity ratio	생산성 지표
products	생산물
products and completed operation liability insurance	생산물 배상책임보험
products liability	제조물 배상책임
profession	직업
professional accountant	직업회계사
professional auditor	직업감사인
professional liability insurance	전문직업인 배상책임보험
professional publication	전문지

professional's market	전문가 상장
professionals	전문가 관련
profit	이익
profit account	이익회계
profit accruing from insurance	보험차익
profit accruing from refund of bonds and debentures	공사채의 상환익
profit accured from valuation	평가익
profit after expenses	경비공제 후 이익
profit after tax	세금공제 후 이익
profit and commissions form	이익 및 수수료 담보양식
profit and loss	손익
profit and loss account	손익회계
profit and loss break-even point	손익기점
profit and loss carried forward	이월손익
profit and loss equation	손익계산서등식
profit and loss method	손익법
profit and loss report	손익보고
profit and loss statement	손익계산서
profit and loss transaction	손익거래
profit available for dividend	배당가능 이익
profit before tax	세금공제 전이익
profit center	이익센터
profit chart	이익도표
profit commission	이익반환
profit control	이익관리
profit control chart	이익도표
profit corporation	영리법인
profit curve	이익곡선
profit debenture	수익사채
profit equation	이익방정식
profit form amalgamation	합병차익

profit from capital reduction 감자차익
profit from consolidation 합병차익
profit from merger 합병차익
profit from private funds offered 사재제공익
profit from redemption 상환차익
profit from sales of stocks 주식매각의
profit from the difference between new and old official prices 가격차임금
profit from trust 신탁이익
profit from valuation of assets 자산의 평가익
profit function 이익함수
profit goal 목표이익
profit growth 이익의 신장
profit growth rate 이익성장률
profit impact 수익효과
profit increase 증익
profit inflation 이윤 인플레이션
profit insurance 이익보험
profit making business 영리사업
profit management 이익관리
profit margin 이익폭
profit maximization 이윤극대화
profit motive 이윤동기
profit on redemption of discount bond 할인채의 상환익
profit on sale 매각익
profit on sale of real estate 부동산 매각익
profit or loss on foreign exchange 외환차 손익
profit per share 주당 이익
profit planning 이익계획
profit potential 잠재적 이익
profit prior to consolidation 연결전 이익
profit prior to incorporation 회사설립전 이익

profit profile 수익구조
profit quota 이익할당
profit rate of total liabilities and net worth 총자본 수익률
profit ratio 이익률
profit ratio of capital 자본이익률
profit responsibility 이익책임
profit slide 이익감소
profit taking 기세매매로 그 차익을 버는 일
profit tax 수익세
profit transferred 대체이익
profit volume graph 한계이익도표
profit-driven market 업적상장
profit-making business 영리사업
profit-sharing 이익 공유, 프로핏 셰어링
profit-sharing bond 이익분배사채
profit-sharing system 이익분배제도
profit-sharing securities 이윤증권
profit-sharing trust 이윤분배신탁
profit-volume ratio 한계이익률
profitability 수익성
profitability and investment analysis ratio 수익성 분석
profitable 수익률이 높다
profitable line of business 채산라인
profiteer 이득자
profits from immovables transactions 부동산매매익
proforma 시계
proforma account sales 추정매출
proforma amount 참고수치
proforma balance sheet 견적대차대조표
proforma bill/draft 견적환수표

proforma estimated cost	견적
proforma statement	견적재무제표
program budgeting	프로그램 예산
program evaluation and review technique	PERT, 퍼트(공정관리)법
program supplier	프로그램 공급자
program trading	프로그램 매매
programed instruction	프로그램 학습
programming method	프로그램 방식
progress payment	공사진행에 따른 지출
progressive average inventory method	총평균법
progressive cost	체증비
progressive income tax	누진소득세
progressive ledger	연속원장
progressive obsolescence	점진적 부진화
progressive tax rate	누진세율
progressive taxation	누진과세
prohibited risks	인수금지물건
prohibition of deposit transfer	예금의 양도금지
prohibition of endorsement	이서금지
prohibitive tax	금지적 세금
prohibitory injunction	금지적 차지명령
project finance	프로젝트 파이넌스
project simulator	프로젝트 시뮬레이터
projected balance sheet	견적대차대조표
projected benefit obligation	예측급부채무
projected demand	예측수요량
projected dividend	예상배당
projected financial statements	견적재무제표
projected holding period rate of return	기대보유기간수익률

projected income statement	견적손익계산서
projective methods	투영법
proliferation	확산
prolixity	불필요진술
promisee	수약자
promisor	계약자
promissory note	약속어음
promissory warranty	약속적 담보
promoter	발기인
promoter's share	발기인주
promoting mergers tax credit	합병촉진세액공제
promotion expenses	창업비
promotion mix	프로모션 믹스
promotional strategy	프로모션 전략
promotools	프로모션 용구
promulgation	공포
proof	증거
proof of loss	손해의 증명
propaganda	선전
propensity to consume	소비성향
propensity to import	수입성향
propensity to investment	투자성향
propensity to savings	저축성향
proper card	자사카드
proper journal	보통분개장
proper law	준거법
proper value	고유값
property	재산
property acquired	취득자산
property and equipment	고정자산
property and liability insurance	손해보험
property damage	재물손해

property depreciation insurance 신가보험
property for advertisement 광고선전용 자산
property for exchange 교환용 자산
property for experimental and research 시험연구용 자산
property for residence 거주용 재산
property for substitution 대체자산
property for transfer 양도자산
property income 재산소득
property insurance 동산보험
property ledger 재산원장
property life insurance 재산생명보험
property replaced by purchase 매환자산
property reserved 담보처리된 재산
property right 재산권
property subject to seizure 차압대상재산
property tax 고정자산세
property tax cadaster 고정자산 과세대장
property ward 재산구
proportional calculation 비례원가계산
proportional expenses 비례비
proportional method 일괄비례배분방식
proportional reinsurance 비례비율재보험
proportional reserve method 비례준비법
proportional reserve system 비례준비제도
proportional tax 비례세
proportional taxation 비례과세법
proportionally equal terms 비례적 평등조건
proportionally variable cost 비례적 가변비용
proposal letter 신청서
proposal method 신청방법
propound 제안하다

proprietary account	자본주 회계
proprietary company	사회사
proprietary insurance company	비상호조직 보험회사
proprietary right	소유권
proprietary trading	자기회계 매매
proprietor	소유자
proprietor deduction	사업주 공제
proprietor of a business	사업주
proprietor punishment	업주처벌제도
proprietors special expenses reserve	사업주특별경비 준비금
proprietorship	개인기업, 소유주 지분
proprietorship account	소유주 계정
proration	비례적 조정
prorogation	폐회
prose model	산문 모형
prosecuting attorney	검찰관
prosecutors office	검찰청
prospective cash receipts	입금예측액
prospective dividend rate	예상배당률
prospective method	장래법
prospective profit	기대이익
prospective rating	경험요율법
prospective return	예상수익률
prospective usable	사용가능기간
prospective yield	예상이율
prospective yield average	예상평균이율
prospectus	내용설명서
prospectus of promotion	회사설립 취지서
prosperous days	호경기시대
protecting the currency	통화방위
protection	보호영장
protection of investor	투자자보호

protective duty 보호관세
protective order 보호명령
protective put trading 프로젝티브 풋 거래
protective tariff 보호관세
protective trust 보호신탁
protectorate 보호령
protest 거절증서
protest charges 거절증서작성 수수료
protestation 이의신청
protested check 지급거절수표
protester 비판적 시청자
protestor 거절자
protocol 조약의정서
provable debt 입증가능한 채권
prove 증명하다
provident benefit 공제 급부금
provision 조건, 담보금
provision account 충당금 계정
provision for bad debts 대손 충당금
provision for surplus 적립금 이월
provision for tax 납세 충당금
provisional attachment 가압류
provisional budget 잠정예산
provisional disposition 가처분
provisional execution 가집행
provisional insurance 예정보험
provisional liquidator 잠정청산인
provisional order 가명령
provisional policy 예정보험
provisional rating 잠정평가(액)
provisional registration 가등기
provisional residence 가주소

provisional return	예정신고
provisional risk book	예정보험인수부
provisional seizure	가압류
provisional settlement of account	가결산
provisional sum	임시총계
provisional tariff	잠정세율
proviso	조건, 단서
provisory clause	단서조항
provocation	도발
proxemics	근접학, 공간학
proximate cause	주원인
proximate damage	직접손해
proximo	다음달의
proximo terms	익월일부 조건
proxy	대리
proxy currency	대용통화
proxy fight	위임장 쟁탈전
proxy solicitation	위임장 권유
proxy statement	주주회의의 소집통지
proxy variable	대용변수
proxy vote	위임장 투표
prudence	주의
prudent man rule	신중성의 원칙
prudent person rule	수탁자 책임
psychic income	심리소득
psychological consumer behavior	심리학적 소비자 행동
psychological element	심리적 요인
psychological laws	심리적 법칙
psychological line	사이컬로지컬 라인
psychological theory of exchange	환 심리론
psychometrics	계량심리학
public accountant	공인회계사

public acknowledgment	인지
public address	장내방송장치
public and corporate bond	공사채
public and corporate bond investment trust	공사채투자신탁
public assistance	생활보호
public auction	공매
public bidding	공개입찰
public body	공공단체
public bond dealing	공채매매
public bond investment trust	공사채투자신탁
public company	공개기업
public compensation bond	교부공채
public corporation	공사·공단
public corporation bond	공사채
public debt securities	공공채
public disclosure	공시
public domain software	퍼블릭 도메인 소프트
public dues	공과
public economics	공공경제학
public enterprise	공적기업
public expenditure	공공지출
public facilities tax	공동시설세
public finance	국가재정
public finance corporation	공고
public finance law	재정법
public goods	공공재
public health service	공중보건기관
public hearing	공청회
public impost	공과
public information	공개정보
public institution	공공기관

public insurance	공영보험
public interest corporation	공익법인
public investment	공공투자
public issue	공모채
public law	공법
public liability coverage	일반 손해배상 책임담보
public market	대중 시장
public measurer	공인검량인
public monopoly	전매
public notary	공증인
public notification	공시최고
public notification of auction	공매공고
public notification of returns	신고서 공시
public offering	공모
public offering business	공모사업
public order	공서
public pension	공적 연금
public policy	공익
public relations	공적 관계
public responsibility	공공책임
public sale	공개매각
public service	공공사업
public spending	공공지출
public subscription	공모
public summons	공시최고
public telecommunication business	공공통신사업
public trust	공익신탁
public utility	공공사업
public utility accounting	공익사업회계
public utility bond	공익사업채
public utility charges	공공요금
public utility rule	공익원칙

public welfare 공공복지
public work 공공사업
publicly held stock 공개주
publicly offered share 매출주
publicly subscribed share 공모주
publicly traded company 상장회사
publicly-held company 공개회사
publishing advertising 출판물광고
publishing cost 출판비
publishing law 출판법
publishing right 출판권
puffer 경매시 바람잡이
puffing 과장
pull strategy 풀전략
pulling-back 후퇴
pulse code modulation 펄스 코드 변조
pulse code modulation broadcasting PCM 방송
pump-priming effect 실마리 효과
punishment on penalty tax 추징처분
punitive damages 징벌적 손해배상
punitive tariff 제재관세
purchase 구매
purchase acquisition 흡수합병
purchase agent 매입 대리인
purchase agreement 매수 계약서
purchase allowance 매입 에누리
purchase amount 매입금
purchase and assumption 예금승계방식
purchase and sale statement 매매계산서
purchase behavior 구매행동
purchase book 매입장
purchase commission 구입수수료

purchase commitments	매입약정
purchase contract	선물매입
purchase cost	매입원가
purchase discount	매입할인
purchase face amount	매수액면 금액
purchase frequency	구매빈도
purchase fund	매입(대량매입) 자금
purchase group	매입 그룹
purchase investigation	매수의 임의조사
purchase ledger	매입처원장
purchase method	퍼처스 법
purchase money	매수대금
purchase money mortgage	토지대금 양도저당
purchase money obligation	매수대금 채무
purchase on credit	외상매입
purchase payment fund	부금적립기금
purchase price	구입대금
Purchasing Power Parity (PPP)	구매력평가
purchase return	구입반품
purchase tax	구입세
purchased parts	매입부품
purchaser	구입주
purchases and sales	매매
purchases budget	매입예산
purchases rebate	매입리베이트
purchasing agent	매수 대리인
purchasing cost	매입원가
purchasing expenses	매입비용
purchasing manager	구매부장
purchasing power gain or loss	구매력 변동손익
purchasing power of money	화폐의 구매력
purchasing power parity theory	구매력 평가이론
purchasing power risk	구매력 위험성

purchasing price	구입가격
purchasing redemption	매입상환
purchasing units	구매단위
pure cap	퓨어 캡
pure deferred life annuity	순수거치종신연금
pure discount bond	순할인채
pure endowment	생존보험
pure endowment insurance	생존보험
pure oligopoly	순수 과점
pure risk	순수 위험
purpose loan pursue	사용목적 특정대부
purview	본문
push money	보상금
push phone telephone line	푸쉬 회선
push pull	푸쉬 풀
put	매도청구권
put bond	상환청구권부 채권
put diagram	풋 다이어그램
put holder	풋 보유자
put option	풋 옵션
put ratio back spread trading	풋 레이쇼 백 스프레드 거래
put swaption	풋 스왑션
put-call ratio	풋 콜 비율
put-value line	풋 가격선
putative	추정상의
puttable bond	풋테이블 본드
puttabel swap	풋테이블 스왑
puttable swaption	풋테이블 스왑션
putting-out system	전대제도
pyramid management method	피라미드형 관리방식
pyramid marketing system	멀티상법
pyramiding	개서
pyramiding process	피라미딩 과정

≪ Q ≫

quadratic cost function	2차 비용함수
quadratic demand function	2차 수요함수
quadratic loss function	2차 손실함수
quadratic programing	2차 계획법
qualification	한정사항, 최격성, 면책사항
qualification criteria	자격기준
quadratic laws	자격법
quadratic process	적격성 확인 프로세스
qualified	적격의
qualified acceptance	조건인수
qualified acceptance heritage	한정상속
qualified acceptance of bill	비단순거래
qualified acceptance of inheritance	한정상속
qualified audit certificate	한정감사보고서
qualified endorsement	한정이서
qualified inheritance	한정상속
qualified opinion	한정의견
qualified pension contract	적격퇴직 연금계약
qualified pension funds	적격퇴직 연금적립금
qualified pension plan	적격퇴직연금
qualified pension system	적격퇴직연금제도
qualified privilege	제한적 면책특권
qualified property	제한적 재산권
qualified report	한정보고서
qualified spouse for deduction	공제대상 배우자
qualifying activity	유망객 결정
qualifying dimensions	제특성

qualifying reserve	한정준비금
qualifying stock option	종업원 자사주 구입권
qualitative analysis	정성(定性) 분석
qualitative credit control	질적 금융통제
qualitative criteria	정성(定性) 기준
qualitative economic policy	질적 경제정책
qualitative substantiality test	질적 실질성의 원칙
quality awareness	품질 의식
quality circle	품질관리 서클
quality class	고품질 클래스
quality control	품질 관리
quality cost approach	품질 비용법
quality description	품질 설명
quality effect	품질 효과
quality improvement	품질 개선
quality loop	품질 루프
quality loss	품질 감소
quality objective	품질목표
quality of earnings	이익의 질
quality paper	고급지
quality policy	품질 방침
quality record	품질 기록
quality related cost	품질관련 비용
quality surveillance	품질 감독
quality system	품질 시스템
quality variable	품질 변수
quantification	수량화
quantitative analysis	정량분석
quantitative approach	정량적 어프로치
quantitative asset allocation	정량 에셋 올로케이션
quantitative boom	수량경기
quantitative economic policy	양적 경제정책

quantitative market analysis	정량적 시장분석
quantitative model	정량 모델
quantitative monetary indicator	양적 금융지표
quantitative substantiality test	수량적 실질성의 원칙
quantitative tool	수량화 수단
quantity adjustment	수량 조정
quantity discount	수량 할인
quantity discount system	단계식 할인방식
quantity limit	수량제한
quantity of production	생산량
quantity sold	판매수량
quantity standard	수량표준
quantity theory of money	화폐수량이론
quantity variance	수량차이
quantize	양자화하다
quantum evaluation	금전적 평가
quantum mechanics	양자력학
quarter	4분기
quarter-days	사계지불 회계일
quarterly real growth rate	4분기토대 실질성장률
quarterly reports	4분기 보고서
quash	각하하다
quasi-arbitrator	준중재인
quasi-cartel	준카르텔
quasi-chain	준체인
quasi-compulsory saving	준강제저축
quasi-contract	준계약
quasi-currency	준통화
quasi-delict	준불법행위
quasi-easement	준지역권
quasi-equity	준주식
quasi-estoppel	준금지반언

quasi-final return	준확정신고
quasi-incompetent person	준금치산자
quasi-insurance	준보험
quasi-integration	반종합
quasi-judicial power	준사법적 권략
quasi-loan for consumption	준소비대차
quasi-member	회원이라 간주되어짐
quasi money	준화폐
quasi-public corporation	제3센터
queuing	(차례를) 기다리는 행렬
queuing model	기다리는 행렬모형
quick assets	당좌자산
quick assets ratio	당좌비율
quick assets to year's cash expenses	년간 지출당좌 비율
quick liabilities	단기부채
quick ratio	당좌비율
quick market	보합시장
quit	면책되다
quitting of business	사업의 폐지
quorum	법정수
quota	출자할당액
quota sample	할당표본
quota sampling	할당추출법
quota share treaty reinsurance	비례특약재보험
quotation	시세값
quotation exchange center	시세교환센터
quotation of over-the-counter issue	점두시세
quotation on overseas markets	해외시장
quote	매매기준가격
quote reporter	시세보고자
quoting high	높은 시세를 말하다

≪ R ≫

rack focus	초점을 맞추다
racketeering	강청
radian	래디안
radio communication	모선통신
raider	적대적 인수를 생각하는 주식취득자
raiding the market	불시판매
rail transportation	철도수송
railroad bonds	철도채
raising of funds	자산조달
raising of interest rate	금리인상
rally	되돌리다
random access memory	램(RAM)
random effect model	변동효과 모형
random fluctuation	불규칙변동
random numbers	난수
random price changes	불규칙한 가격변동
random sampling	무작위 추출법
random variable	확률변수
random walk theory	랜덤 워크이론
range	변동폭
range forward contract	레인지 포워드 거래
rank order	계급순위
ranking system	서열법
ransom insurance	유괴보험
rapid expansion	급증
rare stock	품귀 주
raster	래스터

ratable distribution	비례배당
ratable value	과세견적가격
rate	요율, 세금
rate card	매체요율표, 요금표
rate covenant	금리조항
rate cut	요율인하
rate down	요율저하
rate in foreign currency	외화통화시세
rate in home currency	자국통화시세
rate in overseas market	해외상장
rate of change	변화율
rate of estimated expenses	개산경비율
rate of increase	상승율
rate of inflation	인플레이션율, 물가상승율
rate of listed bond	공사채상장
rate of operating	가동률
rate of output	조업도
rate of premium	보험료율
rate of return	수익률
rate of stock-turn	상품회전율
rate of technical progress	기술진보율
rate of temporary duty	잠정세율
rate of turnover	회전율
rate of variable expenses	변동비율
rate of wage increase	임금인상률
rate papers	납세고지서
rate payment	지방세
rate scale	시청률 측정척도
rate sensitive assets	금리민감형자산
rate sensitive liability	금리민감형부채
rate policy	고료율 적용계약
rate value	정격값

ratepayer 조세부담자
ratification 비준
rating 시청률, 등급
rating agency 등급평가기관
rating of bond 채권등급
rating organization tariffs 등급조직관세
rating system 등급제도
ratio 비율
ratio analysis 비율분석
ratio call spread transaction 레이쇼 콜 스프레드 거래
ratio method 비율분석법
ratio of direct and indirect taxes 직간접 세율
ratio of earnings to dividends 이익금 대 배당금 비율
ratio of fixed liabilities to net worth 고정부채비율
ratio of general expenses to current income 일반경비율
ratio of gross profit to inventory investment 교차비율
ratio of gross profit to net sales 순매출액 총이익률
ratio of net worth to total capital 자기자본비율
ratio of operating profit to revenue 영업이익률
ratio of personnel expenses 인건비율
ratio of profit to capital 자본이익률
ratio of profit to net sales 매출고 이익률
ratio of receivable to inventories 수취회계 대 재고정리 자산비율
ratio of replacement 자산의 경신율
ratio of shareholding 지주비율
ratio of special depreciation deduction 특별상환율
rational motivation 합리적 동기부여
rational valuation 합리적 평가
rationalization 합리화
rationalization of production 생산합리화

rationing	배급제도
raw and processed materials	원재료
raw material	재료
raw material inventory	원재료 재고
Raw Materials Group	1차 상품 그룹
Restrictive Business Productes Code (RBP code)	제한적 거래관행 규칙
reach	도달범위, 누적도달률
reaching the top price	천정부지값
reaction	반작용
reaction curve	반응곡선
reactionary fall	반낙
read only memory	롬(ROM)
readership survey	열람률 조사
readjusting entry	재수정 기입
readjustment of taxation system	세제정리
ready money	즉시현금
ready reckoner	계산조견표
real account	실제계정
real action	대물소송
real assets	실물자산
real balance effect	실질화폐 잔고효과
real capital	실물자본
real chattels	물적동산
real contract	대물제약
real cost	실질원가
real credit	대물신용
real deposits	실질예금
real disposable income	실질 가처분 소득
real distress	부동산 차압
real earnings	실질소득
real economy	실체경제

real entity theory of corporation 법인실제설
real estate 부동산
real estate acquisition tax 부동산 취득세
real estate borker 부동산 브로커
real estate held for sale 판매용 토지
real estate in trust 부동산 신탁
real estate income 부동산 소득
real estate investment trust 부동산 투자신탁
real estate loan receivable 부동산저당 장기대부금
real estate mortgage 부동산 저당권
real estate security 부동산 담보
real estate tax 고정자산세
real evidence 물적 증거
real exchange rate 실질환율
real growth 실질 성장
real growth rate 실질 성장률
real guarantee 물상보증
real hereditament 물적상속재산
real income 실질소득
real income earner 실질소득자
real interest rate 실질금리
real investment 실물투자
real investment return 실질투자수익률
real obtainer of dividend income 배당소득으로의 귀속
real obtainer of interest income 이자소득의 귀속
real property 부동산
real property acquisition tax 부동산 취득세
real rate 실질이율
real right 물권
real term 실질단위
real time 리얼 타임, 실시간
real time communication 실시간 통신

real time processing	리얼 타임 처리
real unit labor cost	실질단위 노동금액
real wage	실질임금
real world computing	실세계 컴퓨팅
real yield	실질이율
real-bills doctrine	상업어음주의
realignment	재조정
realignment negotiation	재조정 교섭
realizable value	실현가능가액
realization	환가
realization basis	실현주의
realization of gains	수익의 실현
realization of tax liability	납세의무의 성립
realization principle	실현주의
realization sales	환금판매
realized appreciation	실현증가액
realized depreciation	실현감가상각
realized price system	실현 가격 시스템
realized profit	실현이익
realized revenue	실현수익
realized volatility	실현변동성
realized yield	실효이율
really rightful person	실질의 권리자
realm of being	존재영역
realty business	부동산업
reappraisal	평가체
reappraisement	재평가
rearrangement of budgent item	예산항목이체
reason for dishonor	지불불가사유
reasonable	합리적인, 상당한
reasonable depreciation	합리적인 상각, 상당한 상각
reasonable doubt	합리적 의심

reassessment	평가체
reassessment of taxes	과세의 재결정
rebalance	재평가
rebalancing strategies	리밸런싱 전략
rebate	환부, 매입리베이트
rebate of premium	보험료 리베이트
rebate on business	매입 리베이트
rebate on sale	매출 리베이트
rebound	반등
rebut	뒤집다
rebutting evidence	반증
recall	회수
recall method	기상법
recapitalization	자본재구성, 자본변경
recaption	자력회복
recapture	출재보해약
recapture clause	상환조항
receipt and payment bookkeeping	수지부기
receipt in full	전액영수증
receipt slip	입금전표
receipts and disbursements break-even point	수지분기점
receipts and payments	수입지출
receivables	수취채권
receivable and payable contract	채권채무계약
receivable from affiliate	관계회사 외상매출금
receivables turnover	매출채권 회전율
receive slip	입금전표
received margin	수입증거금
receiver	파산관재인
receiver in bankruptcy	파산관재인
receivership	채권자 구제수속

receiving	수취계정
receiving bank	수취은행
receiving inspection	구입검사
receiving monitor	상대선택기능
receiving order	재산관리명령
receiving quotation	수취회계 시세
receiving report	수입보고서
receiving stamp	접수인
recession	경기후퇴, 불황
recession cartel	불황 카르텔
recession period	경기 후퇴기
recipient	수취인
reciprocal	역수
reciprocal account	대응계정
reciprocal consignment	상호신탁판매
reciprocal contract	쌍무계약
reciprocal credit	포합신용장
reciprocal decision	상호결정
reciprocal demand	상호수요
reciprocal demand curve	상호수요곡선
reciprocal distribution method	상호배분법
reciprocal duties	호혜관세
reciprocal exchange	상호보험
reciprocal reinsurance	교환재보험
reciprocal transfer of property	자산의 상호교환
reciprocal treaty	교환재보험특약
reciprocity	교환재보험, 상호주의
recital clause	설명문언
recklessness	부주의
reclaimed land	매립지
reclaimed materials	재생원재료
reclamation	회복(만회)하다

reclassification	재분류
recognition of sales	매출액의 인식
recognitive dissonance	인지불협화음
recognizance	서약
recognized private operating agency	민간전기 통신사업자
recommended standard 232C	RS232C
recommended stock	추천주
reconcilement	조합
reconciliation	조정
reconciliation item	조정항목
reconciliation of surplus	잉여금조정서
reconciliation statement for current account	당좌조합표
reconciling type	잔고조정식
reconstruction expense	개축비
reconstruction works	개축공사
recontinuance	상속재산회복
reconversion	재전환
reconveyance	양도저당
record	등록
record a profit	이익을 계상하다
record date	기준일
record high	과거최고(값)
record low	새롭게 등장한 저렴한 가격
record of conviction	유죄판결 기록
record of payment	지불조서
record of seizure	차압조서
record on appeal	상소기록
record on removal	이송신청기록
record price	비싼 가격
record retention	기록의 보유
recorded cost	장부원가

recorder	기록관
recoup	손해를 회복하다
recoupment	공제권
recourse	구상권
recourse loan	리코스 론
recourse right	소급권
recover high	다시 높은 가격을 형성함
recoverable	회수가능한
recovery	회수, 회복
recovery cost	회수가능 원가
recovery expenditure	회수가능 지출
recovery of bad debt	대손회수
recovery of credits	채권회수
recovery legal status	복권
recovery of loss	결손회수
recovery value	회수가능가치
recreation plan	레크레이션 관리
recruiting expense	모집비
rectangular coordinates	직교좌표
recurring profit	경상이익
recurring profit and loss	경상손익
recusation	기피
recycle strategy	자원재이용전략
red B/L	적선하증권
red clause credit	전대신용장
red figure	적자
red green blue	RGB
red herring	가청어
red multinationals	레드 다국적 기업
red tape	관료주의
red-balance	적자잔액
redeem	저당재산을 되찾다

redeem before maturity	중도에 상환하다
redeemable bond	상환채권
redeemable preferred stock	상환우선주식
redeemable stock	상환주식
redemption	상환
redemption at fixed date	정시상환
redemption at market value	시가상환
redemption at maturity	만기상환
redemption before maturity	중도환금
redemption by lottery	추선상환
redemption by purchase	매입상환
redemption by yearly installment	연부상환
redemption date	상환기일
redemption from tax sale	공매한 것을 다시 되삼
redemption of bond	채권상환
redemption of external loan	외채상환
redemption of government securities	정부증권상환
redemption of pledge	전당물을 되찾음
redemption premium	상환 프리미엄
redemption profit	상환익
redemption value	상환가격
redevelopment	재개발
redirect examination	재직접심문
rediscount	재할인
rediscount policy	재할인 정책
rediscount rate	재할인 금리
redistributed cost	재배부 원가
redistribution of income	소득재분배
redress	구제
reduce holding ratio	조입비율을 인하하다
reduce to practice	실시화
reduced asset price	감자산가격

reduced instruction set computer	RISC
reduced old-age benefit	감액노령연금급부
reduced paid-up insurance	감액지불완료보험
reduced rate contribution clause	감률분담조항
reduced tax rate	경감세율
reduced tax rate on dividendpaid	배당경과
reduced tax rate on specified medical corporation	특정의료법인의 특별세율
reducing balanace method	체감잔고법
reducing unemployment rate	실업률 저감
reduction	공제
reduction and exemption of taxes	조세감면
reduction in price	값을 깎음
reduction of incidence	부담경감
reduction of operation	조업단축
reduction of stcok	감자
reduction of taxes	감세
reduction or exemption of tax	조세의 감면
reduction surplus	감자잉여금
reductions in long-term debt	장기차입 반제액
redundancy	여분, 과잉
reengineering	리엔지니어링
referable name	확인(조회)처
referee bond	조정인보증증권
referee in bankruptcy	파산심리인
referee in case of need	예비지불인
reference	조합, 중재합의
reference bank	조회 은행
reference behavior	준거행동
reference index	지표가 되는 지수
reference on consent	합의에 의한 사건부탁
reference period	참고기간

reference price system 참고 가격 시스템
reference rate 기준금리
reference zone 참고시장권
referral premium 소개사례
refinance system 리파이넌스 방식
refinancing 차환
refinancing bond 차환채
refinancing issue 차환발행
refix date 경신일
reflation 리플레이션
reflation policy 리플레이션 정책
reflection 반사광
reflow 환류
reform of the administrative structure 행정개혁
reformation 정정
refresher 특별(추가) 사례금
refund 환부금
refund annuity 상환식 어음
refund bond 선금반환보증증권
refund by final return 확정신고에 의한 환부
refund deferred life annuity 상환거치 종신연금
refund of overpayment 초과지불금 환부
refund of principal 원본상환
refund of taxes 세금환부
refund tax 환부세
refunded corporation tax 환부법인세
fefunding 차환
fefunding bond 상환보증증권
fefunding securities 차환증권
refundment 반환금
refundment guarantee 선금반환보증
refusal to deal 거래거부

regiocentric 지역지향
regional analysis 지역분석
regional bank 지역은행
regional brand 지역 브랜드
regional company 지역기업
regional differences 지역격차
regional economy 지역경제
regional exchange 지역거래소
regional headquarter 지역총괄본부조직
regional issue 지역판
regional market 지역시장
regional office 지역사무소
regional plan 지역계획
regional portfolio 특정지역 포트폴리오
regional station 지역국
regional taxation bureau 국세국
regionalism 지역주의
regionals 지방업자
regioncentrism 지역지향
register 등기부
register of cancellation of attachment 차압말소등기
register of government bonds 국채등록부
register of settlement of mortgage 저당권설정등기
registered 등기완료
registered bond 기명사채, 등록채
registered design 의장권
registered form 기명식
registered gilts 등록길트채
registered issues 등록종목(상표)
registered number 등기번호
registered office 본사사무소
registered owner 등록명의인

registered public accountant 경리사
registered representative 증권외무원
registered securities 기명식증권
registered share 등록주
registered society 등록조합
registered stock 기명주식
registered trade-mark 등록상표
registered trader 등록트레이더
registrar 등록기관
registrar of companies 회사등기소
registration 등기
registration agency 등록기관
registration and license tax 등록면허세
registration certificate 권리증
registration fee 등기료
registration formalities 등기수속
registration of alteration 변경등기
registration of copyright 판권등록
registration of design 의장등록
registration of establishment 설립등기
registration of incorporation 회사설립등기
registration of the right of pledge 저당권 등록
registration of transfer 이전 등기
registration statement 유가증권 신고서
registration tax 등록세
registry 등기부
regrating 매점
regression 회귀식
regression analysis 회귀분석
regression analysis method 회귀분석법
regression coefficient 회귀계수
regression correlation 회귀상관

regression equation	회귀방정식
regression model	회귀모형
regressive expectations	회귀적 기대
regressive taxation	역진과세
regular assortment	정방상품
regular audit	정시감사
regular delivery	통상수수
regular dividend	보통배당
regular fee	통상의 비용
regular member	정회원
regular panel	소집 배심원 명부
regular settlement	익일영업일 인도
regular transaction	보통거래
regular wage	기본급
regular wage standard	기준내 임금
regular way	보통거래
regular way of delivery	통상수수
regulated interest rate	규제금리
regulated investment company	규제투자회사
regulation	규제
regulation by government	정부규제
regulation of debt collection	회수규제
regulation of industrial structure	산업조정
regulation of lending	융자규제
regulation of retirement allowance	퇴직급여 규정
regulation of stock price	주가규제
Requlation Q	레귤레이션 Q
regulations of financial statements	재무제표 규제
regulations on foreign banks	외국은행 규제
regulatory agencies	규제기관
regulatory measure	규제조치
rehabilitation	갱생

rehearing	재심, 속심
rehypothecation	재담보설정
reimburse	구상하다
reimbursed expenses	입체경비
reimbursement	상환, 환불
reimbursement authorization	보상지불수권서
reimbursement benefit	보상급부
reimbursement method	생산고지불제
reimbursing bank	구상은행
reinforcement of response	반응강화
reinstatement clause	부활조항
reinsurance	재보험
reinsurance agreement	재보험 계약
reinsurance bordereau	재보험 보고서
reinsurance broker	재보험 중매인
reinsurance by coinsurance method	공동보험식 재보험
reinsurance by quota	비율재보험
reinsurance clause	재보험 조항
reinsurance commission	재보험 수수료
Reinsurance Exchange	리인슈런스 익스체인지
reinsurance pool	재보험 풀
reinsurance premium	재보험료
reinsurance premium rate	재보험료율
reinsurance recovery	재보험금
reinsurance return	재보험 반환금
reinsurance treaty	재보험특약
reinvested earnings	이익잉여금
reinvestigation organization	이의심리청
reinvestment	재투자
reinvestment rate	재투자 이율
reinvestment risk	재투자 위험
reinvoicing centre	리인보이싱 센터

rejected check	지불거절수표
rejection	기각
rejection certificate	거절증서
related businesses	관련사업
related company	관계회사
related cost	관련원가
related goods	관련재
related issue	관련종목(상표)
related party imports	관련당사자수입
related-item sales	관련상품판매
relation	효력소급
relation income	상대소득
relationship management system	거래처 종합관리
relationship models	관련모형
relative	상대
relative costs	상대적 비용
relative deprivation	상대적 박탈
relative error	상대오차
relative excepted risk	상대적 면책위험
relative income	상대소득
relative income hypothesis	상대소득가설
relative market share	상대적 마켓 쉐어
relative measures	상대적 측도
relative performance	상대적 퍼포먼스
relative price	상대가격
relative quality	상대적 품질
relative revenue	상대 수익
relative revenue curve	상대적 수익곡선
relative share	분배율
relative strength	상대적 강약도
relative viewing distance	상대 시거리
relator	소추대행자

relax 약해지다, 수그러지다
relaxation 완화
relaxation of tight money policy 금융완화정책
relay subsidiary 중계형 자회사
release from debts 채무면제
release of libel bond 차압해제청구보증증권
release of lien 선취특권 포기
release of security 담보해제
release of seizure 차압해제
relegation 추방
relevancy 관련성
relevant information 적절정보
relevant range 적합범위
relevant risk 관련 리스크
reliability engineering 신뢰성 공학
relief merger 구제합병
relief method 제거법
religious corporation 종교법인
relinquishing of business 사업폐지
remain buoyant 계속 호조를 유지하다
remain in surplus 흑자가 계속되다
remainder 잔고
remainder price 비망가격
remainder type 차액식
remaining period 잔존기간
remaining useful life 잔존 내용년수
remand of further proceedings 환송
remargin 추증
remarkably low price 현저히 낮은 가격
remeasurement 재측정
remedy 구제방법
remedy for violation of private right 권리구제제도

reminder advertising	리마인더 광고
remittance abroad	외국송금
remittance bill	송금환
remittance check	송금수표
remittee	수취인
remitter	권원회복
remitting bank	송금은행
remnant	잔존물
remodel	개조
remote area	벽지
remote cause	원인(遠因)
remote sensing	운융심사
removal	이전
removal expenses	제거비용
removal of seasonal effect	계절적 효과의 제거
remove	이전
removed assets	철거자산
remuneration	보수
render	말을 건네다
rendering of service	서비스의 제공
rendition of judgment	판결을 내리다
renewable term insurance	갱신조건부정기 보험
renewal	갱신
renewal after the maturity	기한후 개서 계속
renewal charge	갱신료
renewal commission	갱신수수료
renewal expenses	대체비용
renewal fee	갱신료
renewal of bills and notes	어음의 갱신
renewal premium	계속보험료
renewal projects	통계계획
renounce	거절하다

rent	지대
rent arrears	연체지대
rent charge	지대부담
rent income	임대료 수입
rent on real estate	부동산 임대료
rent payable	미지급 임대료
rent reasonably fixed	정당한 지대
rent roll	지대표
rent-paying capacity	임차료 지불능력
rental	임대료
rental agents' commissions	임차수수료
rental allowance	임대수당
rental expense	렌탈비용
rental income	임대소득
rental income insurance	임대보험
rental market value	임대시장
rental of real property	부동산 대부
rental revenue	리스료
rental service	임대업
rental value	임대가격
rentier class	비노동자층
rents and royalties	임대료 및 사용료 수입
rents of assize	정액지대
rents received	부동산 수입
renumeration	보수
reopen	리오픈
reorganization	재건
reorganization of corporation	회사갱생
reorganization proceedings	갱생수속
reorganization scheme	재건계획
repackage bond	리패키지채
repair	수선

repair equalization reserve	수선평균적립금
repair-shop	수선공장
repairing budget	수선비 예산
repairing expenses	수선비
repairing risks insurance	선박수선보험
repairs and maintenance	수선유지비
reparation	손해배상액
repatriation	이익회수
repayment	상환, 반환
repayment money	상환금, 반환금
repeal	취소
repeat purchase model	반복적 복구모형
repeated calculation	반복계산
repeating audit	반복감사
repercussion effect	파급효과
repetition research	반복조사
replaced property	매환자산
replacement	교체(대체)
replacement assets	대체자산
replacement by purchase	매환
replacement cost	대체원가
replacement cost accounting	대체원가회계
replacement cost coverage	재조달비용보험
replacement demand	대체수요
replacement expense	대체비용
replacement fertility	대체번식력
replacement in kind	현물전보
replacement investment	갱신투자
replacement method	50% 상환법
replacement of business property	사업용 자산의 매환
replacement of collateral	대체담보
replacement of loan	차입금 상환

replacement of property 자산의 매환
replacement potential 매환잠재력
replacement price 대체가격
replacement property by purchase 매환에 의한 자산의 교환
replacement rate 결손보충률
replacement reserve 설비갱신준비금
replacement risk 재취득위험
replacement unit 대체단위
replacement value 대체가치
replacement value insurance 신가보험
replacing 대체
replenish 보충하다
replenishing cost 보충발주비
replenishment 보충
replenishment of stock 재고보충
replevin 동산점유 회복소송
replicate 모조
report 보고서
report form 보고식
report form balance sheet 보고식 대차대조표
report of independent auditors 감사보고서
report on examination 검사보고서
report system 보고제도
reporting audit standards 감사보고기준
reporting currency 보고통화
reporting standards 감사보고기준
repossession 재소유, 회복
representation 표명
representation and warranty 레프리젠테이션 앤 워런티
representation work 표시작업
representative 대표자
representative democracy 대표민주제

representative director	대표관리자
representative liquidator	대표청산인
representative money	대표화폐
representative of corporation	법인의 대표자
representative office	주재원사무소
representative sample	표준견본
representative suit	대표소송
representing issue	대표종목(상표)
reprieve	집행연기
reprimand	견책
reprisal	자력취환
reproduction	재생산
reproduction cost	재생산 원가
reproduction on a diminishing scale	축소재생산
repudiation	거절, 포기
repugnancy	모순
repurchase	환매
repurchase agreement	환매 조건부거래
repurchase obligation	환매의무
repurchase price	환매가격
repurchase right	환매청구권
reputation	평가
reputed owner	표견적 소유자
request	청구
request for correction	경정의 청구
request for decision	품의
request for reconsideration	심사청구
request for reinvestigation	이의신청
request for share distribution	교부요구
request for wage increase	임금인상요구
request payment by securities	증권위탁납부
request repeat system	재송정정방식

requested return	의뢰반각
required accuracy	요구정도
required capital coefficient	필요자본계수
required quality	요구품질
required reserve	법정준비금
required reserve ratio	법정준비율
required reserves	소요준비
requirements	요건
requirements contract	납입계약
requirements of society	사회적 요구사항
requisite	필요요건
requisition	요구
res adjudicata	기판력
resale	재판매
resale price	재판매가격
resale price maintenance	재판매가격유지
resale price method	재판매가격기준법
rescheduling	리스케줄링
rescission	해약
rescue	탈환
research and development	연구개발
research and development expenditures	연구개발비
research cost	연구비
research expenditure	조사비
research method	조사방법
research objectives	조사목적
research on prices	가격조사
research opportunity	조사기회
reseller	재판업자
reservation	유보사항
reservation of ownership	소유권보유

reserve	적립금
reserve account	준비금회계
reserve adequacy	준비금의 타당성
reserve against decline in price	가격변동준비금
reserve assets	준비자산
reserve bank	준비은행
reserve cash	현금준비
reserve currency	준비통화
reserve deposit requirement system	준비예금제도
reserve for accidents	재해적립금
reserve for additions	증설적립금
reserve for amoritization	상각충당금
reserve for bad loan	대손충당금
reserve for bonus payment	상여충당금
reserve for bonuses allotted	보험계약이익배당준비금
reserve for compensation for completed works	완성공사보상담보금
reserve for compensation for default loss	위약손실보상준비금
reserve for construction	신축적립금
reserve for contingency	우발손실준비금
reserve for corporation tax	법인세 담보금
reserve for deferred income tax	압축담보금
reserve for depreciation	감가상각담보금
reserve for electronic computer programs	프로그램보정준비금
reserve for foreign exchange fluctuation	외국환 변동준비금
reserve for guarantee for completed work	제품보증담보금
reserve for intercompany profit	대체이익담보금
reserve for inventory fluctuation	가격변동준비금

reserve for liability	부채담보금
reserve for loss on goods unsold	반품조정담보금
reserve for losses	결손전보적립금
reserve for outstanding claims	지급준비금
reserve for overhead	간접비 준비금
reserve for overseas investment loss	해외투자손실준비금
reserve for pension fund	퇴직급여적립금
reserve for prevention of pollution	공해방지준비금
reserve for price fluctuation	가격변동준비금
reserve for retirement of preferred stock	우선주상환준비금
reserve for self-insurance	자가보험준비금
reserve for specific depreciation	특별상환준비금
reserve for specific purpose	목적적립금
reserve for tax payment	납세담보금
reserve fund	적립금
reserve investments	준비금 투자
reserve on gross premium method	영업보험료식 책임준비금
reserve on net premium method	순보험료식 책임준비금
reserve position	준비포지션
reserve rate	지불준비율
reserve requirement operation	준비율조작
reserve requirement policy	지급준비율정책
reserve requirements system	지급준비제도
reserve system	준비제도
reserve tranche	리저브 트랜쉐
reserved common stock	유보주식
reserved surplus	담보잉여금
reset date	금리경개일
reset frequency	경개빈도
residence liability policy	주택손해배상책임보험
resident	거주자

resident alien	거주외국인
resident auditor	주재감사인
resident foreign corporation	거주외국인
residential investment	주택투자
residential property	거주용재산
residents tax	주민세
residual	재방송할증요금, 잔여의
residual claim	잔여청구권
residual cost	잔여원가
residual equity	잔여지분
residual net imcome	잔여순이익
residual profits	잔여이익
residual property	잔여재산
residual quantitative import restriction	잔존수입제한
residual ratio	잔존율
residual return	잔차수익률
residual share	잔여배분
residual standard deviation	잔차표준편차
residual value	잔존가격
residuary estate	잔여재산
residuary outlay	잔여지출
residue	잔여부분
resiliency	신속한 조정
resistance level	관문
resistance line	상한값 저항선
resolution	해상도, 결의
resource	자원
resource allocation	자원배분
resource consortium	자원컨설시움
resource equity	자원주주 소유권
resources	자원
resources on business	경영자원

respite	변제의 연기
respondent	피공소인
respondent superior	사용자 책임
response elasticity	반응탄력성
response error	회수오차
response function	반응함수
response rate	회답률
responsibility accounting	책임회계
responsibility costing	책임원가계산
responsible and recognized dealer	주요딜러
rest	휴식하다
restitution in integrum	원상회복
responsibility of conjugal rights	동거명령
restoration	복원
restraining order	금지명령
restraint	긴축
restraint measures	긴축정책
restraint of trade	영업제한
restraint on alienation	양도금지
restraint on anticipation	미수이익처분금지
restrict sales	매석하다
restricted account	제한부 회계
restricted distribution policy	제한적 판로정책
restricted letter of credit	매입은행지정신용장
restricted receipts	특정수입고(금액)
restricted share	제한주
restricted surplus	제한부 잉여금
restriction of price range	가격폭 제한
restriction of transfer	양도제한
restriction on the growth of bank loans	대출증가액 규칙
restriction on transfer of shares	주식양도제한
restrictive covenant	한정조항, 무작위약관

restrictive financial covenant 재무제한조항
restrictive monetary policy 금융긴축정책
restructuring 재구축
restructuring related stock 재구축관련주
rests 결산기
resulting trust 추정신탁, 복귀신탁
results of business 영업실적
results of operations 영업성적
results of ordinary operations 경영손익
results of the tax examination 세무조사결과
resumption of dividend 재분배
retail 소매
retail accounting 소매업회계
retail and consumer spending sector stock 소비지출관련종목
retail bank 소매은행
retail banking 리테일 뱅킹
retail broker 소매 브로커
retail cost 소매원가
retail credit 소매신용
retail excise 소매세
retail inventory method 소매재고정리법
retail investor 최종투자가
retail method 매가환원법
retail price inflation 소매물가 인플레이션
retail prices structure 소매가격구조
retail sales 소매매출고
retail selling price 소매판매가
retail stores location strategy 소매점포입지전략
retailing competition 소매경쟁
retailing function 소매기능
retailing strategy 소매업 전략

retained earnings	이익잉여금
retained line	보유액
retained premium	보유보험료
retained profit	내부보유
retained surplus	유보이익
retainer	변호사 위임계약
retaining fee	변호사 고문료
retaining lien	변호사 리엔
retaliation	보복
retaliatory duties	보복관세
retention	보유
retention money	유보금
retention schedule	리텐션 스케줄
retention time	보관기간
retetentive advertising	유지광고
retire	기중에 상환하다, 퇴직하다
retired employee	퇴직한 종업원
retired equipment	폐잔설비
retirement	소각
retirement accounting	제각회계
retirement allowance	퇴직급여
retirement allowance in a lump sum	퇴직금의 일괄지급
retirement allowance regulations	퇴직급여규정
retirement annuity	퇴직연금
retirement annuity business	퇴적연금 업무
retirement annuity reserve	퇴직연금 적립금
retirement by purchase	매입상각
retirement cost	제거비
retirement income	퇴직소득
retirement income deduction	퇴직소득공제
retirement income policy	퇴직소득부보험
retirement lump sum grants	퇴직일시금

retirement method	폐기법, 제각법
retirement of bonds	사채상환
retirement of shares	주식상환
retirement pay	퇴직금
retirement pension	퇴직연금
retirement plan	퇴직금제도
retirement price	제각가액
retirement unit	제각단위
retour sans protet	거절증서 불필요
retracement	되돌림
retractable maturity	단기가능만기
retreat buying	반복적 구매
retroactive adjustments	소급수정
retroactive levy	소급징수
retroactive restatement	소급수정보고서
retrocession clause	반환조항
retrocession treaty	재재보험특약
retrogressive accounting	소급계산
retrospective law	소급법
retrospective policy	소급보험
return	환원, 이익
return after due date	기한후 신고
return and payment	신고 및 납부
return blank	신고용지
return commission	반항수수료
return day	확정일
return form for retirement income	퇴직소득신고서
return freight	반항운임
return inward	되돌아온 물품
return line	리턴 라인
return maximizer	리턴 극대자
return on assets	총자산 수익률

return on equity capital	주주자본 이익률
return on investment	투자수익
return on investment ratios	투자이익률
return on long-term liabilities plus equity capital	장기자본이익률
return on total assets	총자산이익률
return outward	되돌린 물품
return premium for cancellation	해약반여금
return to equilibrium	평균으로의 회귀
return to nature	자연회귀
returned goods unsold	반품
returned materials report	원재료 반환표
returned sales	되돌린 물품
returned unsold goods reserve	반품조정 담보금
returning of premium	프리미엄 환원
returning officer	선거관리자
returns	보수
revaluation	절상, 평가절상
revaluation excess	재평가차액
revaluation profit	재평가익
revaluation surplus	재평가 잉여금
revaluation surplus reserve	재평가 적립금
revealed preference	현시선호
revenue	수익
revenue account	수익계정
revenue agency	세입대리점
revenue and expenditure budget	세입세출예산
revenue bond	특정재원채
revenue curve	수익곡선
revenue deficit	세입결함
revenue expenditure	수익지출
revenue from government enterprise	영업수입

revenue from leases	리스 수익
revenue from operations	영업수익
revenue from public bond	공채수익
revenue maximization hypothesis	매출고최대화가설
revenue officer	수세관
revenue realization	수익실현
revenue recognizing standard	수익의 인식기준
revenue reserve amount	이익적립금액
revenue stamp	수입인지
revenue tax	수득세
reversal	상장의 반전
reversal cost method	역산법
reversal day	반전일
reversal of judgment	판결의 파기
reversal of surplus	적립금의 반환
reversal of taxation	과세처분취소
reversal pattern	반전패턴
reverse direction	역방향
reverse distribution	역유통
reverse engineering	역 엔지니어링
reverse for extraordinary casualties	비상위험준비금
reverse hedge	역 헷지
reverse income tax	역소득세
reverse offset	역상계
reverse operation	역산
reverse remittance	역환
reverse repo	리버스 레포
reverse split	역분할
reverse split of stocks	주식병합
reverse telegraphic transfer	역전신환
reverse zero coupon swap	리버스 제로 쿠폰 스왑
reverse-order perception	가격역전 인지현상

reversed swap	역스왑
reversing entry	반대기입
reversing trade	반대매입
reversion	복귀권
reversionary annuity	생잔연금
reversionary bonus system	보험금증액 배당방식
review	심사
review criteria	실질평균기준
revised average stock price	수정평균주가
revised budget	수정예산
revised statutes	수정법률
revision	정정
revision of office regulation	내규의 개정
revival	보험계약의 부활
revival of judgment	판결의 부활
revived quotation	부활가격
revocable beneficiary	변경가능보험금수취인
revocable letter of credit	취소가능신용장
revocation	철회
revocation of probate	검인철회
revocation suit	취소소송
revoke	취소
revolver	리볼버
revolving collateral	근담보
revolving credit	회전신용장
revolving fund	회전자금
revolving guarantee	근보증
revolving letter of credit	회전신용장
revolving line of credit	극도대부궤
revolving loan	리볼빙 론
revolving trade	회전상
reward	보수

rework	불완전한 것을 고치다
rewriting	개서의
ride down	내려가다
rider	부가조항
right and interest	이권
right in rem	물권
right of access	이용권
right of access to courts	재판청구권
right of auditing	감사권
right of avoidance	부인권
right of beneficiary	수익권
right of cancellation	해약권
right of claim	청구권
right of collective bargaining	단체교섭권
right of credit availability	크레디트 이용권
right of demanding compensation	구상권
right of first refusal	최우선 인수권
right of indemnity	구상권
right of inheritance	상속권
right of lease	임차권
right of nullification	기피권
right of petition	청원권
right of pledge	전당권
right of priority	선취권
right of recourse	상환청구권
right of redemption	권리회수권
right of taxation	과세권
right of telephone	전화가입권
right of trademark	상표권
right of use	사용권
right of way	우선토지사용권
right person in a right position	적재적소

right to begin 개시권
right to counsel 변호사의 원조를 받은 권리
right to obtain foreign money 외화할당권
right to revoke fraudulent act 사기행위취소권
rights 권리
rights and liabilities of members 사원권
rights existing on real property 부동산상의 권리
rights for profit-sharing 공익권
rights of repurchase 환매권
rights off 권리가 없어짐
rights offering 주주할당
rights on 권리가 생김
rigidity of price 가격경직성
ring 입회장
rise in price 가격상승
rise on stock price 주가상승
rise-and-fall market 등락시장
rising of the court 폐정
rising quotation 오름시세
risk 보험사고
risk absolutely excluded 절대적 면책위험
risk arbitrage 리스크 아비트라지
risk asset ratio 위험자산비율
risk assets 위험자산
risk aversion 위험회피
risk capital 위험자본
risk characteristic 위험특성
risk covered 피보험위험
risk disclosure statement 리스크 공시서
risk exposure 위험노출
risk free 신용위험이 없다
risk hedge 위험회피

risk lover	위험 애호자
risk management	리스크 매니지먼트
risk minimization	위험의 최소화
risk penalty	리스크 패널티
risk preference	위험선호도
risk premium	리스크 프리미엄
risk premium insurance	위험보험료식 보험
risk reduction measure	위험경감수단
risk reduction strategy	위험경감전략
risk sector	리스크 섹터
risk sensitive index	위험감응도 지표
risk service contract	리스크 서비스 조약
risk structure	위험구조
risk structure of discount rate	할인율의 위험구조
risk taking	위험부담
risk tolerance	위험허용도
risk weight	리스크 웨잇
risk-based capital	위험기반 자본금
risk-controlled	위험제어
risk-free	무위험의
risk-free assets	무위험 자산
risk-free interest rate	무위험 금리
risk-free securities	무위험 증권
risk-neutral valuation	리스크 뉴트럴 평가법
risk-return group	위험 수익 그룹
risk-return relationship	위험과 수익의 관계
risk-return trade-off	위험과 수익의 교환
risk-weighting	리스크 웨잇팅
riskless arbitrage	무위험 재정
riskless assets	안전자산
riskless transaction	위험 없는 거래
risky	위험이 크다

risky assets mix	위험 자산믹스
risky securities	위험증권
risky shift phenomenon	위험전가현상
rival brands	경합브랜드
road blocking	로드 브로킹
robot teller	로봇 텔러
rocket scientist	하이테크 상품개발자
rogatory letters	촉탁서
role commitment	역할위임
role demand	역할요구
role diffeentiation	역할분화
role involvement	역할관여
role playing	역할 연기법
role theory	역할이론
roll	인명부
rollback	롤백
roller coaster swap	롤러코스터 스왑
rolling readjustment	파동조성
rolling yield	롤링 일드
rolling-forward procedure	선송법
rolling-over	굴림
rollover credit	롤 오버 크레디트
rollover date	금리경개일
rollover loan	롤오버 론
Rome club	로마 클럽
Roosa bond	로사 본드
root cause	근본 원인
root of title	권리의 기초
roster	인명부
rotated merchandise control	윤번상품 재고통제
rotation effect	로테이션 효과
rotten boroughs	부패선거구

rough balance sheet	개산대차대조표
rough cost	개산원가
rough cost book	원가개산표
rough number	개수
round lot	최저거래단위
round turn	반대매매
round-the-clock market	24시 거래시장
roundabout production	우회생산
roundabout trade	우회무역
rounding error	단수처리의 오차
rounding off in calculation	단수계산
rounding reversal pattern	라운딩 리버설 패턴
Round-table of European Industrialists	유럽산업인 라운드 테이블
route sales	루트 세일
router	루터
routing	수순
royalties received for use of patents	특허권 사용료
royalty	로열티
royalty as to know-how	로열티 사용료
royalty interest	소유권리권
royalty of the copyright	저작권의 사용료
royalty on a book	인세
royalty to be paid every fixed time	정시지급사용료
rule	규칙
rule absolute	절대명령
rule against accumulations	영구적립금지 규칙
rule day	명령일
rule nisi	가명령
rule of ejusdem generis	동족의 원칙
rule of law	법의 지배
rule of reason	합리원칙

rule securities trading	매매방법
rule to show cause	이유개시명령
rules	동의제출기
rules for contruction of policy	보험증권해석규칙
rules for the preparation of financial statements	재무제표준칙
rules of court	재판소 규칙
rules of thumb	경험적인 상식
ruling	결정
ruling coalition	여당연합
run	조합
run the book	장부관리
run upon a bank	신용을 잃은 은행에 예금주들이 돈을 찾으려 몰려듬
run-down	상장표 요약
run-off	재보험특약기간종료후의 잔존책임
runaway gap	런어웨이 갭
runaway shop	도망기업
running account	당좌회계
running cost	운전비
running inventory	상시재고정리
running inventory method	계속재고정리법
running of the market	시황상황
running policy	계속보험
running price	시가
running royalty	계속적 사용료
running stock	정상재고
rural-urban shift of population	지방도시간 인구이동
rush order	주문쇄도

≪ S ≫

sabotage	사보타지, 태업, 파괴행위
sacrifice sale	투매
saddle point	안장점
safe custody	보호예수
safe deposit box insurance	대여금고보험
safe harbor lease	세이프 하버 리스
safe keeping	보관
safe-pledge	보석보증인
safeguard provision	세이프가드 조항
safekeeping deposit	보호예수
safety control	안전관리
safety envelop	안전봉투
safety loading	안전할증
safety margin	안전계수
safety nets	예금자보호 시스템
safety stock	안전재고
safety valve	안전판
sag	침하
salaries	급여
salaries and wages	임금
salary and allowances paid abroad	외국 지불 급여
salary plus commission	보합병용 급여제
salary scale	급여지수
sale	판매
sale amount	매출액
sale and lease-back	세일 앤 리스-백
sale and purchase on credit	신용매매

sale and return	해제조건부
sale bond	판매보증증권
sale by agent	대리판매
sale by brand	브랜드 매매
sale by bulk	일괄매매
sale by description	표시제 매매
sale by grade or type	규격매매
sale by specification	사양서 매매
sale by subscription	예약판매
sale for cash	현금판매
sale in gross	일괄매매
sale on account	외상판매
sale on an underwriting basis	인수매출
sale on commission	위탁판매
sale on standard	표준품 매매
sale or return	반환권 매매
sale price	거래가격
sales	매출
sales account	매출계정
sales accounting	판매회계
sales activity index	판매활동지수
sales allowance	가격할인
sales amount	판매
sales analysis	매출분석
sales and purchases on commission	수수료 매매
sales basis	매출기준
sales book	매출장부
sales commission	판매수수료
sales contract	매매계약
sales cost	판매원가(매상원가)
sales cost ratio	매출원가율
sales credit	신용채권

sales discount	판매할인
sales earnings	영업수입
sales finance	판매금융
sales finance company	판매금융회사
sales force	판매력
sales force management	판매원 관리
sales force performance analysis	판매원 성과분석
sales forecasting	매출액 예측
sales growth rate	매출신장률
sales invoice	매출송장
sales journal	매출거래장
sales ledger	매출원장
sales method	판매방법
sales mix	매출배합
sales network	판로
sales of corporate bonds by purchasers	사채소화 상황
sales office	영업소
sales on approval	시용판매
sales on consignment	수탁판매
sales opportunity	판매기회
sales performance	판매성과
sales price	매출가격
sales proceeds	매출액
sales profit ratio	매출이익률
sales promotion	판매촉진
sales promotion expense	판매촉진비
sales quota	판매할당
sales rebate	판매환불
sales record	판매장표
sales response function	매출고 반응함수
sales returns	매출보상

sales revenues	매출수익
sales slip	매출전표
sales subsidiary	판매자회사
sales targets	판매목표액
sales tax	판매세
sales to accounts receivable	외상채권율
sales to cash	현금회전율
sales to fixed assets	고정자산 매출률
sales to inventories	재고자산 매출률
sales to receivables	외상채권회전율
sales to total assets	총자산 매출률
sales to working capital	운영자본 매출률
sales under agreement to repurchase	환매조건부 매출
sales volume	매출고
sales worth ratio	자기자본회전율
sales-force recruitment	판매원 모집
sales-type leases	판매 리스
salesman	판매원
salesman training	판매원 교육
salient ratio	특수비율
Sallie Mae	미국 장학자금금고
salvage charges	구조료
salvage value	처분가치
same day effective order	당일유효주문
same day settlement	동일결제
same day transaction	당일거래
sample	상품견본
sample error	표본설비
sample means	표본평균치
sample shipment	표본적송품
sample variance	표본분산
samples accuracy	표본정도

samples expense	견본비용
samples floater	상품견본 포괄보험
sampling	표본추출
sampling error	표본추출오차
sampling inspection	발췌검사
sampling precision	표본추출정도
sampling sound module	샘플링 음원
sampling survey	표본조사
samurai bond	사무라이 본드
sanction	제재조치
sandwich spread	샌드위치 스프레드
san recourse	상환청구에 응하지 않는
satellite cable network	위성 케이블 네트워크
satellite communication	위성통신
satellite market	위성시장
satellite news gathering (SNG)	위성취재
satisfaction of mortgage	모기지 개방증서
satisfactory	만족할만한
saturation	채도
saturation campaign	집중 캠페인
saving account	저축계정
saving clause	유보사항
saving function	저축함수
savings and loan association	저축대부조합
savings at call	통지예금
savings bank	저축은행
savings bank life insurance	저축은행 생명보험
savings bond and debenture	저축채권
savings deposit	저축예금
savings ratio	저축률
savings-for-tax association	납세저축
savings-type insurance	적립보험

scab	(노동조합) 불참가자, 배반자
scale merit	규모의 이익
scale method	척도법
scale of central and local public finance	재정규모
scale order	소량 주문
scale trading	물타기, 난평매매
scalper	초단기 거래자, 스캘퍼
scalping	스캘핑
scan	스캔, 주사(走査)
scan panel	스캔패널
scan panel research	스캔패널조사
scandalous matter	추문
scanner	스캐너
scanning line	스캐닝선
scarce currency clause	희소통화조항
scarce resources	희소자원
scarce stock	희박주
scarcity of stock	희소주
scenario analysis	시나리오 분석
scenario writing	시나리오
schedule	각종 명세
schedule form	보고식
schedule of bounds payable	사채명세표
schedule of capital	자본금명세표
schedule of concessions	관세양허표
schedule of depreciation	감가상각비명세표
schedule of securities	유가증권명세표
schedule of tangible fixed assets	유형고정자산명세표
schedule of the marginal efficiency of capital	자본한계효율표
schedule of transactions	거래명세
scheduled cost	표시원가

scheduled payment	약정변제
scheduled personal property floater	명세서첨부 동산 포괄보험
scheduled policy	담보조항선택방식증서
scheduled property floater	명세서첨부 고가품 포괄보험
scheduled repayment	정시상환
scheduled income taxation	분류소득세
scheduler income taxation	재무제표 부속명세서
schedules of financial statements	채무정리계획
scheme of arrangement	채무정리계획
scheme of operation	사업방법서
scheme of reproduction	재생산표식
school district	학교구역
science park	과학단지
scienter	고의로
scientific management	과학적 관리
scientific method	과학적 방법
scissors-form difference in price	협상가격차
scope	감사범위
scope of assessment	과세범위
scope of audit	감사범위
scope of authority	권한범위
scope of business	사업범위
scope of exemption of property tax	고정자산 비과세 범위
scope of securities	유가증권범위
scorched earth defense	초토화작전
scout	스카우트
scrap	부스러기
scrap equipment	폐잔설비
scrap value	잔존가치
scrapped property	폐기재산
scrapping	폐기
scrapping of equipment tax credit	특정설비 폐기세액공제

screen angle	스크린 각도
screen ruling	스크린 선수
screen tone	스크린 톤
screening	심사
screening of application for loan	대출심사
scrip certificate	가주권
scrip dividend	증서배당
script	원문서
scrutiny	심사
sea brief	중립선 증명서
sea law	해상법규
sea peril	해상위험
sea-letter	중립국선증명서
seal	검인
seal impression	인감
sealed instrument	검인증서
seaman	선원
search	탐색
search goods	탐색상품
season dating	계절일부
season sale	계절매출
seasonal adjustment	계절조정
seasonal average	계절평균
seasonal discount	계절할인
seasonal duties	계절관세
seasonal fluctuation adjustment	계절변동조정
seasonal fund	계절자금
seasonal goods	계절상품
seasonal index	계절지수
seasonal merchandise	계절상품
seasonal model	계절변동형 모형
seasonal selling pressure	계절적 판매압력

seasonal unemployment	계절적 실업
seasonal variation	계설변동
seasonally adjusted	계절변동 조정완료
seasoned bound	만기도래채권
seasoned issue	통상거래증권
seat	회원권
seaworthy	항해에 적합한
second deliverance	재인도
second generation on-line system	제2차 온라인시스템
second half of the year	하반기
second mortgage	2심 저당
second section	시장 제2부
second surplus treaty	제2차 초과액 특약
Second World	제 2세계
second-distress	제2차 압력
secondary activities	부수업무
secondary beneficiary	제2순위 보험금수취인
secondary bond dealing	유통시장에 있어 채권딜링
secondary boycott	제2차 보이코트
secondary conveyance	제2차적 부동산 이전행위
secondary data	2차 데이터
secondary distribution	2차 분매
secondary drive	2차적 동인
secondary evidence	2차적 증거
secondary financing	제2저당 금융
secondary group	2차 집단
secondary industry	제2차 산업
secondary liability	제2차 부채
secondary market	유통시장
secondary needs	2차적 요구
secondary offering	매출
secondary stimulus	2차 자극

secondary tax liability 제2차 납세의무
secondary trend 2차적 트렌드
secrecy agreement 비밀준수 의무계약
secret account 비밀계정
secret commission 이면수수료
secret language 암호
secret liability 비밀부채
secret partnership 익명조합
secret reserve 비밀적립금
secret service expenses 기밀비
secret trust 비밀신탁
secretariat 사무국
Secretary of State 국무장관
section 섹션
Section 485, Income and Corporation Taxes Act 법인소득세법 제485조
section of revenue 수세과
sectional calculation 부문계산
sectional development 지구개발
sectional income statement 구분손익계산서
sectional journal 분할사역장
sectional ownership 구분소유권
sectional surface rights 구분지상권
sector 섹터
sector balance sheet 부문별 대차대조표
sectoral approach 섹터방식
secular 세속의
secular boom 영속적 효과
secular economic growth 장기적 경제성장
secured account 보증부 계정
secured advance 담보부 대부
secured bond 저당권부 사채

secured credit	담보부 대출
secured debenture	담보부 부채
secured debt	담보부 채무
secured liabilities	담보부 부채
secured loan	담보대출
secured loan on securities	증권담보대출
secured party	담보권자
secured securities	담보
secured transactions	담보거래
securities	유가증권
securities account	유가증권계정
securities acquired by the specified investment in kind	특정현물출자증권
securities administration	증권행정
securities administration trust	유가증권관리신탁
Securities and Exchange Commission	미국증권거래위원회
securities and exchange law	증권거래법
securities borrowed	차입유가증권
securities business	증권업
securities business tax law	증권거래세법
securities capital	증권자본
securities company	증권회사
securities deposited as collateral	담보차입유가증권
securities deposited from others	보관유가증권
securities exchange	증권거래소
securities exchange commission	증권거래심의회
securities finance company	증권금융회사
securities financing	증권금융
securities for fiduciary issue	보증준비
securities for sale	매각가능증권
securities futures	증권선물거래
securities holdings	보유증권

securities house dealer	증권회사딜러
securities in foreign currency	외화증권
securities in portfolio	보유증권
securities in trust	유가증권신탁
securities industry	증권업계
securities investment	증권투자
securities investment advisory service	증권투자상담
securities investment trust	증권투자신탁
securities investment trust sales company	증권신탁판매회사
securities issue	증권발행
securities issued by government related agency	정부계 기관증권
securities ledger	유가증권원장
securities loan	증권금융
securities loaned	대부유가증권
securities market	증권시장
securities market line	증권시장선
securities of affiliated company	관계회사유가증권
securities on property	물적증권
securities purchase	유가증권 매입
securities received as collaterals	보관유가증권
securities received for guarantee	예탁유가증권
securities register	유가증권기입장
securities regulations	증권규칙
securities reserve	유가증권준비
securities transaction loss reserve	주식매매 손실준비금
securities transaction tax law	유가증권거래세법
securities transfer tax	유가증권거래세
securities underwriting business law	유가증권인수법
securities yield	증권이율
Securities and Exchange Commission (SEC)	증권거래위원회

Securities and Investment Board (SIB)	증권투자위원회
securitization	증권화
security	담보
security account	보증계정
security analyst	증권분석사
security credit	증권금융
security credit by banks	은행의 증권금융
security deposits	담보예금
security for costs	소송비용담보
security for obligation	채권담보
security for tax payment	납세담보
security income and expense	유가증권손익
security interest	담보권
security loan	증권담보대출
security of tax payment	납세보증
security right	담보권
security risk curve	증권리스크선
security suretyship	보증인
security yield curve	증권이율선
security-specific risk	증권고유리스크
sedition	선동죄
seed money	초기투입자금
segment reporting	사업구분별 손익보고
segmental breakdown	부문별 내역
segmental information	분류정보
segmental sales	부문별 매출
segmental sales breakdown	부문별 매출내역
segmentation	세분화
segmentation theory	시장분석이론
segregation	격리
seisin	점유
seized	점유한

seized goods	차압물건
seizor	차압인
seizure	차압
seizure note	차압통지서
select table	선택표
selected issue	선정품목
selection	선정
selection of depreciation method	상각방법의 선정
selection of risk	위험선택
selection of valuation method	평가방법의 선택
selection process	선택과정
selective benefits	선택급부
selective bid	지명경쟁입찰
selective buying	선택적 구매
selective channel	선택적 채널
selective competition	선택적 경쟁
selective credit regulation	선택적 신용규제
selective demand	선택적 수요
selective exposure	선택적 노출
selective financing	선별융자
selective function	선택적 기능
selective perception	선택적 지각
selective selling	특약판매
selective tendering	지명경쟁입찰
Self-Regulating Organization	자율규제조직
self-accounting system	독립회계제
self-actualization	재실현
self-addressed check	자기앞수표
self-assessed income tax	신고소득세
self-assessment	자기신고
self-assessment of taxation	신고납세
self-assessment system	자기신고납세제도

self-balancing	독자평균
self-balancing type	증감대조표
self-concept	자기개념
self-consumption	자가소비
self-defense	정당방위
self-disserving evidence	자기에 불이익한 증거
self-employed	자영업의
self-employment income	자가영업소득
self-enforcement	자력집행권
self-finance ratio	자기금융비율
self-inspection	자주검사
self-insurance	자가보험
self-insurance fund	자가보험기금
self-insurance plan	자가보험제도
self-insurance reserve	자가보험준비금
self-liquidating	자기 정산의
self-maintaining growth	자립적 성장
self-management	자영업
self-owned capital ratio	자기자본비율
self-produced fixed assets	자기생산에 관련된 고정자산
self-produced inventories	자기제조에 관련된
self-regarding evidence	자기에 관한 증거
self-regulation	자율
self-regulatory organization	자율기관
self-reliance	자력갱생
self-restraint	자율
self-restraint agency	자율기관
self-restraint interest	자율금리
self-return	자기신고
self-return system	자기신고제
self-service retailing	셀프-서비스식 소매업
self-serving declaration	자기에게 이익이 되는 진술

self-support accounting	독립채산
self-support subsistence	독립생계
self-supporting accounting system	독립채산제
self-sustained personal accident insurance	자손신고보험
sell low	염가판매
sell off	투매
sell on credit	외상판매
sell on the spot	즉매하다
sell order	매매주문
sell signal	판매신호
sell-and-lease agreement	임차계약
seller	판매자
seller structure	판매구조
seller's monopoly	판매독점
seller's option	판매자 선택
seller's option trading	판매자 선택거래
seller's price	판매자 요구값
seller's market	판매자 시장
selling	판매업
selling agreement	판매계약
selling charges	판매자 부담
selling climax	대량판매 매물로 인한 폭락
selling commission	판매수수료
selling concept	판매컨셉
selling concession	판매수수료
selling contract	판매계약
selling cycle	판매순환
selling exchange	매매율
selling expense variance	판매비 차이
selling expenses	판매비
selling group	판매단

selling group agreement	판매단 계약서
selling off	투매
selling offer	매매오퍼
selling on a consignment basis	위탁판매
selling on a rising scale	오름차순 판매
selling on balance	균형매출
selling on credit	외상매출
selling on rally	판매회복
selling on spurt	판매급등
selling operation under repurchase agreement	구매조건부 판매오퍼레이션
selling opportunity	매장
selling order	판매주문
selling out	처분매매
selling overhead	판매간접비
selling pressure	판매압력
selling price	판매가
selling price clause	판매가격약관
selling price inventory	매가재고법
selling price per unit	단위당 판매가
selling rate	판매율
selling right	판매권리
selling sample	판매견본
selling short	공매
selling side	판매자측
selling support	판매자원
sellout	매진
semantic differential	어의상의 차이
semantic differential method	일대비교법
semantic differential scale	어의 차이 척도
semantics	의미론
semi-annual closing of accounts	중간결산

semi-annual compounding calculation	반년 복리계산
semi-annual coupon	반년불 쿠폰
semi-annual report	반기보고서
semi-endowment insurance	만기반액지불 양로보험
semi-facultative reinsurance	반임의 재보험
semi-finished goods	반제품
semi-fixed cost	준고정비
semi-inflation	준인플레이션
semi-installment	반기할부
semi-Tontine dividend	반톤틴식 배당
semi-variable charge	준변동비
semi-variable cost	준변동원가
semi-variable expenses	준변동비 항목
senior	선순위의
senior accountant	상급회계사
senior bond	상위사채
senior citizen	연금생활자
senior co-manager	상급부간사
senior creditor	선순위채권자
senior debt	우선채무
senior issue	상위증권
senior mortgage	선순위양도 저당
senior mortgage bond	선순위담보부 채권
senior securities	우선증권
seniority order wage system	연공서열 임금제도
seniority system	연공제
sensitive market	민감한 시장
sensitivity	감응성
sensitivity adjustment	감응도 조정
sensitivity analysis	감응도 분석
sensitivity coefficient	감응도 계수

sensitivity training	감수성 훈련
sensory characteristic	감응특성
sentiment	감성
sentiment index	감성지표
separable cost	분리가능원가
separate account	분리계정
separate bill	분리계산서
separate financial statements	단독재무제표
separate investment account	분리계정
separate maintenance	별거수당
separate property	특유재산
separate return	개별신고서
separate trading of registered interest and principal of securities	스트리프채, STRIP채
separate valuation	분리평가
separate withholding tax	분리과세
separate withholding taxation at source	원천분리과세
separated taxation on dividend income	배당분리과세
separation between capital and administration	자본경영분석
separation negative	분리반대
sequence of deduction	공제순서
sequence of tax credits	세액공제순서
sequenced entry	단계적 진입
sequenced strategy	단계적 전략
sequencer	순서결정장치
sequencing	순서배열
sequential cost system	공정별 종합원가계산
sequential sampling	순차발췌검사법
serial advertisement	시리즈 광고

serial bond	연속상환채권
serial correlation	계열상관
series bond	연속발행채권
service	서비스, 노무
service area	서비스 지역
service by public notification	공시송달
service contract	서비스 계약
service contribution	노무출자
service cost	용역원가
service delivery	서비스 제공
service department	보조부문
service departmental charge	보조부문비
service division	보조부문
service economy	서비스 경제
service function	서비스 함수
service life	내용년수
service mark	서비스 마크
service office	영업소
service organization	서비스 조직
service report	서비스 보고서
service trade	서비스 무역
service transaction	서비스 거래
service unit	용역단위
serviceability	서비스성
services output method	용역생산고법
servitude	노역, 지역권
servitude for use of water	용수지역권
servitude holder	지역권자
servo mechanism	전자자동제어장치, 서보기구
session	회기
session period	입회기간
set aside	취소하다, 파기하다

set of accounts 회계장표
set of exchange 어음책
set off 상계
setback 하락
sets in use 사용중에 있는 수신기 비율
setting 설정
setting up overdraft 대월설정
settle 청산하다
settle accounts 결산하다
settled account 청산계정
settled additional tax due amount 추가경정결정에 의해 확정된 추가세액
settlement 청산
settlement account 절제하다
settlement date 결제일
settlement day 수도일
settlement discount 결제할인
settlement method 결제방식
settlement of accounts 수지결산
settlement of balance 밸런스상 결제
settlement of claim 채권 변제
settlement of debt 청산
settlement of easement 지역권 설정
settlement of leasehold 대지권 설정
settlement of mortgage 저당권 설정
settlement of subsidy 보조금 변제
settlement of superficies 지상권 설정
settlement of tax amount 세액확정
settlement options 보험금지급방법의 선택
settlement out of court 시담(示談)
settlement price 결산가격
settlement risk 수도리스크
settlement trade 거류지무역

settling	청산
settling term	결산기
settlor	신탁설정자
setup costs	설치비용
setup time	설치기간
Seven Sisters	세븐시스터즈(7대 석유회사)
sever	분리하다
several contract	분할계약
several covenant	가분조항
several fishery	단독어업권
several liability	개별책임
several ownership	분할소유권
severally	단독으로
severally but not jointly	비연대보증
severally liable	개별책임의
severance	분리
severance benefit	퇴직수당
severance of actions	소송분리
shade	조정
shadow account	그림자계정
shadow price	장래가격
shaking-out	투매
shape	형태
share	주식
share account	주식계정
share allotment certificate	주식할당증서
share allotment letter	주식할당통지
share broker	주식브로커
share capital	주식자본
share consolidation	주식합병
share draft account	주식·어음계정
share holding ratio	주식보유율

share in expense of public service	공공시설의 부담액
share index	주가지수
share of audience	시청자수 점유율
share of the residual property	잔여재산
share oriented	쉐어 지향
share price	주가
share price performance	주가동향
share repurchase	자사주 취득
share split-down	주식합병
share split-up	주식분할
share-issuing expense	신주발행비
shared monopolies	공동독점
shareholder	주주
shareholder activism	주주의 행동주의
shareholder resolution	주주결의
shareholder's agreement	주주간 협정서
shareholder's equity	주주자본
shareholder's interest	주주지분
shareholder's list	주주명부
shareholder's meeting	주주총회
shareholder's right	주주권
shareholders ledger	주주원장
shareholders of record	주주명부상 주주
shareholdings	소유주
shares outstanding	발행완료주식
shark repellent	상어격퇴법, 적대적매수에 대한 방어수단
sharp advance market	급등가격
sharp decline	격감
sharp decline market	급락가격
sharp drop	급락
sharp fall	급락
sharp increase	급증

sharp rally	반등
sharp rise	급등
sharp setback	급반락
sharp upward revision	대폭상향수정
shelf life	보관기한
shelf redemption	일괄상환
shelf registration	발행등록
shell branch	외형점포
shell corporation	페이퍼 컴퍼니
Sherman Act	셔먼법
shift system	교체근무제도
shift to yen	엔 쉬프트
shiftability theory	전가성이론
shifting charge	이동비용
shifting of business center	영업 본거지이동
shifting of tax burden	조세의 전가
shinkin bank	신용금고
ship's bill	선장용 선하증서
ship's husband	선박관리인
ship's paper	선박비 부서류
shipment	적송품
shipped quality terms	선적품질조건
shipper	적송인
shipper's usance	수출신용
shipping	해운
shipping articles	선원고용계약서
shipping charge	운송비
shipping commissioners	해사고용감독관
shipping document	선적서류
shipping expense	발송비
shipping market	해운시장
shipping marks	하물인

shipping receipts	해운수입
shipping tax	선박세
ships and vessels	선박
shogun bond	쇼군채, 쇼군본드
shop	공장
shop act	상점법
shop book rule	상품장부법칙
shop cost	공장원가
shop inspection	공장검사
shop talk language	직업용어
shopping around	쇼핑
shopping behavior	쇼핑행동
short	단기
short account	단기매도계정
short bond	단기채권
short call	콜 매도
short covering	환매, 쇼트커버링
short covering at a loss	손실환매
short delivery	부족
short drawing	숏 드로잉
short fall	단기투자이익
short form	간이형
short form audit report	단문식 감사보고서
short forward position	선물매매포지션
short hedge	매도 헷지, 숏 헷지
short interest	공매된 채, 환매되지 않은 주식
short loan	단기대부
short market	약세의 시황
short paper	단기증권
short period	단기
short period insurance	단기보험계약
short position	매도포지션

short position risk 매도 포지션 리스크
short put 숏 풋
short rate table 단기요율표
short sale against the box 현물을 보유한 채 공매도 하는 것
short sale ratio 공매비율
short selling 공매
short squeeze 공매한 사람이 어쩔 수 없이 고가 매입을 하여야 하는 상황
short strangle 숏 스트랭글
short strap 숏 스트랩
short strip 숏 스트립
short supply 공급부족
short swap 단기스왑
short swing 단기거래
short swing profits 단기매매익
short the swap 스왑을 짧게 하는 것
short title 약칭
short-covering 공매의 환매
short-form report 단문식 보고서
short-lined rally 일시적 반등
short-period cost 단기비용
short-run equilibrium 단기균형
short-run optimizing principle 단기최적화원리
short-run supply curve long-run supply curve 단기공급곡선 장기공급곡선
short-term 단기
short-term bond 단기채
short-term borrowing 단기차입
short-term capital 단기자본
short-term capital balance 단기자본수지
short-term capital gain 단기양도소득
short-term capital transaction 단기자본거래

short-term credit market	단기금융시장
short-term debt	단기차입금
short-term economic survey of all businesses	전국기업 단기경제조사
short-term economic survey of principal enterprises	주요기업 단기경제조사
short-term facility rate	단기자금율
short-term finance	단기금융
short-term fund	단기자금
short-term government bond	단기국채
short-term government securities	정부단기증권
short-term interest rate	단기금리
short-term investment	단기투자
short-term investment account	단기투자계정
short-term liabilities	단기부채
short-term liquidity factor	단기유동성요인
short-term loan	단기대부
short-term loan payable	단기차입금
short-term loan receivable	단기대부
short-term money house	단자업자
short-term money market	단기금융시장
short-term note	단기채권
short-term oriented	단기지향
short-term prime rate	단기프라임레이트
short-term returns	단기투자수익
short-term solvency	단기지급능력
short-term transaction	단기거래
short-term yield	단기이율
short-term loan	단기대부
shortage	부족액
shortage economy	부족경제
shortage of funds	자금부족

shortage of special depreciation	특별상각부족액
shortening	단축
shotgun approach	숏건 어프로치
show scan system	전시검사체계
showstopper	매수저지소송
shrinkage barrier	수출장벽
shrinkage of market	시장의 수축
shut for dividend	명의서환정지
shyster	사기꾼
sickness benefit	질병급부
side judge	배석재판관
side liner	부업대리점
sight	일람
sight bill	일람불외환수표
sight credit	일람불신용장
sight draft	일람불어음
sight letter of credit	일람불신용장
sight note	일람불약속어음
sight rate	일람불외환비율
sight-seeing tax	관광세
sign manual	자저
sign of fragility	위약성
signal to noise ratio	신호잡음비율
signature and seal	기명날인
signed and sealed	서명날인
signed check	기명식수표
signed transfer	기명양도
significance level	유의수준
significant	중요한
significant amount	중요한 금액
significant difference	유의차
significant subsidiaries	중요한 자회사

silence	침묵
silent base	묵시적 참가자 베이스
silent participation	묵시참가
silent partner	묵시적 참가자
silver exchange	은교환
silver standard	은본위제
similar goods	유사품
similar investment media	유사의 투자매체
simple accounting	단식부기
simple aggregate	단순총화
simple arbitrage	단순재정
simple arithmetic average index	단순산술평균지수
simple average	단순평균
simple average method	단순평균법
simple average stock price	단순평균주가
simple contract	약식계약
simple correlation coefficient	단순상관관계
simple cost accounting	단순종합원가계산
simple guarantor	단순보증인
simple hypothesis	단순가설
simple index	단순지수
simple interest	단리
simple journal	단순사역장
simple jump model	단순점프모형
simple moving average	단순이동평균
simple multiplier	단순승수
simple obligation	단순채무
simple random sample	단순확율표본
simple regression model	단순회귀모형
simple reproduction	단순재생산
simple reserve method	단순준비법
simple tariff system	단일세율제

simple trust	단순신탁
simplex method	단식법
simplification	단순화
simplified bookkeeping system	간이부기
simplified employee pension	간이종업원 퇴직금
simplified method of depreciation	간편상각
simplified tax system	간이과세제도
simulation	시뮬레이션
simulcast	동시방송
simultaneous distribution	동시분포
simultaneous tax audit	동시조사
simultaneous transmissive communication	동보통신
sinc qua non	필수조건
sine die	무기한으로
sine qua non	필수조건
Singapore Inter-Bank Offered Rate (SIBOR)	싱가폴 은행간 대출금리
single account system	단일회계제도
single balance sheet	단일대차대조표
single banking license	단일은행면허
single bill	채무부담 날인 채무증서
single correlation coefficient	단일상관계수
single entry	단식기입
single entry bookkeeping	단식부기
Single European Act	단일유럽의정서
single exchange rate	단일외환율
single expression	단식
single index method	단일지수법
single index model	단일지표모형
single interest policy	단일이익담보보험
single liability basis	단일책임주의

single life annuity	단생연금
single lump sum credit	일괄지불
single name	단명
single name paper	단명어음
single option	단일옵션
single payment	일괄지급
single payment annuity	일시지급
single payment loan	일시지급대출
single premium	일시급 보험료
single premium annuity	보험료 일시급 연금
single premium deferred annuities	일시급 거치연금
single premium insurance	보험료 일시급 보험
single premium life policy	일시급 종신보험
single purpose	전용의
single rate	단일요율
single step	무구분식
single sum	일시금
single tariff	단일세율
single tax	단일세
single transaction	단일거래
single-customer separate account	단일고객 구분회계
single-employer defined benefit pension plan	단일사업주형 급부연금제도
single-maturity deposit	단일만기예금
single-order term	일정기한지급
single-step income statement	단일구분손익계산서
single-step statement	단일구분계산서
singular concept	단순개념
singular proposition	단칭명제
sinking	침몰
sinking fund	감채기금
sinking fund date	감채기금상환일

sinking fund insurance	감채기금보험
sinking fund method	상각기금법
sinking fund requirements	감채기금적립액
sinking fund reserve	감채기금적립금
sister company	자매회사
sister publication	자매출판물
site	소재지
site audit	현장감사
site survey	실지조사
situation analysis	상황분석
situational variable	상황변수
sizzle	질감
skeleton form account	T자형 계정
skewness	비대칭도
skill inventory	스킬 인벤터리
skill measurement	기능검정
skimming price	스키밍 가격
skimming price strategy	초기고가전략, 스키밍가격전력
skip-day settlement	다음일 결제
skunk work	스컹크 워크
skyrocketing	급등
skyrocketing price	급등가
slack	완만한
slackness of money market	금융완만
slander of title	권리 비훼
slaughter sale	투매
sleeper effect	수면효과
sleeping account	휴면계좌
sleeping member	휴면회원
sliding cheap	슬라이딩 칩
sliding rate	슬라이드 요금
sliding scale	슬라이드제

sliding tariff	슬라이드 관세
slight negligence	경과실
slight ups and downs	소부동
slimmer profit margins	이익률의 저하
slip	무너지다
slip bookkeeping	전표식 부기
slip system	전표제도
slip system of accounting	전표식 회계법
slope risk	경사리스크
slowdown	둔화
sluggish	완만한
slumpflation	슬럼프레이션
small	스몰(100만불단위의 거래)
small-and medium enterprise	중소기업
Small Business Corporation	중소기업
small capital stock	소형주
small enterprise mutual aid plan	소규모기업공제
small group theory	소집단이론
small investor	소액투자가
small loan	소액금융
small loan company blanket bond	소액대부회사 포괄보증증권
small lot order	소액주문
small margin	소폭
small revaluation	소폭상승
small sample	소표본
small savers certificate	소액예금증권
small sized business proprietor	소규모 기업자
small spread	스몰 스프레드
small sum and important property	소액중요자산
small sum deferred assets	소액이연자산
small sum properties	소액자산
small sums of deposits and savings	소액예금

small sums of depreciable property	소액상각자산
small sums of dividend income	소액배당소득
small sums of pension paid to old-age persons	소액노령연금
small sums of savings	소액예금
small talk	잡담
small trend	소추세
smallest space analysis	최소공간분석
smart money	현명한 투자가
Smithsonian system	스미소니언 체제
smoothing constant smorgasbord plan	평활정수
smoothing operation	안정화 개입
smuggling	밀수
snake	스네이크
snapper	스내퍼
snipe	스나이프
snob effect	스노브 효과
snowballing	눈사람 효과
soar	급등
soaring market	고등시장
social accounting	사회회계
social assumption	사회적 가정
social audit	사회감사
social capital	사회자본
social climate	사회적 풍토
social club	사교클럽
social concerns	사회문제
social contract	사회계약
social cost	사회적 비용
social dependent consumer	사회적 의존형 소비자
social ecology	사회생태학

social ethic	사회적 이론
social evolution	사회진화
social expenses	교제비
social imperialism	사회제국주의
social insurance	사회보험
social insurance premiums	사회보험료
social insurance premiums deduction	사회보험료 공제
social insurance tax	사회보험료
social interaction	사회적 상호행위
social judgment theory	사회판단이론
social mobility	사회적 가동제
social movements	사회운동
social multiplier effect	사회적 승수효과
social overhead capital	사회자본
social psychology	사회심리학
social responsibility of enterprise	기업의 사회적 책임
social security	사회보장
social security number	사회보장번호
social security system	사회보장제도
social stimuli	사회적 자극
social system	사회체계
social unrest	사회불안
social value	사회적 가치
social wants	사회적 욕구
social wealth	사회적 부
social welfare function	사회후생함수
socialism	사회주의
socialist common enterprise	사회주의 공동기업
socialization	사회화
socially integrated consumer	사회적 융화형 소비자
societal environment	사회적 환경
Societas Europaea	유럽회사

Societe a responsibilite limitee (Sarl) 유한책임회사
society 조합, 사회
Society for Worldwide International Financial Telecommunications (SWIFT) 국제은행간 금융통신기구
sociodemographic variable 사회인구통계적 변수
socioeconomic classification 사회경제적 분류
socioeconomic process 사회경제적 과정
sociogram 인간관계의 사회학적 도표
sociologist 사회학자
sociometric technique 사회관계측정기법
sociometry 계량사회학
sociostasis 사회정체
soft currency 약한 통화
soft currency country 연화국
soft dollar 소프트 달러
soft landing 연착륙(충격이 심하지 않은 경기조정)
soft loan 연성대출
soft market 약세기조의 시장
sogo shosha 종합상사
soil bank 지방증진금융
sola bill 1통으로 된 수출어음
sold bill 할인어음
sold book 상품매출장
sold ledger 매출원장, 외상매출금원장
sold-out market 매진시장
sole agent 단일판매대리점
sole proprietorship 개인금융
sole right 독점권
solicit 권유
solicitation 교사
soliciting 권유모집

solid model	솔리드 모형
solidity ratio	고정비율
solinton optical communication	광 솔린톤 통신
solution provider	솔루션 공급자
solvency	지급능력
solvency margin	지급능력여유
solvent	지급능력이 있는
sound banking	건전한 은행업무
sound effects	효과음
sound logo	사운드 로고
soundness	건전성
source and disposition statement	원천 및 중도계산서
source effects	정보원 효과
source of funds	자금원
source of income	소득원천
source of information	정보원
source of revenue	재원
source of taxation	세원
sources	원천
South Asian Association for Regional Cooperation	남아시아지역협력연합
South Commission	남쪽위원회
South Pacific Commission	남태평양위원회
South Pacific Forum	남태평양제국회의
sovereign	주권국
sovereign act	통치행위
sovereign immunity	외국주권면제
sovereign loan	독립형 대출
sovereign of taxation	과세주체
sovereign power	주권
sovereign rating	주권순위매김
sovereign risk	주권리스크

sovereignty 주권
space actualization 시장잠재력 실현
space arbitrage 공간재정거래
span of control 관리한계
spare plant capacity 유휴설비
speaker 의장
special 한정된
special account 특별회계
special account for inward portfolio investment 증권특별계정
special account of gains on insurance claim 보험차익특별계정
special assessment 특별과징금
special audit 특별감사
special automobile policy 자가용 자동차종합보험
special bad debts reserve 채권상각특별계정
special bank account firm 특별은행계정회사
special bond 특수채
special bracket group 상위인수그룹
special charges 특별비용
special clause 특별약관
special clearance 특별청산
special collecting agent 특별징수의무자
special collection 특별징수
special committee for public and corporate bond 공사채전문위원회
special conditions of the contract 특별조건서
special contingency reserve 우발손실준비금
special corporation 특수회사
special corporation surtax 법인특별세
special cost studies 특수원가조사
special credit 스페셜 크레디트

special credit of corporation tax	법인세액의 특별공제
special crossed check	특정선할인수표
special damage	실제손해
special damages	특별손해
special day delivery transaction	특약일 결제거래
special deduction	특별공제
special deduction for blue return	청색신고특별공제
special deduction for occasional income	일시소득의 특별공제
special deposit scheme	특별예금제도
special deposits	별단예금
special depreciation	특별상각
special depreciation method	특별상각방법
special depreciation reserve	특별상각준비금
special dividend	특별배당
Special Drawing Rights	특별인출권
special economic benefit	특별한 경제적 이익
Special Economic Zones	경제특구
special endorsement	기명식 배서
special event	특별이벤트
special examiner	특별국세조사관
special exchange	특별교환
special exemption for spouse	배우자 특별공제
special expenses	특별비
special features	스페셜 피쳐스
special incentive measures	촉진세제
special income tax	특별소득세
special indorsement	기명식 이서
special initial depreciation	특별상각
special interest group	특정이해집단
special interest publishing	특정관심층을 대상으로 하는 출판
special intermediary institution	특별매개기관

special item	특별항목
special journal	특수사역장
special landholding tax	특별토지보유세
special letter of credit	매수은행지정신용장
special loan account interest rate	특별대부감정금리
special local consumption tax	특별지방소비세
special local grant tax	특별지방교부세
special loss	특별손실
special margin requirement	특별증거금요건
special methods of computing depreciation	특별한 감가상각방법
special outlay	별도지출
special participant	특별참가자
special payment	특별경제
special performance	특정이행
special policy	개별보험증권
special process	특수고정
special product firm	전문상품 취급업자
special production order	특정제조지도서
special profit and loss	특별손익
special prosecutor	특별검찰관
special quotation	특별청산지수
special repair expenses	특별수선비
special reserve	특별적립금
special reserve fund	별도적립금
special resolution	특별결의
special revenue officer	특별국세징수관
special risks	특별위험
special status system	자격제도
special surplus fund	특별적립잉여금
special tax bond	특별목적세채권
special tax reduction bond	특별감세국채

special tax treatment	특례
special taxation measures	조세특별지위
special treatment	특례
special valuation method	특별한 평가법
special ward	특별구
special ward inhabitants tax	특별구민세
special-purpose financial statement	특별목적 재무제표
specialist	스페셜리스트
specialist block purchases	대구매입
specialist book	스페셜리스트 북
specialist insurer	단수보험자
specialist staff	전문스탭
speciality advertising	스페셜리티 광고
specialization	전문화; 특화
specialized foreign exchange bank	외국환전문은행
specialized fund	특정상표 투자신탁
specialty store	전문점
specie money	정화폐
specie points	금의 현송점
specie reserve	정화준비
specific charge	특정담보
specific consumption tax	개별소비세
specific cost	개별원가
specific duty	종량세
specific foe	특정경쟁상대
specific insurance	물건특정보험
specific media	특수매체
specific performance	특정이행
specific policy	특정보험약관
specific productive factors	특수적 생산요소이론
specific property tax	개별재산세
specific reinsurance	개별재보험

specific risk 고유리스크
specific storage 종량보관료
specific tariff 종량세율
specific-order cost system 개별원가계산제도
specification 명세서; 사양서
specification cost 사양서 원가
specified assets 특정자산
specified disease insurance 특정질병보장보험
specified donation 특정기부금
specified interest 특정이자
specified investment in kind 특정현물출자
specified medical corporation 특정의료법인
specified money in trust 특정금전신탁
specified portion 지정상속분
specified requirement 지점요건
specified stock 특정상표
speculating for difference 차금거래
speculation 투기
speculation for difference 시세폭투기
speculation for margin 차액거래
speculation in stocks 주식투기
speculation transaction 투기거래
speculative buyers 투기적 매입자
speculative buying 투기적 매입
speculative dealing 투기적 거래
speculative demand 투기적 수요
speculative enthusiasm 투기열
speculative gain 투기이윤
speculative import 사혹수입
speculative market 투기시장
speculative money 투기적 자금
speculative motive 투기적 동기

speculative risk	투기적 리스크
speculative stock	투기적 주식
speculative transaction	투기적 거래
speculator	투기가
speculator buying	투기매입
speed resistance line	스피드 레지스턴스 라인
speedy trial	신속한 재판
spending	지출
spending variance	예산차이
spendthrift trust	낭비자 신탁
spike	감당할 수 없다
spill over	스필 오버
spillover effect	스필오버 효과
spin out	스핀 아웃
spin-off	스핀 오프
spinarama	스피나라마
spiral theory	스파이럴 이론
split	스플릿
split ledger account	분해원장계정
split order	대구주문의 소구집행
split rating	다른 등급을 매김
split run	분해 테스트법
split sale	분해판매
split-dollar plan	보험료분담플랜
split-funding	분할지출
split-off	스플리트 오프
split-site production	분산생산
split-ups of stocks	주식분해
splitting a cause of action	청구원인분해
spoilage	공손, 공손품
spoilage expenses	공손품비
sponsor	스폰서

sponsor selectivity	스폰서의 선택력
sponsor tolerance to risk	스폰서의 리스크 허용도
sponsor's role	스폰서의 역할
sponsored research	위탁연구
spontaneous combustion	자연발화
sports gambling	스포츠 도박
spot	직물
spot delivery	현물배달
spot exchange	현물환
spot exchange rate	현물상장; 직물환상장
spot forward	스팟 포워드
spot fund	스팟 펀드
spot market	현물시장
spot next	스팟 넥스트
spot operation	직물거래
spot period	스팟기간
spot position	스팟포지션
spot price	현물가격
spot quotation	현물시세
spot rate	현물시세; 스팟 레이트
spot sale	즉매
spot share	현주
spot transaction	직물거래
spot value	현재가격
spotty	뜸한
spread	가격차
spread	스프레드
spread banking	스프레드 뱅킹
spread effect	파급효과
spread loan	스프레드 론
spread loss cover	스프레드 로스 커버
spread loss reinsurance	초과손해재보험

spread sheet	스프레드 시트
spread trading	스프레드 트레이닝
spread transaction	스프레드 거래
spreader	스프레다
spring offensive	춘투
spurious contagion	의사감염
spurious correlation	의사상관
spurt	급증
square	스퀘어
square an account	감정을 마감하다
square position	스퀘어 포지션
squeeze	몰아침
squeeze-out	배척
STABEX	수출 소득 보장 제도
stability	안정성
stability condition	안정요건
stability of the foreign exchange market	환수급의 안정성
stabilization clause	안정조항
stabilization operation	안정조작
stabilization transaction	안정조작거래
stabilized accounting	안정가치회계
stabilizing	안정촉진적
stabilizing transaction	안정조작
stable dividend	안정배당
stable dollar assumption	화폐가치일정의 공준
stable economic growth	안정경제성장
stable growth	안정성장
stable money principle	안정화폐론
stable stock	안정주
stable stockholder	안정주주
stable stockholder operation	주주안정공작

staff function	스탭직능
stag	권리주 매매인
stagflation	스태그 플레이션
staggered schedule	스태거레드 스케쥴
staggering maturity	만기분산
stagnant industry	정체산업
stagnant market	성장이 정체된 시장, 불황
stakeholder	이해관계자
stale bill of lading	시기경과 선하증권
stale cheque	연체수표
stalemated industry	사양산업
stallage	매장설치권; 장대
stamp	인지
stamp duty	인지세
stamp duty law	수입인지세법
stamp revenue	인지수입
stamping bureau	요율감사부
stand alone investment	단순한 투자대상
stand in debt	채무가 있다
stand-alone company/strategy	프리 스탠딩 기업/전략
standard	기준; 표준율
standard burden rate	표준배부율
standard coin	본위화폐
standard cost	표준원가
standard cost accounting	표준원가계산
standard cross default provision	표준크로스 디폴트 조항
standard currency basket system	표준 바스켓 방식
standard date	표준일
standard deduction	개산공제
standard depletion expenses	표준손료
standard deviation of volatility	변동율의 표준편차
standard documentation	표준서식

standard error	표준오차
standard error of beta	베타의 표준오차
standard error of estimate	추정치의 표준오차
standard industrial classification	표준산업분류
standard interest rate	표준금리
Standard International Trade Classification	표준국제무역분류
standard labor cost	표준노무표
standard lives	표준체
standard machine time	표준기계시간
standard manufacturing expense	표준제조간접비
standard material cost	표준재료비
standard metropolitan statistical areas	통산표준도시권
standard money	본위화폐
standard of price	도량표준
standard part	표준부품
standard policy conditions	표준보험약관
Standard & Poor's Stock Price Index	스탠더드 앤 푸어스의 주가지수
standard population	표준인구
standard profit	표준이익
standard quantity of materials consumed	재료표준소비량
standard rate	기준요금
standard score	표준득점
standard silver dollar	표준은달러
standard stocks	표준주
standard system	본위제도
standard tax rate	표준세율
standard values	표준치
standard wage	기준임금
standard-normal distribution	표준정규분포

standard-run quantity 표준생산량
standardization 표준화
standardized financial statements 표준재무제표
standardized slip 통일전표
standardized volatility 표준화 벌라틸리티
standby agreement 잔액인수; 스탠바이 취결
standby arrangement 차입예약
standby credit 스탠 바이 크레디트; 스탠바이 신용장
standby facilities 스탠 바이 휘실리티스
standby underwriting 청부모집; 잔액인수발행
standing agent 전환부대리인
standing auditor 상임감사역
standing charge 항상비용
standing cost 항상단가
standing expenses 고정비
standing order 계속주문
standing production order 계속제조명령서
standing proxy 상임대리인
standstill 정지
standstill agreement 변제유예
standstill provision 정지조항
staple items 항상상품
star system 스타시스템
stare decisis 선열구속력이 원칙
starting-load cost 당초부담원가
state bank 주법은행
state bankruptcy 국가파산
state branching 주내지점설치
state capital 국가자본
state capitalism 국가자본주의
state enterprises 국영사업
state franchise tax 주법인세

state government bond and debenture	주정부채권
state government securities	주정부증권
state income tax	주소득세
state indemnification	국가보상
state insurance	국영보험
state insurance department	주보험국
state monopoly payment	전매납부금
state of the art	최신의
state of the union message	일반교서
state-chartered association	주면허의 조직
state capital	확정자본금
state liabilities	표시부채
state value	장부기재가격
state value no-par stock	기재식 무액면주식
statement	계산서
statement analysis	재무제표 분석
statement classified by account title	계정과목내역명세서
statement of account	결산보고
statement of cash flow	자금수지표
statement of cash receipts and disbursement	자금조표
statement of changes in financial position	재정상태변동표
statement of facts	합의사실기재서
statement of income and retained earnings	잉여금결합계산서
statement of intent	주지서
statement of items	내역서
statement of liquidations	청산서
statement of operation earnings	경상이익계산서
statement of principles	기본방침

statement of production cost	제조원가보고서
statement of realization and liquidation	청산계산서
statement of retained earnings	이익잉여금계산서
statement of source and application of funds	자금운용표
statement of stockholders' equity	주주지분계산서
statement of surplus	잉여금계산서
statement on auditing procedures	감사수속서
static analysis	정태분석
static market	정태적 시장
static model	정학모형
static multiplier	정학승수
static ratio	정태비율
static risk	정태적 리스크
static statistics	정태통계
stating part	주부
stationary state	정상상태
statistical analysis	통계분석
statistical assumption	통계적 가설
statistical decision theory	통계적 가설이론
statistical laws	통계법칙
statistical procedure	통계처리
statistical sampling	통계 샘플링
statistical technique	통계기법
statistical terminology	통계용어
statistics	통계학
statistics of foreign currency reserves	외화준비통계
statistics on international balance of payment	국제수지통계
statistics on money supply analysis	통화공급분석통계
statistics on national income	국민소득통계

status quo 현상
status system 지위체계
statute 제정법
statute book 법령전서
statute of limitation 시효
statute of limitations on collection 징수권의 소멸시효
statute of limitations on refund claim 환부청구권 시효
statutes at large 법령집
statutory 법령에 의한
statutory accounting principle 법정회계원칙
statutory audit 법정감사
statutory bond 법정보증증권
statutory company 사법률에 의한 회사
statutory debt limit 법정발행한도액
statutory depletion method 법정상각법
statutory deposit 법정공탁금
statutory depreciation method 법정상각방법
statutory due date of tax payment 법정납기한
statutory merger 강제합병
statutory notice 법정통지서
statutory rate of interest 법정이율
statutory reserve 법정준비금
statutory tariff 법정세율
statutory useful life 법정내용년수
statutory valuation method 법정평가방법
statutory valuation method of securities 유가증권의 법정평가방법
stay of execution 형집행정지
stay of proceedings 소송중지
steady 견고
steady market 견고한 시황

steady rise	착실한 신장
steady sales	순조로운 매상
steady state	항상상태
step function	단계함수
step-ladder payment method	단계상환
step-up bonus	생존급부금
step-up coupon	스텝-업 구폰
step-up swap	스텝업 스왑
stepped cost	단계원가
stepped coupon bond	단계적 이자채
stepping stone company	스탭핑 스톤 컴퍼니
stereogram	입체시화상
sterling balance	파운드 잔고
sterling exchange standard	파운드본위제
stet processus	소송종결기재
steward	토지관리인
Stichting Onderzoek Multinationale Ondernemingen	다국적기업조사연구소
stiffen	오르다, 강세를 보이다
stiftung	재단
stimulated demand	자주 수요
stimulatory marketing	자주 판매
stipulated damage	약정손해배상액
stipulated price	협정가격
stipulated security	약정담보권
stipulation	조항
stochastic calculus	확률해석
stochastic method	확률적 기법
stochastic model	확률모형
stochastic process	확률 프로세스
stochastics	추측통계학
stock	주식 · 재고

stock abbreviation	주식약어
stock account	자본계정
stock acquired by the investment in kind	현물출자취득주식
stock acquisition	주식취득
stock adjustment	주식조정
stock allotted to third persons	제3자 할당주
stock arbitrage	주식재정거래
stock at par	액면주
stock authorized	수권자본
stock bonus plan	주식보너스 플랜
stock book	재고품 장부
stock broker	주식중매인
stock buyback	주식재매입
stock capitalization	자본금
stock certificate	주권
stock certificate to bearer	무기명주권
stock clearing corporation	대체결제회사
stock collateral loan	주식담보금융
stock compensation plan	주식보상제도
stock controlling other business	기업지배주식
stock cum rights	증자권리부 주식
stock dealing	주식거래
stock dealing on credit	주식신용거래
stock dividend	주식배당
stock equity	주주지분
stock equity value	주식지분가치
stock exchange	주식거래소
Stock Exchange Automated Quotation	런던증권거래소 시황정보시스템
stock exchange clearing house	주식청산소
stock exchange daily official list	주식거래소 공보

stock exchange holiday	주식거래소 휴일
stock exchange loan	주식거래소 대부
stock exchange panic	주식공황
stock exchange seat	주식거래소위원장
stock exchange share	당소주
stock exchange transaction	거래소 거래
stock for guarantee	보증주
stock for inflation hedging	인플레이션 헷 지주
stock for margin trading	신용거래
stock futures transaction	주식선물거래
stock holding ratio of foreigners	외인지주비율
stock in hand	재고품
stock in process	재공품
stock in the inventory	재고품
stock index	주가지수
stock index futures	주가지수선물
stock inflation	주식인플레이션
stock investment	주식투기
stock investment trust	주식투자신탁
stock issue at market price	주식의 시가발행
stock issue expenses	신주발행비
stock ledger	주식대장
stock level	수지재고수준
stock loan	주권대부
stock loan market	대주시장
stock manipulation	주가조작
stock market	주식시장
stock market fluctuation	주식시장의 변동
stock mind	스톡 마인드
stock name	주식명
stock of affiliated company	관계회사주식
stock on hand	수지주

stock option	주식매취선택권; 스톡옵션
stock option plan	주식구입선택권
stock power	주권양도위임장
stock price	주가
stock price analysis	주가분석
stock price average	평균주가
stock price index	주가지수
stock price index arbitrage transaction	주가지수 재정거래
stock price index futures trading	주가지수 선물거래
stock price index option transaction	주가지수 옵션거래
stock price manipulation	주가조작
stock purchase option	주식매취 옵션
stock purchase plan	주식구입계획
stock purchase warrant	신주인수권
stock quotations	주가정보
stock rating	주식등급매기기
stock receipt	주권양도증
stock recommended for purchase	추장주
stock register	주식원장
stock repurchase plan	주식환매계획
stock right	증자신주매취권
stock risk estimation	주식리스크 추정
stock speculation	주식투기
stock split-up	주식의 분할
stock subscription	주식응모
stock swap	주식스왑
stock symbol	주식이름
stock taking	실재고조사
stock transfer	명의서한
stock turnover	잔고품 회전율
stock used in the average	평균주가채용명

stock valuation	주식평가
stock valuation based on dividend	배당환원주식평가
stock valuation summary	주식평가개요
stock warrants	주식 워런트
stock with par value	액면주식
stock without par value	무액면주식
stock yield	주식이윤
stock-book	상품장부
stock-flow	주식흐름
stock-market crash	주식공황
stock-to-sales ratio	재고율
stockdraw	비축취 붕괴
stockholder	주주
stockholder's equity	자본주감정
stockholder's right	주주권
stockholding limit for foreign investors	외인지주제한
stockpile financing	체화금융
stockpower	위임장
stocks	저장품
stocks in hand	재고품
stolen check	도난수표
stop loss cover	초과손해율보험
stop loss order	손절주문
stop loss reinsurance	초과손해재보험
stop order	공탁금지불금지명령
stop-and-go policy	스톱 앤 고 정책
stop-limit order	역지가주문
stop-loss order	손실한정주문
stop-payment order	지불정지통지
stoppage of business	영업정지
storage	보관료

storage accounts receivable	미수보관료
storage charges	보관비
storage costs	저장경비
storage management	저장품관리
storage of inventories	재고자산보관
store arrangement	점포배열
store audit	점포감사
store business interruption insurance	점표휴업보험
store modernization	점포근대화
store preference	점포선고
store saturation	점포포화상태
store traffic	점내교통
storecasting	점내방송
stored and forward switching	축적교환
stored goods	저장품
storekeepers' comprehensive insurance	점포통합보험
stores ledger	원재료원장
stores purchase book	재료취입장
storyboard	스토리보드
stowage	하적표
straddle	스트래들
straddle position transaction	스트래들 포지션 거래
straight average cost method	단순평균법
straight bankruptcy	단순파산
straight bill of lading	기명식 선하증권
straight bond	보통사채
straight climb	시세가 갑작스레 오름
straight commission	보합제도
straight corporate bond	보통사채
straight credit	매수불능신용장

straight currency swap	스트레이트 커런시 스왑
straight fall	시세가 갑작스레 내림
straight government bond	보통국채
straight life annuity	종신연금
straight life insurance	보통종신보험
straight-line depreciation	정액감가상각법
strait-line method	직선법
stranding	좌초
stranger	제3자
strangle	스트랭글
strangle position transaction	스트랭글 포지션 거래
strap	스트랩
strategic advantage	전략우위제
strategic advertisement	전략광고
strategic alliance	전략적 제휴; 전략동맹
strategic beachhead	전략적 교두보
strategic business unit	전략사업단위
strategic buyer	전략적인 구매자
strategic competition	전략적 경쟁
strategic decision	전략적 의사결정
strategic field	전략분야
strategic group	전략적 집단
strategic information system	전략정보시스템
strategic management	전략경영
strategic performance	전략적 성과
strategy	전략
strategy analysis	전략분석
strategy development	전략개발
strategy formulation	전략형성
stratification	층화
stratified sampling	층화추출
stratum	계층

straw bail	공보증인
straw man	무사력사
street	금융가
street broker	장외중매인
street name	명의
street price	인후시장
strengthen	굳어지다
strengthening	시세가 오를 듯한 기세
strengthening of managerial function	관리기능강화
strict construction	엄격해석
strict foreclosure	대물변제담보물건의 취득
strict liability	엄격책임
strike a balance	대차를 공제하다
strike price	권리행사가격
stringent policy	긴장정책
strip player	스트립 플레이어
strip yield	스트립 일드
stripped cap	스트립트 캡
stripped interest rate cap	스트립트 금리캡
stripped zero-coupon	스트립트 제로 쿠폰
strips	스트립스 채
strong and weak	강약
strong feeling	강한 기운
strong form	스트롱 폼, 강형
strong growth	높은 성장
strong incentive	호재료
strong market	강세시황
strong sentiment	강한 기운
strong tone	시세가 오를 듯한 기세
strong yen	엔고
structural	구조적

structural adjustment facility	구조조정융자
structural analysis	구조분석
structural change	구조변화
structural determinant	구조요인
structural equation	구조방정식
structural factor	구조인자
structural flexibility	구조탄력성
structural impediments initiative talks	구조협의
structural inflation	구조적 인플레이션
structural outline	구도
structural unemployment	구조적 실업
structural-functional analysis	구조기능분석
structure	구축물
structure of industry	산업구조
structure of interest rates	금리구조
structure of price	가격구조
structured transaction	사조거래
struggle for existence	생존경쟁
stuck	스턱상황
student comprehensive insurance	학생종합보험
student's distribution	학생분포
studio standard	스튜디오 규모
stuffer	첨부광고
style sheet	스타일 시트
sub-contrary	소반대명제
subcenter	부도심
subcontract	하청
subcontract factory	하청공장
subcontracting	하도급
subcontractor	하청업자
subculture	하위문화
subduct	공제하다

subheading 소견출
subject 과목
subject market 서브젝트 마켓
subject-matter 계쟁물
subject-matter of insurance 보험의 목적
subjective perception 주관적 지각
subjective probability 주관적 확률
sublease 부동산 전대차
sublet 전대하다
subliminal 서블리미널
subliminal advertisement 의식하광고
subliminal advertising 잠재의식광고
subloan 서브론
submission 중재부탁합의
subobjective 하위목적
suboptimization 부분 최적화
subordinate debenture 노후조항부사채
subordinate ledger 보조원장
subordinated 후순위의, 열후의
subordinated bond 후순위사채
subordinated clause 후순위조항
subordinated creditor 후순위권자
subordinated debenture 후순위사채
subordinated debt 후순위채권
subordinated discount bond 노후할인채
subordinated payment-in-kind bond 노후 페이먼트 인 카인드 채
subordinated stock 노후주
subordinated unsecured debenture 노후성 무담보사채
subordination 종속; 열후
subpart 'F' income 섭파트 F 소득
subparticipation 배참가
subrogated performance 대위변제

subrogated right 대위채권
subrogation 대위
subrogation arising out of salvage 잔존물 대위
subrogation payment 대위납부
subrogation receipt 대위영수서
subrogation right of obligee 채권자 대위권
subscribe 서명하다
subscribed capital stock 미불입 자본
subscriber's yield 응모자 이자
subscription 출자
subscription agreement 모집계약
subscription blank 주식신청서
subscription book closed 주식모집마감
subscription book open 주식모집개시
subscription certificate 출자증권
subscription for shares 주식응모
subscription money 신청금
subscription period 판매기간
subscription price 응모가격
subscription right 신주인수권
subscription television 유료방송
subscription warrant 신주인수권증서
subscription's receivable account 주식인수감정
subscriptions 지불미제자본금
subsequent events 후발사상
subsequent measurements 사후측정
subsequent taxable year 차사업년도
subsidiary 자회사
subsidiary accounts 보조 원장 계정
subsidiary book 보조부
subsidiary coin 보조화폐
subsidiary company 자회사

subsidiary corporation	관계회사
subsidiary department	보조부문
subsidiary journal	보조기입장
subsidiary ledger	보조원장
subsidiary material cost	보조재료비
subsidiary money	보조화폐
subsistence money	생계비
substance	본질
substance over form	실질우선
substandard	표준하체
substandard loan	회수에 문제있는 대부
substantial damages	실질적 손해배상금
substantial evidence	실질적 증거
substantial performance	실질적 이행
substantive	주요적
substantive evidence	실질증거
substantive law	실체법
substitute assets	대체자산
substitute certificate for government bond	국채대용증서
substitute fixed assets	대체고정자산
substitute property	대체자산
substitute securities	대용유가증권
substituted expenses	대체비용
substitution	대체
substitution curve	대체곡선
substitution effect	대체효과
substitution of land lot	환지처분
substrategy	하위전략
subsystem	서브시스템
subtitle	하부제목
subtraction	공제

subunderwriting	하인수
suburban paper	교외지
suburban population	교외인구
suburban store	교외점포
subvention	보조
subzero growth	마이너스 성장
succession	승계
succession of endorsement	배서연속
succession of liabilities	채무인계
succession of national tax liability	국세채무승계
succession of property	유산상속
succession of right of taxation	과세권 승계
succession of tax liability	납세의무승계
successive inheritance	상차상속
successor	후계자
suck	재산을 탕진하다
suction to cash	썩션으로의 부착
sue and labor charges	손해방지비용
sue and labor clause	손해방지조항
sue out	신청하여 취득하다
suffer	인용하다
suffrage	투표행위
suggested resale price	추장재판가격
suggestion scheme	제안제도
sui generis	그 자신에 특유한
suit	소송
suitor	소송인
Sullivan Principle	설리반 원칙
sum	총액
sum insured	보험금액
sum insured left	잔존보험금액
sum insured method	보험금액 비례주의

sum payable at death	사망보험금
sum total	합계
sum up	계상하다
sum-of-the-years-digits method	산술급수법
summary	총괄감정; 요약
summary account	집합계정
summary journal	일괄분개장
summary judgment	즉결판결
summary measure	집약척도
summary of earnings	영업성적
summary procedure	독촉수속
summary proceeding	약식소송수속
summary reports	개략보고
summary sheet	집계표
summary statement of business	사업개황설명서
summated rating	평정가산법
summer time	하시간
summing-up	증거의 요약
summons	호출장
sundry account	잡계정
sundry expenses	제잡비
sundry goods	잡화
sundry income	잡수입
sundry supplies	소모품
sunk cost	회수불능가격
super 301 Article	슈퍼 301조
super floater swap	슈퍼 플로터 스왑
super gold tranche	슈퍼 골드 트랜체
super impose	슈퍼 임포우즈
super majority provision	슈퍼 메이져리티 조항
super NOW account	슈퍼 NOW 감정
super prime rate	슈퍼 프라임 레이트

super royalty	슈퍼 로얄티
superannuation	노령퇴직자연금
superannuation payment	퇴직금 적립금
supercargo	화물상승인
superficiary	지상권자
superficium	지상물
super-imperialism	대제국주의
superior character	상부문자
superior courts	상급재판소
superior obligation	재단채권
superior risks	우수물건
supernational bond	국제기관사채
supersede	사서 바꾸다
supertax	부가세
supervisor	슈퍼바이저
supplemental	보족의
supplemental contract	부수계약
supplementary budget	보정예산
supplementary call	보충부담금
supplementary cost	간접원가; 보족적 비용
supplementary financial measure	보족융자
supplementary income statement information	손익계산서의 보족자료
supplementary insurance	보족적인 보험
supplementary payment	부수적 급부
supplementary proceedings	보충수속
supplementary regulations	부칙
supplementary special deposits scheme	추가특별예금제도
supplementary statement	부속명세서
supplier's credit	연불신용
supplies	저축품

supplies expenses	소모품비
supply	지급
supply and demand	수급
supply bond	공급보증증권
supply function	공급관수
supply of investible funds	자금공급
supply-side economics	공급주의 경제학
support	지지
support buying	지원매입
support line	하가지지선
support operation	주식시세가 떨어지려 할 때 주식을 필요한 만큼 매입하여 시세를 안정시킴
support price	유지가격
support trust	부조신탁
supporter	부양자
supporting documents	부속서류
supporting order	매지주문
suppression of deposition	공술녹취서금지
suprafirm	수프라펌
supra-national firm	초국적 기업
Supreme Court	(연방) 대법원
supreme law of the land	나라의 최고법규
surcharge	가중세; 과징금
surety	보증인
Surety Association of America	아메리카 보증보험협회
surety bond	보증증권
surety company	보증회사
surety money	보증채무
surety obligation	구상권
suretyship	보증
surface communication	표면적 커뮤니케이션
surface model	표면모델

surface right	지상권
surgical expense insurance	수술비보험
surplus	잉여금
surplus account	잉여금 계정
surplus adjustment	잉여금 수정
surplus analysis	잉여금 분석
surplus appropriated for redemption fund	재무상환적립금
surplus appropriation statement	잉여금처분계산서
surplus at liquidation	청산잉여금
surplus available for dividend	배당가능이익
surplus charge	잉여금부과
surplus equipment	유휴설비
surplus finance	흑자재정
surplus from capital reduction	감자잉여금
surplus from consolidation	연결잉여금
surplus from merged company	합병차익
surplus from revaluation	재평가잉여금
surplus funds	잉여금
surplus insurance	잉여인슈어런스
surplus line	주내 보험자가 소비할 수 없는 보험
surplus profit	잉여이익
surplus reserves	잉여적립금
surplus reserves transferred to income	적립금 환원
surplus section	적립금 구분
surplus statement	잉여금 계산서
surplus transaction	잉여금 거래
surplus treaty reinsurance	초과액 특약 재보험
surplus value	잉여가치
surplusage	과잉
surprises in earnings	이익의 예상외의 변동
surrender	권리포기

surrender charge	해약공제
surrender profit	해약익
surrender provisions	해약조항
surrender ratio	해약율
surrender value	해약반환금
surtax	과징금
surtax on land tax	지조부가세
surtax on national tax	국세부가세
surveillance	감시
survey bias	바르지 못한 조사
survey fee	감정료
survey repot	감정보고서
surveying	측량
surveying fee	감정료
surveyor	사정인
survival bond	서바이벌 본드
survival of the fittest	적자생존
surviving company	존속회사
surviving entity	존속실체
survivor annuity	유족연금
survivor benefit	유족급부금
survivorship	생존자에게 권리가 귀속됨
survivorship annuity	생잔연금
suspended trading	매매정지
suspense account	미결제계정
suspense payment account	가불금계정
suspense payments	가불금
suspense receipts	가수금
suspense receipts account	가수금계정
suspension	정지
suspension of banking transaction	은행거래정지처분
suspension of business	사업의 중지

suspension of convertibility	교환성 정지
suspension of execution	집행정지
suspension of payment	지불정지
suspension of prescription	정지시효
suspension of right	권리정지
suspension of seizure	차압유예
suspension of statute of limitations	시효의 정지
suspension of transactions	입회정지
suspension of work claims	중단 클레임
suspicion	혐의
sustain	유지하다
sustainable equilibrium exchange rate	유지가능한 균형환율
sustainable growth	지속적 성장
sustainable growth rate	지속적 성장율
sustaining program	스폰서가 붙어있지 않은 프로그램
sustenance	생계
swap	스왑
swap agreement	스왑 협정
swap broker	스왑 브로커
swap cost	스왑 비용
swap coupon	스왑 쿠폰
swap fund	스왑 펀드
swap loan	스왑채
swap of bond	채권 스왑
swap portfolio	스왑 포트폴리오
swap position	스왑 포지션
swap rate	스왑 레이트
swap strike	스왑 스트라이크
swap trading	스왑 거래
swap-in-arrears	스왑 인 어리어
swaption	스왑션
sweat	땀에 젖은

sweep	시청율 조사
sweep account	스왑 계정
sweetener	감미료
swing	스윙
swing line	신용공여
switch	환승
switch finance	스위치 금융
switch from yen to dollars	엔 달러 시프트
switch pitch	스위치 핏치
switch reversal	역교체
switch trade	스위치 무역
switching cost	매입선변경 코스트
syllabus	판결의 두 주
symbiosis	공생
symbol system of accounts	감정기호법
symbolic communication	심볼릭 커뮤니케이션
symbolic delivery	상징적 인도
symbolic logics	기호논리학
symbolic model	기호모델
symbolic simulation	심볼릭 시뮬레이션
symmetrical distribution	대칭분포
symmetrical triangle pattern	대칭 트라이앵글
symptomatic behavior	증후형 행동
synchromarketing	동조형 마케팅
synchronize	공기를 취하다
synchronizer	싱크로나이저
synchronousity broadcasting	공기방송
syndic	파산관재인
syndicate	인수단
syndicate of banks	은행단
syndicate survey	신디케이트 조사
syndicate underwriting	신디케이트단 인수

syndicated loan	신디케이트 론
syndicated term loan	중장기 협조융자
syndication	신디케이트단
synergy	상승
synergy effect	상승효과
synopsis sheet	개요시트
synthesis tax rate	종합세율
synthetic assets	합성자산
synthetic bond	신세틱 본드
synthetic cash arbitrage transaction	합성현물 재정거래
synthetic cash instrument	신세틱 캐쉬
synthetic instrument	복합상품
synthetic long	신세틱 롱
synthetic position	합성포지션
synthetic propositions	종합적 명제
synthetic put	신세틱 풋
synthetic rubber	합성고무
synthetic short	신세틱 숏
synthetic useful life	합성내용연수
system approach	시스템 어프로치
system audit	시스템 감사
system engineering	시스템 공학
system issue	시스템 품목
system of accounts	회계조직
system of blue return	청색신고제도
system of fixed rate of exchange	고정환율제
system of interest rates	이자율체계
System of National Account	신국민경제체계
system of note issue	발권제도
system of taxation	조세체계
system operation	시스템 조작
system repos	시스템 레포스

system risk	시스템 리스크
systematic analysis	조직적 분석
systematic calculation	계통적 계산
systematic risk	시스터메틱 리스크, 체계적 위험
systematic sampling	계통적 표본
systemic	계통했다
systems competition	시스템간 경쟁

≪ T ≫

T form account	T자형 계정
table	계산표
table of present value	현가표
table of price factors	환산계수테이블
table of random numbers	단수표
tabloid size	타블로이드 판
tabular cash book	다행식 현금출납부
tabular ledger	표식원장
tabular standard	계표본위
tabulating machine	회계기
tabulation	제표
tachistoscope	순간노출기
tacit	묵시의
tacit collusion	암묵의 공모
tacking	후순위 저당우선
tact system	택트 시스템
tactical asset allocation	전술적 자산배분
tactical planning	전술계획
tail hedge	테일 헷지
tailgating	동반이익
tailing	테일링
tailor made	특별주문의
take a capital stake in	자본출자하다
take-home pay	실수입
take-off strategy	초기단계전략
take-ones	테이크 원즈
take-or-pay contract	산출물 인수 및 지불계약

takeout	차액수입
takeout loan	장기융자
takeover	인수
takeover bid	주식공개매입
taking a bath	투기매매의 손실
taking a flier	투기행위
takings	소득
talk down	구두 하락개입
talk up	구두 상승개입
tally	조회
tally audit	검수감사
tally man	검수인
tangible assets	유형자산
tangible depreciable property	유형상각자산
tangible fixed assets	유형고정자산
tangible loss	유형손실
tangible property	유형고정자산
tangible value	유형재산가격
tap	탭 발행(분할발행방식의 일종)
tap bills	탭 빌
tap certificate of deposit	탭 CD(양도성 예금증서)
tap issue	탭 발행
tap stock	탭 채
tapping of resources	자원개발
target assets value	대상자산가액
target company	대상회사
target cost	목표원가
target group	표적집단
target income	목표이익
target issue	타겟발행
target payout ratio	목표 배당성향
target portfolio	목표 포트폴리오

target price 목표 가격
target profit 목표 이익
target range 목표 변동폭
target securities 대상 상품
target stock 대상 주석
target yield 목표이율
target zone 목표 시세권
tariff 관세
tariff autonomy 관세자 주권
tariff barrier 관세 장벽
tariff by agreement 협정요율
tariff commission 세율위원회
tariff escalation 경사관세
tariff harmonization 관세조화
tariff in jeopardy 긴급관세
tariff negotiations 관세교섭
tariff preference 관세 특혜조치
tariff premium 영업보험료
tariff quota 관세할당
tariff quota system 관세할당제도
tariff rate 관세율
tariff war 관세전쟁
tariffication 관세화
tarnished halo effect 역 할로 방법
task 사업
task environment 사업환경
task method 태스크 매소드
tax 조세
tax accountant examination 세무사 시험
tax accountant fee 세무사 보수
tax accounting 세무회계
tax adjustments 세무조사

tax administration system	세무행정조직
tax advisor	세부고문
tax agency	세무대행
tax agent	납세관리인
tax amount	과세액
tax amount settled	조정세액
tax and public dues	조세공동부과
tax and stamp revenues	조세 및 인지수입
tax anticipation bill	조세준비증권
tax arbitarage	세금 재정
tax assessment	조세사정
tax audit	세무감사
tax authorities	세무당국
tax avoidance	조세회피
tax base	과세기준
tax basis	과세표준
tax bearer	납세자
tax bearing capacity	조세부담능력
tax benefit	조세특전
tax bond	세수채
tax bracket	세율등급
tax burden	조세부담
tax burden rate	세부담률
tax burden ratio	조세부담률
tax claims	조세채권
tax clause	조세조항
tax collection	징세
tax collection by stamp	인지징수
tax collection system	징세기구
tax collector	세금징수원
tax computation basis	세액계상기준
tax consultation	세무상담

tax convention 조세조약
tax court 조세재판소
tax credit 세액공제
tax credit for dividend 배당공제
tax credit for minor 미성년자 공제
tax criminal 조세범
tax cut by law 감세
tax cutback 세액삭감계산
tax deductible items 과세공제비용
tax deductions 세액공제
tax deed 공매증서
tax delinquency 체납
tax dispute 세무소송
tax documents 세무서류
tax due 납세액
tax effect 세효과
tax effect accounting 세효과회계
tax evasion 탈세
tax examination 세무조사
tax exempt 비과세
tax exempt bond 면세채
tax exemption 면세
tax exemption for agricultural income 농업소득면세
tax exemption for dependents 부양가족공제
tax exemption for speciffic use 특정용도면제
tax exemption limit 면세점
tax for default 가산세
tax for transfer of securities 유가증권이전세
tax forms 납세 신고 용지
tax free 비과세
tax free article 비과세품
tax free corporation 비과세 법인

tax free purchase	비과세 취득, 비과세 매입
tax harmonization	세의 조화
tax haven	조세 회피지역, 조세 피난처
tax holiday	텍스 홀리데이 세제장려 조치
tax in arrears	연체세
tax in jeopardy	긴급과세
tax in kind	물납세
tax incentive	세제상의 우대조치
tax incidence	조세의 귀착
tax increase	증세
tax items	세목
tax jurisprudence	세법학
tax law	세법
tax lease	세액 리스
tax liability	납세의무
tax lien	조세선취특권
tax loss carry-forward	결손금 차기 이월
tax loss carryback	결손금 전기 이월, 환입
tax manager	납세관리인
tax obligation	납세의무
tax office	세무서
tax on admission	입장세
tax on bank note system	태환권 발행세
tax on capital gain	자본이득과세
tax on construction	건축세
tax on depost	예금이자세
tax on dividend	이익배당세
tax on excess issue	초과 발행세, 제한외 발행세
tax on goods and possessions	물품세
tax on property	자산세
tax on redemption profit	상환차익과세
tax on the write-up	자산 재평가세

tax on undistributed profits	유보소득에 관한 세
tax on unutlized land	미이용토지세
tax oriented transaction	절세거래
tax papers	납세고지서
tax paradise	조세천국
tax payable	미지급세금
tax payable account	미지급세금계정
tax payer's suit	납세자 소송
tax payment	납세
tax payment by securities	증권납부
tax payment by self-assessment	신고납세
tax payment by stamp	인지납부
tax payment by transfer account	이체납세
tax payment in kind	현물납부
tax payment in money	금전상납, 금전납부
tax payment place	납세지
tax payment slip	납부서
tax policy	조세정책
tax practitioner	세무사
tax procedures	세무수속
tax proxy	세무대리
tax rate	세율
tax rate applied to upper part of income	상적세율
tax rate higher than standard	초과세율
tax rate of gift tax	증여세율
tax rebate(refund)	조세환급
tax reduction	감세
tax reform	세제개혁
tax refunded	환급된 세금
tax regulations	세법
tax reimbursement	조세환급

tax relief	조세부담경감
tax relief bonds	감세채권
tax requisition	과세요건
tax reserve	납세충당금
tax resort	세금 리조트, 특별조세혜택부여지역
tax return form	납세 신고서
tax revenue	세수입
tax roll	과세대장
tax rule	세법규
tax sale	환가처분
tax saving	절세
tax saving association	납세저축조합
tax seal	인지
tax selling	세금을 위한 매각
tax shelter	세금회피수단
tax sparing	대내투자장려조치
tax sparing credit	간주외국세액공제
tax spinning	텍스 스피닝
tax state	조세국가
tax structure	조세구조
tax suit	세무소송
tax surcharge	부가세
tax swap	세금 스왑
tax system	세제
tax system council	세제조사회
tax table	세액표
tax take	세징구액
tax threshold	과세 최저한도
tax treaty	조세조약
tax tribunal examiner	국세심사관
tax unpaid	미지급납세
tax value	과세가격

tax-gathering season	세수입기
taxable	과세가능한
taxable amount	과세가격
taxable capacity	세부담능력
taxable depreciation	과세상각
taxable document	과세문서
taxable estate	과세유산
taxable goods	과세품
taxable income	과세소득
taxable item	과세대상
taxable minimum of property tax	고정자산세 면세점
taxable period	과세기간
taxable property	과세자산
taxable purchases	과세취득, 과세매입
taxable sales	과세매출, 과세판매량
taxable undistributed profits	과세대상유보금액
taxable unit	과세단위
taxable value	과세가격
taxable year	사업년도
taxable year of merger	합병사업년도
taxanticipation note	세수예정어음
taxanticipation warrant	세수예정 워런트
taxation	과세
taxation allowance for life insurance premium	생명보험료 공제
taxation allowance for nonlife insurance premium	손해보험료 공제
taxation at the source	원천과세
taxation at time of receipt from bonded area	거래과세
taxation by applying upper bracket	누적과세
taxation by estimate	추정과세

taxation division	수세과
taxation of income basis	소득세
taxation on a per capita basis	균등세
taxation on aggregate income	종합과세
taxation on capital gain	자본이득세
taxation on corporation tax basis	법인세
taxation on enterprise	기업과세
taxation on government monopoly	전매세
taxation on retirement annuity	퇴직연금과세
taxation on shipment	선적세
taxation on small business	중소기업과세
taxation rate	세율
taxation system	세제
taxation upon the general-public	일반과세
taxation upon total income	종합과세
taxbenefit rule	세효과규제
taxcollector	세무관
taxdodging	탈세
taxes	공과
taxes and rates	국세와 지방세
taxes assessed by taxpayers	신고세
taxes collected	세금예금
taxes receivable	미수세
taxexempt organization	비과세기관
taxflation	택스플레이션
taxfree income	면세소득
taxfree investment	면세투자
taxfree reserve	비과세 충당금
taxpayer	납세자
taxpayer filing a blue return	청색신고서
taxpayer indentification number system	납세자 번호제도

taxpayer with limited tax liability	제한적 납세의무자
taxpayer's association	납세조항
taxpayer's option	납세자 선택
taxpayer's suit	납세자 소송
teaser advertising	티저광고
technical analysis	기술분석
technical assistance	기술지원
technical change	기술적 변화
technical cooperation	기술제휴
technical forecast	기술적 예측
technical graph	기술분석용 그래프
technical index	기술지표
technical indicator	기술적 분석지표
technical innovation	기술혁신
technical position	시장내부요인
technical progress	기술진보
technical quality	기술의 질
technical rally	자율반등
technical reaction	자율반응
technical rebound	자율반등
technical specification	기술 사양서
technical theory	기술 이론
technical trading	기술 훈련
technocrat	기술 관료
technological changes	기술 진보
technological fixity	기술적 고정
technological forecasting	기술 예측
technological gap	기술 격차
technological rent	기술적 지대
technology assessment	기술적 평가
technology transfer	기술 이전
technology transfer agreement	기술이전계약

telecine translation 영화 텔레비전 변환
telecommunication business 전기통신사업
telecomputing 컴퓨터 통신
telegraphic transfer 전신환
telegraphic transfer buying rate 전신환 매입률
telegraphic transfer payable 전신환 지급
telegraphic transfer receivable 전신환 수급
telegraphic transfer selling rate 전신환 매도요율
telematique 텔레마티크
telephone market 전화사업시장
telephone rates 전화요금
telephone subscription right 전화가입권
teleport 텔레포트
teletext 문자다중방송
television conference 화상회의
television system 텔레비전 방식
teller 현금출납계
temporal law 시간적 법칙
temporal method 속성법
temporary 잠정적
temporary account 가계정, 일시계정
temporary advance 일시대체
temporary annuity 정기생명연금
temporary bond 일시채권
temporary boom 일시적 호황
temporary borrowing 일시 차입금
temporary income 임시 소득
temporary injunction 가집행
temporary investment 일시투자
temporary layoff 일시적 이직
temporary leave from work 일시귀휴
temporary loan 일시 대부금

temporary loan before bond flotation 기채 관련 융자
temporary loan on property 재산의 일시적 대부
Temporary Money Rates Adjustment Law 임시금리조정법
temporary payment 가지급금
temporary rally 일시적 반품
temporary receipts 가수금, 가영수증
temporary receipts account 가수금계정
temporary repairs 가수선
temporary residence 임시거주지
temporary seal 가봉
temporary tariff rate 잠정세율
temporary tax accountant 임시 세무사
temporary use 임시 사용
10-K report 10-K 보고서
10-Q report 10-Q 사분기 보고서
tenancy 부동산권
tenancy in common 전구성원에 의한 공유
tenant 임차인
tenant right 임차권, 임대권
tender 입찰인수, 면적서
tender bill 텐더빌
tender clause 입찰약관
tender panel 텐더패널
tender security 입찰증권
tenement 보유재산
tenor 상환기한
tension 긴박
tentative agreement 잠정합의
tentative balance sheet 가대차대조표
tentative budget 잠정예산
tentative validity 공정력

tenure of office	재직기한
term	기간, 조건
term annuity	정기연금
term bonds	단일만기채
term deposits	정기예금
term fed	텀 페드
term federal fund	텀 페드럴 펀드
term financing	중장기 금융
term financing rate	기간차입금리
term for evaluation	평가시기
term insurance	정기보험
term loan	기간대출
term of execution	집행기한
term of insurance	보험기한
term of office	재직기한
term of payment	지급기한
term of validity	유효기간
term policy	정기생명보험계약
term risk	기간 리스크
term sheet	조건 개요서
term structure	기간구조
term-end	기말
term-end account	기말계정
term-end settlement of accounts	기말결산
terminal dividend	소멸배당
terminal funding	연금원가 적립방식
terminal funding method	연금현가 충족방식
terminal pay allowance	퇴직수당
terminal reserve	연말책임준비금
termination	기간만료
termination claim	만기청구액
terminal dividend	계약종료배당

terms and conditions	조건
terms of access	수입허가조건
terms of delivery	인도조건
terms of trade	교역조건
terrier	토지대장
territorial limitation	지역제한
territorial multiplier	지역배율
territorial right	지역특약권
territorial waters	영해
tertiary beneficiary	제3순위 보험금 수취인
tertiary industry	제3차 산업
test data	시험 데이타
test marketing	시험판매
test of hypothesis	가설검정
testament	유언
testify	증언하다
testimonial advertising	추천광고
testimony	증언
testing	시험
testing audit	시사
testing expenses	시사비
testing hypothesis	검정가설
text editor program	텍스트 편집 프로그램
theoretical	이론적
theoretical economics	이론 경제학
theoretical future price	이론선물가격
theoretical hypothesis	이론적 가설
theoretical price	이론 가격
theoretical rate of exchange	이론적 환율시세
theoretical support	이론적 지시
theoretical value	이론가치
theories of insurance	보험학설

theory of achievement motivation	동기달성이론
theory of action	행위이론
theory of approximation	근사치이론
theory of asset valuation	자산평가
theory of comparative cost	비교생산비
theory of consumption	소비이론
theory of games	게임이론
theory of indemnity	손해배상원칙
theory of international indebtedness	국제대차설
theory of liabilities taxation	조세채무관계설
theory of multiplier	승수이론
theory of optimum tariff	최적관세이론
theory of portfolio selection	자산선택이론
theory of rate-making	보험료율 결정이론
theory of role enactment	역할실현론
theory of tax accounting	세무회계론
theory of ultimate cause	최호조건설
thesaurus	(지식의) 보고, 사전
thin	한산, 빈약
thin capitalization	과소자본
thin industry	취약산업
thin margin	낮은 이윤, 이익이 없는 상태
thing in action	무체동산
things real	부동산
think tank	두뇌집단
third country bill	3국 수표
third generation	제3세대
third generation on-line system	제3세대 온라인 시스템
third market	점두거래시장
third party	제3자
third party claimant bond	제3자 이의신청소송 보증증권
third party legal liability insurance	제3자 배상책임보험

third party liability cover	제3자 배상특약보험
third party liability insurance	제3자 배상책임보험
third party sales credit	할부구입알선
third sector	제3섹타
third world	제 3세계
third world countries	제 3세계 각국
third world multinationals	제 3세계 다국적 기업
threat	협박
3D scanner	입체스캐너
three digit PER	백배대의 주가수익률
three line converting method	3선전환법
three-fourths loss clause	3/4 보상약관
three-month moving average	3개월 이동평균
threshold	한계
threshold of divergence	괴리한도
through bill of lading	통과선증권
through transportation	일괄수송
through-put contract	스루-풋 조항
throughout accounting	일괄회계
through the target issues	대상품목 전체의
throw-back rule	스로-백 원칙
throwaway product	일회용 제품
thumbnail	아주 작은, 간결한
tick	외상거래
ticker	주식상장표시판
ticket	전표, 티켓
ticket of leave	가석방 허가증
ticket sale finance	티켓 판매금융
tie-in	포함의
tie-in clause	타이 인 조항
tie-in sale	끼워팔기
tie-up loan	제휴론

tied loan	조건부대출
tied purchase clause	타이드 구매조항
tied-agent	전속중개자
tier	계층
tight	긴축
tight budget	긴축재정
tight fiscal policy	긴축재정정책
tight money policy	긴축금융정책
tightened inspection	세밀검사
tightening	튼튼하게 조이다, 강화하다
tighter monetary policy	긴축강화 금융정책
tightness of money	금전압박
timber delivery tax	목재거래설
timber income	산림소득
time bargains	정기거래
time base business	시차 비즈니스
time bias	시간 바이어스
time bill	기한부 수표
time card	타임 카드
time cost	시간원가
time deposit	정기예금
time deposit account	정기예금계정
time deposit certificate	정기예금증서
time division multiple access	시간분할 다원접속
time draft	일람후 정기 환어음
time expired	기한종료
time filter	타임 필터
time for tax payment	납기한
time horizon	거래시간
time limit	기한
time limitation	기간제한
time limited	기일

time loan 정기대부
time of adoption 채용시간
time of presentation 표시기간
time of receipts 수입시기
time of recognizing gain 수익계상시기
time of recognizing loss 손실계상시기
time perception 시간지각
time policy 기간보험
time preference 시간선호
time priority 시간우선원칙
time rate system 시간임금제
time sales 할부판매
time series analysis 시계열분석
time series behavior of earnings 이익의 시계열 변동
time series data 시계열 데이타
time span 시간대, 기간
time spread 시간 스프레드
time study 시간연구
time to expiration 잔여기간
time to maturity 잔존기간
time transaction 정기거래
time value 시간적 가치
time value of option 옵션의 시간가치
time variance 시간차이
time-series analysis 시계열 분석
time-series behavior 시계열 변동
time-weighted return 시간가중수익률
timely disclosure 시간적인 정보개시
Times 1000 타임즈 1000사
times per year 연간의 회전회수
times-interest earned 이자부담배율
times-interest earned ratio 이자부담률

timing differences	기간차이
timing option	시간옵션
tip	정보누설
title	부동산 등의 소유권
title deeds	부동산 권리서
title insurance	소유권 보증
title insurance company	소유권 보험회사
title of account	계정과목
title paramount	우월한 권리
tobacco consumption tax	담배소비세
token order	명목발주
tokkin	특별금융
tolerance	허용차
tolerance limit	허용한도
toll	통행료
toll charges	통행세
toll gate	도로요금소
toll traverse	사유지 통행료
tomorrow-next	익일 차입, 익익일 변제
tone	시장분위기
tonnage due	선박세
Tontine dividend	톤티식 배당
tool	수법
tool for analysis	분석도구
top	상위
top bidder	최고치 입찰자
top-down forecasting	하향식 예측
top-down technique	하향식 기법
top management	수뇌부
top straddle	상향제한 스트래들
top vertical combination	최고 수직 결합
top-reversal day	천장반전일, 고가반전일

topless	한정이 없는
topography	지세도
topology	위상
topping out	최고 상승세
tort	불법행위
total	합계
total amount of insurance in force	보유계약
total asset turnover ratio	총자산 회전율
total assets	총자산
total audience	총시청자
total capital	자본금 합계
total capital profit ratio	총자본 수익률
total capitalization	총장기 자금
total correlation	전체상관
total cost	전체비용, 전체원가
total cost curve	총비용곡선
total cost of transaction	총거래비용
total costing	총원가계산
total deposit	총예금
total earnings	총수익
total liabilities and net worth	총자본
total loss	총손실
total loss only	총손실담보
total market delta	총시장 델타치
total market value	총시장가치
total maximum liability	책임한도액
total money supply	총통화 공급
total net income	총소득금액
total net worth	자기자본합계
total payment of installments	할부가격
total rate of return	총수익률
total receipts	총수입

total receivables	미수수취 계정합계
total reserve system	총액준비제도
total reserves	총준비
total return	종합이자회수
total sales	총매출액
total selling contract	총 매도 계약
total stocks issued	총발행완료주식수
total sum	총계
total taxable income	과세총소득금액
total turnover	총회전율
touching the bottom	바닥치기
tourist income	관광수입
tourist tax	여행자세
tout	강매하다
towage	예선료
town	마을
town planning scheme	도시계획
traceability	추적가능성
traceable cost	관리가능비, 추적가능원가
traceable theory	귀속이론
tracking	트래킹
tracking error	연동오차
tracking stock	트래킹 스톡
trade	영업
trade acceptance	인수완료
trade acceptances payable	인수수표
trade account	영업계정
trade account payable	외상매입금
trade account receivable	외상매도금
trade advertising	유통광고
trade against the trend	추세에 역행하는 거래
trade assets	영업자산

trade associations	증권거래업자협회
trade balance	무역수지
trade barrier	무역장벽
trade by agreement	협정무역
trade channel	거래경로
trade claim	무역크레임
trade contractor	무역업자
trade control	무역통제
trade creation effect	무역창출효과
trade credit	무역금융
trade creditor	무역거래처, 매입처
trade date	약정일
trade debtor	외상거래처
trade deficit	무역적자
trade description	상품기술
trade discount	업자할인
trade expansion act	통상확대법
trade expenses	영업비
trade figure	무역수지실적
trade friction	무역마찰
trade imbalance	무역불균등
trade liability	영업채무
trade mark	상표
trade matrix analysis	무역연관분석
trade name	상호
Trade Negotiations Committee	무역교섭위원회
trade on commission	위탁무역
trade payables	지급채무
trade receivable	매출채권
trade rights	영업권
trade secrets	기업비밀
trade show	견본

trade statistics	무역통계
trade surplus amount	무역수지흑자폭
trade tax	영업세
trade terms	정형무역조건
trade union	노동조합, 직업별 조합
trade-in	신규구입대금의 일부로 내놓는 것
trade-in articles	신규구입대금의 일부로 내놓은 물품
trade-mark	상표
trade-mark infringement	상표권 침해
trade-mark registration law	상표등록법
trade-off	상충관계, 타협적 거래
trade-related investment measures	무역관련 투자조치
traded securities	유통증권
trader	거래업자, 매매담당자
trading	거래
trading account	매매계정
trading area	상세권
trading conditions	거래조건
trading day	거래일
trading down	박리다매
trading firm finance	상사금융
trading floor	거래소
trading halts	거래정지
trading know-how	거래 노하우
trading limit	가격폭 제한
trading market	유통시장
trading on equity	자기자본대용
trading on the over-the-counter market	점두거래
trading partner	무역상대국
trading post	교역소
trading profit	증권매매이익

trading profit and loss account	매매손익계정
trading range	트레이딩 레인지
trading securities	거래목적 유가증권
trading stamp	경품
trading system	거래시스템
trading tax	거래세
trading unit	거래단위
trading volume	총매출액
trading-up	상향구매
traditional channel	전통적 경로
traditional market	전통시장
traffic personal accident insurance	교통사고 상해보험
trailing PER	실적기준 PER
trailing expenses	훈련비
trailing program	훈련계획
trailing within industry	감독자 훈련
traitor	신뢰를 배신한 자
tramper	부정기선
tranche	분할발행
tranche issue	분할발행
Trans Africa	트랜스 아프리카
transaction	거래
transaction account	결제계정
transaction approach	개별거래 리스크 평가
transaction characteristics	거래특성
transaction cost	거래 비용
transaction fee	거래수수료
transaction in assets	자산거래
transaction motive	거래동기
transaction of near delivery	단기거래
transaction on a dealer basis	자기매매
transaction on exchange	거래소 거래

transaction shift	거래변경
transaction tax	거래세
transaction with delayed settlement	착지거래
transactional efficiency	거래효율
transactions tax	거래세
transcript	등본
transfer	양도
transfer account	이체계정
transfer agent	명의개서대리인
transfer at low price	저가양도
transfer books closed	주권명의개서정지
transfer books open	주권명의개서정지해제
transfer contract	양도계약
transfer effect	이전효과
transfer entry	대체기입
transfer expensditure	이전적 경비
transfer expenses	양도 비용
transfer fee	양도 수수료
transfer income	이전 소득
transfer ledger	대체원장
transfer machine	일관작업용 자동공작설비, 트랜스퍼 머신
transfer number	대체번호
transfer of a share-certificate	주권명의 개서
transfer of assets	자산양도
transfer of business	영업양도
transfer of current account	당좌계정대체
transfer of endorse note	배서양도
transfer of fixed assets given in pledge	담보부 고정자산양도
transfer of fund	자금이동
transfer of land tax	토지세 양도
transfer of name	명의서환

transfer of operations	영업양도
transfer of property	자산양도
transfer of real property	부동산 양도
transfer of rights	이권양도
transfer of securities	유가증권양도
transfer of seized goods	차압물건 인계
Transfer of Technology(TOT) Code	기술이전기준
transfer of transferable credit	신용장 양도
transfer parking	트랜스 파킹
transfer payment	이전지출
transfer price	양도가격, 이전가격
transfer pricing	이전 가격 조작
transfer pricing tax	이전 가격 세제
transfer pricing taxation	이전 가격 세제
transfer problem	대체 문제
transfer profit	대체 이익
transfer risk	대체 위험
transfer savings account	대체 저축 계좌
transfer slip	대체 전표
transfer tax	양도세
transfer transactions	대체 거래
transferable account	대체 가능 계정
transferable credit	양도 가능 신용장
transferable loan	양도 가능 대출
transferable loan facility	양도 가능 대부
transferable RUF	양도 가능 RUF
transferee	양수인
transferee corporation	합병법인
transferor	양도인
transferor corporation	피합병회사
transferred debt	이관채권
transfers between geographic areas	지역간 대체

transgression	침해
transient rate	단발요금
transit account	미달계정
transit advertising	교통광고
transit clause	운송약관
transit insurance	운송보험
transit trade	통과무역
transition	경과조치
transition matrix	추이 확률 행렬
transition model	추이모형
transition period	과도기
transition probability	추이확률
transitional benefit	과도적 급여
transitional measure	경과조치
transitory	일시적인
transitory income	변동소득
translation	재무제표의 환산
translation adjustments	환율환산조정
translation method at historical rates	취득시 환산법
translation of foreign currency statements	외화표시부분 환산
transmission mechanism	파급경로
transmitting bank	통지은행
transnational bank (TNB)	초국적 은행
transnational company	초국적 기업
transnational corporation (TNC)	초국적 기업
Transnational Information Exchange-Europe (TIE-Europe)	유럽다국적기업정보센터
transponder	중계 증폭기
transport	수송
transport insurance	운송보험
transportation	운송

transportation business	운송업
transportation charges	운송료
transportation claim	운송 크레임
transportation company	운송업자
transportation cost	운송비
transportation equipment	운송설비
transportation in bond	보세운송
transportation insurance	운송보험
transportation model	운송모형
transposition	배치전환
transshipment	이적, 환적
travel advances	선불여비
travel tax	통행세
traveling audit	순회감사
traveling benefits	여비수당
traveling expenses	여비교통비
traveling expenses for business	출장여비
traveling salesman	순회판매인
traveling tax	통행세
traveller's letter of credit	여행신용장
traverse	부인하다
treason	반역죄
treasurer	재무부장
treasury	출납소
treasury auction	국채입찰
Treasury Bill	재무성 단기채권
Treasury Bill issued	재무성 증권발행고
Treasury Bond	재무성 장기채권
Treasury Bond Investment Series	재무성 투자채권
Treasury Certificate of Indebtedness	재무성 채무증서
Treasury Euro-dollar Spread	TED 스프레드
treasury fund remittance	국고금 송금

treasury investment and loan	재정투자융자
Treasury Note	재무성 중기채권
Treasury Savings Notes	재무성 중기 저축채권
treasury securities market	재무성 증권시장
treasury stock	자기주
treasury surplus	국고여유금
treasury tax and loan account	조세공채계정
treasury yield	재무성 증권 이율
treating	향응
treaty	조약
treaty of Rome	로마조약
treaty reinsurance	특약재보험
treaty shopping	조세조약의 맹점 이용
treaty wording	재보험 특약서
treble indemnity	3배보상
treble tariff	3중 관세율
tree structure	3중 구조
trend	추세
trend analysis	추세분석
trend channel	추세경로
trend follower	추세를 좇는 투자자
trend line	추세선
trend model	추세 모형
trend of earnings	수익의 추세
trend pattern	추세선
trend series	추세지수
trend towards luxury spending	고급품 소비지수
trespass	침해소송
trespass for mesne profits	중간이득반환 청구소송
trespasser	침해자
trial	시산
trial at bar	공판

trial balance of balances	잔고시산표
trial balance of totals	합계시산표
trial balance of totals and balances	합계잔고시산표
trial balance sheet	시산표
trial consignments	위탁품
trial employment period	시용기간
trial manufacture	시작
trial product	시작품
trial running expenses	시운전
trial running of manufacturing equipment	생산설비 시운전
triangle	삼각형(기술적 분석의 도표유형)
triangular trade	삼각무역
tribunal	심판기관
trickle down	통화침수설의
trigger price	트리거 가격, 수입최저기준가격
trilateral commission	미·유·일 위원회
trilemma	트릴레마
trimming	정돈
tripartite agreement	삼국간 협정
tripartite Declaration of Principles Concerning Multinational Enterprises and Social Policy	다국적기업과 사회정책의 원칙에 관한 3자 선언
triple bottom	삼중바닥형
triple crossover method	삼중교차식
triple merit	삼중이익
triple settlement	삼각결제
triple top	삼봉천정형
trouble shooter	분쟁조정
trough	경기주기의 골
trover	동산침해소송
truck system	현물급여

true and fair	진실 공정한
true group insurance	정규단체보험
true installment premium	정규분할불 보험료
true panel	순수패널
true reserve	순준비금
Truman Doctrine	투르만 선언
trust	신탁
trust account	신탁계정
trust accounting	신탁업 회계
trust accounts of all banks	전국은행 신탁계정
trust agreement	신탁계약
trust assets	신탁재산
trust bank	신탁은행
trust by act of law	법정신탁
trust company	신탁회사
trust company administered pension plan	신탁은행 이용형 기업연금
trust contract	신탁약관
trust deed	신탁증서
trust deposit	신탁예금
trust estate	신탁재산
trust fee	신탁보수
trust for value	유상신탁
trust fund	신탁기금
trust fund bureau	자금운용부
trust fund plan	신탁형 연금
trust indenture	신탁증서
trust joint	합동
trust money	위탁금
trust property	신탁재산
trust receipt	트러스트 리시이트, 담보선적서류 예탁증
trust under agreement	계약신탁

trust-fund plan	신탁식 연금제표
trustee	수탁자
trustee company	수탁회사
trustee for bond issuance	사채발행 수탁자
trustee group insurance	수탁자 단체보험
trustee in bankruptcy	파산관재인
trusteed plan pension	신탁형 연금
trusteed surplus	신탁 잉여금
trustor	신탁 설정자
truth in lending	진성 대부법
tungsten light	텅스텐 라이트
turn around	반전
turn to red figures	적자전락
turn-key contract	완공인도계약
turndown	침체
turning point	전환점
turnkey contract	턴키계약
turnover	총매출고
turnover increase rate	매출증가율
turnover of capital	자본회전율
turnover of commodity	상품회전수
turnover of funds	자금회전율
turnover of payables	매입채무회전율
turnover of receivables	매출채권회전율
turnover of total capital	총자본회전율
turnover of total operating assets	경영자본회전율
turnover period	회전기간
turnover rate	회전율
turnover rate of capital	자본회전율
turnover ratio	회전율
turnover ratio of capital	자본회전율
turnover ratio of total liabilities	타인자본회전율

turnover ratios	회전율
turnover tax	매출세, 거래세
turnovers of net worth	자기자본회전율
twig	소규모지점
twin deficits	이중적자
twisting	수수료를 목적으로 과도한 매매를 권하는 행위
two factor contribution plan	2요소식 이원별 배당
two tier market	이중구조시장
two way account	상호계정
two way price	이중가격
two-item form	2항목방식
two-level inventory control system	2단계 재고 콘트롤 시스템
two-tailed test	양측검정
two-tier offer	2단계 청약
two-way layout	이원배치
two-way market	쌍방호가시장
tying arrangement	구속부협정, 연대협정
type	활자
type face	서체
type of holding	보유형태
typology	유형론

≪ U ≫

U.S. dollar short-term interest futures	미달러 단기금리선물
U.S. savings bond	미국 저축채
U.S. term	아메리카 방식
ulterior motive	숨겨둔 동기
ultimate consumer	최종소비자
ultimate fact	주요사실
ultimate objectives	최종목적
ultimate table	종국사망표
ultra definition television	초정밀 TV
ultra high frequency	UHF
ultra long-term national bond	초장기국채
ultra vires activites	월권행위
ultra-imperialism	초제국주의
umbrella cover	포괄보험
umbrella liability policy	기업포괄배상책임보험, 포괄책임보험
umpire	심판인
una voce	전원일치
unabsorbed burden	간접비 배부부족액
unadmitted asset	비공인자산
unallocated benefit	포괄급부
unallocated claim expense	제2차 사정비
unallocated funding instrument	비할당적립방식
unamortized	미상각
unamortized bond discount	미상각사채할인
unamortized cost	미상각원가

unamortized debt discount and expenses	미상각부채할인
unamortized discount on debenture accounts	채권조정계정
unamortized interest during construction	미상각건설이자
unamortized premium on bonds	사채발행차익
unanimous	만장일치
unappropriated deficit	미처리결손금
unappropriated earned surplus	미처분 이익잉여금
unappropriated earned surplus for current term	당기미처분 이익잉여금
unappropriated income	미처분 이익
unappropriated retained earnings	미처분잉여금
unappropriated surplus	미처분이익잉여금
unassigned surplus	미분배잉여적립금
unaudited	비감사
unauthorized card	무권한 카드
unauthorized member	무효회원
unauthorized use	부정사용
unavoidable accident	불가피한 사고
unavoidable circumstances	어쩔수 없는 사정
unavoidable cost	회피 불가능 원가
unavoidable dangers	불가피한 위험
unbalanced	미결산의
unbalanced account	미결산계정
unbalanced book	미결산장부
unbalanced budget	적자예산
unbalanced open	미결산
unbundling	비패키지형 경영자원의 요소선별
uncertain	불확실한
uncertain factor	불투명 요인

uncertainty	불투명
unchange	수준유지
unchanged to slightly higher	강보합
unchanged to slightly lower	약보합
unclaimed	소유자 불명의
unclaimed dividends	미청구 배당금
unclaimed wages	미지급임금
unclassified expenses	잡비
unclear energy insurance	원자력 보험
unclear energy liability insurance	원자력 손해배상책임보험
uncollected balance	미수금
uncollected commission	미수수수료
uncollected funds	미수자금
uncollected income	미수수익
uncollected interest	미수이자
uncollected premium	미수보험료
uncollected rent	미수지대
uncollected revenue	미수수익
uncollectible accounts	불량채권계정
uncollectible loan	회수불능대출
uncompleted works	미완성공사
unconditional	무조건
unconditional contract	단순계약
unconditional debt	무조건 채무
unconditional drawing right	무조건 인출권
unconditional estimate	무조건 추정
unconditional liquidity	무조건적 유동성
unconditional operation	무조건적 조작
unconditional reserve	별도적립금
unconfirmed credit	미확인 신용장
unconsolidated subsidiaries	비연결 자회사
unconstitutional	위헌의

uncontrollable expenses	관리불능비
uncorrelated return	무상관 수익률
uncovenanted benefit	무계약 급부
uncovered interest arbitrage	무방비 금리재정
uncovered option	무방비 옵션
uncovered position	무방비 포지션
uncrossed check	미횡선 수표, 보통수표
undated bill	무일부 수표, 날짜가 없는 수표
undepreciated balance	미상각잔고
undepreciated wasting property	미상각감소자산
under absorbed	배부부족
under development	개발중
under hedge	과소 헤지
under insurance	일부보험
under liquidity	과소유동성
under protest	지불거절
under repair	수선중
under reserve	유보조건
under separate cover	별봉으로
undercapitalization	과소자본
underdepreciation	과소상각
underemployment	과소고용
underemployment equilibrium	과소고용균형
underemployment multiplier	불완전 고용승수
underestimation	과소평가
underground economy	지하경제
underhedging	과소헷징
underinsurance	일부보험
underinvestment	과소투자
underlease	전대차
underlining security	현물증권
underlying	기초의

underlying assets	기초자산
underlying index	대상지표
underlying premium	기준보험료
underlying retention	보유손해액
underlying securities	원증권, 대상증권
underlying stock	대상주식
underlying swap	대상스왑
underpayment	과소납부
undertaker	사업자
undertaking	약속
undertaking of corporate bonds	사채응모
undertenant	전대차인
undertone	시장의 기조
undervaluation	과소평가
undervalued	염가할인
underwrite	인수하다
underwriter	인수업자
underwriting	인수업무
underwriting account balance	영업계정수지잔고
underwriting agreement	인수계약서
underwriting business	인수업무
underwriting commission	인수수수료
underwriting company	인수회사
underwriting contract	증권인수업자 수수료
underwriting firm	인수회사
underwriting group	인수단
underwriting of government securities	국채인수
underwriting of new issue securities	신증권인수
underwriting spread	발행비용
undischargeable claim	비면책 채금
undisclosed reserve	비밀적립금
undisposed	미처분

undisposed deficit	미처분 결손
undistributed profits	유보금액
undivided	미처분
undivided bequest	미분할 유산
undivided interest	불가분권
undivided profits	미처분 이익
undue influence	부당 위압
unduplicated audience	중복되지 않은 시청자수
unearned	미수
unearned discount	미경과 할인료
unearned income	불로소득
unearned interest	미경과 이자
unearned premium	미경과 보험료
unearned premium reserve	미경과 보험료 준비금
unearned revenue	이전수익금
unemployment benefit	실업급여
unemployment insurance	실업보험
unemployment rate	실업률
unequal probability	불균등 확률
unexpected property loss	임시자산손실
unexpired	미경과
unexpired cost	미소멸원가
unexpired expenses	미경과 비용
unexpired insurance premium	미경과 보험료
unexpired interest	미경과 이자
unfair advantage	부정이익
unfair call	무당이행청구
unfair competition	부당경쟁
unfair dismissal	부당해고
unfair labor practice	부당노동행위
unfair trade	부당영업행위
unfavorable balance	지급초과

unfavorable factor	악재료
unfavorable leverage effect	부(負)의 레버리지 효과
unfilled orders	미처리 주문
unfixed interest bearing	불확정 이자부
unforeseen event	예견되지 않은 사고
unfunded debt	단기채무
UNICE EC	내산업연합
unified brand	통일상표
uniform	일률적
uniform accounting	통일회계
uniform accounting regulations	통일회계기준
uniform accounting system	통일회계제도
Uniform Commercial Code	통일상법전
uniform cost accounting	통일원가계산
uniform cost accounting system	통일원가계산제도
unilateral	국내법상
unilateral contract	편무계약
unilateral record	일방적 기록
unilateral transaction	일방적 거래
unimodal	단봉형의
unincorporated company	법인격이 없는 회사
unincorporated joint venture	비회사형 합병사업
uninscribed stock	무기명주식
uninsured peril	비담보위험
union	조합
Union Europeenne des Experts Comptables Economiques financiers (UEC)	유럽회계연맹
union label	조합증표
union mortgage clause	표준저당권자 지불약관
union shop	유니온 샵
unique chattel	불대체물

unique factor	고유인자
unissued capital stock	미발행자본
unissued certificate	예비주권
unissued stock	미발행 주식
unit	단위
unit banking	단일은행제도
unit banking system	단일은행제도
unit benefit plan	연금액 방식
unit cost	단위원가
unit depreciation	개별상각
unit investment trust company	투자회사
unit linked life insurance	단일연계보험
unit load	단선로
unit merchandise planning	단일상품계획
unit method	개별감가상각법
unit of account	계산단위
unit of account bond	표시채권, 통화단위표시채
unit of production method	생산고 비례법
unit of taxation	과세단위
unit of trading	매매단위
unit price	단가
unit pricing	단가적산법
unit sales	매상수량
unit type investment trust	단위형 투신
unit-price contract	단가계약
unitary taxation	합산과세
United Nations Capital Development Fund	유엔자본개발기금
United Nations Commission Transnational Corporations (UNCTC)	유엔다국적기업위원회
United Nations Conference on the Law of the Sea (UNCLOS)	유엔해양법회의

United Nations Conference on Trade and Development (UNCTAD) 유엔무역개발회의
United Nations Draft Code of Conduct on Transnational Corporations 유엔다국적기업행동기준초고
United Nations Economic Development Administration 유엔경제개발국
United Nations Industrial Development Organization 유엔공업개발기구
United States trustee 연방재무관
unity of seisin 점유통합
unity of title 권원합동
universal agent 총대리인
universal banking 유니버설 뱅킹
universal legacy 포괄유증
universal life policy 유니버설 생명보험
universal notation 국제공통기호
unjust disbursement 부당지출
unjust enrichment 부당이득
unjustified 부당한
unknown clause 부지약관
unlawful 불법의
unlawful act 불법행위
unlawful assembly 불법집합
unlawful detainer 불법유치
unlawful entry 불법점유
unlawfulness 불법
unless otherwise specified 달리 정해진 것이 없는 한
unlimited legal tender 무제한 법화
unlimited liability 무한책임
unlimited liability company 무한책임회사
unlimited partnership 합명회사

unliquidated claim	불확정채권
unliquidated damages	불확정 손해배상액
unlisted assets	부외 자산
unlisted company	비상장회사
unlisted liability	부외 채권
unlisted loan	부외 차입금
unlisted securities	장외증권
unlisted stock	비상장주
unloading	대량매도처분
unofficial capital flight	비공식 자본의 유출
unpaid	미지급
unpaid capital	미지급 자본
unpaid claims	미지급 보험금
unpaid dividend	미지급 배당금
unpaid donation	미지급 기부금
unpaid draft	부도어음
unpaid returns	미지급 반환금
unpaid tax	미지급 세금
unproductive capital	미가동자본
unprofitable company	업적이 나쁜 회사
unqualified financial statements	미감사재무제표
unqualified opinion	무한정 의견
unrealizable assets	환가불능자산
unrealized gross profit on installment sales	할부매출 미실현이익
unrealized income	미실현 이익
unrealized revenue	미실현 수익
unreasonable taxation	부당과세
unreasonably	비합리적으로
unrecovered cost	미회수 원가
unregistered	미등기
unregistered stock	미등록주

unrelated business income	비관련 사업이익
unsalable stock	미판매재고
unsealed deposit	개봉예금
unseasoned security	발행직후의 증권
unseaworthy	내항력이 없는
unsecured	무담보의
unsecured account	무담보 계정
unsecured bond	무담보 사채
unsecured credit	무담보 신용
unsecured creditor	일반 채권자
unsecured liability	무담보 부채
unsecured loan	무담보 융자
unsecured trading	무담보 거래
unsettled	미결제의
unsettled account	미결제 계정
unsold	판매재고
unsual casualty reserve	비상위험준비금
unsubordinated	비(非)열후
unsystematic risk	비시스템적 리스크
untied loan	비연계 융자
untrue	사실에 반하는
unused buildings	유휴건물
unused land	유휴토지
unused land tax	미이용 토지세
unusual gains or losses	임시손익
unusual item	이상항목
unusual loss	이상손실
unusual profit or loss item	이상손익항목
unusual risks reserve	비상위험준비금
unvalued policy	미평가보험
unwritten law	비제정법
up front	일괄선지급

up load	업로드
up-down ratio	등락률
up-tront payment	계약일시금
up-tront premium	선지급 프리미엄
up-pressure	상승력
up-tick	상향
update	갱신하다
upkeep	유지비
ups and downs	성쇠
upset price	최저경매가격
upstairs market	계상시장
upswing	상승
upswing on business results	업적상승
uptrend	상향
upturn	호전
upward pressure	상승압력
upward revision	상방향 수정
upwards	상승기조
urban fringe	도시주변지대
urban remodeling enterprise	도시개량사업
urbanization	도시화
Urugugy Round	우루과이 라운드
usable years	사용기관
usage	관습
usage rate	사용요금
usance	어음 기간
usance bill	기한부 어음
usance bill rate	기한부 어음가격
usance buying rate	기한부 어음매입가격
usance letter of credit	기한부 신용장
use and file	사용후 신고제
use and occupancy insurance	사업중단보험

use of funds	자금용도
use value	사용가치
used hours	사용시간
used property	중고자산
useful life	내용년수
useful life table	내용연수표
user	소비자
user cost	사용자 원가
user instruction	취급설명서
usual covenants	통상약관
usufruct	사용수익권
usurer	고금리 대출
usury	법정이율초과이자
usury law	이자제한법
utilities bond	전력채
utilities stock	전력, 가스주식
utility	공익기업, 유용성
utility consumption	효용소비
utility curve	효용곡선
utility function	효용함수
utility maximization	효용극대화
utility model	실용신안
utility model patent	실용신안권
utility service	용역제공
utility theory	효용이론
utility value	사용가치
utilization variance	조업도 차이
utilized cost	이용원가
utmost good faith	최대선의
utter	사용하다, 발행하다
U-turn investment	U턴 투자

《 V 》

vacant land tax	나대지세
vacant lot	나대지
vacation	휴가
vacation pay	휴가수당, 유급휴가
vacation with pay	유급휴가
vacuum packing	진공포장
valid	유효한
validate	정당하다고 인정되다
validation	타당성 확인
validation test	타당성 테스트
validity	정당성
valuation	평가액
valuation account	평가계정
valuation actuary	보험계리인
valuation at cost	원가법
valuation at selling price	시가법
valuation basis	평가기준
valuation by multiplier	배율평가
valuation by road rating	노선가방식에 의한 평가
valuation characteristics	평가특성
valuation clause	보험평가액 조항
valuation form	적하가격 신고서
valuation item	평가항목
valuation loss	평가손
valuation modeling	평가모형
valuation of assets	자산평가
valuation of bond	공사채 평가

valuation of call option	콜 옵션 평가
valuation principle	평가원칙
valuation profit	평가익
valuation reserve	평가성 충당금
valuation standards	평가기준가액
value	가치
value added	부가가치
value added advantage	부가가치 우위
value added chain	부가가치 연쇄
value added network	부가가치 통지망
value added tax	부가가치세
value analysis	가치분석
value approach	가치 접근법
value at	견적을 내다
value chain	가치연쇄
value date	기산일
value declared	신고가격
value diagram	가치 다이아그램
value engineering	가치공학
value exchange system	가치교환시스템
value in use	사용가치
value investor	가치투자가
value judgment	가치판단
value line average	가치선 평균
value line composite index	가치선 종합지수
value line index	가치선 지수
value line option	가치선 옵션
value line ranking	가치선 순위
value next month	익월수표
value of assessment	과세가격
value received	대가수령
value today	당일수표

value tomorrow	익일수표
value variance	액면가액 차이
vampire video	뱀파이어 비디오
variability	불안정성
variable	변수
variable annuity	변액연금
variable budget	변동예산
variable capital	가변자본
variable cash reserve requirements	가변적 현금준비제도
variable charge	변동비
variable constant	가변상수
variable cost and expenses	변동비
variable cost ratio	변동원가율
variable costing	변동소득계산
variable expenses	변동비
variable insurance	변액보험
variable interest rate	변동이율
variable investment tax	가변투자설
variable life insurance	변액 생명보험
variable overhead	변동관리비
variable premium	변동보험료
variable profit	변동이익
variable rate mortgage loan	변동금리형 부동산론
variable universal life insurance	변액 유니버설 생명보험
variable zone	변동가격권
variance	차이
variance account	원가차액계정
variance analysis	분산분석
variance of cost	원가차액
variance of the estimate	평가차액
variation from budget	예산차이
variation margin	변동증거금

various kinds of income 변동소득
various kinds of tax benefits 세법상의 특전
varying annuity 예정변동연금
vector 벡터
vehicle selection 매체선택
velocity 속도
velocity of circulation 유통속도
vendee 매입자
vendor 판매자
vendor analysis 거래처 분석
venture 사업
venture business 벤처 비지니스
venture capital 벤처 캐피털
venue 행위지
verbal 구두의
verdict 평결
verification 검증
verification by telephone 전화확인
verification of a seal impression 인감조회
versus 대하다
vertical analysis 수직분석
vertical angle of view 수직각도
vertical blank interval 수직귀선 소거기간
vertical channel system 수직적 경로시스템
vertical integration 수직형 통합
vertical marketing system 수직적 마케팅 시스템
vertical merger 수직적 합병
vertical publication 전문업계지
vertical specialization 수직적 국제분업
vertical spread 수직스프레드
vertical territorial customer restrictions 수직적 고객제한

vertical trade horizontal trade	수직적 무역 수평적 무역
very high frequency	VHF
vessel	선박
vessel unknown	적재선명 미상
vest	권리를 수여하다
vested benefit	기득권
vested benefit obligation	확정급부채무
vested in interest	발생확정시키다
vested in possession	현소유의
vested interest	확정권리
vested interests	기득권
vested remainder	확정잔여권
vesting	수급권 부여
vesting deed	계승재산부여증권
vesture	토지점유
veto	거부
viable	성장가능한
vicarious liability	사용자 책임
vice chairman	부의장
vice president	부총재, 부사장
vice-consul	부영사
vicinity of the upper limit	천정권
vicious member merchant	악질가맹점
video dial tone service	비디오 다이얼 폰 서비스
video display terminal	비디오 단말
video editing	비디오 편집
video on demand	주문형 비디오
video random access memory	V-RAM
video system control architecture	비디오 통제기기
video tape recorder	VTR
video tax	비디오 조세
video transmission service	영상전송 서비스

view	검증
view of lowering interest rate	저금리 전망
viewfinder adopter	시도조절
viewing distance	시거리
viewing model	시야 모형
viewing transformation	시야변환
vintage	자본의 평균연령
violation	권리침해
violation of a contract	계약위반
violence	불법행위
virtual interface environment workstation	가상환경 웍스테이션
virtual private network	가상전용선
virtual reality	가상현실
virtually unchanged	큰 변화 없는
virus	바이러스
vis major	불가항력
visible supply	유형공급
visual curve-fitting method	작도법
vital statistics	인구동태통계
voice	발언
voice mail	음성메일
voice over	바깥소리
voice recognition	음성확인
voice recognition & response system	음성응답시스템
void	무효한
void agreement	무효한 합의
void contract	무효한 계약
void transaction	무효한 법률행위
voidable	무효로 하다
voire dire	예비심문
volatile market	변동시장

volatility	변동률
volatility value	변동성 가치
volume	조업도, 매출액
volume accumulation	누적매출액
volume cost	양산원가
volume discount	수량할인
volume efficiency	양산효과
volume indicator	조업도지수
volume of business	거래액
volume of inventories	재고량
volume of issuance	발행규모
volume of over-the-counter transaction	점두판매고
volume of sales	매출액
volume of trading	거래액
volume ratio	거래량비율
volume variance	조업도 차이
voluntary	임의의
voluntary accumulation plan	임의형 계속투자계획
voluntary additions	자발적 추가
voluntary adjustment	자기부인
voluntary association	자발적 조직
voluntary audit	임의조사
voluntary bankruptcy	자기파산
voluntary chain	임의연쇄
voluntary conveyance	무상양도
voluntary depreciation	임의상각
voluntary depreciation method	임의상각법
voluntary dissolution	임의해산
voluntary export restraint	임의수출규제
voluntary insurance	임의보험
voluntary liquidation	임의정리

voluntary partnership	임의조합
voluntary place of tax payment	임의 납세지
voluntary reserve	임의준비금
voluntary restraint program	자율규제계획
voluntary restriction of export	수출자율규제
voluntary saving	자발적 저축
voluntary settlement	무상계승적 부동산 처분
voluntary tax payment	자주납부
voluntary unemployment	자발적 실업
voluntary waste	적극적 손실
voluntary winding	임의해산
volunteer	무상취득자
Vostro account	상대편 계정
voting	투표
voting company	결의권 회사
voting right	결정권, 투표권
voting stock	경정권 주식
voting trust	결정권 신탁
voting trust certificate	의결권 신탁증서
vouch	증명하다
voucher	전표
voucher for disbursement	지불증표
voucher payable register	지불전표 기입장
voucher system	지불전표제도
vouching	증빙추적
voyage policy	항해보험
Vredeling Proposal	프리딜링 법안

≪ W ≫

wage according to job evaluation 직능급
wage assignment 급여공제
wage ceiling 임금의 상한설정
wage contract 임금협정
wage cut 임금삭감
wage disparity 임금격차
wage earner 임금생활자
wage freeze 임금동결
wage in kind 현물급여
wage income 임금소득
wage increase 임금인상
wage level 임금수준
wage negotiation 노사교섭
wage rate 임금률
wage stabilization system 안정임금제
wage structure 임금체계
wage unit 임금단위
wage variance 임금차이
wage-bracket table 간이세류표
wage-hike drive 임금투쟁
wage-price control 임금・물가 통제
wage-price guideline 임금・물가 가이드 라인
wage-push inflation 임금 인플레이션
wages attached to a post 직무급
wages lodger 임의원장
wages on job evaluation 직능급
wages payable 미불임금

wait and see	경과를 관망하다
waiting period	대기기간
waiver	권리방기
waiver clause	권리방기조항
waiver of obligation	채무면제
waiver of premium	보험료불입면제
walk-out	동맹파업
wall flower	인기하락종목
Wall Street	월가
Walrasian auctioneer	왈라스의 경매인
want of procesution	소송불이행
wanton negligence	무관심과실
wantonness	무시
war clause	전쟁약관
war perils	전쟁위험
warehouse charges	참고사용료
warehouse expenses	보관비
warehouse fee	창고료
warehouse financing	창고금융
warehouse receipt	수탁증권
warehouse rent	보관료
warehousing	입고
warrant	위임장
warrant agent	위임대리인
warrant agreement	위임동의서
warrant bond	위임채, 위탁채
warrant in bankruptcy	파산자 재산차압영장
warrant of attachment	차압영장
warrant of attorney	위임장
warrant parity	보증동가
warranted rate of growth	적정성장률
warranty	보증

warranty of legality	위법성 담보
wash order	위장매매주문
wash sale	가상매매
waste	폐기물
waste circulation	무효부수
wasting assets	감소자산
watch list	요주의 종목
water concession	수리권
water expense	수도료
water right	수리권
water-bailiff	수리감시관
water-utilization tax	수리이익세
watered assets	가공자산
watered capital	가공자본
watered stock	수증주식
wave function	파동함수
Wave Theory	파동이론
waveform	파도형
way	통행권
ways and means	재원
weak form	약형
weak stockholders	부동주주
weak tone	약세
weaken	지치다, 약해지다
weaker economy	경기후퇴기
weaker U.S. dollar	달러약세
weakness	약세
wealth tax	부유세
wear and tear	마모
weather insurance	기상보험
wedge	쐐기
wedge formation	쐐기형

Wednesday-factor	수요일 요인
week order	주별주문
weekend effect	주말효과
weekly accounting	주간결산
weekly chart	주간차트
weekly payment	주급
weight of evidence	증거의 비중
weighted	가중
weighted arithmetic average	가중산술평균
weighted average	가중평균
weighted average cost method	가중평균원가법
weighted average method	가중평균법
weighted average number of common share outstanding	가중평균보통주수
weighted average of market capitalization	시가총액가중평균치
weighted basis trade	가중평균베이스 무역
weighted index	가중지수
weighted mean	가중평균
weighted mean method	가중평균법
weighted stock price average	가중평균주가
welfare economics	후생경제학
welfare expense	복리후생비
welfare facilities	복리후생시설
welfare pension	후생연금
welfare pension insurance	후생연금보험
welfare program	복리후생
Western European Union	서구동맹
Western Hemisphere Free Trade Area	미주자유무역권
Western Hemisphere Trade Corporation (WHTC)	서반구무역회사
WFTU	세계노동조합연맹

wharfage	부두세
wheel of retailing	소매차륜
when-issued basis	발행일 기준
when-issued transaction	발행일 거래
while clause	위험부담정지약관
whisky tax	위스키 세
white knight	백기사
white list	우량자 리스트
white paper on economic cooperation	경제협력백서
white return	백색신고
Who Owns Whom	기업계열 편람
WHO/UNICEF Code of Marketing Breastmilk Substitutes	세계보건기구/UNCEF모유대체품 마케팅에 관한 연구
whole issued stock	총발행완료 주식수
whole life annuity	종신연금보험
whole life insurance	종신보험
wholesale	도매
wholesale accounting	도매회계
wholesale bank	도매은행
wholesale business	도매업
wholesale dealer	도매상
wholesale establishment	도매사업
wholesale group insurance	단체계약
wholesale price	도매가격
wholesale price index	도매물가지수
wholesale trade	도매업
wholesaler	도매업자
wholly owned subsidiary	완전소유자회사
WHTC Western Hemisphere Trade Corporation	서반구무역회사
wide area distribution center	광역물류센터
wide fluctuation of market	대폭등락

widening gap	확대격차
wider band	변동폭을 가진 고정제
wider margin	확대가격변동
widow	과부, 미망인
widow deduction	과부공제
widow-and-orphan stock	안정배당주
width of currency movements	환율변동폭
wild card option	와일드 카드 옵션
willful	고의의
willful false	고의적 허위
willful misconduct	고의적 불법행위
willful negligence	고의적 과실
willingness to pay	변제의지
wind storm and flood insurance	풍수해 보험
windfall loss	의외의 손실
windfall loss or gain	우발적 손익
windfall profit	우연한 이익, 예기치 않은 이익
winding up	해산
winding-up by the court	강제청산
winding-up of pending affairs	잔무정리
winding-up order	청산명령
window	창구
window dressing	분식(粉飾)
window dressing deposit	분식예금
window dressing financial statement	분식재무제표
window dressing settlement	분식결산
window guidance	창구지도
win-win	윈-윈
wire houses	개인고객상대 증권회사
wire transfer	전신송금
with a proviso	조건부
with average	분손담보

with discount	액면이하
with holding tax	원천소득세
with premium	액면이상
with recourse credit	상환의무 불면제 신용장
with warrants	권리부
withdrawal of portfolio	자산인출
withdrawal plan	인출계획
withdrawals	철회
withholding	원천징수
withholding agent	원천징수의무자
withholding and payment	원천징수와 납부
withholding at source	원천징수
withholding exemption certificate	원천징수표
withholding income tax	원천징수소득세
withholding of customs appraisement	관세평가차 중시
withholding system	원천징수제도
withholding tax	원천과세
withholding tax on income	원천소득세
withholding tax option	원천세 선택
withholding tax system	원천징수제도
within-group stratification	집단내 계층분화
without compensation	무보수
without credit at sight buying rate	신용장없는 일람불수표 매입률
without prejudice	권리손실 없는
without prejudice to preliminary	기득권 손해 없는
without recourse	상환의무를 지지 않는
without recourse credit	상환의무 면제신용장
without reserve	가격무제한
witness	증거
witnessing part	증거본문
word of mouth	구전
words of limitation	내용표시문언

work	작업
work in process ledger	시제품 원장, 재공품 원장
work instruction	작업지시서
work order	제조지도서
work rules	취업규칙
work sheet	정산표
work study	작업연구
workable competition	유효경쟁
workaholism	일중독
worker's property accumulation savings	재형저축
workers' accident comprehensive insurance	노동재해종합보험
workers union	종업원조합
working account	사용계좌
working assets	적용자산
working balance	운용자산
working budget	실행예산
working capital	운전자금
working capital analysis	운전자본분석
working capital control	운전자금관리
working capital position	운전자본상태
working capital ratio	유동비율
working condition	작업조건
working cost	영업비
working days	작업일수
working document	작업문서
working fund	운전자금
working hour curtailment	단시간
working hours	작업시간
working hypothesis	작업가설
working interest	임차권리자

working inventory	운영재고자산
working place	사업장
working rules of audit procedures in reporting	감사보고준칙
working student	근로학생
working student allowance	근로학생공제
working trial balance sheet	시산표
working year	영업연수
working-capital ratio	운전자본비율
working-hours method	운전시간법
workmanship	기량, 솜씨
workmen's compensation acts	노동자 재해보상법
workmen's compensation insurance	노동자 재해보상보험
workmen's compensation law	노동자 배상법
worksheet method	정산표 방식
workshop	작업장
workshop subsidiary	분공장형 제조 자회사
World Bank	세계은행
world company	세계기업
World Council of Churches Program on Transnational Corporations	다국적기업에 관한 세계종교회의 연구 프로그램
world crisis	세계공황
World Directory of Multinational Enterprise	세계다국적기업명단
World Federation of Trade Unions (WFTU)	세계노동조합연맹
world index	월드 인덱스
World Intellectual Property Organization	세계지적소유권기관
World Intellectual Property Organization (WIPO)	세계지적재산권기구
world market portfolio	세계 시장 포트폴리오

world market price	세계 시장가격
world marketing	세계 마케팅
World Trade Organization	세계무역기관
World Wide Fund for Nature	세계자연보호기금
worth and fixed assets ratio	자본고정자산비율
worth debts ratio	자본부채비율
wreck	난파
writ of entry	부동산 점유회복 소송
write-down	장부가격을 깎다
write-off	상각
write-up	과대평가
writer	판매자
writing	집필, 문서
written agreement	서면계약
written application	서면신청
written assignment	양도증서
written contract	서면계약
written decision	결재서
written examination	필기시험
written inquiry	서면조사
written premium	계상보험료
written-down value	평가감후가격
wrong	위법행위
wrong doing	부정행위
wrongful dismissal	부당해고

≪ X ≫

X-efficiency X효율

《 Y 》

Yankee bond	양키본드
Yankee bond market	미국달러채 시장
yard transportation	공장내 운송비
year	년도
year end stock	연말 재고
year in brief	당년도 개황
year's opening session	신년회
year-end	연말
year-end dividend	연말 배당
year-end market	연말 상장
year-end settlement	연말 조정
year-to-year changes	경년 변동률
year-to-year percentage change	전년대비 변화율
yearly earnings	연간 순익
yearly installment	연(할)부
yearly taxation	연세주의
yeas and nays	찬반투표
yield	생산고
yield auction	이자입찰
yield based on weighted average	가중평균이율
yield book	이율표
yield by simple interest	단리이자
yield curve	이자곡선
yield curve risk	이자곡선 리스크
yield curve swap	이자곡선 스왑
yield differential	이자격차

yield factor	이자요인
yield for average life	평균 잔존년한 이율
yield for holding period	소유기간 이율
yield improvement switch	이율개선 스위치
yield on already issued bond	기발행채 이율
yield on bond	채권이율
yield on investment	운용이율
yield on public and corporate bond	공사채응모자 이율
yield rate	보류
yield spread	이율격차
yield standard	이자구조
yield structure	이율구조
yield to call	임의상환이자
yield to maturity	만기이율
yield to subscriber	응모자 이율
yield-to-call	매수청구이자
yield-to-put	매수청구이자
yo-yo stock	요요주식
youth orientation	청년지향

≪ Z ≫

zaibatsu	재벌(한국), 자이바쯔(일본)
zapping	재빠르게 움직이는
zero cost option	제로코스트 옵션
zero coupon bond	제로 쿠폰채
zero defects	무결함 운동
zero-beta portfolio	제로-베타 포트폴리오
zero-cost collar	제로비용고리
zero-cost option trading	제로-코스트 옵션거래
zero-coupon bond	무이자 할인채
zero-coupon curve	무이자 할인 곡선
zero-order model	제로발주모형
zero-plus tick	제로-플러스 틱
zero-sum game	제로섬 게임
Zillmerized reserve	질멜식 책임준비금

<편저자 약력>

김영래(金榮來)

전공 : 국제경영
일본 WASEDA 대학 상학박사
미국 UNIVERSITY OF OREGON객원교수(81/82), (06/07)
고시출제위원 (행정자치부)
일본 Waseda 대학 초빙교수(94)
일본아시아 경제연구소(IDE) 초청연구원(95/96)
교과과정 심의위원(교육부 97/99)
충북대학교 경영대학장(91/93)

현, 충북대학교 국제경영학과 교수

100人 포럼 공동대표(02/04)　(사) 국제 e-비지니스학회 회장(01)
(사) 한국국제통상학회장 (02)　(사) 한일 경상학회장(03)
(사) 한국 경영사학회장(04/05)

＊저 서

- 글로벌시대 한국기업과 경영, 법문사, 2006(편)
- 글로벌경영(개정판), 법영사, 2006
- 글로벌비즈니스 개론, 법문사, 2003, 2005 (저)
- 글로벌 전략경영, 두남, 1999, 2000, 2002 (저)
- 국제경영, 두남, 1997, 1998, 2000 (공편저)
- 기업국제화의 전개-무역경영, 법영사, 1995, 1996(저)
- 종합상사론, 법문사, 1987, 1990 개정 (저)
- 국제경영론, 박영사, 1985, 1987, 1988 (공편저)
- 무역경영론, 박영사, 1983, 1984, 1988 개정(저)
- 무역용어사전, 학문사, 1982, 1984, 1987, 1989 (편저)

조강필(趙康弼)

전공 : 국제금융
미국 Pittsburgh 대학 경제학 석사
미국 Pittsburgh 대학 경제학 박사
대통령 직속 금융개혁위원회 전문위원
보험개발원 대외정책연구팀장
한국 경영사학회 편집위원

현, 충북대 국제경영학과 교수

임달호(林達鎬)

전공 : 국제전략경영
일본Waseda 대학 국제경영 석사
일본 Rikkyo 대학 국제경영(전략) 박사
한국국제경영학회 이사
한국국제통상학회 이사
한일경상학회 이사

현, 충북대 국제경영학과 교수

英·韓 글로벌 비즈니스 辭典

2006년 10월 1일 초판인쇄
2006년 10월 10일 초판발행

편저자 김영래 · 조강필 · 임달호

발행인 고 준 영

발행처 **법 영 사**

(135-280) 서울시 강남구 대치동 611
전화 (501) 8898(대) FAX (501) 8895
등록 1987. 11. 5 제3-125호(윤)
Site : www.bubyoungsa.co.kr
E-mail : bypuco@chol.com

파본은 교환해 드립니다. **정가 18,000원**

ISBN 89-7032-226-4